THE POLITICS
OF SORROW

STUDIES OF THE WEATHERHEAD EAST ASIAN
INSTITUTE, COLUMBIA UNIVERSITY

STUDIES OF THE WEATHERHEAD
EAST ASIAN INSTITUTE

The Studies of the Weatherhead East Asian Institute of Columbia University were inaugurated in 1962 to bring to a wider public the results of significant new research on modern and contemporary East Asia.

THE POLITICS OF SORROW

UNITY AND ALLEGIANCE ACROSS TIBETAN EXILE

TSERING WANGMO DHOMPA

Columbia University Press   *New York*

Columbia University Press
Publishers Since 1893
New York   Chichester, West Sussex
cup.columbia.edu

Copyright © 2025 Columbia University Press
All rights reserved

Library of Congress Cataloging-in-Publication Data
Names: Dhompa, Tsering Wangmo, author.
Title: The Politics of sorrow : unity and allegiance across Tibetan exile/
Tsering Wangmo Dhompa.
Other titles: Unity and allegiance across Tibetan exile
Description: New York : Columbia University Press, [2025] | Series: Studies of the
Weatherhead East Asian Institute | Includes bibliographical references and index.
Identifiers: LCCN 2024023259 (print) | LCCN 2024023260 (ebook) |
ISBN 9780231212465 (hardback) | ISBN 9780231212472 (trade paperback) |
ISBN 9780231559393 (ebook)
Subjects: LCSH: Tibetans—India—Societies, etc. | Bhod Dedon
Tsogpa (Organization) | Cholsum Chigdril Tsogpa (Organization) |
Gungthang Tsultrim, 1923–1978. | Exiles—India—Societies, etc. |
Nationalism—China—Tibet Autonomous Region—History. | Tibetans—
India—Ethnic identity. | Tibetans—India—History—20th century.
Classification: LCC DS432.T5 D46 2025 (print) | LCC DS432.T5 (ebook) |
DDC 320.951/5—dc23/eng/20240606
LC record available at https://lccn.loc.gov/2024023259
LC ebook record available at https://lccn.loc.gov/2024023260

Cover design: Milenda Nan Ok Lee
Cover photo: Tibetan Welfare Association

CONTENTS

Preface vii
Note on Transliteration, Titles, and Names xv
Timeline of Texts and Events xvii

Introduction 1

1 A Government in Exile 33

2 Unity in Exile 67

3 The Group of Thirteen 97

4 The Seven Resolutions and Supporting Documents 119

5 Against the Grain of History: Mutiny at the Ockenden School 145

6 The Convergence of the Thirteen Leaders 169

7 A Politics of Sorrow 197

8 The People's Government 227

Conclusion: A Statement of Real Truth 245

Acknowledgments 265
List of Thirteen Founders and Settlements 269
Appendix: Who's Who 271
Notes 275
Bibliography 307
Index 331

PREFACE

Every now and then, someone I have interviewed in the course of doing this research has asked: "Why are you writing *this* story?"

My decision to work for a nonprofit organization in San Francisco upon graduation from university in 1998 was not accidental. The choice was shaped by my mother's lifelong service to the Tibetan people and her desire that I work for the community as well. The foundation worked with the Tibetan exile government to provide funding for humanitarian and cultural projects for Tibetan refugees. During my first week of employment, a prominent Tibetan diplomat met with my bosses. Upon learning that the foundation had hired me, the diplomat told them: "Her mother was antigovernment."

An antigovernment designation for my mother could only mean that, as her daughter, I was a questionable hire for an international organization working with the Tibetan government and Tibetan-led projects. Tsering Choden Dhompa, my mother, had served in the exile government as a member of parliament, then known as the Commission of Tibetan People's Deputies, from 1972 through 1979 in its fifth and sixth terms. She rejoined politics in 1992 after a long hiatus. On January 1, 1994, she was on her way to a parliament session in Dharamsala, the capital of the Tibetan exile government in India, when she met with a car accident on the Grand Trunk Road entering

Karnal in the state of Haryana in India. Afterward, exile officials consoled me, saying I should be proud she had died while serving the nation. I was twenty-three. I had lost my only family.

Prior to her service as a member of parliament, my mother had looked after Tibetan children in an orphanage funded by Save the Children in Shimla in Himachal Pradesh and then taught in a Tibetan school in Clement Town, in Uttarakhand. Given her decades-long history of governmental work and community service, the diplomat's dismissal of her contributions to the Tibetan community was surprising. I asked someone who had worked with my mother why the diplomat had identified her as antigovernment. My mother's colleague thought it had to do with her association with Tsokhag Chusum.

Tsokhag Chusum, or Group of Thirteen, was established in India by thirteen Tibetans who were lamas, leaders, and chieftains from Kham and Amdo, two of the three regions of Tibet. The group's leaders independently sought help from the Tibetan Industrial Rehabilitation Society (TIRS)—an organization established in 1966 and funded by foreign aid groups to help Tibetan refugees run small-scale industries—to build settlements where they could live with members of their regional or monastic communities. Identification with their clan was an important feature of the social systems these Tibetans belonged to. Their hope was that when Tibet's freedom was regained, they could leave together for their ancestral lands. This decision to build their own settlements was interpreted by the Chigdril Tsogpa, Tibetan United Association, the largest political organization in the exile community, as an attempt to split from the Tibetan society in exile and to destroy its unity. The Tibetan United Association was well received by the Tibetan exile population—the organization had branches in many Tibetan settlements—and their statements about the Thirteen carried weight. To protect themselves from further damaging denunciations, the Thirteen leaders registered themselves as the Tibetan Welfare Association with the Indian government under the Charitable Societies Act in 1966. In this book, I will refer to the

Tsokhag Chusum interchangeably as the Thirteen, or the Group of Thirteen. The Thirteen is also how members of the group refer to themselves. I will refer to the Tibetan United Association as the United Party.

Relations between the Thirteen and the United Party were tumultuous during my mother's parliamentary term in the 1970s. My mother's family had maintained ties to the lineages of Chokling Rinpoche, Drawupon Rinchen Tsering, and Pon Namkha Dorje (three of the thirteen leaders) over many generations. Her familiarity with the histories of all the leaders had provided a frame through which she interpreted their actions, concerns, and intentions. She sympathized with their desire to live with their clan and knew these were relations forged over hundreds of years. She also sympathized with their willingness to trust the exile government in return for recognition of their desire to build and maintain forms of community that they considered integral to their survival in exile. My mother served as an intermediary between the Thirteen and the government.

Not until I was interviewing the few remaining members of the Thirteen did I realize my own connections to their settlements. The first three years of my life were spent in Clement Town, the first of the settlements established by the thirteen groups. I had met many of the Thirteen leaders, including Gungthang Tsultrim, as a child. I also knew well my mother's colleagues in the Tibetan parliament such as Alak Jigme Rinpoche, Deyki Dolkar, and Drikung Genyen Choden, who represented the Amdo and U-Tsang regions. I was aware of the different perspectives they might have held of the Group of Thirteen. My mother and Alak Jigme Rinpoche would joke that they challenged each other when they stepped into the office but turned back into friends when they stepped out. They remained friends until my mother died.

In 1991, His Holiness the Dalai Lama inaugurated a new auditorium in Lady Shri Ram College in New Delhi. The college principal asked me to read a poem on the occasion. After reading, I genuflected as best as I could on the stage. I offered the poem, written on a scroll, to His Holiness. He asked where I was from.

"From Kham Nangchen," I responded instinctively, giving the name of my family's ancestral kingdom.

"Which settlement in India?" he asked.

I had not lived in a settlement since I was three. I had no answer. I offered my mother's name instead.

Later, a Tibetan friend in Delhi told me I should have said I was from Kathmandu, where I had been living since the age of twelve. Saying I was from Kathmandu was less divisive than saying I was from Nangchen. *Less divisive for whom?* I had wondered. I did not understand then what she meant.

While doing this research, I have grappled with why a connection to the Thirteen is cast as a dissident form of Tibetan-ness. Belonging is a conundrum, even to Tibetans of my generation, born as refugees in India and Nepal. We are not the Tibetans who had to flee from homes tucked deep within the folds of mountains and walk over the Himalayas to keep alive. We are not the ones who through our labor helped build a nation in exile under the leadership of His Holiness the Dalai Lama. We are not the ones whose life choices were shaped by estrangement. Yet we learned from the generation who fled Tibet that being a Tibetan in exile was not the same as being a Tibetan in Tibet. They became refugees; we were born refugees. Born in settlements and educated in schools established by the exile government, many of us feel gratitude to the government and His Holiness for having nurtured us. It is easier for us to think of a pan-Tibetan identity because we have not been to the villages our parents came from, do not have any contacts inside Tibet, and have not been fully exposed to the histories and languages of places in the regions outside Central Tibet.

I observed a certain forlornness in the Tibetan elders I spoke to, a feeling I have come to understand more clearly after my own experiences writing this book that to speak of Khampa concerns or express desire for fuller representation or recognition in exile is still seen as choosing a narrow, protective regionalism at the expense of a broader Tibetan identity. Regionalism implies a strained tension between regions and a center. It reinforces the notion that the center should hold people's allegiance, not the parts. By this interpretation, "regionalism" today is applied to expressions of cultural or political difference from dominant forms of what it means to be Tibetan. The dominant group or entity applies the label of "regionalism" and accepts (or rejects) identities into a community of value. Then what does it mean to be a Tibetan in exile?

In the early 1960s the United Party advocated for Tibetans to shed their affiliations to their regions (Amdo, Kham, U-Tsang) and reconstitute themselves into a homogenous national identity. Tibetan unity depended on this conversion. This national identity in exile, as observed by historian of Tibet and anthropologist Carole McGranahan, privileged Central Tibetan norms. McGranahan explains that Central Tibetan or U-Tsang social and political forms "were recast in exile as a shared, pan-Tibetan identity."[1] This meant that U-Tsang norms were transformed from being particular and a regional identity to being a general and a national identity, and being particular and regional became associated with Amdo and Kham identities. McGranahan's observation that this conversion of particular to general is one of the "means by which regional identities were criticized and devalued" is vital to understanding one of the organizing principles of the concept of regionalism in exile.[2] Regionalism or showing affinity with a regional identity came to be understood as a sign of resistance to unity or a unified Tibetan identity. This is at the core of what I call in the title of this book the politics of sorrow.

Unity is a trope presented in exile political discourses as an antidote to regionalism. But what does it mean that unity is held out as something that must be protected from the threat of plurality and regional allegiances? What would unity look like if it began with an invitation to inclusion that encompasses different histories and experiences of being and feeling Tibetan? Does the conception of a Tibetan refugee-citizen entail a stripping of difference in order to be enfolded into unity? Settled in me like a worm, these questions uncoiled whenever the topic of regionalism emerged, as it did with increasing frequency, in discussions among Tibetan refugees. By no means an uncritical endorsement for pluralism, this book nonetheless suggests that national homogeneity, even when it serves a purpose as important as the Tibetan national struggle, still deserves scrutiny—if for no other reason than for all involved to understand its stakes, as well as the roads not taken.

Some readers might swiftly deem this book to be "antigovernment." Some might hold the view that I should bury this story. Yet is the very act of telling a story from the perspective of minor or peripheral characters in the history of the Tibetan nation dismissible as mere regionalism, or does it invite a rethinking of the terms of belonging in exile? This book suggests that the Thirteen carried the dream of Tibet's independence alongside all Tibetans in exile. The Thirteen was committed to the well-being of Tibetans, as the United Party is believed to have been. Both narratives are Tibetan narratives.

This narrative of the Thirteen is based on reading letters, pamphlets, manifestos, autobiographies, and minutes of meetings written by Tibetans in exile, and is supported with present-day conversations with Tibetans from the settlements established by the Thirteen. The elderly Tibetans I interviewed look back at events, their intentions, and how their actions were interpreted within the Tibetan society. The Thirteen's position was unusual then, for the ideas they were challenging but also for their challenge to certain people in power, in particular Kasur Gyalo Thondup, brother to His Holiness the Dalai Lama, who was thought to be the leader of the United Party. Critiquing an organization that had the Dalai Lama's approval and questioning policies established by a government led by him could be viewed as sacrilegious. The Tibetan society's unshakable and profound love for His Holiness the Dalai Lama is bolstered by a ferocity and fidelity that interprets slight deviations from devotion as offenses against the nation. This feeling has intensified over time in exile because His Holiness has been the one constant source of comfort, guidance, and strength to the Tibetan people since 1959. He has been the only Dalai Lama for Tibetans in exile. Such watchfulness is also extended toward the *yabshi*, the families of the Dalai Lamas. There is an unspoken consensus to maintain a decorum around forms of public critique acceptable or allowable by the Tibetan society toward the *yabshi*.

In exile, Tibetan nationalists had to learn the normative language of self-determination and democracy in an attempt to forge a nationalism that served the Tibetan people. This has resulted in the dominion of certain ideas, sentiments, and efforts over what it means to be a community. The story about the Group of Thirteen is one sectional history in relation to the ideological development of Tibetan nationalism rooted in a struggle for independence. The difficult passage to a new political status for all Tibetans, but especially those on the margins, is also a tale about the significance of not only external but also internal recognition. Indeed, the story of the Thirteen dramatizes the perceived struggle between two individuals who were born in Amdo and were of the Gelug school of Tibetan Buddhism: Gungthang Tsultrim, who headed the Thirteen, and Kasur Gyalo Thondup, the putative power behind the United Party.

Tibetans live with the fear that our stories, especially those that reveal us in unflattering ways or disclose the fissures among us, will hurt His Holiness the Dalai Lama, or that they will be used against us by China. Unity in the face of China is crucial, but the Tibet we build in exile must also be more than the sum of our fears. Unlike Tibetans in Tibet, Tibetans in exile, both as individuals and as collectives, can construct the diverse histories and desires that make us Tibetan and in so doing prefigure a self-affirming Tibetan nationalism. Tibetan internal struggles are evidence of our hope for a future for all Tibetans, and of our resourcefulness in dealing with the hopelessness that is to be expected every now and then in such a long exile from our homeland. Our internal struggles point to the changes that Tibetans have gone through and will continue to experience as we work toward a nation forged out of many Tibetan homelands. And they point to the need to reevaluate how we see and think about regions and what we mean by unity. The exile government serves as a fulcrum for this process of becoming unified. Unlike China, which has neither historical legitimacy to rule Tibet nor the will of the Tibetan people under its control, the exile government expresses the will of the Tibetan people.

Our struggles are painful but offer opportunities to learn and do better to care for one another. Stories are one way of working toward unity. The Tibetan elders who helped my mother raise me gave me the stories that animate the history I relay in this book. They also often spoke of the meadows of their *phayul,* or homeland, filled with a variety of flowers. It is my small hope that this book will prompt Tibetans, especially those of us in exile, to imagine and realize a Tibet that, like its meadows, is a space where flowers of all varieties bloom.

Tsering Wangmo Dhompa
Ardmore, PA

NOTE ON TRANSLITERATION, TITLES, AND NAMES

In this book I have used a simple phonetic rendering of Tibetan words for English readers. The bibliography carries some titles in both the Wylie system (*bka'blon*) and their pronounceable spellings (*Kalon*). Most of the words may be pronounced close to their English values.

There are some unavoidable and deliberate inconsistencies in spellings. "Derge" refers to the region but is also a part of an individual's name, and spelled "Dege." Likewise, "Dorje" is sometimes spelled "Dorje" and other times "Dorjee." The names of individuals, organizations, and monasteries are transliterated according to their respective preferences.

Tibetans' naming preferences are also maintained. Some Tibetans go by their full personal name, such as Tsering Dorjee, or are referred to by one personal name, such as Jinpa. Some Tibetans have a family name, a title, or an honorific title. Drawutsang Rinchen Tsering may also be referred to in conversations or texts as Drawupon Rinchen Tsering (the *pon* is his honorific title as chief). In this case, the family name (Drawutsang or Drawupon) comes first and is followed by the personal name (Rinchen Tsering). Similarly, lamas may have and use their personal names but are known by their titles.

TIMELINE OF TEXTS AND EVENTS

April 18, 1959	The Dalai Lama arrives at Tezpur, Assam, in India.
February 3, 1960	The Great Oath offered in Bodh Gaya, Bihar.
May 1960	The Tibetan government-in-exile, also known as the Central Tibetan Administration (CTA), established.
September 2, 1960	The Tibetan parliament formed in exile.
November 9, 1963	The conference of the four major sects of Tibetan Buddhism held in Dharamsala.
April 23, 1964	*Five Aims of the Tibetan United Association* published by the Tibetan United Association in Darjeeling, West Bengal.
March 12, 1965	*Seven Resolutions and Supporting Documents* published by the Tibetan United Association in Darjeeling.
June 2, 1966	"A Report by Gyaltsen Choden" published in the *Tibetan Freedom* newspaper, Darjeeling.
June 6, 1966	"The Reason Why Kelsang left Ockenden" published in *Tibetan Freedom*, Darjeeling.

1966	Bhod Dedon Tsogpa (Tibetan Welfare Association/The Thirteen Group) established in New Delhi.
1974	The Chushi Gangdrug disbanded in Mustang, Nepal.
May 18, 1977	Article on the Thirteen published in the *Young Army Journal* in Taiwan.
February 6, 1978	New Year's greeting advertisement published in *Tung-yang Nyin-rai Sar-Shok* in Calcutta, West Bengal.
June 16, 1978	Gungthang Tsultrim shot in Clement Town, Uttarakhand.
July 1978	*The Assasination [sic] of Gungthang Tsultrim* (also referred to as *The Black Friday*) published by the Group of Thirteen in Clement Town.
August 9, 1978	"In Reply to Allegations Contained in the Pamphlet 'The Assassination of Gungthang Tsultrim'" published by the exile government in Dharamsala.
September 20, 1978	"Declaration of the Thirteen Group" published by the Group of Thirteen in Dharamsala.
December 7, 1978	*A Statement of the Real Truth* published by the Group of Thirteen in Tashi Jong, Himachal Pradesh.

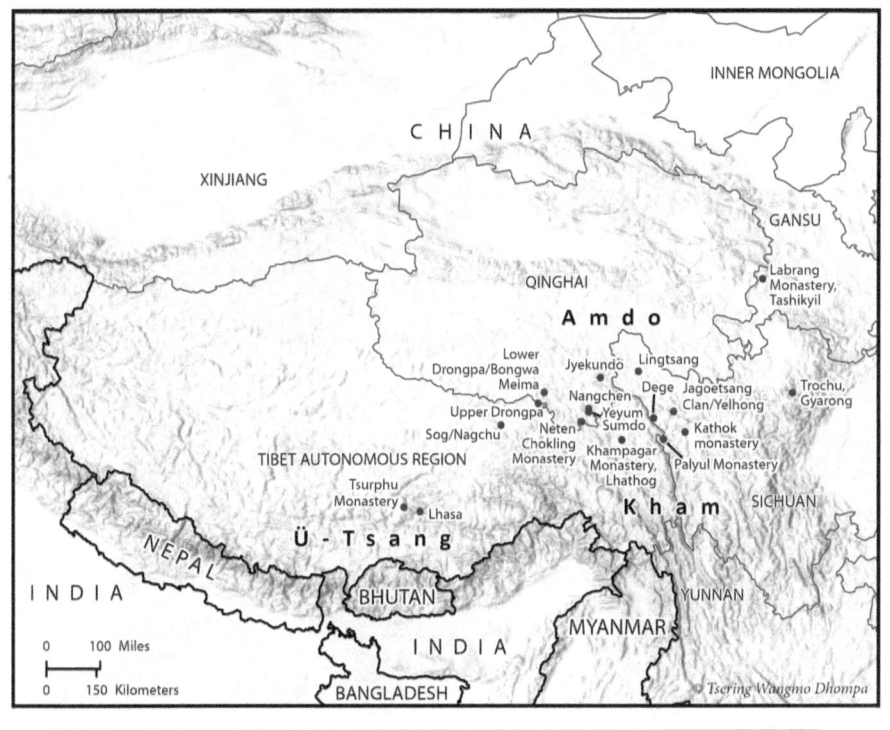

MAP 1 Tibet (Chol Kha Sum/Three Regions Model)

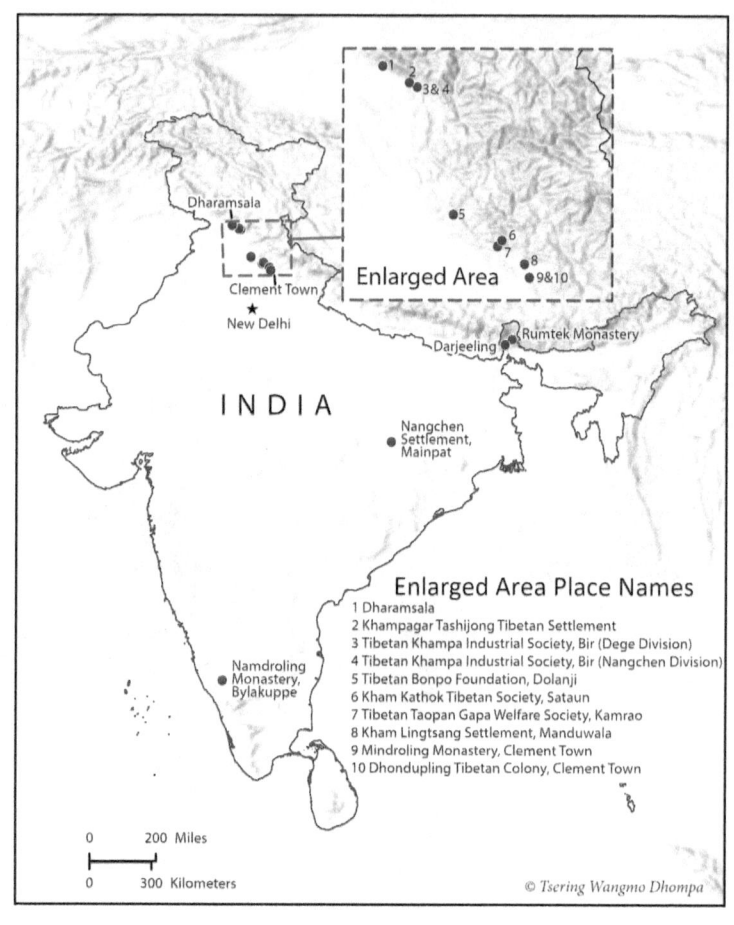

MAP 2 The settlements established by the Group of Thirteen in Exile

THE POLITICS
OF SORROW

INTRODUCTION

On the evening of June 16, 1978, Gungthang Tsultrim—Akhu Tsultrim to his friends—was fatally shot in the backyard of his house in Clement Town, India. Hours before his death on the hospital bed, Gungthang Tsultrim had given his statement to the area's superintendent of police and district magistrate naming three individuals he suspected of hatching and executing a plan to murder him: Wangdu Dorjee, Gyemi Dhondup (also known as Amdo Dhondup), and Phakte (also known as Gara Phakte). Wangdu Dorjee was the Minister of Home Affairs in the exile government and the representative at the Bureau of His Holiness the Dalai Lama in New Delhi. Dhondup was a senior army officer stationed at Establishment 22, the base for an elite regiment of Tibetan commandos in Chakrata, India (created in 1962 after the Sino-Indian War with help from the Central Intelligence Agency of the United States and the Research and Analysis Wing, the foreign intelligence agency of India). Phakte was a businessman who lived close by in Rajpur.[1] Gungthang Tsultrim had no evidence to support his accusations against the three men, but his pointing them out to police indicated that his murder was of the order of a political assassination.

Gungthang Tsultrim's death was described as the "first mysterious murder" of this nature committed among Tibetan refugees in a two-column report in the July 1978 issue of the *Tibetan Review*, the most popular English-language journal devoted to Tibetan affairs, at that time run by the government-in-exile, officially known as the Central Tibetan Administration (CTA).² The article appeared in the "News Report" section and introduced Gungthang Tsultrim as one of "the most controversial figures among Tibetan refugees," with as many friends as foes who either admired him for his achievements in exile or accused him of being a traitor for working with and receiving "payment from the Taiwan Government."³ (The Taiwanese government shared the Chinese Communist Party's view that Tibet was part of China, so Tibetans saw them as the same entity.) The *Tibetan Review* indicated there were many suspects involved in his death, including the possible hand of Taiwan. Gungthang Tsultrim's followers had traced the motive for his murder to 1971, when he and many from his group had applied for Indian citizenship. The *Review* also noted that this event had been followed by an unsuccessful attempt on his life.

A month later, the *Tibetan Review* ran a five-page article entitled "Gungthang Tsultrim—A Political Victim?" It stated that most Tibetans had only become aware of Gungthang Tsultrim's death in late July following the publication of an article in *The Current*, an Indian weekly from Bombay (now Mumbai), that insinuated he was killed for upsetting certain exile officials and for leading an organization that was seen to challenge the exile government.⁴

Before escaping to India, Gungthang Tsultrim had been an important administrator for Gungthang Rinpoche in Labrang Tashikhyil Monastery, located in Tibet's Amdo region. He had also been among the fighters from the monastery to join the Chushi Gangdrug, the grassroots resistance movement in Tibet. Gungthang Tsultrim's teacher had advised him to leave Labrang when the new Chinese Communist government began to arrest Tibetan leaders in the region. Gungthang Tsultrim had reached India via Bhutan in 1959. He established the Tibetan refugee settlement in Clement Town in 1964. He was also recognized as the leader of the organization Bhod Dedon Tsogpa (Tibetan Welfare Association), known to Tibetans as Tsokhag Chusum or the Group of Thirteen. Gungthang Tsultrim had formed the group in 1966 with twelve Tibetan political and religious luminaries from Kham, Eastern Tibet.

The Thirteen was perceived by dominant Tibetan political and social groups as being antigovernment for disrupting Tibetan unity in exile, for three main reasons: their alleged relations with Taiwan's Mongolian and Tibetan Affairs Commission (MTAC); building their own self-sufficient settlements; and their attempts to attain Indian citizenship in the mid-1970s. These acts were viewed as detrimental to the authority of the exile government at a pivotal moment when a great deal was at stake for the Tibetan nation.

The Thirteen's supposed transgressions against unity in exile turned out to be less impactful than their critics imagined. Over time, having relations with Taiwan and seeking Indian citizenship were found to be less consequential. This was particularly the case once it was revealed that the exile government's department of security had secretly established relations with the Taiwanese National Security Bureau in 1982 and received financial aid. Similarly, Gungthang Tsultrim had been condemned for seeking Indian citizenship in the early 1970s, but by and by, many Tibetans (including those who had censured him) sought to secure Indian citizenship for their families. This was made much easier in March 2017 when the Ministry of External Affairs (MEA) of the Indian government received a Delhi high court ruling accepting Tibetan refugees born in India between January 26, 1950, and January 1, 1987, as Indian citizens. Lastly, the dedication of Tibetan Buddhists to their diverse religious traditions and teachers is not viewed with concern today.

Yet the narrative of the Thirteen as antigovernment persists.

Gungthang Tsultrim's assassination brought to the surface the pain of belonging even within the Tibetan exile nation that was constituted following China's invasion and seizure of Tibet. Unity was regarded as a prerequisite for the nonviolent national struggle for freedom, but the process of national integration was seldom tranquil even for people who had much in common. It is this contradiction—that unity is not free from violence—that I follow in this book.

I met more than fifty Tibetan elders who had joined the settlements of the Thirteen group in the 1960s to hear their stories and perspectives on representations of the Thirteen in exile texts. Only two of the group's founding members, Lopon Tenzin Namdak Rinpoche and Drawupon Rinchen Tsering (who passed away in November 2023), were alive when I began. The elders I approached in the settlements in 2015 and 2022 were willing to speak to me either because we had an existing relationship or because they had known my mother, or both. They counted her as one of them or as being sympathetic to the Thirteen. I knew several people in Bir, Bylakuppe, Clement Town, Kamrao, Mainpat, and Tashi Jong, and had fewer contacts in Chauntra, Dolanji, Munduwala, Sataun, and Rumtek. Often, individuals I interviewed in one place would recommend I speak to their friends or relatives in other settlements.

My role as the daughter of a supporter of the Thirteen, and as someone who knew many of the founders, placed me in relation with this community. It enabled me to ask questions and to be entrusted with answers that many were otherwise reluctant to share, partly because the Thirteen settlements are integrated into the exile community today and partly because they feared that returning to the past would awaken dormant feelings of resentment toward them. And yet, they also spoke of their desire to be free of the itch from old wounds. This book seeks to tell their stories as a first step to that end.

The documents that survived in their dusty cupboards or makeshift shelves—pamphlets, posters, letters, scraps of notes—were perhaps not meant to be shared beyond their intended readers. Written in cursive Tibetan script, some documents were impenetrable due to the poor quality of their writing and neglect—the handwriting and the materials having etiolated over time. The archive I draw from is full of innuendos, repetitions, and rumors that often serve not to clarify as much as to point to the difficulty of maintaining a linear narrative or a singular truth of the past. I relied on readers equipped with the contextual knowledge to interpret the many allusions and to identify the abbreviated names that the texts offered as half-revealed clues in a partial puzzle. These documents were also a form of speculation and, much like rumors, they were read in the company of people. Most often, the texts map a binary of those in favor of and against the exile government. Synecdoches for the nation—the exile government and the Dalai Lama—are the backdrop against which individual characters and public organizations rise and fall.

The details of Gungthang Tsultrim's death and information about the events leading to it were made public in a pamphlet entitled *The Assasination [sic] of Gungthang Tsultrim* (also referred to as *The Black Friday* because he was killed on a Friday) from the Tibetan Welfare Association. The pamphlet was published in Tibetan as well as in English. *The Black Friday* indicated that Gungthang Tsultrim had been assassinated because he opposed the "ministers" of the Tibetan exile government, who feared he "might awaken" the Tibetan people to corruption within the exile administration.[5] The pamphlet took four controversial positions while providing the background political and social environment. One, elite members of the exile administration were linked to Gungthang Tsultrim's murder. Two, His Holiness the Dalai Lama was described as a prisoner of exile administrators. Three, high-level officials within the government were said to discriminate against the people of Kham and Amdo. Last, although the pamphlet did not state outright that the Lhasa government did not have control over Kham and Amdo, it suggested that the distance between the regions resulted in the Lhasa government having "effective authority only over one province, i.e., Lhasa" and that the people of Amdo and Kham considered themselves "free."[6]

Unlike the texts produced by Tibetan refugees in the 1960s and the 1970s, whose primary function was to gain support for Tibet's cause for independence and draw internal support for a unified nonviolent resistance policy under the leadership of the Dalai Lama, the *Black Friday* writers drew attention to discrepant identity formations and questions of loyalty within the exile community in linking Gungthang Tsultrim's death to a high-ranking exile government official. The *Tibetan Review*'s editor, Tsering Wangyal, commented on this in his editorial "Politics of Sorrow," published two months after Gungthang Tsultrim's death. Wangyal asserted that never before had a text voiced so openly the "suppressed grievances of various Tibetan groups."[7] He intimated that the *Black Friday* pamphlet might have been written in a burst of emotion and without consent from all members of the Thirteen. Wangyal drew a damning conclusion: "If Gungthang Tsultrim was murdered because of his independent views, it was indeed a deplorable act, not entirely dissimilar to the practices of a regime from which we have fled in exile." At the same time, the editorial noted that unless proven, such opinions and "rash pronouncements" should be kept private. Even if true, the allegations should have been "done in a proper and dignified manner."[8]

In Wangyal's editorial, the politics of sorrow referred neither to the tragic death of a man nor to the fears expressed by the Thirteen but to the fact that they chose to privately publish the pamphlet. He described the Thirteen as Tibetans who liked to "function as a unit separate from the Tibetan Government," suggesting they diverged from the masses who stayed faithful to the goal of independence.[9] A month later, in its September issue, the *Tibetan Review* reported that a twenty-five-year-old Tibetan named Tenzing had been arrested in Kathmandu, Nepal, in connection with Gungthang Tsultrim's murder. Tenzing was said to have confessed to the murder, according to the *Review*. It also noted, "According to the police, Tenzing was allegedly hired by some persons, whom Mr. Tsultrim named in his dying declaration, to commit the crime."[10]

Other commentaries published in Tibetan and English and circulated among exile Tibetans in the wake of Gungthang Tsultrim's murder focused on his purported subversive character and the Group of Thirteen's adversarial relationship with the exile government. Not much was said about what the Thirteen represented, or their efforts toward self-sufficiency after barely a few years in exile. The absence of any reflection on the loss of life or the concerns expressed by the Thirteen illustrated the hostility toward Gungthang Tsultrim that was indicated by the group as the reason for his murder in *The Black Friday*. The one exception was a letter in the September 1978 issue of the *Tibetan Review* in which Samten Gyaltsen Karmay slightly shifts the relationship between the Thirteen and the government. This small but significant change in narrative makes room for contextualizing Gungthang Tsultrim and the Thirteen beyond the backdrop of national history and politics as understood by the Tibetan majority in exile.

In "Who are the Amdowas?," Samten Gyaltsen Karmay presupposes His Holiness's importance to all Tibetans, thereby suggesting the Thirteen were not anti-Dalai Lama. Samten Karmay sought to clarify the status of Amdowas, or people from the Amdo region, by providing a brief overview of Amdo's political, cultural, and social ties with Lhasa prior to the Chinese invasion of Tibet in 1950. Backdating the history, he explained that Lhasa remained Amdo's cultural center even though Central Tibetan authorities lost political control over the region after the ninth century. Even as he emphasized the government's success in caring for all Tibetan refugees, he indicated that not all Tibetans depended solely on the exile government. There were people who took the initiative to take responsibility for their communities. In doing so, they developed their own policies, which sometimes clashed with those proposed by the exile government.

Amdo Gungthang Tsultrim, the leader of the Thirteen, was one such individual.

Having established Gungthang Tsultrim's role in the Group of Thirteen, Samten Karmay then importantly suggested that the "undercurrent" that brought the Thirteen together was a desire to counteract an "old fear of abandonment" that may have taken root after Chinese incursions in Kham in the mid-1950s.[11] This fear was that one day the Tibetan government-in-exile would negotiate with China to gain Central Tibet's independence and give up Amdo and Kham lands. He described it as being profoundly divisive, and one of which the exile leadership was aware. Samten Karmay didn't provide a basis for the "old fear" but did mention the Lhasa government's dismissive response to the Chushi Gangdrug's—the grassroots military movement that began in Kham in the mid-1950s—call for help in fighting the Chinese army. He also mentioned that the Chushi Gangdrug was among those who escorted His Holiness the Dalai Lama safely from Lhasa to India in 1959. Showing that the group was both relied upon and dismissed touched upon old wounds and anxieties for many of the exiles from Kham.

Defined by post-1959 nationalism in exile, most discussions about the Thirteen judge them for their agreement with or indifference to new exile policies or power figures. In contrast, Samten Karmay's letter alluded to the Thirteen as entities with their own distinctive historical and political organizational character—chiefdoms, principalities, and clans—reflecting the variety of forms that had existed in Tibet, with a variety of relations to imperial China, Nationalist China, and the Lhasa government. Samten Karmay's observation that the people of Amdo had become a minority within the Tibetan exile population also shed light on the significant demographic shifts in exile that contrasted with the regional populations of pre-1950 Tibet. Likewise, the reference to the Chushi Gangdrug brought the Thirteen into orbit as individuals who were integral and important participants in the Tibetan struggle, thus disturbing their new denomination as dissidents. In other words, Samten G. Karmay's brief analysis of Gungthang Tsultrim and the Group of Thirteen took both post- and pre-1959 Tibetan history into account, including the psychological and existential aspects of dispossession.

The Tibetan Empire, whose boundaries correspond roughly to U-Tsang plus Tibetan-speaking areas outside the Central Tibetan Autonomous Region (TAR) created by China in 1965, developed between the seventh and the ninth centuries, contemporaneously with China's Tang dynasty era. In this period, Tibet was constituted ethnically, culturally, and linguistically and unified under a single Tibetan ruler. After the breakdown of the empire in the ninth century, many Tibetan regions within what came to be known as Kham and Amdo became independent or were divided into administrative entities. In the subsequent centuries, the relationships these diverse regions had with the Chinese imperial court and the Central Tibetan rulers were varied and inconsistent. Matthew T. Kapstein, a noted scholar on Tibet, comments that even though there was political fragmentation and unrest in the mid-ninth century, Tibetan regimes reappeared and held power over vast territories from the thirteenth century until the formation of the Fifth Dalai Lama's government in 1642. The first of these systems rose to power through the "interventions of China's Mongol rulers."[12]

In 1252, Tibet was incorporated into the Mongol empire by Möngke Khan. Representatives of the religious groups competed to win the favor of prominent members of the Mongol royal family. Sakya Pandita (1182–1251), a master in the Sakya tradition, obtained support from factions of the Mongol court, but it was the Pandita's nephew, Pakpa, who was elevated to secular and religious authority over Tibet in 1264 after giving a formal initiation to Khubilai Khan (1215–1294). The Khan granted Pakpa rule over the thirteen myriarchies (administrative districts of Tibet under the Sakyapa-Mongol regime) of U and Tsang, along with Amdo, Kham, and western Tibet. The Sakyapa became the "chief agents of Mongol rule" in Tibet.[13] The Mongol-Sakyapa administration was not the first example of the relationship characterized by the term *cho yon* (priest-patron), but it solidified the importance of foreign patronage for Tibetan lamas seeking political power.

Sakyapa rule ended in 1350, and the administration fell to Tai Situ Jangchup Gyaltsen (1302–1364) of the Pakmodrupa order of the Kagyu lineage. The Pakmodrupa rulers' relationship with the Ming (1368–1644) after the fall of the Yuan dynasty was, according to Kapstein, mostly ceremonial. Both Sakyas and Kagyus had their domains of power during this time. In the fifteenth century, a new Buddhist order that became known as Gelugpa, or the "Virtuous Ones," grew in popularity in Tibet. The Mongols reappeared in the form of Altan Khan, the leader of the Tumed Mongols, and by the mid-sixteenth century had returned to power. Like his predecessor Khubilai Khan, Altan Khan looked to Tibetan Buddhism for spiritual legitimacy. The timing was serendipitous.

In 1578, Altan Khan embraced the Gelugpa school after meeting lama Sonam Gyatso. He created the title "Dalai Lama," and in turn, the Dalai Lama granted Altan Khan the title "King of Dharma, Brahma Among the Gods." This relationship, according to Kapstein, altered the "balance of power in Tibet."[14] The power was shifted indisputably in 1642 when Gushri Khan, the Khoshot Mongol leader, crushed all opposition to the Gelugpa and presented the thirteen myriarchies to his spiritual teacher, Losang Gyatso, the Fifth Dalai Lama, also known as the Great Fifth. This historic moment reunified Tibet after some two centuries of strife.[15] The Dalai Lama's political and religious authority over Tibet, based in Lhasa, dates from 1642.

The politico-religious relationship between China and Tibet then went through phases of ebb and flow. For most of that period, sovereignty as understood in the era of the modern state applied to neither Tibet nor China. This changed in the late nineteenth century when the British, referring to the Chefoo Convention Treaty signed with the Chinese imperial government in 1876, demanded trading rights in Tibet. A Western power's recognition of China's authority over Tibet and a subsequent shift in China's attitude, more along the lines of Western notions of political sovereignty, greatly altered the older relationship between China and Tibet. As historian Tsering Shakya explains in *The Dragon in the Land of Snows*, the political and cultural terms of the traditional relationship did not survive the arrival of Western colonialism and the political and social alterations in the Chinese polity that led to a Republican China and the rise of a new form of Chinese nationalism.[16] This transformation did not go unnoticed by the Tibetan government in Lhasa. The 1911 revolution in China presented Tibet with the opportunity to sever political ties. From 1911 to 1950, Tibet was a de facto independent state. This is clear in the Thirteenth Dalai Lama's declaration of independence in 1913.[17]

Following China's invasion of Tibet in 1950, many Kham and Amdo polities, which were already provinces as de jure Chinese territories enjoying an "incredible degree of independence both from Peking [now Beijing] and Lhasa," were incorporated into the modern Chinese state even as the Chinese revolution claimed to depart from the structure of the empire.[18] China then claimed its sovereignty over the Lhasa government with the Seventeen-Point Agreement of 1951, which specifically related to the Central Tibetan territories under the Tibetan government. Therefore, a sensitive problem for Tibetans arose as to whether the Chinese authorities would grant autonomy to all three Tibetan regions—U-Tsang, Kham, and Amdo (also known as U-Tsang, Dotoe, and Domey respectively)—as demanded by Tibetans in exile, or whether autonomy would be limited to Central Tibet or what the Chinese government has mapped as the Tibetan Autonomous Region (TAR). The Chinese considered Amdo and Kham to be "legally Chinese" rather than Tibetan.[19] The fear of abandonment expressed by some Tibetans from Kham and Amdo is linked to these realities.

Prior to the Chinese invasion of Tibet in 1950, most members of the Thirteen belonged to the eastern region of the Tibetan plateau. Consisting of agricultural, pastoral, and semipastoral societies with diverse forms of authority, Kham is referred to as a frontier to regimes based in China (Yuan, Qing, Republican) and the Lhasa government; as microcosms defying a unifying history or sociospatial narrative; and as self-governing societies.[20] Kham's internal diversity and the fact that it was not studied as much as U-Tsang or Amdo placed it, until recently, in a peripheral or marginal position within imaginings of the Tibetan world. Indeed, Kham (and Amdo) were referred to as borderlands of U-Tsang. As argued by Stéphane Gros, Kham's unclear boundaries meant that it remained "an ill-defined region" to outsiders.[21] Gros suggests that from a Chinese perspective Kham was a Tibetan "Other" that was vital but not completely outside the Chinese Self, and that from a Tibetan perspective, Kham was part of greater Tibet through what Gros describes as a sense of "a naturalized link between identity and territory."[22] His point is that no singular term—frontier, boundary, borderland—captures the multifaceted composition of Kham's many locales.

Almost all the leaders of the Thirteen were considered as centers of power in their roles as kings, lamas, chieftains, and headmen in their regions. Scholar of Tibet Dawa Norbu's description of Kham as self-governing societies that had prioritized "local and tribal interests" over "national concerns" captures the mostly decentralized political systems and the varying autonomy the Thirteen leaders had known in Tibet.[23] Their communities were organized politically into clans with varying freedom in governing their people according to the Tibetan traditions and law in their regions. Their leaders had the power to pass their title down the family line.

The regionally specific political formations of Kham and Amdo did not contradict Khampa or Amdowa recognition of themselves as Tibetan and of Tibet as a land that included three Tibetan regions. A shared religion and historical memory including origin myths, a single writing system, and imagination of a geographical territory kept alive a congruous social system and a larger Tibetan ethos and feeling consistent with those of a nation or a nationality.²⁴ Indigenous leaders across the Tibetan plateau traced their lineage to the Tibetan Empire, creating bonds of collective belonging firmly held together by a historical and religious legacy. For example, the Nangchen kings traced their lineage to the Yarlung dynasty. While this technique of using history and broader cultural narratives was a way for indigenous rulers to bolster their authority, it was foremost a means to highlight their autonomy and placed them within what scholar Maria Turek describes as "a larger Tibetan constellation of politics."²⁵ Whether under the Tibetan government or in self-governing societies, Tibetans responded to these broader feelings and spaces of belonging in defining their identities.

As with other exile Tibetans, the lives that the Thirteen members had known and the ideas of self they had held were profoundly disrupted when they became refugees. Unmoored from their territories and uncertain of their relations with the new and unfamiliar locus of power in exile, these leaders had to accustom themselves to being peripheral characters while negotiating new terms of belonging to a nation in exile. On the one hand, they identified themselves as Tibetan and accepted the Dalai Lama as their leader. On the other hand, their fear that the nationalizing process in exile might not affirmatively recognize their regional identities was being realized.

Early Tibetan nationalists in exile might have found the differences between the Lhasa government and Kham polities, which included overlapping forms of authority, irrelevant or inconvenient to the struggle to gain support for the Tibetan independence movement. Perhaps they found no easy way to translate Kham's diverse forms of belonging into notions of sovereignty, nationhood, and territory based on international law and hegemonic Western concepts of nation-states. While the Dalai Lama had tremendous influence over the Gelugpa population in these regions, the Lhasa government had few to no political rights in or privileges over the territories. The historical and religious autonomy of eastern Tibetan regions did not align with the national narrative of a politically united Tibet proposed by exile nationalists. This meant that narratives of Khampas or people of Kham as members of dynamic economic, cultural, and religious centers came with the burden to prove their allegiance to the exile government.

The exile government initiated two simultaneous projects: to recover the geographical territory occupied by the Chinese Communist regime and to protect the "cultural territory," a phrase used by Edward W. Said to describe the efforts at the heart of decolonization.[26] The latter, as described by Said, included efforts to reconstitute a dispossessed people in exile and regain a sense of community that would help establish "new and independent stakes," integral to nation building.[27] Unity in the face of China's occupation of Tibet was vital to recovering both geographical and cultural territories. Defined by external historical pressures, the Tibetan nation in exile was also shaped by internal tensions. Keeping Amdo and Kham to the margins, the government anachronistically mobilized unity as something Tibetans had known in an earlier past, now retrieved to bind the people and nation in the unstable present. This also meant transforming Amdo and Kham societies led by hereditary chieftains, kings, and clans into a modern society informed by concepts of democracy, rights, and equality.

In a statement the Thirteen published a year after Gungthang Tsultrim's death, they described their goal as preserving and protecting the diversity of Tibet's "ancient culture" and religion, something they held to be more precious than their own lives.[28] It is possible that in restricting their roles and reconstructing their authority into something like cultural guardians in exile, they unintentionally stepped into a role that the government deemed important for itself. After all, the work of cultural protection is crucial to nation building.

Vietnam's independence from France in 1945 and India's independence from the British in 1947 were followed by as many as sixty other countries' political independence by 1968. In an era when China was seen as an anti-imperialist beacon to postcolonial nations in Asia, Latin America, and Africa, Tibetans were swimming upstream in their effort to draw global attention to the Chinese occupation of Tibet in the 1960s and to render their own exilic nationalism legible in the anticolonial terms of the day. As an uncommon movement for anticolonial nationhood forged in exile, Tibetan nationalism was born in this knot.

For individuals I interviewed, the politics of sorrow stemmed from having been marked as "factions." Compounding their pain was the perception that it was unwarranted. Gungthang Tsultrim's death was the price for their dream of diversity in unity. His death was acutely personal to them and remains so even decades later. It was a loss they could name. Many of them marked Gungthang Tsultrim's murder as the concluding chapter of the Thirteen. Even if it was the end for the organization, the story of the Thirteen continues to unfurl a testimony to both losses and feats along the path toward a Tibetan homecoming.

The Bhod Dedon Tsogpa or Tibetan Welfare Association was formed in 1966 in a covert meeting in Delhi. The collective of thirteen Tibetan groups, each represented by a core leader, expressed what might have appeared as a paradoxical need to organize themselves to protect their regional histories and religious practices while living within the Tibetan exile society whose objective was to build a Tibetan national identity and movement, in order to oppose China's destruction of Tibetan ways of life. Critics of the organization named them Tsokhag Chusum, "Group of Thirteen," or simply "The Thirteen," for the thirteen leaders. The elders say that the moniker was given to them as a kind of curse by the Cholsum Chigdril Tsogpa, the Tibetan

United Association, also called the United Party. However, the Western superstition about the number thirteen did not hold the same valence for the Thirteen leaders as it did for those who had given them the name.

The formation of the Thirteen meant there were two competing narratives for the Tibetan nation to come in the first two decades of exile politics: the dominant vision of the United Party, seen to represent the democratic and progressive goals of the exile government, and the marginal vision of the Thirteen, believed to represent regional interests of elite leaders from Kham. The Thirteen's reservation that unity would suppress intracultural and religious differences and lesser-told histories was interpreted as a sign of their resistance to modernity and change. Their resolve to protect their religious and regional cultures was interpreted as an attempt to preserve their traditional positions of power. To no small degree, this narrative ascribes modernity to the United Party and assigns retrograde traditionalism and communalism to the Thirteen.

Telling the story of the Thirteen through their voices offers a more complex tale of Tibetan nationalism in the latter half of the twentieth century. It draws attention to marginal narratives of the Tibetan struggle for belonging and democratic self-governance in exile and asks how such accounts place pressure on narrow conceptions of unity. I use the term "marginal" to recognize this group's new configuration of themselves as a minority within the majority U-Tsang and Gelug exile population, while keeping in mind that the leaders of the Thirteen held positions of power within their own clans and groups. Not all the leaders and their members were from Kham—a region that does not stand for a monolithic religious, cultural, or political identity—but the Thirteen came to stand for Khampa politics in the larger exile imagination because eleven leaders came from that area.

Far from being dismissible as a regional matter or a self-serving attempt to retain traditional power, the Thirteen's assertions of Tibetan-ness throw into relief the typology of Tibetan nationalism in exile. The ideation of the future state was shaped not only by the exile government and institutions such as the United Party but also by alternate narratives of Tibetan struggle, whether by armed resistance to the Chinese within Tibet or broad ideological ambivalence toward the exile government's vision of unity.

Individuals I interviewed expressed concern that I was attempting to revive the story about the Thirteen. Those who had been members of the United Party, not coincidentally historically aligned with the dominant faction in the exile polity, felt the story of the Group of Thirteen and the death of Gungthang Tsultrim exposed an ugly conflict they preferred to forget. They believed the Thirteen had been a political organization aspiring to power and that this still had potential to work in favor of the Chinese. They shared the opinion expressed by politician and diplomat Lodi Gyaltsen Gyari, known to Tibetans as Gyari Rinpoche, in his autobiography that the Thirteen "literally broke away from Dharamsala."[29] Gyari Rinpoche explains that there was no "CTA presence" in the Thirteen settlements and that Tibetan exile officials avoided going there for fear "of being harassed."[30] Such indirect obloquies were more prevalent than I had expected from Tibetan elders who had lived through the period. Such views have served to cement the Thirteen's character as dangerous, reinforcing the existing stereotype of Khampas as hectoring, aggressive, and capricious regionalists. Often those who felt this way declined to speak to me.

In contrast, members of the Thirteen felt that talking about their banishment in exile broke open the old canker they labored to keep hidden. They showed me with unmasked bitterness the cumulative toll of being labeled as traitors in the exile government's official texts and informal narratives, which elided their perspectives. They suggested that in adopting state-like processes to realize its national goals, the government made diverse ways of belonging difficult. The subtext that emerges from their conversations with me is about belonging: their desire for recognition from the exile government, affirming not just their societal and cultural values but also their desire for meaningful integration. They did not expect that creating their own settlements would be translated as breaking away from a government formed to protect Tibetans. All the individuals I interviewed agreed that the Group of Thirteen was formed as a cultural entity to protect their multiple regional histories and religious traditions.

Individuals who identified as belonging to the Thirteen spoke the same grammar of pain. People who had never met face to face, people who had only heard of the other settlements, began their stories the same way. They voiced a similar weary acknowledgment of what they identified as misjudgment, namely, their having been accused of receiving funds from Taiwan or of opposing the exile government. In turn, they blamed the United Party for many injuries but stopped short of offering any evidence. They used the pronoun "we," implying the collective nature of the Thirteen.

"We were driven together to shield ourselves from the United Party," they said.

"It's the government who made us outcasts. They did not keep in touch with us," said Jadur Sonam Zangpo in Dolanji, who had served in the CTA as a supreme justice commissioner and a member of parliament.[31]

They expressed that their requests to the exile government to protect them from the United Party were not taken seriously. They also spoke of the exile government and the United Party interchangeably.

The elders repeated questions they had posed among themselves in the early years of exile life: "Who has power over the Tibetan polity—the exile government or the United Party?" "Where does the latter's power come from?" (They wanted the exile government to confirm its special relation with the United Party.) Indeed, by 1969 the United Party had representatives in Kathmandu and the Khumbu valley in Nepal, and in Rajpur, Ola Pari, Mainpat, Mysore, and Bylakuppe in India: branch offices in most places where the exile government ran settlements. In 1968, the United Party had also moved its headquarters from Darjeeling to Dharamsala, where, according to the party, they were given a room in a house that belonged to the Private Office of the Dalai Lama.[32]

The elders' questions regarding the United Party are not crucial today as they were then; now the organization is barely known. That is why it is possible to write this book and to ask if alternative steps could have been taken to achieve Tibetan unity without falling into the worn plot of nation-states. The United Party's expressed intention was to move beyond the sectarianism of regional identities by building a community based on shared histories, cultures, and future dreams, but it might not have recognized that the unifying vision it held out was marked by a Central Tibetan and Gelug provenance. Furthermore, what the party labeled treachery could have alternatively been understood as the need of Tibetan refugees to be with members of their clans. It was not just political ambition driving people together; it was simple human longing to be comforted, and to find a way to survive forced dispersal and heartbreak. Likewise, the Thirteen's expressed intention was to serve the nation by preserving the unique features of their regions and religion, but they might have misinterpreted the call for unity as negatively implicating them and tearing them away from their traditional leaders and members. Be that as it may, the imbalance of power between the two groups also played a role in how events unfolded.

Even decades after the difficult years, many elders hesitated to speak about the hardships they experienced. They narrated their stories to me in careful generalities and often abandoned their sentences midway, discouraged that their sorrow could not be captured in words. Those who were part of the Thirteen felt that I would tell my own version of the story, not theirs. Labeled as traitors, they recounted having themselves felt betrayed. Listening closely to these many elders in the Tibetan settlements and repeatedly returning to their interviews, I learned that they understood themselves as people caught in a pivotal phase of their nation's story. I want this book to make their experience of nation building an inseparable part of the history of Tibetan exile.

The events and particular aspects of the Thirteen's experiences are not easily reconciled to a recognizable past or present features of nationalism elsewhere. Nor can their ongoing and unpredictable journey be viewed through one discipline. The theorist and political historian Benedict Anderson alludes to the philosophical difficulties in writing about nationalism in the introduction to *Mapping the Nation*. He asks the open-ended question whether there is a discipline best equipped to address the phenomenon.[33] This is not an easy story to write even from my positions as a Tibetan, writer, and scholar.

The narratives I listened to have multiple exits and entries. Often only emotions are legible. Perhaps this is because even though goals of Tibetan nationalism have undergone change—for example, the official Middle Way Approach in place of independence—the Thirteen remain fixed in a particular infamous role in exile history. They were never freed from that role as promised. There are also many secrets, rumors, speculations, and misunderstandings about them and their past. The problem is not restricted to perspective. Then, there's language. I listened to elders who spoke in the various dialects of Kham I am familiar with, Nangchen, Derge, and Gawa, as well as the dialects of Amdo, such as Labrang, that I struggled with. Even within these dialects there are many differences. Many words went through multiple translations; some remain approximates, some emotions live as metaphors. I tried to capture the common threads in the narratives. I followed departures from a shared plot if they emerged.

The elders were curious about what I had learned from other settlements: How had the settlement leaders met one another? Had the Karmapa really gone to get the Dalai Lama's consent to be the leader for the Thirteen? If His Holiness had given permission for the Thirteen to form, why were they known as antigovernment? Did some members of the Thirteen take money from Taiwan? Was Gyalo

Thondup behind all decisions made by the United Party? The elders were also curious to see the pamphlets produced by the Thirteen or the texts produced by the United Party. They had known of the contents but had not seen the texts. Often we would puzzle over a question together. For example: Why do Khampas feel marginalized when there are many minority groups even within U-Tsang? Why did the Thirteen hold Gyalo Thondup accountable for all their struggles? What proof did Tibetans in Clement Town have to blame Tenzin for killing Akhu Tsultrim? They offered theories: a pair of spectacles belonging to Tenzin was found outside Akhu Tsultrim's house the evening of the murder; Tenzin was known to Amdowas in Clement Town; someone in Nepal admitted it was him; and so on.

Perhaps the nation and its parts were more fully revealed to Tibetans when they had to flee from it. What had they overlooked previously that they longed for in its absence? What had they seen necessary to disavow in order to begin anew? How did Tibetans read the indistinct relations between their regions and the new exile government in those early years? If unity meant the construction of an integrated identity, as the Thirteen suspected, who was being asked to assimilate and toward what end? To ask these questions and to write alongside the Thirteen, I have drawn from various disciplines, including literature, cultural studies, history, psychology, sociology, anthropology, and Buddhism. But most of all, this book is informed by what was shared with me as I listened to how Tibetans reflected upon, understood, and narrated events from their own lives. I turned to the archive of ephemeral texts they produced: handwritten notes, letters to the government, speeches, their memory, and their heartache. This archive is fragmented and filled with gaps, as are the lives of its displaced authors.

"The group had been established out of necessity," my friend Sodam responded after I asked him why the Thirteen was formed. Now eighty-three years old, he had been the secretary for the settlement in Kamrao and had attended most of the meetings held by the

Thirteen. I met him in Dharamsala in 2015 and then again in Clement Town in 2017 and 2022.³⁴

"It's not a long story," Lobsang Gyatso in Dolanji stated. "It began in 1964 and ended in 1979," after Gungthang Tsultrim's death.³⁵

"Killing Gungthang Tsultrim meant killing all of us. Each person felt the gunshot aimed at them," recalled Chime Luthoktsang, who was living in Boudhanath, Kathmandu, when we met in the summer of 2017.³⁶

Contrary to stories that the Thirteen received funds from Taiwan, the leaders struggled to raise the money to find Gungthang Tsultrim's murderer(s) and file a case against them. Sodam said that each leader was requested to offer 10,000 Indian rupees (Rs.) if they could. A Tibetan man who had friends in Clement Town was arrested. Sodam said that he was set free after five years in jail.

"It's not a story that matters today," another elder in Bir said. What he meant was that the Thirteen was now integrated into the Tibetan exile community.

External observers often commend the Tibetan refugee and diasporic community for its cohesion. Tibetan unity, like democracy and a reasonably safe refugee existence in exile, is attributed to the Dalai Lama. His life has been tied to the Tibetan nation and its people since he was recognized as the Fourteenth Dalai Lama in 1937 at the age of three in Taktser, a village in Amdo, the northeast region of Tibet. He was formally enthroned when he was four-and-a-half years old and had to assume political leadership of Tibet at the age of fifteen, at the nation's most crucial moment.³⁷ The Dalai Lama was seen as the only person who could bring Tibetans together under a single government in exile, and since 1959 he has remained the glue keeping Tibetans together. His vision continues to guide both personal and national perspectives even though he stepped down from his political responsibilities in 2011.

After just five years in exile, Tibetan refugees had, with the help of the Indian government and international aid agencies, acquired land that they had begun clearing for refugee settlements, procured access to medical care, and established schools. These resources were also possible because the Dalai Lama prioritized them in exile. Like his predecessor, the Thirteenth Dalai Lama, the Fourteenth Dalai Lama used his position to improve life for ordinary Tibetans.

The Thirteenth Dalai Lama led numerous initiatives to modernize Tibet. There were many firsts under his rule: a telegraph line was built between Lhasa and Gyantse; a hydroelectric plant was planned; and an English school was established in Gyantse in 1924. However, the Thirteenth Dalai Lama's efforts to bring change were opposed by conservative religious monastic bodies and sections of the Tibetan government in Lhasa. The religious leaders particularly resisted Western-style schools and military expansion, as they believed that Tibet was a Buddhist country and wished to preserve its religious character. Their primary loyalty was to Buddhism and the Gelugpa monastic order, not the nation, according to anthropologist and historian Melvyn C. Goldstein.[38]

The Thirteen are sometimes compared to conservative religious leaders of the past. Their resistance to unity in exile, characterized as an unwillingness to give up their power by Gyari Rinpoche and as conservatism by the United Party, leaves out important details. The religious Gelug institutions in Central Tibet *were* the government. As Tsering Shakya writes, all monk officials in the Tibetan government were "exclusively recruited" from the Gelugpa monasteries in Lhasa's vicinity.[39] The Kashag (cabinet) and other officials were also more than likely to be Gelug. Gelug rule had been the norm in Central Tibet since the seventeenth century. This was not so for the Thirteen leaders representing the schools of Bon, Gelug, Kagyu, Nyingma, and Sakya. They had little power over the narrative of Tibet in exile. Their critique of the discourse of unity was, in part, that it did not adequately challenge the norms of the Lhasa system.

Unlike his predecessor, the Fourteenth Dalai Lama was able to implement changes and bring considerable stability and democracy in the Tibetan community. The 1960s was a crucial decade for the formation of the Tibetan nation in exile and of a modern polity for Tibetans. This is when the Tibetan government in exile, officially known as the Central Tibetan Administration (CTA), undertook the concurrent initiatives to rehabilitate dispossessed Tibetans in temporary settlements, provide work for the able-bodied, educate Tibetan children despite scarce material and human resources, and establish its legitimacy. Several Tibetan civil, social, and political organizations were established after being vetted by the exile government.

The Fourteenth Dalai Lama's initiative to change a system over which his institution has provided political leadership for nearly four centuries is extraordinary. He began to draft a constitution for a future Tibet based on the principles of justice, equality, and democracy as laid down by the Universal Declaration of Human Rights as well as the doctrine of Buddha. This strategic framing allowed for flexible interpretations and consideration of the needs of the people while also getting international support. On the one hand, the features associated with modern states such as egalitarianism, freedom, and rights could be highlighted to present the modernity of the Tibetan constitution as well as the unity of people so that it could gain recognition from entities such as the United Nations, other established powerful states, and educated Tibetans in favor of political as well as social reform. On the other hand, tracing the genealogy of these features, in particular (Western) democracy, to traditional Buddhist precepts could satisfy Tibetans who held Buddhism as a dominant and long-standing influence on Tibetan identity and history.[40] The Dalai Lama hoped that Tibetan refugees would elect a representative assembly and build an "interim constitution" for the country they wished to return to.[41] In his statement on the second anniversary of the Tibetan National Uprising Day on March 10, 1961, he asked Tibetans to prepare for the day "when we can return to our country and build a happier and greater independent Tibet."[42]

Unlike many national movements, Tibetans have not had to invent a national spirit to represent their nation. The Dalai Lama already existed as the political leader as well as the incarnation of the bodhisattva Avalokitesvara guiding Tibet. The devotion Tibetans feel toward the Dalai Lama is rooted in his role as part deity, part leader, and part parent. As deity, he is beyond reproach; all ideas and wishes expressed by the Dalai Lama are received as truth and blessing. This has meant that any attempt to critique or question the policies of the Dalai Lama is received by the exile community as a kind of unfaithfulness punishable by community members. He is often referred to as the head as well as the heart of the national body. He is the heartbeat of the nation. He binds the Tibetan people, those inside Tibet and those in the diaspora. This gives Tibetan unity its precarity, its potency, and its preciousness.

For Tibetans, loyalty to the Dalai Lama means loyalty to Tibet. This has meant that he has borne the task of raising and shaping his people's political awareness in a variety of ways. His message to Tibetans to realize their own aspirations and exercise their powers and responsibilities are goals they hope to achieve. Tibetans believe in the Dalai Lama's hope to create a just society and a robust and progressive administration. They also continue to lean heavily on him for both spiritual and political guidance. The Dalai Lama's efforts in exile have served to exemplify his exceptional leadership and deepened Tibetans' sense of gratitude and indebtedness toward him.

Democracy, Tibetans assert, is a gift from the Dalai Lama.

Trine Brox, a scholar in Tibetan studies, suggests democracy is a gift that is largely unopened by Tibetans. She observes that the more they accept the gift, the more they seek the Dalai Lama as the "ultimate authority."[43] In his examination of democracy, scholar Jigme

Yeshe Lama observes that Tibetan exiles curb democratic rights of individuals in the "name of the Dalai Lama" out of loyalty to him and the need to stay united. The naming of democracy as a gift limits Tibetans' "questioning the democratic policies of the exiled government" but also leads to "criticism, and sometimes even excommunication or violence" against individuals who question the government.[44] Naming democracy "a gift" implies to some degree that the leader has no will to dominate, and therefore this makes the idea of an equal society more available. Tibetans also seem to interpret an equal society as one that feels the same way about things, and while there is unanimity about the idea of homecoming, it is harder to find agreement on other ideas, such as recognizing a diverse population, new cultural struggles, or considering U-Tsang and Gelug dominance as a hegemonic construction. Unity was seen as paramount for freedom. All efforts, even democracy, were seen to exist to promote unity. This is probably why in the first two decades of life in exile Tibetans feared factionalism from two sources: communalism and diverse voices.[45]

A society of Tibetans or the Tibetan nation had existed in many forms long before the national movement. However, under the new historical conditions of dispossession, being Tibetan is being incorporated as refugee-citizens administered by a centrally organized government. Diverse people from the three regions of Tibet had to be woven together as equal citizens in exile. Whether nationalism is understood in Eric J. Hobsbawm's definition, as a political arrangement where groups that see themselves as nations have the right to form territorial states, or in Dawa Norbu's view, as a history of "rising social consciousness" goal-driven to produce social power for the public and political including the desire for a new political community, Tibetan nationalism in its present form is tied to the Chinese occupation of Tibet.[46] Tibetans had to realize and attempt to meet their purpose as refugees in the in-between space of exile. I believe they did what they had to do, what was in their power to do. They were learning too, amid the disintegration of everything they held familiar, how to imagine a future and build a nation without living on their nation's territory.[47] It was and is a tremendous undertaking.

Legibility is important to transform a nation into a state. It is also crucial for individuals who are expected to follow terms of belonging to a state. Most members of the Thirteen had lived in nomadic communities in Tibet. Their livelihoods, choices, and practices were not always legible to those outside their regional systems. The elders taught me that the Thirteen saw themselves as people who had stories about who they were. Not unlike the populations of other forming states, Tibetans faced the process of negotiating between deference and dissent and between unity and difference. Not unlike people in other national liberation movements, many advocates of Tibetan independence saw sectarian or regional identities as a threat. They feared those separate identities would disrupt Tibetan unity and possibly serve others instead, such as the interests of China.

Minutes of meetings of the Tibetan cabinet in the 1970s reveal their awareness of the United Party's power within Tibetan society. They discussed warning the United Party to restrain themselves from overstepping boundaries. Such conversations suggest the Thirteen's assessment of the party's power was not misplaced or unfounded. However, the Thirteen's critique of the United Party's power was also a critique of the government for overlooking or inviting the party's efforts to be a stakeholder in the Tibetan future while questioning the Thirteen for harboring similar ambitions. Thus, their opposition to the United Party was seen as challenging the Tibetan government. Minutes of meetings also reveal that exile political leaders sensed there were Tibetans who lacked faith in the government. Unlike the present—when skepticism about exile leaders is exercised, even exulted in by Tibetan people—revealing any uncertainty regarding the government in the early years was interpreted as a failure on the part of the individual, not the government. This is likely because the leaders, the Kashag, were nominated by the Dalai Lama. To express doubt in their capacity was seen to indirectly express a lack of faith in the Dalai Lama. The majority of Tibetans viewed this as a form of a moral and spiritual failure on the part of the individual.

According to historian Prasenjit Duara, national integration has a peaceful ring to it, but it rarely has been a peaceful process. In an essay on deconstructing the Chinese nation, Duara pushes back against the notion that national identity is a new form of consciousness. He writes that not just modern societies are capable of creating self-conscious political communities. Nor does he privilege the grand narrative of the nation as "a collective historical subject."[48] He counters that nationalism represents the space where different views of the nation confront each other.

Duara suggests that the people can have very diverse ideas of the nation, but their sense of identification with the nation can override the differences. For example, one can feel Australian or Chinese, but the differences in what that entails are often "temporarily submerged" when there is a common outside threat.[49] The power of the feeling for nation, which Duara suggests is also the very same feeling dividing fellow nationals, comes from what it means to be of a particular nationality. These feelings are formed from cultural signifiers that include narratives, symbols, and practices. Duara states that the master narrative of a nation mobilizes a community by "privileging a particular practice" as its constitutive principle, which shapes who belongs and who doesn't.[50] In an earlier work on nation formation, Duara identifies historical education as one of the main means to "identity formation," in that it teaches individuals to love the new national self and to hate the enemy.[51]

Anthropologist Clifford Geertz identifies two powerful dialectical desires that animate people of new states: the "desire to be recognized as responsible agents" whose hopes, opinions, and wishes matter in the world, and the desire to build a "dynamic modern state."[52] He suggests that the first desire is oriented toward the search for identity and for that identity to be "publicly acknowledged," and the second is practical and linked to having a better standard of living, a more effective political life, and social justice over time. The tension between these two desires becomes important in shaping the new state because people's sense of self is bound to locality, religion, language, or tradition. Geertz contends that independence movements built on directing the energy of the people against foreign domination obscure the "frailty" of the movements' cultural foundations.

The answer to the question of who we are, or the quest to seek a collective subject from within (after independence), is often built out of cultural forms that take the routes of indigeneity or history. Both these forms, according to Geertz, are entangled in new states.[53] National unity is mostly maintained by "vague, intermittent, and routine allegiance" to a civil state and not to primordial attachments (religion, region, kin, and so on).[54] But in societies where civil politics is weak and the technicalities necessary for an effective welfare state are not understood well, primordial attachments, he suggests, become bases for autonomous political units. This conflict between "primordial and civil sentiments" becomes a source of concern for the state, because although these formations don't threaten the nation, they have the potential to undermine governments.[55] Both Duara and Geertz are talking about the longing that sits in the heart of a new state and the tensions that have to be negotiated in cultivating the "fellow feeling" crucial to keeping the national heart beating.

The answer to the question of who we are was acceptable insofar as it focused on the integration of a differentiated Tibetan population in early exile life. The form as well as the elements of Tibetan national identity focused on known and dominant features that were also linked to Central Tibet. In his discussion on Irish identity in *Anomalous States*, the poet and scholar David Lloyd focuses not on the question, "Who or what are we?" but instead on the function of an "unanswerable question" that has to do with the assimilation of subjects as citizens.[56] He illustrates how the formation of identity is a process that, among other processes, requires the "negation of other possible forms of existing."⁵⁷ Lloyd points out that the state becomes the end of representation, and cultural forms that question the state are in danger of being suppressed or viewed as out of step with the national values.

The Tibetan exile community's continued focus on unity and its framing of regionalism as an act of disunity can be viewed as part of the process of the creation of a new polity and a new form of citizenship. That focus is shaped by the values given to unity within a limited definition of what it means to be a Tibetan in exile and, perhaps more pertinently, it divests primordial attachments that could be in the way of the new government. The tension in the Tibetan independence movement and the narrative of what it means to be a Tibetan, in relation to China, also came from obscuring the differences of Tibetan regional identity. While it was easy to galvanize everyone to identify a shared timeline to the loss of nation or feel certainty in not being Chinese, building solidarity behind the idea of what made a Tibetan, Tibetan proved more complex.

What it means to belong to a political community and what it means to belong to a community are different questions and experiences for Tibetans inside Tibet and Tibetans living in exile. These questions are not theoretical but experienced in quotidian tasks. By promulgating an alternative vision of Tibetan exile nationalism—one inclusive of religious and regional autonomy and plurality—the Thirteen leaders and its people found themselves between a rock and a hard place: between Chinese incursions against Tibetan sovereignty and the exile government's marginalization of their historical experience and of Khampa politics as traitorous concerns. In attempting to write a part of the story about a Tibetan nation to come, I am reevaluating and inserting their position, deemed recalcitrant and harmful, into the national narrative. I am also simultaneously asking: What constitutes a literary archive for a people who are dispossessed, and in what way does the in-betweenness of their lives shape the ideals and structure of the future nation? The texts produced by the Thirteen and the United Party allow for examining the practice of belonging and the development of rights-bearing individuals as refugee-citizens in the formative years of Tibetan exilic life. This entails studying not just what the Thirteen set out to accomplish and remember and their interactions with members of the group and with the exile government, but also what the Tibetan society and the exile government knew of the Thirteen's existence and histories, and how it viewed their contributions to that national narrative.

The United Party maintained that its goal was to bring Tibetans together in exile to secure an independent Tibet that would give every Tibetan a place in society. The party pushed for social reform, education, limiting the power of traditional leaders, and a democratic government. They were asking Tibetans to turn their attention to the needs of building a different Tibetan nation. The Thirteen were attempting to express questions linked to changes in personal and political lives: Who is the exile government serving and preserving—the Tibetan people, individual people, or institutions in power? What is the relationship between the government and the people? Where are we going? Who is included in the story of the nation? These questions indicate loss. They are also questions that touch the nerve of political life in any complex society.

These questions remain relevant even or especially today, when achieving the reality of a free Tibet appears more challenging.

Will there come a time when Tibetans accept life in exile as a Tibetan way of life?

What then will be the category by which we know ourselves?

1

A GOVERNMENT IN EXILE

One of the first accounts of the Dalai Lama's dramatic escape from Tibet in 1959 was written for *Time* magazine by Heinrich Harrer, an Austrian who had spent seven years in Tibet between 1946 and 1952. Harrer had come to know the young leader personally in his brief role as tutor. The Dalai Lama, holding a bouquet of flowers in his arms, smiles into a crowd in the cover photo of the magazine's April 29, 1959, issue. Describing the Dalai Lama's comportment in the tumultuous time, Harrer writes, "The god-king's manner, distinguished but as natural as that of a warm-hearted Westerner seemed to make light of his recent adventure."[1]

Tenzin Gyatso, the Fourteenth Dalai Lama, the spiritual and political leader of the Tibetan government and people, left Tibet in disguise and on horseback on March 17, 1959. In his autobiography *Freedom in Exile*, the Dalai Lama writes that he had consulted the Nechung oracle on whether he ought to stay in Tibet or leave. The oracle had instructed him to flee that very night and written down the route he was to take. Thus was charted the way by which the twenty-four-year-old leader and thousands of other Tibetans would travel to a life in exile. Author Jamyang Norbu suggests that Lord Chamberlain Phala Thupten Woeden might have already planned for the Dalai Lama to leave on March 17, including the route. He playfully notes an element of supernatural revisionism in the Dalai Lama's reference to the oracle's prophetic charge.²

The Dalai Lama was accompanied out of Norbulingka, his summer residence, by his chief of staff, his chief bodyguard, the lord chamberlain, and two soldiers. The small party was met on the other side of the river Kyichu in Lhasa by a band of Tibetan military and resistance fighters from the Chushi Gangdrug. The Dalai Lama's older brother Gyalo Thondup writes in his book *The Noodle Maker of Kalimpong* that by the time the party reached Lhokha in southern Tibet, they had an entourage of a hundred people and were guarded by 350 Tibetan Army soldiers and 50 Chushi Gangdrug warriors. Chushi Gangdrug men were posted at every pass. Lithang Athar Norbu, one of the key figures of the people's armed movement, messaged the CIA about the Dalai Lama's safe arrival at the Indian border.

The Dalai Lama recalls entering India on March 31, 1959, "in a daze of sickness and weariness and unhappiness," deeper than he knew how to express, in *My Land and My People*.³ By the year's end, as many as fifty thousand Tibetans had followed him to seek refuge in the neighboring countries of Bhutan, India, and Nepal.

The Dalai Lama's first political action in exile was to formally repudiate the Seventeen-Point Agreement with China at a press conference in India on June 20, 1959, thereby establishing that it no longer was binding. Declaring that the agreement had been signed under duress gave the Dalai Lama room to argue that the Tibetan claim to sovereignty had not altered from the time before Tibetan delegates had signed the agreement. His second significant political action was the establishment of the Tibetan government-in-exile in India, first informally, when he declared, "Wherever I am, accompanied by my government, the Tibetan people recognize us as the government of Tibet" at his first press conference in Mussoorie.⁴ Not long after, the Dalai Lama formally re-established the government-in-exile, also known as the Central Tibetan Administration (CTA), in Dharamsala,

India, as the continuation of the government of independent Tibet. He was clear in his address to Tibet support groups in Bonn in 1996 that the Tibetan government had a history over three hundred years; it was not a new entity.

The CTA is a continuation of this earlier establishment, but it is an altered polity with new policies and a new historical course. First, the Dalai Lama chose not to rule as he had done in Tibet. Under his leadership, the exile government shed many older traditions that conflicted with democratic principles, including the scope of his own power. The Dalai Lama's leadership is unique in that he has encouraged and led Tibetans—who had no prior experience of democracy and democratic leadership as we know it today—to take individual responsibility in building the future independent Tibetan nation-state.

As early as November 1959, the Dalai Lama reminded civil employees of the CTA that Tibetans had not come to India for "mere survival" but to restore independence to Tibet.[5] He also advised them to avoid creating hostility in the name of regional divisions, monastic institutions, or military affiliations. He encouraged Tibetans to set their personal interests aside and to work toward a common goal through actions, not mere words.

The Dalai Lama has stated that he began building a "qualified administration in harmony with the time" as soon as he could so that the exile government could "gather greater credibility, respect and recognition" from the Indian government as well as from "the free world countries around the globe" to counter China.[6] The twofold political initiative to achieve full democratization of the CTA and the liberation of Tibet was initially led by men. The first and second cabinet members he picked were men who had served in the Lhasa government. Zurkhang Wangchen Gelek had been a cabinet minister in Lhasa and became the chair of the cabinet in exile; Neshar Thupten Tharpa had served as the foreign secretary in Lhasa and became the minister of foreign affairs in exile; Shenkha Gurmey Topgyal had been a deputy minister in Lhasa and became the minister of religion; and Gadrang Lobsang Rigzin, who had been the head of ecclesiastical affairs in Lhasa, became the minister of finance.

The highest legislative body of the government, the Commission of Tibetan People's Deputies, was established on September 2, 1960, with members representing the three regions of Tibet as well as the four Buddhist religious schools (Gelug, Kagyu, Nyingma, and Sakya); Bon (also an organized religious movement from Tibet) was added in the 1970s.[7] The first elections for the representatives took place on September 2, observed annually in exile as Tibetan Democracy Day. Ordinary Tibetans had never voted for any politician before. In the first few elections, many wrote the names of people from their region whom they respected to represent them. According to John F. Avedon, who wrote the first biography of the Dalai Lama, this meant that "all of the thirteen men whose names appeared most frequently were either important lamas, aristocrats or tribal chieftains from Kham and Amdo."[8] (There were thirteen members of parliament: one representative from each of the three regions and one representative from each of the four religious schools.)

In March 1963, four years after the Dalai Lama had left Tibet and on the fourth anniversary of the Lhasa uprising against the Chinese, the draft constitution was presented to the Tibetan public. The document included socialist guidelines to ensure equitable distribution of wealth as well as to secure a democratic process for a representative government.[9] This blend reflects the Dalai Lama's personal belief in the importance of people and of freedom. Democracy and reform were also wishes expressed by young nationalists in exile. The Tibetan exile government, a stateless entity, had to establish its legitimacy and prove that Tibetans had a national history with a deep past. Writing a state discourse in the conceptual space of exile—unhampered by the topographical challenges of manifold rugged terrain, distance between regions, plural self-identifications, and multiple political and cultural centers—also meant articulating what served the interest of the Tibetan people and nation to both an internal audience and a global audience.

Significant changes were made in the Tibetan exile administration in its first decade, including ending the traditional practice of requiring equal numbers of monks and lay officials in government, and abolishing hereditary titles in 1963. One of the important and difficult tasks of moving to full democracy was making legislative clauses to establish changes to the office of the Dalai Lama. This too was initiated by the Dalai Lama himself in a synopsis of a Draft Constitution of Tibet that included a clause limiting his own powers. Article 36, section (e) stated that the national assembly could decide, by a majority of two-thirds of its total members in consultation with the supreme court, that the executive function of His Holiness the Dalai Lama be "exercised by the Council of Regency" if that was seen to be in the best interests of the state.[10] Exile officials refused this clause. In *Freedom in Exile*, the Dalai Lama mentions that he insisted on leaving it in.[11] The seventy-seven articles of the constitution declared the "fundamental rights of all Tibetans to include those of universal suffrage, equality before the law, life, liberty and property, as well as freedom of religion, speech and assembly." All these changes entailed that the newly constituted government differed from what in Tibet has been described as a "working theocracy" by Dawa Norbu.[12]

The changes made by the Dalai Lama were unconventional and radical. Not all Tibetans were ready for them at the same time. The Dalai Lama mentions in his memoir that some were suspicious and suggested the government was practicing communism. John Avedon states that the reforms introduced by the Dalai Lama were not embraced by "a few noble families and Khampa chieftains, who thought that their power would be eroded."[13] Avedon's identification of the chieftains as challenging the reforms most likely reflects what his sources in Dharamsala believed. Doubts about Khampa cooperation appear to have been expressed even before Tibetans had cast off their heavy *chubas* (robes) upon entering India. Chamberlain Phala Thupten Woeden is alleged to have reminded newly arrived Khampa and Amdowa monks in Buxa, West Bengal, that they were now considered part of the Tibetan community and should not bring shame to Tibet.

Tibetans know their country as composed of three regions: U-Tsang (Central Tibet), Kham (Eastern Tibet), and Amdo (Northeastern Tibet). The terms "political" Tibet and "ethnographic" Tibet are used by some scholars and historians to distinguish between U-Tsang, ruled by the Dalai Lama until 1951, and the neighboring regions of Kham and Amdo. This differentiation was first made by Hugh Richardson, who served in Lhasa as a diplomat for the colonial Indian government in the 1930s and 1940s. According to Richardson, political Tibet was the area the Tibetan government ruled from an earlier time until 1951 and ethnographic Tibet was the regions over which the Tibetan government ruled only in "certain places and at irregular intervals."[14] The Tibetan government, however, did not accept these as permanently lost territories, as is evident in its claim to Kham and Amdo in the Simla Convention of 1913 to 1914 drawn up among Great Britain, China, and Tibet.[15] The Tibetan exile government's use of the term "Tibet" also includes all regions, eliding Richardson's historical differentiation.

Chinese leaders consider Tibet (or Xizang in Chinese, which means the "treasure in the west") as the western and central parts of the Tibetan plateau (U-Tsang), the regions ruled directly by the Tibetan government of the Dalai Lama until the Seventeen-Point Agreement in 1951. This is also referred to as the Tibetan Autonomous Region (TAR) today. It comprises less than half of the 2.5 million square kilometers of the combined Tibetan areas. Of the approximately 6 million Tibetans, 2.7 to 3 million live in the TAR while the rest live in Kham and Amdo.[16]

In contrast to their promises made to and agreement signed by the Lhasa government's representatives, the Chinese had no similar agreement with leaders in Kham. The Seventeen-Point Agreement had assured the Lhasa government that its political system would not be altered, its religious beliefs and culture would be respected, and reforms would not be imposed. Most significantly, it assured Tibetans that the Dalai Lama's position would stay as it was. But reforms were initiated in Amdo and Kham as early as 1953. These included dismantling the local political authority of monasteries and traditional systems and collectivizing monastic and elite holdings, which set off a series of isolated resistance movements all over Kham and Amdo in the mid-1950s, ultimately organized into an armed movement known as the Chushi Gangdrug. Some Khampa leaders had initially surrendered to Communist China, and many of them would later fight the Chinese by joining the resistance.[17]

The grassroots military resistance movement that erupted in the mid-1950s illustrates that Tibetans in Kham and Amdo did not accept the new terms of Chinese rule. The continuing pattern of revolts on the Tibetan plateau indicates that China has not yet won the hearts and minds of the Tibetan people. Regardless, as far as China is concerned, territories outside U-Tsang are not up for discussions involving Tibetan independence because they had not been under the jurisdiction of the Tibetan government in 1950. This is why debates over the Kham and Amdo regions become so crucial and challenging for both the Chinese and the Tibetan governments.

Recent scholarship on Kham polities and history examines their centrality in the late-nineteenth and early twentieth-century relations between China and Tibet. Works such as Yudru Tsomu's on Jago Tobden of the Derge kingdom and on Gönpo Namgyel of Nyarong in the 1920s help demonstrate power changes within polities and show how certain regions of Kham found themselves caught in the middle of competing forces that included the Tibetan government in Lhasa, the Chinese Nationalist government, Chinese warlords, and the Khampa elite. Tsomu's research on representations of Kham by Chinese Republican intellectuals shows how the political differences between the local polities and the Lhasa government were seen as advantageous to these scholars and administrators' project to recover Kham into the Chinese imagination during the Chinese Republican period.[18]

Present scholarship on Kham and Amdo as borderlands also points to the complexity and diversity in the multiethnic composition of its peoples and systems. Yudru Tsomu describes Derge, ruled by a king, as a "feudal state with a decentralized bureaucracy" where hereditary officials were given land in exchange for administering them.[19] The region had a total of thirty-three local chiefs or headmen and forty-three nomadic tribes in the 1940s. A scholar of Buddhism and of Nangchen, Maria Turek, describes Nangchen, also ruled by a king, as more akin to a federation of twenty-five pastoral clans and eighteen monastic districts under "a royal banner."[20] The terms "tribe," "clan," and "regions" have been used to speak of the polities even though they might not encompass their particular sociocultural realities.

Understanding Kham's diversity, and the state-resistant attitude of many nomadic pastoralists, might also help contextualize the initial tentativeness of certain Khampa leaders toward the CTA in the first decade of life in exile. Although nomads, or *drokpas* in Tibetan, can be seen as subalterns because they are "targets of cultural assimilation" and because their voices are not included in written historical records for the most part, historian Mark E. Frank focuses instead on *drokpa* agency in his study of Tibetan nomads in Kham. He views nomadism as a technology that helped produce state-resistant spaces and one honed over centuries of "human adaptation to the local environment."[21] Frank writes that nomadism was taken as an unfortunate consequence of isolation by Chinese modernists and intellectuals. They figured that nomadic pastoralism would disappear when the people came into contact with farming. Agriculture, Frank suggests, was a "technology" of assimilation.[22]

Frank notes a spatial feature to *drokpa* or nomad life that is resistant to assimilation. He does not attribute this "state-resistant space" to environmental determinism or human exceptionalism but suggests that nomads were able to produce these spaces because of their knowledge of the environment and their ability to sustain their herds.[23] In that aspect Frank departs from James C. Scott, who argues that the rugged terrain of the Southeast Asian Massif, which he names Zomia, became the refuge for individuals who wished to escape capture or control by lowland states, in particular, the Chinese empire.

Frank understands resistance to the state not by choosing to focus on either humans or the environment but by seeing human and nonhuman actors as transforming one another. He points out that Khampa nomadic pastoralism included "humans, bovids, and grasslands" as the most "salient members" of the space.[24] This interdependent nature is a crucial feature. The spatial element in nomadic life and its resistance to assimilation is understood as *drokpa* feeling by the elders in the Thirteen settlements, who predominantly came from nomadic communities in Kham. The bond among land, human, and herd is reflected in their histories, their myths, and their love for their homeland. And, although nomadic communities were headed by indigenous leaders, nomads knew that their mobility was foundational to their life. It kept them close to their clan and permitted them to leave without too much trouble to seek refuge with another lord or *behu* if they needed to. In Nangchen, the practice of seeking refuge in another clan was known as *gotakpa*.

For many Khampa polities, the power of rule was counted in terms of population, particularly important in nomadic communities hungry for members. This meant that mobility was useful as leverage against those in power: not only could Tibetan nomads move without losing much, but also they were easily accepted into another community.[25] Disputes between clans in Nangchen were often resolved by mediators who brokered the one at fault giving an agreed-upon number of families to the other clan leader. Thus the population ruled diminished in one and grew in the other. Nomads understood that their mobility gave them power. Indigenous justice systems such as this kept the ecosystem of humans, bovids, and the grassland in mind even if their mediation traditions or systems were viewed as outdated or barbaric by others.[26] That is to say, justice operated on a set of values and principles that departed from that of the state. In the same way, it might be helpful to read against the grain when thinking about place and allegiance.

The belief in the coexistence of an animated landscape (of local mountain deities, indigenous territorial spirits assimilated into Buddhism) and its people shaped how communities in Kham understood authority, held relations within and outside the clan, and developed a sense of belonging. Local narratives do not indicate with any certainty that Kham polities sought a stable political unity. Allegiance to their respective local chieftains and indigenous territorial spirits was sometimes even held above loyalty to the local king in the diverse kingdoms of Chakla, Derge, Nangchen, Lingtsang, and Lhathok. Within Khampa polities, group identities rarely extended far beyond their clans or regions and did not develop into allegiance to a singular Kham or Amdo nation, as indicated by the elders I spoke to and in the texts of McGranahan, Dawa Norbu, and Tsomu. This is also evident in the armed struggle against the Chinese that spread through regions of Kham and Amdo in the 1950s. The Chushi Gangdrug, McGranahan reminds us in *Arrested Histories*, was not a creation of the CIA, the Tibetan government, or later leaders such as Andrugtsang Gompo Tashi or Gyalo Thondup.[27] The Chushi Gangdrug was a movement of the people organized alongside independent and autonomous resistance efforts in response to Chinese occupation and oppression. This system continued to shape the organization in exile until it was no longer manageable. The category of a homogenous Khampa identity is likely a recent phenomenon, first offered by non-Khampas. In exile, it has further developed due to broader regional identifications and also been galvanized by Khampas from different regions to secure their identity.

With the Chinese invasion of Tibet, being or feeling Tibetan obtained an additional meaning: a shared suffering of losing a homeland. The nature of exile forced Tibetans into a different spatial and temporal reckoning, and from this new space, they plotted their way back to the home from which they had been thrust. Home, however, held different images and narratives for the thousands of Tibetans tossed like barley grains out of their ancestral lands, and the loss meant that their stories had different political stakes. Out of the many images of home and homeland that Tibetans tried to make recognizable to one another, they had to select the stories that could prove they were an independent people. The Dalai Lama captures the situation poignantly: it had not occurred to Tibetans that they would have to provide "legal proof to the outside world" that they were an independent nation because their freedom had seemed so obvious to them.[28]

The proclamation issued by the Thirteenth Dalai Lama in 1913 had affirmed his absolute rule in Tibet and over all Tibetans, and although the document may not have conformed to Western norms of a declaration of independence, it indicated, according to Melvyn C. Goldstein, the Dalai Lama's wish for freedom, as well as his plan to rule Tibet without Chinese interference given the political framework of the country in that era.[29] The proclamation can also be seen as introducing the notions of national agency, national independence, and the rights and responsibilities of citizens. It was both an expression of Tibetan national self-determination and an assertion of Buddhist values as requisite for national peace and happiness. The proclamation articulated the desire and need for social and political change in Tibetan society. The Fourteenth Dalai Lama's exile government made these changes a reality. The unification of the three Tibetan regions into a Tibetan polity under the circumstances of dispossession is one of the most significant political achievements in recent Tibetan history.

Yet exile officials rarely celebrate this unification. Instead, the biography of the nation outlined in speeches and texts, especially in the first two decades of life in exile, is the story of an always intact Tibet. Most national narratives begin with the Tibetan empire, linger on the advent of Buddhism in Tibet and its demise at the hands of King Lang Darma, and then, with the kind of leap that Tibetans make daily between the temporal and spiritual, tell the story of the nation suffering a tragedy with the Chinese invasion in 1950. That texts produced in exile in the 1960s and '70s overlooked or avoided the interruptions and discontinuities of foreign intimacies that shaped the territorial borders, sovereignty, and politics of the three regions of Tibet was not commented on by Tibetans. Lhasa had, after all, existed as the center of the Tibetan cosmos in the Tibetan imagination and in narratives since Buddhism's entry in the seventh century, despite changes in political leadership. Furthermore, study of Tibetan history is mostly concerned with Central and Western Tibet. In the 1960s exile landscape, scholarship and written histories on other regions were not readily available, in contrast to the present.

THE GREAT OATH

The official story of Tibetans in exile begins with the formal establishment of the exile government and the Dalai Lama's announcement that he was the leader of the Tibetan people. An alternative beginning is when Tibetans gathered in Bodh Gaya, India, to make an oath to follow every wish of the Dalai Lama.

A pilgrimage to Bodh Gaya is rarely a happenstance for Buddhists; it is a journey intended to accumulate merit for both the present and future lives. Traditionally identified as the place where Buddha gained enlightenment, Bodh Gaya is one of the most sacred Buddhist sites. The Bodhi tree, which serves as a symbol of the tree under which Buddha was enlightened, offers the comfort of continuity as well as simultaneity of time to believers. Cheme Dorjee, known to Tibetans as Dege Cheme—who once served with my mother in the Tibetan parliament and is the only Tibetan I know personally who was present in Bodh Gaya at the time when the oath was made in 1960—had set off from Buxa in West Bengal to Bodh Gaya in Bihar when he heard that the Dalai Lama was going to address the Tibetan public. (When asked, he said he was happy to be known as Dege Cheme because there were many people named Cheme Dorjee, even within the Derge community, but he is the only one recognized as Dege Cheme.)

Dege Cheme described his journey to me during a phone call in 2020 from Shillong, India, as being spontaneous but spurred by the possibility of seeing His Holiness the Dalai Lama, something he would never have dreamed of in his home in Derge, Kham.[30] In his reconstruction of that trip across an unfamiliar landscape, he narrated events as though they had taken place just the previous day. He spoke as though everything had been new and was being revealed simultaneously. Dege Cheme recalled he didn't have to pay for the journey. He and his friends had chanted "Gaya, Bodh Gaya, *babuji*," to ticket collectors before hopping onto trains.[31]

It is impossible to locate a policy that exempted Tibetans from paying for train tickets, but in his mind the wonder of the time was that he could travel to his destination without paying a fare. I suspect many Tibetans were not yet familiar with public transportation systems. My mother too had mentioned how she and her group of more than fifty people made their way from Kathmandu to Dharamsala in 1961–1962 by chanting "Dalai Lama, Dalai Lama" and "Dharamsala" before forcing their way into buses and trains. She had never seen a train before that journey and had not known then that each train had multiple stops and a final destination. It had taken her a while to get to Dharamsala. She reasoned that they might have zigzagged their way across India before reaching Pathankot. She conceded to me that she and her companions had looked desperate and formidable to passengers and train conductors.

Dege Cheme's personal accounts of the trip to Bodh Gaya and of other events in exile are shaped by feeling as much as by fact or information. A night before the oath-taking event he had listened to Wangdu Dorjee and Jagoetsang Namgyal Dorjee address an audience gathered in a large white tent belonging to the Chushi Gangdrug. In a different conversation with Dege Cheme in February 2023 on WhatsApp he told me that Chushi Gangdrug leaders Andrugtsang Gompo, Sandutshang Lo Nyendrak, and Gyen Yeshi, as well as two Lhasa aristocrats (he didn't know their names) and a few Gelug monks, had also been present. He described that evening in the tent as monumental and poignant. He had felt something important was being created. He speculated that the Chushi Gangdrug might have organized the event or come up with the idea for taking the oath. The evening had tilted toward a fracas when Chushi Gangdruk members Martham Thoesam and Gyen Yeshi aired the news of disappeared CIA funds, but others had redirected the tautness of that moment into something of a celebratory feeling of hope that Tibet could be taken back from China.[32] All Tibetans in that room had been in solidarity to follow the Dalai Lama's leadership. When I asked Cheme who had written the script for the vow, he said it had not been discussed during the meeting. He had not considered that to be important information. The symbolism of an impending vow had mattered; it had felt beautiful and powerful to him.

On February 3, 1960, Tibetan refugees representing the three provinces of Tibet and four major schools of Tibetan Buddhism offered an oath to the Dalai Lama. The sixty representatives, all men, pledged to continue their fight for Tibet's independence and offered *ten-shug*, or long-life offerings, to the Dalai Lama. The representatives also took an oath, commonly referred to as the *nagen thumo che*, "great oath of unity," or great oath, to make every possible effort toward freedom under the leadership of His Holiness the Dalai Lama.[33] The oath claimed that China was able to invade Tibet because the Tibetan people from the three provinces of U-Tsang, Kham, and Amdo had not been united and promised that Tibetans would henceforth eschew parochialism, sectarianism, and personal differences. The representatives promised to unite and stand together, solid as an iron ball. Ordinary Tibetans were not present at this event, Dege Cheme explained as though it should be obvious. Indeed, ordinary Tibetans scattered across India didn't know the oath was made on their behalf, yet when reflecting on this moment they embrace it as evidence of a shared Tibetan spirit.

Not quite a full year into exile, Tibetans were still figuring out the geography of the new lands they were forced into, still quelling their forlornness about not having the wherewithal to conduct prayers for their loved ones who had died on the journey and were dying upon arrival in India and Nepal, still searching for family members separated from them during their journey. Heartsore but grateful to be alive, they gathered to offer what they had in service to the nation.

An oath is not a unique feature in the story of human relations, national struggles, or the life of modern citizens. Moreover, Tibetans are intimately familiar with stories of oaths. They are how Buddhism was established in Tibet and how bitter enemies are made into allies. An oath is a promise, a first step, a binding element when needed. It is also a performative speech act. The great oath is a resolution. Tibetans were recognizing their task of having to simultaneously establish a refugee state and fight a national movement outside Tibetan territory. They turned inward and resolved to first unite the Tibetan body before concentrating on the enemy.

The oath can be interpreted in a few ways. First, it is yet another example of Buddhism's role in harnessing Tibetan anticolonial energy to unite all Tibetans against China's occupation.[34] Resistance to Chinese hegemony and rule since 1950 has been fueled by a sense of what Dawa Norbu calls "cultural sovereignty," at whose center Tibetans place the Fourteenth Dalai Lama.[35] Dawa Norbu suggests that antiimperialist nationalist leaders of the "Third World" recognized that "religion-induced culture that constituted the cultural hegemony of a given society" was effective in mobilizing the people. His point is that the core of any national identity, at least in its formative stages, is cultural, in addition to having other ideological dimensions.[36]

Dawa Norbu explains that Tibetans view the Dalai Lama as the symbol of their culture, religion, and sovereignty and that this helped produce a psychological basis among the people to oppose Han domination. On more than one occasion, the Dalai Lama has served as the symbol of Tibetan resistance. At the height of Chinese incursions into Tibet in 1950, the Lhasa government's first concern had not been to secure Tibet's territory or protect the Tibetan people but to ensure the safety of the Dalai Lama.[37] This was also the sentiment expressed by ordinary Tibetans in Lhasa who protested on March 10, 1959, when they realized he was in danger of being kidnapped by Chinese authorities. In his examination of the events, historian Tsering Shakya writes that one reason that prompted people to rise that day was their belief that 1959 was an obstructive year for the Dalai Lama. It was held that not only he but also the entire Tibetan nation would suffer. Hence, Tibetans turned up outside Norbulingka palace to express their anger when they heard rumors that Chinese officials meant to kidnap the Dalai Lama. They were also expressing their "resentment against the Tibetan ruling elite," whom they determined had betrayed him.[38] Such responses indicate that they believed the Dalai Lama was the only person with any influence over the entire Tibetan population.

The oath of allegiance in Bodh Gaya can also be read as the first significant political act in exile undertaken by Tibetans from all regions of Tibet to express a shared political goal and dream. The democratic Tibetan government-in-exile was initiated not long after this traditional contract of unwavering loyalty, burden of debt, and renouncement of dissent to obtain unity.[39] Tibetan diplomat and politician Gyari Rinpoche interprets the oath as a "collective affirmation" that all Tibetans were united under the Dalai Lama and that this unity was imperative for opposing their common enemy.[40] He suggests in his autobiography, *The Dalai Lama's Special Envoy*, that the oath led to a "powerful sense of nationalism" among the Tibetan people. It also allowed the Dalai Lama to bring considerable political and social changes to Tibetan society.[41] For example, the composition of governance in exile polity altered when he included individuals of nonaristocratic backgrounds in leadership positions.

Lastly, the oath may be read as a political commitment made to a religious leader by the people in the medium of a religious ceremony. In taking this oath, Tibetans can be seen as constituting a national culture whose foremost value is moral and religious. In pledging unquestioned loyalty and indebtedness to the Dalai Lama, they could be seen as establishing a moral code of obedience as a regulatory feature of the Tibetan polity and individual political life. By such an interpretation, Tibet's new political struggle is shaped by the spiritual. The oath brought Tibetans unswervingly into a direct relationship with the Dalai Lama, and not necessarily with the government or nation. Ironically, the oath to follow all his wishes contradicted the Dalai Lama's expressed wish for democracy. Thus, the oath casts significant light on shifts and continuities in Tibetan self-perception, particularly the continuing role of Tibetan Buddhism in the now democratic Tibetan nation. While it offered ordinary Tibetans the opportunity to participate in the exile government, it also left its imprint on what was acceptable as standards and codes of participation.

The men taking the oath were representatives from the famous Gelug institutions of Drepung, Sera, Ganden, Gyuto, and Gyume; from other religious schools; from the three Tibetan regions; from the Chushi Gangdrug, and from the government.[42] They expressed their debt to the Dalai Lama for helping Tibetans through the unimaginable loss of homeland. They expressed their belief that if all Tibetans were to unite, they would be able to find a path back to a free Tibet. Most of the people who took the oath are dead at the time of writing this book.

More than half of those sixty representatives were affiliated with religious institutions and likely familiar with oath taking as a means of social and political binding in Tibetan society. They would have been aware of various oaths that served as the glue between religious and internal politics in the courts of the early Tibetan kings. Some of them knew oath taking ensured fealty; they might have relied on it to build stability among their people in Tibet as well as to maintain their power. These men would have known that such vows are binding, that historic debt underlies the ritual of oaths.

The story of the gathering of recently dispossessed Tibetans and their pledge to the Dalai Lama is alluded to every now and then in political speeches as an example of the collective spirit of the Tibetan struggle. The event symbolizes the significance of the Dalai Lama to the Tibetan people. This is evident in the oath's emotional and intimate language. Addressed directly to the Dalai Lama, the oath expresses the need for Tibetans to abandon their self-serving and short-term interests for the benefit of all Tibetans.

> We profoundly regret our past mistakes and in future in accordance with your Holiness' deep vision, we will avoid engaging in any petty regionalism and remain united like a solid block of iron. There is no better way to bring short- and long-term benefits for all Tibetans than if we carry our responsibilities in accordance with His Holiness' vision and under his genuine and undisputed leadership. This is our common outlook, and we will never waver from this decision taken spontaneously and voluntarily with our hearts filled with bliss. In the event that anyone, whether high or low or whether of a religious or lay community, breaks even a tiny part of this pledge they will be subject to the dual system of the laws of the land as well as the religious systems. The concerned will be treated with the precision of an incision by a lancet removing pus from a body.

"PURE GREAT OATH," BODH GAYA, 1960[43]

The representatives take full responsibility for all past failings, which they describe as "petty regionalism" and animosities. The claim that ordinary Tibetan people brought the loss of homeland upon themselves—not the power struggles and inefficiency of ruling institutions and leaders, and not the wars involving lamas, aristocrats, and chieftains—tells us something about Tibetan society.[44] The oath in part answers the hypothetical question: Why was Tibet so easily invaded and colonized by China? Tibetans went inward for the answer. It is upon this acceptance of culpability—that ordinary people were at fault—that the campaign of unity rests. The new imperative toward unity led to the categorization of certain traditional ways of life and values, such as kinship and local affinities, as a newly pejorative regionalism. But these lifeways and values were considered necessities for many Kham communities, even as they have also been divisive.

The use of the term "regionalism" is important because it implied that Tibet had been lost because of internal tensions. This might be true in the longer story of the Tibetan nation, but the occupation of Tibet had not been uniform for the three regions. Democratic reforms were carried out in Kham and Amdo as early as 1953, while U-Tsang was given an extension of "six years of no-reform period."[45] The oath does not mark the time or the events it refers to. More important, it sets up regionalism as a problem to be combated without identifying what it really means.

The oath takers promise to take responsibility into the future and to be in harmony with the wishes of the Dalai Lama.[46] The oath intimates there is no better way to achieve both short-term and long-term benefits for Tibet than for Tibetans to adhere to the Dalai Lama's vision.[47] Dissenters are warned that they will be viewed as the enemy of the Tibetan people and nation, and of Buddhism. The pledge to be united is simultaneously a commitment to identify the dissenting "other" as such. There is little room for negotiation for those unable to or unwilling to become enduring as iron. A subtext of anxiety underpins the oath.

Although this event was an immediate celebration or resolve by the people to choose—given the extraordinary circumstances as well as the faith they had in the Dalai Lama—there are no details of who initiated it or if certain individuals were asked to be present. The representatives stated that the pledge to work in accordance with the Dalai Lama's vision arose spontaneously. Given the tumult of the time, with no government in charge, it is moving that individuals unknown to each other for the most part were able to be present in Bodh Gaya at the same time and all felt compelled to offer a pledge. Ordinary Tibetans such as Yugyal or Dege Cheme, who previously would not have been invited to partake in politics and had little power, now stepped forward to shoulder the loss of the nation. Unfortunately, there is insufficient information around an event that was a significant moment in early exile political life.[48]

Nevertheless, it is a moment that feels "Tibetan." By that I mean the act has many precedents. It is possible that, as suggested by Dege Cheme, the Chushi Gangdrug inspired this gathering. They were the only organized group in 1960, and they had both financial and human resources to make it happen. And after all, in February 1958, forty-three representatives (some say sixty men) from different Khampa groups had met in the Andrugtsang house in Lhasa to pledge their support for one another and to fight the Chinese together. (Many Tibetans had already died fighting the People's Liberation Army in Kham and Amdo.) At an unstable moment in Tibetan history, the leaders of the armed movement took the first action or oath to unity in the form of a united national resistance movement. Not long after this meeting, they formally established the movement in Lhokha, Central Tibet.

Gyari Rinpoche tells a story in his autobiography about his father, Gyari Nyima's, response to the events in Bodh Gaya that signifies the political, existential, and social significance of the oath. Gyari Nyima, who was a chieftain of Nyarong in Kham, gathered members of his clan around him and declared he was no more their *pon*, their chieftain. They protested, but Gyari Nyima insisted they listen to him. Gyari Rinpoche commends his father for his wisdom in looking beyond his personal interests and for encouraging his clan members to "integrate into the mainstream community and extend full loyalty" to the exile government.[49] It was an invitation to shift from identifying with a particular chieftain, clan, or group to seeing themselves as part of a national community.

Unlike his father, Gyari Rinpoche writes, other Khampa chieftains "formed settlements of their own clans."[50] In this differentiation he suggests that these Khampas did not want to give up their power but does not explain what power amounted to or meant to the chieftains without their homeland and as refugees in a foreign territory. Nevertheless, his analogy shows that the oath was a step in envisioning a new Tibetan identity as an equal people of a democratic nation in exile loyal to the exile government. In conflating loyalty to the government and giving up the desire for one's own clan, Gyari Rinpoche suggests that Khampa chiefs formed settlements for reasons other than community.

Questions of loyalty—here defined as allegiance to the exile government—among Tibetans living in all regions of the Tibetan plateau are taken for granted today, but this was not established in 1950 at the time of the Chinese invasion, when political relations between some of the independent chiefdoms and kingdoms of Kham and the Tibetan government in Lhasa were barely existent or already extenuated. What helped ameliorate this political reality was a shared past when all Tibetan regions had been under Tibetan rulers and belief by Tibetan Buddhists across Tibet that the Dalai Lama was the incarnation of the Buddha of Compassion. There was also an older existing narrative of Tibetans distinguishing themselves as *tsampa* (barley) eaters and as *nangpa* (insiders), a reference to Buddhists as national insiders. According to Dawa Norbu, the shared Buddhist foundation made eastern Tibetans, who were geographically closer to Chinese provinces than to Lhasa, behave like any other Tibetan.

Dawa Norbu describes the Tibetan rebellion that sprang up in areas of Kham as defending "Tibetan Buddhist values, and the political and sacred institutions founded upon such values."[51] He points out that uprisings were concentrated in areas where "democratic reforms" were more widespread. Tibetans fought back against the Chinese because the reforms were affecting their value systems and because both social life and political institutions were premised on Tibetan Buddhism, there could be no social change without "undermining" or touching the foundations of religion.[52] The Chinese leaders had not realized that even though the eastern areas were outside the Tibetan government's control in Lhasa, their common religious beliefs shaped their social life and the diverse political formations. Dawa Norbu explains that there were no revolts in U-Tsang until 1959 because the Chinese leadership had not tampered with the social and value systems as they did in Kham. He suggests that Tibetans, regardless of their social class and regions, were united in their religious beliefs.

Dawa Norbu's analysis that social change in the Tibetan context comes at the risk of touching the base of religion and religious beliefs is extremely significant for understanding the Tibetan movement. He cites the example of Khampas, who were loath to organize yet did so in Lhokha to fight for Buddhism, and arrives at a stunning conclusion: for Tibetans to rise against Tibetan "theocracy" they would have to be secularized, and to have an "indigenous revolution, Tibetans must become anti-Buddhist." In other words, the value system permeating Tibetan everyday life would have to be dramatically emptied of its religious "meaning and sanctity" for radical social change to happen.[53]

China's suppression of and control over religious practices and institutions inside Tibet has further cemented Buddhism's role in imagining a future Tibetan state. The destruction of religious schools and restrictions on monastic institutions make religion and rights an integral part of the Tibetan anticolonial stance. Furthermore, the Fourteenth Dalai Lama's international status as an exemplar of peace links Buddhism and Tibet in the imagination of non-Tibetan communities. For the majority of Tibetans, the Dalai Lama is the symbol of Tibetan Buddhism and Tibetan civilization, aspiration, and struggle. Tibetan Buddhism both grounds the inner domain and provides a framework for a contemporaneous national culture. Inside and outside Tibet, when Tibetans shout, "Long live the Dalai Lama," they often also mean "Long live Tibet."

The Dalai Lama's success in bringing Tibetan Buddhism onto the world's stage as a system with universal values does not always inspire international political support. While it is true that the Dalai Lama has brought visibility to Tibet and its plight, Buddhism as a religion of peace is a powerful idea that can also keep representations of Tibetan identity and expressions of culture and political will within a dominant framework. I point this out to show that even today Tibetan nationalism and identity are not easily disentangled from Buddhist identity. The reasons that had driven many eastern Tibetans in small nomadic villages across Kham to join the local resistance and fight the organized People's Liberation Army did not vanish when they left Tibet. In exile they had to build back their communities, and it was clear that much-needed political and social reforms in exile would have to be done carefully so as not to shake the bedrock that Tibetans thought would help them rebuild for a homecoming.

The United Party's action to bring unity within the order of religion made it possible for unity to be seen as protecting Tibetan values. Unity was interpreted as eschewing forms of regionalism and religious affinities. Unity was also expressed as the Dalai Lama's wish. But some communities from Kham felt they were being asked to make profound and fundamental changes in their political as well as their religious spheres. These communities had their own *samaya* (religious pledge or bond) to consider, and they could not give up their diverse lineages just because the United Party insisted unity was the only way to ensure freedom.

The establishment of a democratic exile government did not replace Buddhism's centrality in Tibetan society; that was not the goal. Rather, many Tibetans continue to approach democracy and reform in the spirit of receiving blessings from a religious teacher. Tibetans wear democracy as a talisman because the Dalai Lama has led them toward it. By continually reminding them that democracy is a gift given by the Dalai Lama, Tibetan leaders keep the focus on their responsibility to protect it, not so much by learning and practicing what that might entail as by holding each other to observing the CTA's policies. The vow exemplifies how religion is entwined in Tibetan social systems and political institutions. Even as the United Party led the way to a future egalitarian society, it used the Bodh Gaya pledge to remind the Tibetan community that they were already bound to the task of maintaining unity. The documents that the party produced, such as the *Bhod Cholsum Chigdril Tsogpae mig yul dontsen gna* (*Five Aims of the Tibetan United Association*) and *Drochoe dhon tsen dun dang dhe gyab non chey shug so* (*Seven Resolutions and Supporting Documents*), reinforced their work through repeated acts of oath taking. The effects of these documents are evident today even if the texts themselves have slipped away from memory. Tibetans still expect their leaders and community members to adhere to the policies initiated by the Dalai Lama. Expressions of alternate views are seen as disruptive to unity and often as regional, especially when they come from Khampas and non-Gelugs.

The meaning of democracy and secularism in a dominant Tibetan Buddhist society is not contained within the experiences and terminologies of Europe. As in India, secularism in theory in the Tibetan context could become the equal existence of all religious schools of Buddhism, as well as other religions and belief systems. The distinction that Romila Thapar, a leading scholar on ancient India, makes between secularism and the secularization of a society could be applied in part to the Tibetan experience. Thapar describes secularism as "an ideology whose concern is with secularizing society" toward a shift in the identity of a citizen.[54] This process is not opposed to religion or its place in individual lives, but it does not privilege religion as the priority in society. Instead, it is concerned with the rights and duties of individuals as citizens. In its most optimistic and distant future form, Tibetan unity might be open to such a form of secularization.

Thapar suggests that the values endorsed by secularization cannot be imposed; they must come from the people as they change into citizens. For the recently formed Tibetan refugees, secularization would entail shifting loyalty from local and regional authorities they had known in Tibet to the exile Tibetan society, in exchange for equality and equal membership. This would also involve prioritizing larger value systems.

The Dalai Lama briefly mentions the momentous event in his autobiography, *Freedom in Exile*. He does not specify the oath but states that sixty or more Tibetan leaders pledged their lives to the struggle for a free Tibet.[55] But, as Gyari Rinpoche observes, the people of that generation who took the oath made the vow to His Holiness the Dalai Lama's personhood and not to the office of the head of state, the people, or the nation. However, the Dalai Lama was the head of state and the leader of a people, just not elected to his position. Yet it would also be true to suggest that there was nobody else Tibetans would have accepted as their leader, and thus the boundary between personhood and head of state is blurry. A significant feature, then, of the Tibetan polity in the early years of life in exile was that membership in the community was a relationship between an individual and the CTA, but exemplified foremost by allegiance to a single leader. For the recently dispossessed Tibetans coming from a variety of political formations, membership in a political community took priority, but it was perhaps through the Dalai Lama that they built these relations. Thus, the question of sovereignty was not limited to the nation or the people.

The oath in Bodh Gaya helps to illustrate the struggle that every society faces: how to live with difference, how to be united without subjugating the other, and how to imagine the nation. Today details of the oath are rarely offered; nor does it feature as a significant act in the story of exile. The few Tibetans who remember the event refer to the beauty of the act; they see the strength of the people who were willing to give up their own personal ambitions for the good of the nation. They speak of the goodness of the leader. This ethos reverberates in the ways Tibetans think about and apply unity in political and cultural discourses.[56]

But there is also the other story, the one that sixty men spoke for all Tibetans.

Sixty men took a vow of unity stipulating that any individual who broke it would be removed from the Tibetan society like pus from a wound. Vows, being both a promise and a threat, an act and a gesture to future action, also contain the possibility of being broken.

CHOL KHA SUM

Following the oath-taking event, Chushi Gangdrug leaders, predominantly from Amdo and Kham, are believed to have met in Kalimpong, a hub of Tibetan resistance and intelligence activity. Kuomintang agents, Chinese Communist agents, Japanese agents, aspiring agents, agents from the old Central Intelligence department, and those from the State Intelligence Bureau all scurried in and out of Kalimpong. It was a "local parlour game," Jamyang Norbu writes in *Echoes from Forgotten Mountains*, to try to guess who was working for which agency.[57] Many Tibetan aristocrats from Central Tibet, lamas, and Khampa traders such as Andrugtsang Gompo Tashi, also referred to as the founder of the Chushi Gangdrug, had settled there.

The meeting's agenda was to discuss the new conceptual boundaries of Kham and Amdo and to deliberate on whom to elect to represent the regions in the exile administration. The CTA's electoral process was divided along the geopolitical divisions of *chol kha sum*, the three regions of U-Tsang, Kham, and Amdo. (Even though there were fewer people from Kham and Amdo in exile, the Dalai Lama had ensured equal representation of each region. This was part of the strategy to have a more equitable and united Tibet in the future.)[58] *Chol kha sum* is a concept that existed during the Sakya-Yuan period from the late thirteenth to the mid-fourteenth century. Scholar Eveline Yang writes that the term *chol kha* is a transcription of a Mongol word, *colga*, which means "district." The *colga* was a geo-administrative unit of decimal structures the Mongols used to determine a district's population.[59] According to Yang, *chol kha* is described as a Mongol loanword that does not seem to appear in texts predating the 1360s.

A popular Tibetan verse, attributed to Sumpa Khenpo Yeshe Peljor (1704–1788), a scholar from Amdo, captures the regional strengths of Tibet: U-Tsang is the *chol kha* of religion (or where religion spreads), Kham is the *chol kha* of people, and Upper Kham (Amdo) is the *chol kha* of horses. Stéphane Gros suggests that before the idea of a Greater Tibet comprising *chol kha sum* (three regions), Tibet was "spatially divided" into the upper region of Ngari to the west, the middle region of U-Tsang with Lhasa at its center, and the lower region of Dokham in the east.[60] Dokham includes both Amdo and Kham. As observed by Carole McGranahan, Tibetans use the term *chol kha sum* today as a culturally and politically organizing force. It is also, as she points out, the frame used by the government to organize the exile society. Today it is increasingly used as an identity marker.

The boundaries of Kham had altered before and during the nineteenth century, and yet again in the twentieth century under Chinese rule. For example, Nangchen is believed to have come under the administrative structure of the Mongols during Godan Khan's rule in 1240 and likely was organized into its twenty-five pastoral clans during this period. Maria Turek mentions that Nangchen was under the Ganden Phodrang government in Lhasa under the Fifth Dalai Lama (1617–1682) and then placed under the Qing amban in 1724. In 1911, Nangchen fell under Xining's Hui Ma clan's authority. Given the multiple historical changes, discussing where it would be situated in the territoryless nation in exile was important to those who were from Nangchen.

According to former cabinet minister and politician Juchen Thupten Namgyal, Gungthang Tsultrim had remarked that since the twenty-five Nangchen clans were under Qinghai province in contemporary China, along with many regions of Amdo, Nangchen should be categorized as part of Amdo. Jagoetsang Namgyal Dorjee (who had just returned from the oath-taking event in Bodh Gaya) had argued that if so, the territories of Labrang, where Gungthang Tsultrim was from, and other places such as Chone, Dzorge, and Meu, which considered themselves part of Amdo but were under Gansu, Qinghai, and Sichuan provinces in contemporary China, should be categorized under Kham, not Amdo. Similarly, Trochupon Dorje Pasang, chieftain of Trochu and Somang in Gyalrong before 1950, stated that since Gyalrong historically had not considered itself part of Amdo or Kham, it should be a separate region of its own.[61]

Ultimately, it was decided that Amdo would include areas extending to upper and lower Gyalrong, and that the twenty-five clans of Nangchen, and upper and lower Golok, would continue to be part of the Kham-in-exile polity.[62] The leaders agreed to select the following individuals in this first election in exile: Tongkhor Rinpoche, Gungthang Tsultrim, and Trochupon Dorje Pasang as representatives of Amdo; and Sadutshang Lobsang Nyendak, Jangtsetsang Tsering Gonpo, and Drawupon Rinchen Tsering as representatives of Kham. All had held prominent positions in their respective regions in Kham and Amdo, and they were the first representatives in the new democratic polity that was to usher in a more egalitarian society.

According to the erstwhile chieftains I spoke to, Khampa leaders, whose hereditary authority had centered around their people and land, had felt some uncertainty about their roles in the new exile nation. Some harbored a niggling concern that the CTA would give up regions of Kham to China to secure U-Tsang's (or TAR) freedom or autonomy, despite the lack of evidence of such plans.[63] That boundaries and territories were discussed, although virtually, and without violence by people who came from warring regions is both extraordinary and instructive about the character of the Tibetan nation. It indicates their willingness to be an integral part of the government. Perhaps this was possible because leaders from Amdo and Kham were familiar with the regions' history of flexible and changing relations with both the ruling Chinese and the Tibetan government under the Dalai Lama. Perhaps they realized their old chiefdoms and kingdoms were already gone.

The new configuration of rule by the people, not by traditional kings and chiefs, initiated by the Dalai Lama was acknowledged to have the potential to free Tibet and create a different Tibetan society. But without the cooperation of the people, including sometime chiefs and local kings, the exile government's authority would have been less certain of bringing the three regions together under one administration.

Tibetan nation building, sandwiched between two newly independent nation-states who also had to consolidate themselves internally and externally, was impacted by the two neighbors' every decision.[64] Both China and India had to create a body of citizens out of a diverse social, political, and religious population to fit an international standard that linked a state to boundaries.[65] Prasenjit Duara suggests that the definition of national territories was problematic because it meant extending the doctrine of nationality to parts of the old empires.[66] The Nationalist and the Chinese Communist leadership found this to be the case with the Qing dynasty's peripheral regions of Tibet, Mongolia, and Xinjiang. Their relations with the old empire had included multiple and "flexible positions" with religious and symbolic premises that did not correspond neatly to the terms of belonging of modern territorial states.⁶⁷ Adopting an interpretation of itself as a multinational state and not an empire, China presented Tibet and other neighboring conquered states as integral parts and incapable of forming a state on their own.⁶⁸ This situation, according to Yudru Tsomu, called for an assessment of control as well as a shift in the concept of Chineseness and in the narrative of nation on many levels. Such reimaginings brought the hitherto small Tibetan regions of Kham into prominence as strategic zones of contact that would provide access to the more prized Central Tibetan territory. Chinese attempts at drawing Kham's borders took place in this context. Tsomu illustrates the efforts of the Chinese Republican Party to portray Tibet as an old member of the new state of China to the Chinese public, who had previously viewed frontier races as different and as barbarians.⁶⁹

Similarly, the Chinese Communist Party's (CCP) rhetorical shift from self-determination to unity of the nation meant they had to continue with some very salient features of the Nationalist regime that they had initially repudiated as oppressive. Uniting the nation meant that Tibet had to be "liberated" from its own past. It also meant defining the territory and the configuration of the nation found in the historical legacies of the Qing empire.⁷⁰

Wang Hui, a prominent public intellectual and scholar in China, provides a long view of the ideas, values, and historical forces that made up the relation between the Qing dynasty's empire-building and modern China's state-building projects in *China from Empire to Nation-State*. Exploring the metanarrative of nation-states, he writes that the narrative of empire and nation-state has been formed as oppositional due to the dominant narratives of European nationalism.⁷¹ Wang Hui describes modern sovereignty as resulting from a new form of "international relations of recognition" of the treaty system,⁷² which the tribute system, or the trade and diplomatic relations between empires, is seen as opposing. He proposes viewing the two systems as parallel.

According to Wang Hui, the Qing dynasty's recognition of multiple political structures and cultural identities within its borders in the earlier period changed with its state-building efforts in later years. The move to bring the diverse political and social institutions into something of a unitary political formation meant reevaluating society.[73] Thus, while traditional dynasties had maintained local autonomy, the late-Qing reforms eliminated the eight banners system of the Manchus as well as Tibet's "Kashag system" in order to centralize power and create an identity that was linked by the state rather than rooted in what Wang Hui calls "local relationships," such as family, religion, or clan.[74] The power of local clans remained suspect in the time of the Nationalist 1911 revolution as well as during the Chinese Communist Revolution. Mao Zedong saw powerful local clans as "leftover of China's 'feudal' tradition" detrimental to the social mobilization at the heart of the Chinese revolution.[75]

The modern nation-state, Wang Hui writes, reorganizes individuals into collective institutions guided by the state, leading ultimately to securing power over the individual. But it does so by working in the name of legal rights, revolution, and liberation. In China, this meant that "foundational social organizations and institutional diversity" in its older imperial traditions were eliminated.[76] Wang Hui's assessment of the changes China has had to make in its move toward becoming a state is illuminating for a few reasons. It illustrates the ways Tibetan intellectual traditions and social and political institutions are ultimately subsumed by the Chinese state, even as it mobilizes both tribute system relations between the Chinese empire and Tibetan regions and treaties signed between the Tibetan government and the British to protect and justify China's occupation of Tibet.

Wang Hui's insight helps us understand the importance of the Kham and Amdo regions in discussions about Tibet. Many regions of Kham had enjoyed a time of sufficient autonomy after the collapse of the Yuan dynasty (1271–1368) and during the Ming (1368–1628). In the early seventeenth century, sections of Kham were pulled under

Tibetan control, and in the late seventeenth century they were drawn in under the Qing (1644–1911).[77] The Qing continued the Yuan dynasty's imperial policies of control over its minority peoples and frontier elites through granting hereditary titles and chieftaincies known as *tusi*. Under the *tusi* system, imperial expansion was managed indirectly by appointing native hereditary chieftains (such as those among the Thirteen) and recognizing them as owners of the traditional lands. Stéphane Gros identifies this system of indirect rule as a device intended to lead to the leaders' eventual integration.[78] The process was not uniform across Kham areas.[79]

The imperial centers might have seen the chieftains as representatives of the imperial state, but the Tibetan chieftains and kings, who had their own historical trajectories, saw themselves as mostly independent. Their varying relations with the Chinese imperial centers contributed to Kham's internal diversity,[80] which had always allowed the small and big nomadic clans in Kham to thrive and survive. The description of Dokham of Greater Tibet—upper Kham, middle Kham, and Amdo—in famous Nyingma lama Dilgo Khyentse Rinpoche's autobiography illustrates how the people of Kham might have seen their landscape. The vast area, he writes, is filled with many "kinds of communities, people of diverse ethnic groups and dialects," bearing little similarity to each other. Some live scattered over the plains while some live in close clusters. His analogy is a reminder of how the land was crucial to the people of those regions. The various people "are like a multicolored variety of flowers in summertime."[81]

The initial wariness displayed by some Khampas toward the exile government is more understandable when seen within this longer historical reality. Considering eastern Tibetans' spirit of belonging helps in understanding their gradual cooperation with the exile government as a process that depended on forging new structures and styles of trust and familiarity, which included formal and informal expressions of recognition. Likewise, the exile government's representation and definition of unity can be understood as being less straightforward within a landscape that is not limited to Central Tibet.

Unless Tibetans recognize such complex histories and experiences in context, the realization of unity might not be able to rise above the boundaries we have currently created. If unity can only be achieved by constructing regions as potential problems, sections of the Tibetan national family will be in danger of continually being relegated to the category of antigovernment instead of being brought into the community as valued members. Studying such histories allows for deeper understanding of the particular structure of belonging—the establishment of Tibetan values, the difficult job of gaining loyalty—and the struggle to prove the sovereignty of a people within a fixed and universal framework to which aspiring nations are expected to conform.

The establishment of national subjects and national traditions as unified, unique, and legible to the language of states entails what scholar Homi K. Bhabha calls acts of "affiliation and establishment," as well as "moments of disavowal, displacement, exclusion, and cultural contestation."[82] To view a nation as unified and transcending all difference is to have a single narrative that can only happen by conflating or suppressing multiple histories into one.[83]

In forming itself along the lines of a state, the exile society can be seen to have created its own category of nonmembers, those slow to embrace their concept of unity. The stories of chieftains and kings who yielded their power, first by force to the invading Chinese and second, symbolically and willingly, to the future Tibet under a Tibetan government are crucial chapters in the production of the democratic Tibetan nation in exile. These are also the stories rarely discussed.

2

UNITY IN EXILE

Narratives in the exile community presume that the Thirteen turned away from the government. My friend Yugyal in Mainpat said that if that were true, there wouldn't be so many heartbroken Tibetans. Like many of the other Thirteen elders, Yugyal had been trying to convey to me the intensity and uncertainty of the early years in exile. He found it difficult to articulate the emotions of that time because they don't exist in the present in the same way. His heartache sprouted from sensing that what he had lost was irrecoverable. The loss of his home was an event that left traces on all subsequent decisions, actions, and meaning in his stories. He used the word *phayul* (fatherland) as my mother did to speak of her village in Nangchen. *Phayul* intimates a profound closeness among the land, people, animals, and spirits. He was a teenager when he left Yeyonsumdo in Nangchen, with his chieftain, Bongsarpon Namkha Dorje.

The Bongsar pon (chief) was given the hereditary title of *bechang* or *baihu* most likely during the reign of the Yongzhen emperor (1722–35). Maria Turek explains that such titles were first used as military decimal units in the Jurchen Jin state (1115–1234). Tsodi Bongsar, the chieftain's daughter, who was twelve years old when her family left Yeyonsumdo, writes about the journey to exile in her memoir *Nangchen Sremo: The Story of Tsodi Bongsar from Nangchen*. In 1958, Pon Drakpa Namgyal, the younger of Tsodi's two fathers, who were brothers (polyandry is practiced in Nangchen), had a premonition that he should excuse himself from a meeting of clan leaders and chieftains that the Chinese Communist Party had called in Xining. Drakpa Namgyal, known for his clairvoyance, had declared the family should instead visit their guru, the Karmapa in Tsurphu Monastery near Lhasa. That decision altered their future.[1]

Nomads in Nangchen, like Khampas elsewhere, had feared the democratic reforms imposed by the Chinese would erode Tibetan ways of life. Tibetans had resisted, step by step, as the reforms and the PLA swept through Kham. The Great Khampa Uprising in February 1956 in Litang, Batang, Lingksashi, Chatreng, Nyarong, and other villages had been a rejection of Chinese reforms. The PLA had suppressed Tibetans brutally with bombs and a flood of machine guns. The second uprising had been launched in the autumn of that year in Markham, Drayab, Gonjo, Sho-ta-lho-sum, Derge, Khyungpo Tengchen, Dzachukha, Jyekundo, and Kandze.[2] Nangchen had been poised for action.

Tsodi explained to me that by 1958 nomads in her region were suffering after being forced into collectives of big and small communes she called *rerog tsochen* and *rerog tsochung*. Drakpa Namgyal had confided to a Chinese friend, who had been an officer with the former Nationalist Party, that the time had come for him to either take up arms and fight against the PLA in Nangchen or slip away to Lhasa. His friend advised him to leave without drawing anyone's attention. Drakpa Namgyal asked the former officer's help in obtaining permission to go on a pilgrimage to Lhasa.

Tsodi's fathers had organized nine tents and several months' food supply for a party of thirty people that included Yugyal. Two days into the journey, they stopped at the family's yak farm to take yaks with them—the female *dris* would provide milk and the male *khee* could be exchanged for food or money. Tsodi's fathers had promised clan members that they would call for them when it was safe. They were certain to draw attention from the PLA if the entire clan left together. After four weeks they arrived at a beautiful pasture, and Drakpa Namgyal sent five men on horseback back to their village to escort clan members to join them. Tsodi remembers they waited for a long time at that spot, but only two families came. The Chinese army had apprehended several men from their village after their chieftain had left. Other families had stayed back to care for yaks afflicted with *kha tsa*, hoof-and-mouth disease. Tsodi's group set off for Lhasa on foot and on horseback once they were certain nobody else was to join them.

More than a month into their journey they met Gawu Bechang and Bongrum Bechang, also clan leaders from Nangchen, who were escaping with their people. The men in the two groups carried guns and rifles. Tsodi remembered hearing that one of the women had plucked a gun out of her husband's hands to shoot a PLA soldier. After walking for a few more months, they reached Lake Nam Tso, about 220 kilometers from Lhasa in Central Tibet. The cerulean blue of the sky and the frozen lake was their backdrop to news about uprisings in Lhasa. This was followed by information that the Dalai Lama had reached India safely. Tsodi recalls meeting people from different parts of Nangchen and Derge at Lake Nam Tso, such as Orgyen Nyima, a clan leader from Nangchen Shornda, and the famous treasure revealer, Ratro terton. (*Tertons* are mystics usually in the Nyingma or Drukpa Kagyud schools who receive prophecies enabling them to discover religious treasures and texts believed to have been concealed by masters in the eighth and ninth centuries.) They camped at the lake for two months, deliberating whether to take the southern route or the more treacherous northern route to India, or return to their *phayul*. The southern route to India had two advantages—it was believed to be safer, and it would also allow them to return to Nangchen if the Chinese left Tibet. Orgyen Nyima and Ratro terton had decided to take the southern route. Drakpa Namgyal insisted his group take the northern route to India. Much later Tsodi heard that Tibetans, including a few of her relatives, who had taken the southern route, were captured or killed by the PLA.

Tsodi and her clan arrived in Mustang, Nepal, in 1959, a year after leaving Yeyonsumdo. Her fathers had rejoiced with prayers. Tsodi recalls that Drakpa Namgyal's melodious voice had carried high into the sky and soothed their hearts. They recuperated in Mustang for four months and were helped by the people and King Jigme Dorje Palbar Bista, whom her fathers had befriended. Tsodi joked that they must have smelled unusual because the animals in Mustang would sniff them from afar and bolt. The men in their group handed their guns over to the king of Mustang and the group made their way to the Kathmandu Valley, and from there to India, where they heard that the Dalai Lama had established a Tibetan government in exile.

Tsodi's father Bongsarpon Namkha Dorje and his people heard they could find work building roads and joined other Tibetans from Nangchen already working in Manali in Himachal Pradesh around 1962. The first group of Tibetans—3,394 individuals—had been hired as early as September 1959 to build roads in Sikkim. By 1964, about 18,000 to 21,000 Tibetans were employed to build roads in temperate places in the states of Himachal Pradesh, Jammu and Kashmir, West Bengal, and Uttar Pradesh.[3] Road construction camps were organized into collectives of 100 workers called *gyashok* in Tibetan. The groups were managed by a representative appointed by the exile government who served as intermediary between the Tibetan laborers and Indian government officials. The exile representative distributed work, took care of the workers, and influenced social and cultural life at the camps.

The Dalai Lama was heartbroken when he saw the workers at one of the road construction sites. In his autobiography he describes the air as "fetid and thick with mosquitoes" and reports that Tibetans working with dynamite suffered injuries.[4] The living conditions in the makeshift road camps were extremely difficult and perilous especially for children, many of whom died from malnourishment. At the Dalai Lama's behest, the Indian government organized an exclusive transit camp for children. As many as 5,000 children were taken from their parents to live in such camps.

Tibetans I interviewed in Bir, Dolanji, and Mainpat recalled that they got into trouble with exile officials while working in Manali. An elder in Mainpat complained that officials made derogatory comments about his dialect and attitude. Comments like this were probably not restricted to people from Nangchen or Derge because every region of Tibet has multiple dialects. He also said that exile supervisors questioned him about skipping prayer sessions they had organized to attend to his own personal practice as a Kagyu. A few followers of Bon—also known as Tibet's oldest spiritual tradition—in Dolanji felt they could not say they were Bonpos for fear of being discriminated against by the Buddhist majority. They found that the more they protested against small impositions, the more they were scrutinized. The exile officials may have hoped that community prayers would help create a sense of belonging, but their supervision manifested as discriminatory.

After unabating small misunderstandings with officials, Pon Namkha Dorje hit upon what he thought was a novel idea: he would get permission from the exile government to oversee his clan! Members of his clan had found each other after crossing the borders of Tibet, Nepal, and India. They were a family of approximately two hundred people, more than half working on building the roads. Namkha Dorje's assistant Yugyal recalled accompanying him to Dharamsala in 1961 or 1962 to request from Kalon Wangdu Dorjee, then Home Minister, the ability to form a work unit composed solely of their clan. Namkha Dorje had explained that his people wanted to work and live together in Manali. His request was turned down for practical reasons. He was told that a work unit over a hundred people would be difficult to manage. He was also reminded that the government had already placed representatives to assist them.[5]

According to Yugyal, Pon Namkha Dorje stayed in Dharamsala for three months hoping he could reverse Wangdu Dorjee's decision.[6]

(Two other elders from Mainpat suggested it was at a later time, when Namkha Dorje requested the group be settled together, that they spent three months in Dharamsala. It was also possible, as they said, that Namkha Dorje had gone to Dharamsala on two occasions.) Namkha Dorje had explained that many of his people had escaped together from their nomadic village in Nangchen in order to live together. His request was dismissed, and he returned to Manali disheartened. His clan decided to form their own work unit, for there was no law preventing them from doing so. After all, they had maintained their community since the fifteenth century. They called their own work unit Nangchen *gyashok*, and that is how they came to join the ranks of independent workers known as *khushi* Khampas, which Tibetans translate as "independent" or "carefree" Khampas. "*Khushi* Khampa" also referred to Tibetans who had come to India before 1959 and had been working on the roads as independent contractors before the arrival of Tibetan refugees. They were known to Tibetans as *Gyagar* Khampas, or "Indian" Khampas. This differentiated them from Tibetan refugees. As independent laborers, *khushi* Khampas didn't have dependable access to medical and educational facilities, and the job's seasonal nature meant they had to search for other temporary jobs when needed.

Tibetan refugees who became *khushi* Khampas grew in numbers in two years. The Bonpo community, which increased to approximately sixty-two individuals, formed their own group under the leadership of Pon Sangye Namgyal, as did the Chokling *gyashok* under the third Neten Chokling Rinpoche. Chokling Rinpoche had also asked the exile government if he could form a work unit with his group, and not receiving a favorable response, his people too opted to work independently. The status of *khushi* Khampa brought these groups autonomy, but it also served to alienate them from Tibetan refugee laborers represented by the exile government. Yugyal explained to me that *khushi* Khampas were accused of being antigovernment and un-Tibetan for organizing themselves. Restricted access to refugee aid was one of the first indications of their exclusion. They felt that Indian officials did not discriminate against them, whereas some Tibetan exile officials, who had control over aid resources, used their authority to punish some of the *khushi* Khampas.[7]

Namkha Dorje and Chokling Rinpoche's group had their second conflict with exile officials over their slowness to move to the Tibetan refugee settlements established by the exile government. Haunted by the difficulties Tibetans were facing, the Dalai Lama had requested the Indian prime minister to help resettle refugees into more stable settlements in India. The Tibetan government wanted Tibetans to live in one area as a large integrated community, but the Indian government, perhaps for its own reasons, including security, offered to help secure several agricultural settlements scattered across India. Karnataka was the first Indian state to make an offer of 3,000 acres in Bylakuppe, and the first Tibetan agricultural settlement was set up in a stretch of jungle in December 1960. A total of 3,217 Tibetans were resettled there by the end of 1965. The first six hundred Tibetans to arrive had come from the road construction sites of Shimla, Kullu, Chamba, and Dalhousie. A special officer designated as a divisional commissioner was sent by the Indian government to administer the camp, along with secretaries, engineers, and a small police force. The Dalai Lama sent two representatives, Thubten Nyima and Phala Wangchuk Dorji, to serve as liaisons between Tibetans and the Indian officials.[8] Two other agricultural settlements were set up by the end of 1965: 2,500 Tibetans moved to Mainpat and 3,000 Tibetans moved to Chandragiri in Chhattisgarh. Most Tibetans on the road camps went willingly to the settlements, but a few groups hesitated to move to South India, providing the rationale that they were afraid of the heat, they were nomadic people from Kham with no farming skills, and they didn't want to be separated from members of their clans. They decided to find a way to live with their community.

Indeed, by 1964, Tibetans were showing how fantastically resourceful, plucky, and independent they were. For example, Namkha Dorje acquired land in Mainpat in Madhya Pradesh to establish a settlement for his clan. He had written a petition directly to Prime Minister Jawaharlal Nehru.⁹ Reaching out to the Indian prime minister, however, had been a last resort. He had first approached Wangdu Dorjee, the Tibetan home minister, with a request to allow his clan to live together in one settlement. That was rejected, just as his earlier request to form a work unit had been. Lama Asi, who was a young monk in the 1960s, recalled witnessing his father's umbrage and disappointment when he was told by an exile official (Lama Asi guessed it was Chamberlain Phala) that he couldn't live with his chieftain and his clan. Lama Asi's father had stated that he had escaped from Tibet with his family and clan without help from any government and didn't find any reason to be held back from being with his community.¹⁰ There were whisperings that Gungthang Tsultrim had also acquired land to build his settlement.

Namkha Dorje had also managed to get refugee rations sent directly to him instead of going via the exile government. He had made this decision because his group had not received refugee aid, despite their requests to Tibetan officials distributing aid to Tibetan groups at the construction work sites.

Such independent projects are mentioned in the United Party's 1965 publications as threats to the Tibetan national integration in exile. Establishing autonomous settlements that contrasted with the exile government's centralizing resettlement projects for all Tibetan refugees understandably could be seen to undermine the attempts of the exile government to care for its people. Carving out different territorial refugee resettlements could create different spaces of power. Perhaps exile officials and the United Party suspected the lamas' and chiefs' potential to become separate sources of traditional authority within the Tibetan exile community. After all, Namkha Dorje and Gungthang Tsultrim revealed their ability to understand how power worked even in an unfamiliar country. They knew how to work with Indian leaders precisely because they had been leaders in their own lands.

For newly dispossessed Tibetans, mobilizing social and political change took the shape of reassessing who could organize as a group or institution, what aspects of culture and tradition had to be safeguarded and conserved, and what had to be reformed. Assimilation and preservation were seen as going hand in hand. This meant in practice that while the categories of Kham, Amdo, and U-Tsang were territorial identifications necessary to electoral representation in the CTA, they were received less enthusiastically as social or cultural identities. Tibetans who did not confine their religious and regional pluralism to the inner life felt they were in danger of having to prove their loyalty as Tibetans. In regard to this point, Carole McGranahan asked me an important question: "Across history, when did Tibetans from Kham find it necessary to define themselves as Tibetan?" Her question invites a deeper look into the terms, conditions, and categories of Tibetan social and political life over a longer period than I offer here.

Chigdril (unity) was presented as the key to the future by exile leaders. *Chigdril* was also the prophecy from the oracle. This powerful invitation to come together also came with a threat.

UNITY OF REGIONS AND RELIGION

In the early months of 1965, the Nechung oracle stated that there were threats to the Dalai Lama's life. When the leaders of the Tibetan polity consulted the oracle on how to protect the Dalai Lama, he instructed Tibetans to offer long-life prayers and ceremonies. He also advised them to pledge to build unity within the community. The Tibetan government immediately held a general assembly meeting where the cabinet addressed the need for conducting religious activities by the government as well as by the public. Most important, the cabinet emphasized the need for unity and passed a six-point resolution. The resolution was printed in the Tibetan newspaper, *Bhod-mi*

Rangwang (*Tibetan Freedom*), and distributed to settlement offices. This was not the first time the Nechung had spoken for unity, but the reference to an obstacle to the Dalai Lama drew everyone's attention.

The tradition of consulting the Nechung oracle, considered to be the Dalai Lama's protector divinity, is hundreds of years old. The Dalai Lama and the oracle bear common responsibilities but carry them out differently in their respective roles. The Dalai Lama's role is that of leader, which he executes peacefully, while the Nechung oracle is the wrathful "protector and defender" of Tibet.[11] In their hierarchical relationship, if the Dalai Lama could be understood as the commander, the Nechung is the lieutenant. The Nechung and the gods are the "upper house" of government and the Tibetan cabinet is the "lower house."[12]

The Dalai Lama describes the oracle in *Freedom in Exile* as the medium between the two realms of the natural and the spiritual and hence more accurately a spirit than an ordinary mortal. The Tibetan word for oracle, *kuten*, is translated as "the physical basis." Oracles, known also as protectors and healers, foretell the future and help people in their dharma practice.[13] There were many oracles in Tibet; today the Nechung, the principal protector divinity of the Tibetan government and the Dalai Lama, is the preeminent working oracle for Tibet.

Almost immediately after the general meeting, the United Party held a meeting of Tibetan officials and representatives working in the recently established refugee settlements in India. The party had, fortuitously, pushed for unity a year earlier in its manifesto, *Bhod Cholsum Chigdril Tsogpae mig yul dontsen gna* (*Five Aims of the Tibetan United Association*). Their goal, as the organization's name suggested, was to unite all Tibetans.

The objective of the meeting held on February 11, 1965, in Dharamsala was to discuss how the community would follow the oracle's suggestions to abide by the wishes of the Dalai Lama, organize long-life prayers, and secure unity among all Tibetans. Participants also identified individuals responsible for endangering the Dalai Lama's life and discussed measures to prevent them from succeeding in their efforts. Those identified as impediments or opponents to unity, and therefore also putting the Dalai Lama in harm's way, fell into three main categories: those who held religious and regional allegiances above national goals; those who spoke or taught histories that contradicted the exile government's narrative; and those who opposed the new policies and plans of the exile government. The call for unity was presented as important not only because it was the Dalai Lama's wish but also because it was necessary for his longevity. Thus, a connection was made between the Dalai Lama's life and the project of unity among Tibetans.

These discussions of the United Party's meeting contributed to a document published by them later in 1965, *Drochoe dhon tsen dun dhang dh'e gyab non chey shug so* (*Seven Resolutions and Supporting Documents*). This text develops the goals and ideas expressed in *Five Aims of the Tibetan United Association*, into a conceptual framework for Tibetans to follow as well as into concrete actions for the community. Whereas the pledge to unity was confined to the form of a personal oath in the *Five Aims of the Tibetan United Association*, unity was mandated as a national agenda in this second document, which was signed by 180 Tibetans and submitted to the Dalai Lama.

Most Tibetans did not challenge the United Party's role in managing civic life. However, some felt that the party's call for Tibetans to remember who their lama, friends, and enemies were (*gon, nyen dra sum*) and that they work to give up regionalism and sectarianism was suggesting that historical, cultural, and social differences and conflicts could be transcended. They understood the call for assimilation to mean that some Tibetans represented a threat to Tibetan unity.

THE FIVE AIMS OF THE CHOLSUM CHIGDRIL TSOGPA (TIBETAN UNITED ASSOCIATION)

Now diminished in significance—though it still runs an office in McLeod Ganj in Dharamsala—the United Party played an important role in shaping the self-consciousness and behavior of Tibetans as new refugee-citizens in the first two decades of life in exile. The organization was formally established by Tibetans in Darjeeling on April 23, 1964, to follow what would become their "five aims" and to educate Tibetans on the concept of a united Tibet.[14] In *Arrested Histories*, the powerful account of the Chushi Gangdrug, Carole McGranahan describes the United Party as a political party "generated" by Dharamsala and handed over to Gyalo Thondup to lead.[15] Phenpo Lobsang Yeshi, who was an official in the exile government's security department, moved to Darjeeling from Dharamsala to lead the organization; this intimated a relationship between the exile government and the United Party. While Gyalo Thondup was not officially linked to the United Party in its publications, it was widely believed in the Tibetan community that he was the force behind it. Chanzoe Ngawang Tenpa, who served the United Party for over two decades, referred to Gyalo Thondup as the party's founder when I spoke with him in 2015 in Dharamsala.[16]

Ugyen Topgyal Rinpoche, a former member of parliament in exile and the son of Chokling Rinpoche who established the Bir settlement, recalled that he used to refer to the leaders of the United Party as "slim ankles" because those men wore stylish fitted tapered trousers.[17] Many of them had been educated in English-medium schools in India; a few had returned from universities in the United States. He believed Gyalo Thondup to be behind the United Party. Ugyen Topgyal Rinpoche thought the United Party had formed in opposition to politically conservative Lhasa aristocrats who did not agree with Gyalo Thondup's socialist ideas. He believed the party's goal had been to establish a democratic Tibetan national movement for a

Buddhist society and that they anticipated religious institutions and aristocrats would oppose social change. Ugyen Topgyal Rinpoche also thought that the United Party was targeting Lhasa aristocrats who had been lukewarm or unfriendly to the arrival of the Dalai Lama's family into Lhasa aristocracy.

Gyari Rinpoche, whose father was among the early members of the United Party, writes that Gyalo Thondup had less influence over the party than it seemed in the popular perception. He suggests that the United Party sought guidance from Dharamsala, particularly from individuals such as Phuntsok Tashi Takla, who was in the security department and was married to the Dalai Lama's older sister.[18] Drawupon Rinchen Tsering, a former member of parliament and a leader in the Chushi Gangdrug and the Group of Thirteen, worked briefly with Phenpo Lobsang Yeshi in the security department. He told me that he had been surprised when Phenpo Lobsang Yeshi had resigned from his government position to lead the United Party. Drawupon recalled Yeshi as a wonderful person with a brilliant mind. He had seemed poised for a brighter future within the government. He wondered, echoing Gyari Rinpoche, if Phuntsok Tashi Takla had asked Lobsang Yeshi to head the party.[19]

Gyalo Thondup had held no position in the Tibetan government in Lhasa. Thondup's presumed closeness to the Dalai Lama as his brother and his position as the head of security for the Dalai Lama as well as the head of Tibetan intelligence made him one of the most influential Tibetans in exile. He described his role in the new exile government as being in "charge of foreign affairs."[20] He seemed to be in possession of powers that came not only from the government but also from his being the sole liaison for the resistance movement with foreign intelligence agencies, namely the CIA and the Indian Intelligence Bureau. The closeness to Thondup provided the United Party weighty recognition even long after he had left Tibetan politics in the late 1960s to live in Hong Kong. From the mid-1960s to the 1970s, the party was believed either to be synonymous with the exile administration or to exert more influence over the exile population than the government. Interestingly, Gyalo Thondup does not mention the United Party in his autobiography.

The founders of the United Party were from the three regions of Tibet, and their diverse backgrounds were showcased as evidence of the organization's commitment to unity in exile.[21] The standing committee comprised Tibetans from all religious schools. Noteworthy among them was Dudjom Rinpoche, head of the Nyingma school, considered one of Tibet's great scholars, meditation masters, and *tertons*.[22] One of the tasks that the United Party hoped to undertake was to educate people on democracy and how it functioned; the new democratic constitution had been recently presented by the Dalai Lama. These goals were possible because the United Party was the only political party in the refugee community at that time, and it was in charge of the newspaper *Bhod-mi Rangwang* (*Tibetan Freedom*), overseen by Gyalo Thondup.

The organization's manifesto, *Five Aims of the Tibetan United Association* was published on April 23, 1964, followed by an organizational charter of seventeen-point rules and regulations. Gyari Nyima Gyaltsen, Phenpo Lobsang Yeshi, and Gendun Zoepa went to Dharamsala from Darjeeling to present the United Party's aims and regulations to the parliament, the Kashag, and through the Kashag to the Dalai Lama. The Dalai Lama approved of their goals and gave permission to the government to recognize the association.[23] Once it was ratified by the exile government, the members undertook a robust door-to-door campaign to educate Tibetans about their party's goals and to recruit more members. The United Party was also given permission to have a seat at the *lokhor laydhom* (annual general meeting) of government officials, a privilege not granted to other nongovernmental organizations. This exception gave the United Party leaders the opportunity to present their views directly to both CTA administrators and the Tibetan people. By the end of their first year, the United Party had as many as 1,337 members making voluntary cash contributions from the Darjeeling and Kalimpong regions, including Ghoom, Kurseong, Sukhay, Mirik, and Sonada.

The party's promotion of adult and early education in Kalimpong and Darjeeling won it favorable attention and strengthened its momentum. It educated Tibetans on terms such as "democracy," "freedom," "unity," "feudalism," and "revolution," which were first translated from the Chinese into Tibetan. Over time, the Tibetan counterparts of these concepts, *mangtso* (democracy), *rangzen* (freedom), and *chigdril*, were resignified largely by defining them in contrast with Chinese practices.[24] Over the years in exile, these terms subtly shifted to incorporate traditional Tibetan as well as more universal Western inflections. The United Party also printed and distributed religious texts for daily prayers and informed Tibetans on world events and news related to Tibet through the *Tibetan Freedom*.[25]

In *Five Aims of the Tibetan United Association*, the group referred to itself as a voluntary organization formed to advocate for the freedoms granted in Article 5 of the new constitution for a future Tibet as part of the democratization of the Tibetan polity, and as a fulfillment of the Dalai Lama's wishes. The manifesto was distributed among Tibetans in the refugee settlements in India and Nepal. Although the organization claimed that it had been formed to promote the freedoms granted in Article 5—notably the freedoms of expression, to assemble without arms, and to form associations and societies—the five aims are paradoxically bound to obeying the wishes of the Dalai Lama per the conventions of Tibetan Buddhism. This was a strategic decision. Members of a deeply religious society might have been seen as more receptive to a democratic form of governance that they thought contrary to their religious beliefs if guided or mediated by religious leaders.

The manifesto's five goals were to follow the leadership of the Dalai Lama and the new democratic Tibetan government without hesitation in order to regain independence for Tibet; to respect and abide by the constitution put into place by the Dalai Lama; to prioritize unity by leaving aside differences in religious schools and regional origins and to work together to identify protector, enemies, and friends; to pray for the long life of the Dalai Lama; and to be willing to sacrifice their individual lives, if need be, for Tibet. Tibetans were cautioned against being fooled by officials representing Communist China or the Nationalists or KMT Party in Taiwan. Tibetans working for the Chinese, referred to as "running dogs," were to be stopped.[26] The resolution ended with the warning that every Tibetan joining the United Party would have to make a pledge to follow these aims before (an image of) His Holiness the Dalai Lama and the two national protector deities of Tibet. Going against the five aims would qualify as a sin, the consequences of which the sinners would have to bear.[27]

The United Party focused on two true narratives in its short manifesto. It established the Dalai Lama as the sole leader working tirelessly to raise awareness of Tibet's political struggle in the international arena to secure food, clothing, and education for all Tibetan refugees, and to prepare the draft constitution that would democratize the exile political system. And it reminded Tibetans that China had taken away their common heritage and was torturing, killing, and imprisoning Tibetan people, and destroying the Tibetan way of life.

The manifesto reminded Tibetans of their duty toward the struggle and the means to achieve freedom: "Tibetans must work in unity, leaving aside differences in religious sects, and regional partisanship, with total dedication to remove temporary and long-term sufferings of Tibetans. All Tibetans from the Three Provinces must unite and bond like water flowing in a canal and act together to identify their protector, enemies, and friends."[28]

The United Party explained that the success of a Tibetan democratic system was contingent on the people's unity and collective strength. It demanded that all Tibetans dedicate themselves to removing one another's temporary and long-term suffering. Tibetans were to work in unity to obtain unity, presented as a transformative, moral, and collective weapon that would fulfill the goal of freedom and create a path to transform the Tibetan society, socially and politically. Unity was a duty, not a process or an accommodation made over time by ordinary Tibetan people.

The form of the text and its flexibility to function as both a manifesto and an oath is a choice that binds together political and religious duties. It was an effective strategy to get Tibetans united under the guidance of a single system or leader. Such a view was believed to reflect the needs and desires of the majority and not to contradict the practice of democracy because the goal of independence was the primary focus. Besides, Tibetans sought a democracy with a Tibetan twist.

The United Party advanced the belief that Tibetans were fighting in a just movement that would become self-evident over time. The manifesto successfully linked national unity and compliance with the Dalai Lama's vision as a value that would provide a sense of belonging and would serve to govern Tibetans in exile. The five aims can be interpreted as positioning the Dalai Lama as both the symbol and the motivation and goal of the Tibetan struggle for freedom. The politicization of the people was built on normalizing a synecdochical relationship between the Tibetan nation and the Dalai Lama as necessary to a Tibetan present and future.

The United Party, casting itself as modern and politically democratic, professed its aims were to educate Tibetans—many of whom were nonliterate and to a great degree shaped by the values of a Buddhist society—and to bring them into the arena of emancipatory politics. Indeed, the party was important in politicizing Tibetans to recognize the benefits of democracy and its potential to maintain internal unity. It helped bring the language for the new global transitions that came from outside to the population. However, in practice, the United Party's unity, imposed as a guarantor of national freedom and democracy, functioned simultaneously to discipline personal freedoms and establish nonnegotiable terms for inclusion. Unity was presented as the path to freedom, but opposition as a betrayal that was punishable. To no small degree, the five aims offered substitution, not change. The United Party promulgated a different form of subordination of the people in place of the older rule of lamas, aristocrats, and chieftains they sought to transform.

It is possible today, given the vantage point of time and distance from the precarity of the early years of exile life, to trace the United Party's ideological development of unity as reflecting the desire of Tibetan refugees. Documents such as the *Five Aims of the Tibetan United Association*, were focused on a Tibetan future that began with Tibet's freedom. These documents, however, were approved by the Dalai Lama and the exile government. This gave the United Party the appearance of being not just sanctioned by but also close to the government. Furthermore, the party's plans to set up branches wherever Tibetans settled indicated its confidence in having both the people's and the government's support.

Over the following decades, the Dalai Lama has cautioned against naming the exile government as the institution of the Dalai Lama and advised instead that the government register under the Indian Registration Act to ensure the longevity of the organization. His decision to retire from politics was also made in the interest of ensuring the continuity of the Tibetan administration in exile. In an address to Tibetan officials attending an annual meeting organized by the Tibetan cabinet on March 21, 1976, the Dalai Lama explained, "If we act as if everything depended on one single person, then there is a risk of the collapse of the whole structure when that individual dies."[29] But in 1965, the United Party's five aims were creating a form of national subject whose relation to other individuals and to the nation was mediated by a single individual.

In the *Five Aims of the Tibetan United Association*, the nation's sovereignty does not derive from its own name or its people as much as it is imagined as emanating from the Dalai Lama. The United Party's assertion that the Dalai Lama was central to Tibetan culture and civilization in addition to holding political sovereignty over all Tibetans was not a new belief. For the generation who came from Tibet, particularly those from Central Tibet, the figure of the Dalai Lama was already pivotal to Tibetan Buddhism and to the nation.

Symbols and histories, however, are created; they do not self-arise.

For the Thirteen members, their clan identities were significant to their individual identities. They had barely recovered from the break in their history. They primarily leaned on their chieftains and religious teachers before anyone else. They were uneasy with the campaign for unity's underlying assumption that regional or religious affiliation was harmful to the nation.

Ugyen Topgyal Rinpoche, who was in Bir when I met him in 2022, was succinct in summarizing the questions that the leaders of the Thirteen had been attempting to pose: Did *chigdril* (unity) mean to blend into a singular Tibetan identity? If so, who was doing the blending or conversion, and to what end? Was the culture that the United Party was claiming to defend and revive as Tibetan culture an invention or a modification? Was the United Party creating a Tibetan identity whose allegiance was to be built around one center at the cost of multiple regional and religious loyalties and characteristics?[30]

Some people, he added, went so far as to compare the actions of the United Party with those of the Chinese Communist Party. They stated that the Chinese Communist Party was indoctrinating Tibetan children inside Tibet and Tibetans in exile were privileging Gelugpa teachings over those from other schools of Tibetan Buddhism. Ugyen Topgyal Rinpoche felt the statements and actions around unity were a strategy to create deep dissension among Tibetans, not to promote unity as professed.[31] I understood him suggesting that unity as expressed in *Five Aims of the Tibetan United Association*, was not an invitation to belonging or inclusion in a capacious sense of democratic self-rule. The Thirteen's objection to the United Party's method found little endorsement outside of their groups. The need for unity signified a crisis of values. The different attitudes toward unity illustrate how communities alter features that make up their constitution, whether we use the term "national character" or "national consciousness" to describe it.

Juchen Thupten Namgyal, a veteran in exile politics, mentions in his autobiography that the United Party had national ambitions as early as 1963. The founding members had organized a meeting in Dharamsala that year to discuss the need to develop the collective strength of the Tibetan people. Juchen Thupten alleges that United Party leaders were critical of lamas, chieftains, and aristocrats during this meeting. Its leaders indicated that traditional religious and non-religious power holders had historically used their resources to benefit themselves and rarely to strengthen the collective whole. They hinted that some lamas and chieftains would continue to use their religious and regional distinctiveness to carve their spaces of power in exile. Juchen Thupten writes that the speaker pointed at Dudjom Rinpoche, who was sitting in the audience, when he mentioned there were people starting their own settlements.[32]

It is possible to read the underlying tensions between the United Party and Khampa chiefs and lamas as stemming from the fact that both entities were learning about democracy and citizenship and developing a political practice. While the United Party and the exile government were defining the boundaries of rights and duties of the new citizens and consolidating their power, the Thirteen learned about exercising their rights and eschewing limits placed on them as citizens.[33] Having a voice is crucial to the practice of politics, and the Thirteen were attempting to self-represent or to find a voice that would express their position as they realized that clan identification, long in practice among nomadic communities in Kham, was increasingly viewed as an obstacle to the struggle for Tibetan independence and unity. Perhaps the United Party's suspicion of lamas and chiefs had to do with their power to evoke profound loyalty among their people. Loyalty, a trait valued in nomadic communities in Kham, began to feel like a problem.

The Thirteen's objection to unity could have been a response to the effects of the exile government's reconfiguration of itself in the mold of the modern state. Khampa chieftains might have suspected that the rule of law established under the exile government would end the rule of chieftains that had been the source of their traditional power and their identity. It is possible the Thirteen leaders were falling back on tactics that had been central to the preservation of their clans. They would have been familiar, for example, with interclan mobility and the division of clans into smaller groups to evade political and social incorporation. They may have wanted to keep their options open.

The national project of unity depended on conformity and a certain level of uniformity. Tibetans were expected and called on to give up, without resistance, their traditional roles and values that could not be accommodated under the new polity. The United Party suggested unity could be achieved if all people bonded like water flowing in a canal, and if people acted together to identify their protectors, enemies, and friends. The metaphor of different regions melding into one entity was an agreeable symbol to many Tibetans in exile; after all, regaining their country was a shared goal. It was also a pragmatic step; most Tibetan refugees were from Central Tibet and of the Gelug school. Identifying enemies, likewise, was accepted as a necessity in the struggle for freedom. However, symbols when taken out of the realm of story are not the same structures.

The United Party's *Five Aims of the Tibetan United Association* indicated they already knew of a few small-minded people in the exile community aligning with the enemy. In the follow-up document, they identified the people by name.

This is the opening act of unity in exile.

For Khampa leaders, caring for their clan was an asset to their identity. My sense is that it never occurred to the Thirteen leaders that their desire to live with people they had known in Kham would find resistance in exile. Kinship, a crucial principle of relations shaped by regional histories and their movements, was vital to them. Perhaps it occurred to them only after they were criticized and understood that their desire to be with their clan was also interpretable as an act of exclusion.

Chanzoe Ngawang Tenpa, a leader in the United Party, felt that even though the Thirteen had begun with a good aim to preserve the languages as well as the religious practices of different regions, things went wrong, but he couldn't pinpoint the problem. He thought that the leaders had *shengog*—"allegiance to" or pride in their own regions. He said this as though it was a shortcoming. He declined to speak about the Thirteen on my first visit to see him in his house in Dharamsala in 2015, but on the second visit he was more open to the idea after he learned my mother had been married to a United Party member. Chanzoe Ngawang Tenpa described my father, Gyalpo, as one of the "good ones."[34] Chanzoe Tenpa had joined the organization in the early 1960s and served as its leader for decades. He said he knew most people in it. I let it slip, intentionally, that I had not seen Gyalpo for over twenty years.

"The Thirteen had gone the wrong path," said Chanzoe Tenpa, suggesting that advocating for a smaller group or for a region, often Kham, was not right for Tibetan unity.[35] He intimated that the Thirteen wanted the benefits of belonging to the Tibetan refugee community but had not been willing to make any personal accommodations or sacrifices. He murmured that many conflicts could have been resolved, for many problems had been the result of misunderstandings between the two groups, a helpful insight. Tensions between the United Party and the Thirteen were over differences in ideas about the past and the Tibetan future. Members of the Thirteen felt that the United Party believed what they promoted was the right path for freedom and expected all Tibetans to follow their vision. This expectation may also have been one of the factors tearing the Chushi Gangdrug apart.

THE CHUSHI GANGDRUG, THE UNITED PARTY, AND THE THIRTEEN

The Thirteen's story is often linked to the Chushi Gangdrug through its members. That is to say, some founders and members of what would become the Thirteen were already leaders of the Chushi Gangdrug, namely Jagoetsang Namgyal Dorjee, Drawupon Rinchen Tsering, Barchungpontsang Thutop Gompo, and Sey Dhonyo Jagoetsang. These individuals had led local military campaigns inside Tibet, and although they initially worked with Gyalo Thondup in strengthening the military movement in exile, they would eventually become critics of his leadership. There are also other connections between the two groups that can be illustrated better through a detour to the story of Rashi Karma Kandor, also known as Rashi Kandor.

Rashi Kandor was born in a nomadic region halfway between the towns of Shornda and Jyekundo in Nangchen. The elders I spoke to didn't linger on Rashi Kandor's brief time as a monk in his pastoral land but focused on his life as a successful trader in Lhasa and his fierce loyalty and bravery. He moved to Lhasa with his family in the late 1940s and built his reputation there as one of the successful traders from Nangchen. When the Chushi Gangdrug uprisings began in Kham, he used his personal funds to purchase guns and ammunition and formed an army of thirty or more men from Nangchen. His band of warriors managed a few attacks on the PLA soldiers despite their modest size, but they were not able to sustain their fight for too long. Rashi Kandor joined the Chushi Gangdrug army and eventually escaped to India and found his way to the Chokling work unit in Manali. He was something of a legend in the Bir Nangchen settlement, where he lived until his death.[36]

There were a number of men like Rashi Kandor, traders and wealthy landowners from regions of Kham, who organized and funded their own armies to fight the Chinese before the formal establishment of the Chushi Gangdrug army. Such independent initiatives show the ways Tibetans responded to the Chinese invasion in their local areas and also reveal the ethos of autonomy in Kham. These individuals did not wait for their regional kings or chieftains to lead them. Some of their chiefs and kings had, in fact, surrendered without much resistance. People like Rashi Kandor often joined the Chushi Gangdrug movement in India or belonged to the communities of the Thirteen. Thus the relationship between the two groups was formed through not strategic alliances so much as responses to older bonds and affections between place and people.

Carole McGranahan is sensitive to the importance of such affiliations in Kham in her work on the Tibetan resistance movement. She also recognizes the Chushi Gangdrug guerrillas' "view of the resistance as an autonomous organization"[37] and describes the army's formation as a version of Tibetan nationalism in which individuals didn't sacrifice other identities even as they stood in support around the state. It was a nationalism that recognized regions and nation as "complementary," not as "competing projects." However, by 1965 there were competing actors with competing projects within the organization that could not be reconciled.

One of the first disturbances within the Chushi Gangdrug organization in India came in the form of embezzlement charges against some of its leaders in 1960 from a group of veterans that included Martham Thoesam, Gara Lama, Lhabso (Lhasang) Gyaltsen, and Sersang Lobsang Dorjee. These men insisted on questioning the leaders about their involvement in the disappearance of some portion of money airdropped by the CIA from East Pakistan into Tibet. The controversy is referred to in Tibetan as *ghur serpo* (yellow tent, for the yellow airdrop parachutes). Gyalo Thondup mentions in his memoir that "some Tibetans in Kalimpong" spread a rumor that he had taken the money. He writes that the rumor was baseless because he was in Darjeeling, not Tibet, when this airdrop was made. He had "never seen the money."[38] He explains that the four men responsible for creating this rumor were "expelled from India [by the Indian government] not for their false accusations but as Communist agents. Intelligence agents from all sorts of places were stirring up rumors and fostering dissension then."[39]

Supporters of the jailed men insisted the only crime they had committed was challenging the Chushi Gangdrug, which at that time also meant challenging its leader, Gyalo Thondup. They believed that Thondup took advantage of his credibility with Indian and U.S. intelligence agencies to put away individuals who disagreed with him by identifying them as Communist agents.[40]

Other signs of a rift within the leadership arose when Gyalo Thondup decided to merge the Chushi Gangdrug press Sungkyop Parkhang, established in Kalimpong in 1963 (it published *Rangwang Sungkyob* or *Defend Tibet's Freedom Press*), with Rangwang Parkhang or Rangwang Sarshok, started by himself in 1960. A writer who worked for Rangwang Parkhang soon afterward revealed to me that Thondup believed that two newspapers were unnecessary and inefficient. In the *Truthful History of the Tibetan United Association*, the United Party states it was a waste of funds to have two newspapers from one place and so the two were merged. This resulted in *Bhodmi Rangwang* or *Tibetan Freedom Press*, which became affiliated with the United Party. Thondup's critics felt the merge was a ploy to get rid of Chushi Gangdrug affiliates who ran *Defend Tibet's Freedom Press*: Barchungpontsang Thutop Gompo, Dhondup Phuntsok, Amdo Khato, and Tedrung Yeshi Trinley.[41] The writer also remarked that Thondup had complained that the men who ran the press had no work ethic, that they just talked big and horsed around.[42]

Dege Cheme, who worked for Rangwang Parkhang for a few years, recalled the printing machines were unwieldy and bulky to operate. It was backbreaking work. He contends there were differences in opinion and misunderstandings that led to the restructuring of the press. But he equivocated: he did not say outright that both sides were unyielding and authoritative.[43]

Rinchen Norbu, then a young writer for the press, surmised that Gyalo Thondup was upset at Chushi Gangdrug leaders, like Barchungpon, because they were not afraid to challenge his position.[44] Gyalo Thondup was not used to being questioned. Barchungpon left his job at the press after an argument with Thondup. Barchungpon's late wife, Dorjee Lhamo, recalled that the water and electricity in their rented home were cut off. She was certain it was done on purpose in retaliation for her husband's resignation. She told me when I visited her in her home in Kathmandu, Nepal, in 2015, that her family left Darjeeling soon after these events.

By 1964, the Chushi Gangdrug was divided into two groups: new CIA-trained and U.S.-educated administrators and volunteer soldiers who supported Gyalo Thondup and soldiers who supported Baba Yeshi, also known as Gyen Yeshi.[45] Gyen Yeshi, a monk and veteran from Batang in Kham, had been chosen to run the military base in Mustang, Nepal, after Andrugtsang Gompo Tashi died. Each side accused the other of embezzling funds, and each side fought for authority over the funds. Gyen Yeshi's supporters accused Gyalo Thondup of misusing Tibet's treasure in gold and losing jewels worth eleven to thirty million dollars in "dubious business ventures."[46] They also believed that Thondup was using funds meant for the Chushi Gangdrug to run United Party activities. (The organization, supposedly run on people's contributions, made sizeable purchases of property in India, which it still owns.)

For Tibetan leaders and soldiers, Andrugtsang Gompo Tashi was the head of the resistance movement. Gyalo Thondup held the other important position as an intermediary between the movement and their foreign funders and the exile government. Officers who had been trained by the CIA in Colorado accused Gyen Yeshi of running the Mustang camp like a clan leader and wanted more accountability.[47] Gyalo Thondup's right-hand man, Lhamo Tsering, was given the responsibility of overseeing the work in Mustang, but he and Gyen Yeshi did not see eye to eye. Lhamo Tsering sent a young warrior,

Gyato Wangdu, to assist Gyen Yeshi, but Gyen Yeshi would not cede power to the younger man and the internal conflicts blistered. In *The Noodle Maker of Kalimpong*, Gyalo Thondup remarks that Gyen Yeshi was under criticism from the operation centers for being an ineffectual leader who buttressed his own private funds with money meant for the soldiers.[48] It was also believed that U.S. intergovernmental organizations supporting the guerrilla movement wanted someone younger in his place, preferably someone they had trained who could speak English.[49] Jamyang Norbu explains in his book that a delegation of the Colorado officers in Darjeeling requested that Gyalo Thondup visit Mustang to sort out the mess.

McGranahan's *Arrested Histories* provides an in-depth look at the longer history of the people's resistance movement. At its core, she writes, the problems within the Chushi Gangdrug were also about the soldiers who were on the ground fighting and the administrators who had limited understanding and sympathy for the movement's complex structure shaped by Khampa systems of authority and values. The army's units were based on "native-place affiliations" reflecting the sociopolitial frameworks of Eastern Tibet, where "trust, loyalty and familiarity" were crucial.[50] The relationships between the leaders of the units and the soldiers were deeply personal in that they were linked to places with regional histories predating the 1950 Chinese invasion. Their allegiance to their regional and local systems of power could not be easily organized along the CIA's unfamiliar system of ranking and status. This latter position was less legible to the fighters.

By 1970, the contention between the two main factions led to killings on both sides and affected the entire exile population.[51] In addition to the embezzlement accusations, there were power struggles between the Markham and Bawa groups on one side and the Litang groups on the other side. Gyalo Thondup is believed to have favored Tibetans from Litang, which left other Khampa groups resentful. Many freedom fighters didn't know whether to stay in Mustang or to leave. The final years of the Chushi Gangdrug's military efforts read like a complex mystery novel, rife with charges and countercharges of murders, embezzlement, and deception. Gyen Yeshi bore the brunt of the blame. His supporters among the leaders of the Chushi Gangdrug—Jagoetsang Namgyal Dorjee, Sadutshang Lo Nyendrak, Drawutsang Rinchen Tsering, and Bawa Chakzoe Tashi—went to Dharamsala in 1970 to present their support for Yeshi. They were castigated by Tibetans who campaigned against them through letters to the government of India and to the Tibetan administration. A statement issued from the Kashag in 1971, based on Lhamo Tsering's report, claims that Gyen Yeshi killed as many as thirty-eight people, embezzled public money, took Buddhist artifacts for himself, and caused confusion among Tibetans, all the while saying he was following the Dalai Lama's wishes, and that Lhamo Tsering and Wangdu were following Gyalo Thondup's orders.[52] It is unclear if the Kashag took into consideration the reports provided by Yeshe's supporters before dismissing him on charges of embezzlement, robbing precious items from unsuspecting Tibetans, and killing "a number of [Tibetan] people."[53] The Dalai Lama supported the Kashag's position during an address to exile officials on March 17, 1971, where he referred to Gyen Yeshe as a "man of achievement" but not without fault. He explained that Yeshe "has lost huge amounts of money and even we cannot say that he has not secretly killed some of his rivals."[54] The dissolution of the Chushi Gangdrug in 1974 in a standoff with the Nepalese army is described by the Dalai Lama as "one of the saddest episodes in the history of the Tibetan diaspora."[55] In *Arrested Histories,* McGranahan links the tensions within the Chushi Gangdrug, where individuals identified others as being either for or against Gyalo Thondup, with the split between the Thirteen and the exile government. She suggests that the United Party represented "an effort to bring together Tibetans from across regional and sectarian divides."[56] However, this was perceived by some Tibetans to still maintain the "Lhasa/Dharamsala status quo." She quotes a "Khampa government official" who suggests that exile altered the domains of power held by various Khampa power holders.⁵⁷ This was true for both Khampa traders who had more influence in Lhasa than they did in exile and Khampa chiefs who still commanded the loyalty of their local clan but not much beyond that in exile. McGranahan writes that the Group of Thirteen formed an oppositional political party to distance themselves from the United Party, Gyalo Thondup's reforms, and the exile government. This sounds very similar to Gyari Rinpoche's claim in his autobiography that the "seeds of discontent" among Thirteen members are traceable to the founding of the Chushi Gangdrug.⁵⁸ He writes that the styles in which the two main Chushi Gangdrug leaders, Andrug Gonpo Tashi and Gyalo Thondup, ran the organization (favoring certain Khampa leaders over others) led to resentment among the Khampa population and that the KMT operatives and Tibetans working for them fueled the budding animosities.

My friend Sodam thought that the rift in the Chushi Gangdrug between Gyalo Thondup and Gyen Yeshe had a different timeline and character from the rift in the exile community between Gyalo Thondup and Gungthang Tsultrim, but Gyalo Thondup was the common factor in both. Sodam felt that the trouble for ordinary Tibetans began when the United Party imposed its version of unity and led a smear campaign against individuals who didn't unquestioningly embrace their authority.⁵⁹ He felt that the Chushi Gangdrug was already in turmoil before the existence of the Thirteen and that the Thirteen pursued goals that were independent. However, the majority of the people in the Thirteen settlements were loyal to the Chushi Gangdrug and to the dream of Tibetan independence.

The leaders of the Thirteen, who were also leaders of the Chushi Gangdrug, were more preoccupied with the latter's affairs. For example, Drawupon Rinchen Tsering rarely attended the Thirteen's meetings, for as he told me when I visited him for a week in Kamrao in August 2015, he had been overwhelmingly busy with the Chushi Gangdrug. People who lived in the settlements of the Thirteen seem to hold the view, as expressed in Chushi Gangdrug veteran Shangri Lhagyal's biography, that the group was formed to "counter the new sociopolitical reformatory party" led by Gyalo Thondup and some exile officials.[60]

3

THE GROUP OF THIRTEEN

I met Tenzin Norbu in 2015, outside his quarters in the Chokling Monastery, also known as Pema Ewam Chogar Gyurme Ling, in the Bir Nangchen settlement. He was in his late seventies and was a little reluctant to talk until I told him that friends in Bir had recommended that I speak to him because of his excellent memory.

"How would you describe the Thirteen?" I asked.

I often began my interviews with a question such as the one above, believing that it offered multiple openings into a story they recalled, and yet almost every person I spoke to responded with a personal answer. To ask a person to locate the exact moment when they began to feel a certain way is to assume that events are transparent and fully apprehended when they take place, that there is a linearity to our experiences, and that our personal lives in time find a way to align with the places and nation we live in, even or especially a nation to come. I realized that in asking them to describe the Thirteen, I was asking them to describe themselves.

"We came together as a group to protect our many religious practices," Tenzin Norbu said in the Nangchen dialect.[1] He had first heard of the organization called the United Party in 1964. Tibetan refugees were being pressed to take an oath of unity. Tenzin Norbu referred to the pamphlet published by the United Party that had outlined its goals for the Tibetan exile society. He admitted he had not read it, but that had not altered the conclusions he had drawn about it in 1964 and still held at the time of our conversation. He understood the text as follows:

1. All Tibetans were asked to take a vow to uphold the goals of unity expressed by the United Party.
2. Tibetans were dissuaded from saying they were Khampa, Amdo, or from U-Tsang. They were encouraged to say they were Tibetan.
3. The Nyingma school was deemed unnecessary.
4. Unity meant Tibetans were to unite to obey His Holiness the Dalai Lama.

He also said that Tibetans who hesitated to take the oath were labeled as anti-Tibetan unity. Tenzin Norbu spoke more about the United Party than the Thirteen during our conversation. He felt that the party had contradicted their expressed goal of building a democratic society by asking Tibetans to take a religious oath of loyalty. Tenzin Norbu's priority as a monk and a practitioner of the Nyingma school was to uphold his religious practice. He had not been willing to take oaths to religious protectors unless he was certain he could uphold them and felt the same way about this new oath. Tenzin Norbu had felt the sting of being identified as the internal enemy simply for questioning the party's rules. He referred to the United Party and the exile government interchangeably. He also referred to the United Party and Gyalo Thondup as being the same entity. A sentence from him would move in the following manner: What was the point of a government if the United Party was above reproach, and "they" could do whatever "he" wanted?[2]

Tenzin Norbu felt his identity was being misconstrued as an internal *dra*, "enemy." When he said *dra*, I heard *dre*, "demon."

Many of our stories indeed begin with demons and their subjugation, I thought. And those stories too often begin with an oath.

According to Tibetan legend, the Chinese princess Wencheng Kongjo, bride to the famous seventh-century Tibetan monarch Songtsen Gampo, announced that Tibet resembled a demoness lying on her back. Kongjo was troubled that the cart carrying her gift, the statue of Sakyamuni, from the Tang dynasty capital Chang'an or nearby between 635 and 636 was taking a long time to reach Lhasa. Upon her arrival, Kongjo referred to Chinese divination to determine that the spirits of the land had been obstructing the Sakyamuni's journey. She identified the geomantic features of the Tibetan landscape and believed that the demoness would have to be subdued for Buddhism to take hold in Tibet.[3]

The demoness, who was also the land, was not dismembered into parts but held to the ground by temples built on key points of her body. Her heart, which was also the center of the land, is where the Jokhang temple, Tibet's holiest shrine, was constructed and stands today. Lhasa, the center of Buddhist Tibet, would also become the center of political Tibet under the Dalai Lama in the seventeenth century.

Tenzin Norbu explained that he had never questioned His Holiness the Dalai Lama's position as the legitimate Tibetan leader of the Tibetan people. He had disagreed with the United Party's perspective on unity. Tenzin Norbu conceded that the definition of "enemy" used by the party might have been a tactic to control Tibetans. He felt their attention had been disproportionately placed on new minority populations in exile. For him, unity had spelled erasure, and thus he had not signed the oath to unity petitioned by United Party members.

Tenzin Norbu insisted he desired to be "heard" by the exile government, which I interpreted as his and the Thirteen's desire to be included in the narrative of the united nation. Separation was most certainly not on his mind. The project of unity had appeared exclusionary to him. Tenzin Norbu never got a chance to explain why he was hesitant about following the United Party. Besides, rumors had already defamed him and his friends as being antigovernment. In other words, actions that may or may not have occurred were preceded by *koka*, a term used by Tenzin Norbu, which translates as "gossip" or "rumor." It was through the circulation of stories that he also learned about Tibetans who got into trouble with the United Party in other places. He spoke of *Five Aims of the Tibetan United Association* as being composed of innuendoes intended to foment disorder within the Tibetan community.

Tenzin Norbu interpreted *chigdril* (unity) as a political strategy to dilute regional identities and affiliations to religious schools. His understanding was that the United Party had an implicit goal of controlling all religious activities and bringing them under the authority of a singular religious framework because its leaders believed that the power struggles between the religious schools in the past had weakened Tibetan unity. But instead of uniting people, the party would tear them apart. Tenzin Norbu was not willing to give up his religious beliefs and his monastic community. He said the United Party had hoped to discard the Nyingma lineage "like an old shoe."[4] He did not furnish concrete examples as context for how he'd arrived at that conclusion, but during our two-hour-long conversation, he mentioned that many of Dudjom Rinpoche's students were upset upon hearing that Dudjom Rinpoche had not been offered a chair to sit on at a meeting organized by the United Party in Dharamsala. They had been offended that one of the most important lamas of the Nyingma school had been ignored and insulted and felt that exile officials and United Party members gave recognition to only the Gelug lamas. Lodi Gyaltsen Gyari too mentions in his autobiography that Dzongnang Rinpoche, a respected Nyingma lama and a founding member of the Thirteen, had witnessed and testified to the disrespectful treatment of Dudjom Rinpoche at a public gathering in Dharamsala.[5]

In Tenzin Norbu's understanding, the fusion of Tibetan regions and respective religious practices entailed a privileged imposition of

Central Tibetan cultural practices as the constitutive principle of the Tibetan community. Likewise, he intimated that the United Party, and the government by extension (because it did not curb activities initiated by the party) had wanted to standardize the Gelug doctrine for Tibetan Buddhist practice in exile.

What Tenzin Norbu expressed was the fear of a standardization of Tibetan identity to a Gelug-centric and U-Tsang-centric formation. The exile government was Gelug by virtue of being the continuation of the Lhasa government, with a Gelug majority population and cabinet members who were all from Central Tibet and Gelug in the early years. Tenzin Norbu felt he was expected to give up his religious traditions and his loyalty to familiar regional leaders under the name of unity of Tibetans. He had been in Tibet in the 1950s when the Chinese had enforced the collectives and was in India when exile officials asked Tibetans to form collectives of one hundred people while building the roads in the 1960s. The similarities in the vocabulary and the attitude toward refusal had concerned him.

"How do you make sense of the madness that was taking place in Tibet?"

"And," he added before his reply, "in exile."[6]

The Great Proletarian Cultural Revolution or Cultural Revolution in China was a complex phenomenon and is understood in a variety of ways, but Tibetans interpret it as a deliberate project to destroy Tibetan ways of life and to convert Tibetans into new Chinese subjects. In his annual address to Tibetans on March 10, 1967, the Dalai Lama described the occupation of Tibet as "one long catalogue" of miseries and sufferings and expressed his concern that the persecution of Buddhism and of Tibetan culture had reached a new level of intensity with the arrival of the "so-called Cultural Revolution."[7] He explained that the destruction of religious monuments and institutions inside Tibet was clear evidence "of the depth to which the Chinese rulers have fallen in their efforts to wipe out all traces of Tibetan culture."[8]

The Cultural Revolution from May 1966 to 1976 resulted in the destruction of 90 percent of monasteries, temples, and historical monuments. The Chinese Communist Party's campaign to destroy old ideas, culture, habits, and customs was presented as its efforts to reform Tibet. The Cultural Revolution was the opportunity for the Sinicization and forced integration of Tibetans into China.

I was unsettled by Tenzin Norbu's comparison and did not follow up with a question, just waited for him to elaborate. He said the imprisonment of Dudjom Rinpoche in India was an event that had chilled his heart.

"If they could imprison Dudjom Rinpoche, a beloved lama of the Nyingma lineage, for no reason, they could do anything to ordinary monks like me," he reasoned.[9]

According to Khenpo Tsewang Dongyal Rinpoche, who worked closely with Dudjom Rinpoche as his translator and attendant, Dudjom Rinpoche's followers had asked him to join them in the exile government's new settlement in Orissa established in 1962. At the time of receiving this request, Rinpoche had committed to helping the exile government prepare texts for Tibetan schools. Dudjom Rinpoche had reasoned that he would ask exile officials about joining his followers in Orissa while he was in Dharamsala. The fact that such a highly respected and powerful figure in Tibet sought the exile administration's approval provides a sense of the importance of the government to all Tibetans.

After working on the curriculum, Rinpoche traveled to Ladakh for two weeks, giving Buddhist empowerment and teachings to his followers in the region. Kathok Ontrul Rinpoche, who was from Kathok Monastery in Derge, Kham, had been traveling with Dudjom Rinpoche. Dudjom Rinpoche is believed to have asked Kathok Ontrul Rinpoche to read their situation in a mirror divination. Kathok Ontrul Rinpoche had responded worriedly that he saw a Padmasambhava statue swaddled in barbed wire. The premonition had startled the lamas' students, but the lamas, as writes Khenpo

Dongyal in his biography of Dudjom Rinpoche, had continued their separate journeys. Dudjom Rinpoche had set off for Siliguri, from where he was to continue onward to his home in Darjeeling. He was met by the Indian police at the Siliguri railway station and to his surprise, taken to jail. No reasons had been provided for his detainment.

Khenpo Dongyal intimates that Dudjom Rinpoche's popularity in Ladakh, Darjeeling, and Kalimpong had come as a shock to exile administrators. The then-dominant Gelug administrators had not expected non-Gelug lamas to have such an influence over the Buddhist communities of Nepal and India. Khenpo Dongyal hints that jealousy and fear prompted the arrest.[10]

Khenpo Dongyal suggests that the early 1960s was a time when Tibetan culture was beginning to take root in exile. The questions of how, and who was shaping this culture, were of great concern to many Tibetans, particularly a few high-ranking officials who held their own ideas about what Tibetan culture and politics meant. Exile nationalists believed that Tibet had lost its freedom due to a lack of unity and felt that the time for change had come. Tibetans were urged to call themselves Tibetan rather than to identify with their local regions. Tibetans were also told to think of a "single school of Tibetan Buddhism" rather than the multiple traditions that existed in Tibetan society, particularly in Kham.[11]

Khenpo Dongyal writes that non-Gelug Tibetans began to speculate that the campaign for unity was a disguise to destroy the schools of Nyingma, Kagyu, Sakya, and Bon. Followers of these schools had begun to ask each other, "If we make one school, which will it be? What happens to us?"[12]

As he describes, it sounds like in the exile atmosphere of the 1960s fear felt thick in the air, and like the mosquitos of India, new to Tibetan skin, it left stinging and itchy bumps that would not heal before the next bite. Khenpo Dongyal's observation of the heterogenous religious practices and players within the Himalayan Buddhist community helps us understand the different ways Tibetan

Buddhist teachers were received within the regions. While the Dalai Lama's authority in both the secular and the religious spheres was unquestioned in Tibet, responses to it were less predictable in the Himalayan regions of Nepal, India, and Bhutan. For example, Mustang in Nepal was dominated by adherents of the Sakya school, and both Sikkim and Bhutan leaned toward Nyingma and Kagyu traditions. This is not to suggest that the diverse Buddhist communities in the Himalayan region did not hold the Dalai Lama in high esteem; as Tibetan Buddhists, they never disputed his position as the spiritual leader of all of Tibet and of Tibetan Buddhism. Khenpo Dongyal suggests that administrators from the earlier Gelug-and-Lhasa-centric government were faced with a new equation and challenge; they had little control over non-Tibetans who were Buddhists and devoted to the lamas of Bon, Nyingma, Sakya, or Kagyu schools and were willing to help establish their communities.

Tenzin Norbu believed that the Indian Intelligence Bureau had been notified by a Tibetan who alleged that Dudjom Rinpoche was collaborating with the Chinese Communist Party and was receiving money from them.[13] Dudjom Rinpoche was released when the Dalai Lama, the king of Sikkim, and the king, queen, and ministers of Bhutan all wrote separately to the Indian prime minister about this false allegation. Although Dudjom Rinpoche's arrest might not have had anything to do with the United Party, its framing within national security concerns led individuals with preconceived ideas about Gyalo Thondup's far-reaching powers within the Indian government to see his involvement in this as in many other arrests. Tibetans I spoke to believed he had the power to overturn their individual lives with a call to the Indian Intelligence Bureau. Jamyang Norbu explains in his blog *Shadow Tibet* that the common belief in Tibetan society at the time was that Gyalo Thondup's "near monopoly connection to Indian intelligence, and his control of the Chushi-Gangdrug" gave him the power "to make bad things happen to those who crossed him."[14]

The elders I spoke to from the Thirteen, who had also been Chushi Gangdrug veterans, referred to the joke among Khampas in the mid-1960s: if you opposed the United Party, you'd find yourself on a list marking you for the next life or a jail in the Thar desert.[15] A few were convinced their names were on one such list created by the United Party. The clandestine nature of the work meant that they could not provide evidence. Gyalo Thondup himself writes in his memoir that much of his work remained "highly secret, though keeping those secrets was never easy."[16]

Such accusations against Gyalo Thondup, according to diplomat and politician Gyari Rinpoche, are unwarranted. Gyari Rinpoche asserts that Gyalo Thondup deserves "greater recognition and appreciation" than he receives for his contributions to the Tibetan society. He is misunderstood and miscast as a "vindictive person," which Gyari Rinpoche insists he is not.[17] Gyari Rinpoche writes that it was the Indian government that arrested Dudjom Rinpoche.[18] In response to the attacks from the People's Liberation Army (PLA) and the occupation of disputed border territory in October 1962, The Defense of India Act 1962 was passed, allowing the government to detain anyone suspected to be of "hostile origin."[19] People's movement in and out of Darjeeling and Kalimpong, where many Tibetans lived, was curtailed. Thousands of Indian nationals of Chinese ethnicity living in India were arrested and sent to prison camps. Many Tibetans were also detained. Gyari Rinpoche believed that Dudjom Rinpoche happened to be one of them.

Gyari Rinpoche dismisses as ludicrous the idea that the exile government wanted to create a single Buddhist entity—a belief still held by some members of the Thirteen. He suggests that "a group of Tibetans mainly from Kham and Amdo" and some former Lhasa aristocrats were responsible for spreading this rumor. He is most likely referring to the Thirteen as the "group" tarnishing the United Party's reputation. This "rumor" was not limited to the above groups.

Jamyang Norbu mentions in his blog that politically active Tibetans were almost required to join the United Party, whose goals he outlines as: "1) Confiscation of private money to create a balanced class; 2) Neutralization of traditional class differences; 3) Unification of all religious sects."[20]

Gyari Rinpoche also blames the Kuomintang (KMT) for devoting their resources and efforts to discredit the United Party through its Mongolian and Tibetan Affairs Commission (MTAC). Established under the Chinese Nationalist Party after it designated Nanjing as its capital, the MTAC was the party's way of claiming Mongolia and Tibet as Chinese territories even though it had no control over both regions at that time. In 1949, some MTAC members left for Taiwan with the KMT government. Thereafter based in Taiwan, MTAC continued to symbolize KMT's ideology of a united China, including Mongolia and Tibet as territories.[21] The KMT government pledged support for Tibetans in their struggle against the Chinese Communist Party (CCP), but like the Communists, it claimed Tibet as an integral part of China. Jamyang Norbu mentions in *Echoes from Forgotten Mountain* that the Kuomintang had worked to undermine Tibet's appeal to the United Nations in 1949 because it feared that supporting Tibet in the UN had the potential to "weaken Nationalist China's claims of sovereignty," as it too was under threat of an invasion by the PLA.[22] Taiwan's position led the Tibetan exile government to categorize the KMT, alongside the CCP, as the enemy. Any relation with MTAC was seen as an antinational activity.

Gyari Rinpoche states that the MTAC was successful in creating the impression that the United Party was the "CTA's instrument" to end the regional-oriented system of government and to establish the Gelug sect as the dominant religious tradition.[23] He also writes that it was an "undeniable fact that a number of prominent people within the Thirteen" were receiving financial support from the KMT through the MTAC.[24] He does not indicate the timeline nor does he provide names. Gyari Rinpoche believed His Holiness the Dalai

Lama was attempting to create a society that was more inclusive and that gave all the religious schools equal presence in the new political and social system.[25] Gyari Rinpoche evades a critique of the United Party's actions by talking about the Dalai Lama's vision but admits that some of the activities led by the United Party could have created an impression that they were against religious leaders.[26] He contends that in many cases, members of the Thirteen misinterpreted certain actions by senior exile officials as prejudicial or arrogant when in reality, the officials might have acted out of ignorance or failed to "understand and appreciate the changed circumstances resulting" from the unified administration.[27] Gyari Rinpoche's perspective is important because he worked in and for the Tibetan community in various capacities. He had the pulse of the community and the government, and perhaps more keenly that of the United Party because of his family's close connection with Gyalo Thondup. His father was among the founders of the United Party, and Gyari Rinpoche himself worked as a writer for the newspaper *Bhod-mi Rangwang* or *Tibetan Freedom* while still in high school.

Gyari Rinpoche's dismissal of the Thirteen's belief in Gelug hegemony and his suggestion that they might have imagined or misinterpreted slights forecloses a meaningful exchange about how Tibetans were negotiating living in unity. Exile leaders too were paying attention to the tensions playing out in the community, and they attempted to address and understand concerns over religious discrimination. On July 20, 1967, cabinet members and select members of parliament discussed a complaint from a Tibetan from Manali who reported that Kathok Ontrul Rinpoche had rented a room for thirty Indian rupees to perform the *yarney* or religious summer retreats, and a United Party representative stormed in and insisted Rinpoche join monks performing prayers in a neighboring town. Ontrul Rinpoche refused, explaining that he had to follow certain rituals particular to the Nyingma practice. Some cabinet members brought up this story to illustrate that discriminatory and bullying tactics by the United Party were not limited to ordinary non-Gelug Tibetans but also were used against religious teachers.[28] Exile officials discussed curbing the party's activities but took no action at that time.

Even if the United Party was consciously running a campaign to make Tibetan society more inclusive, the distrust voiced by Tenzin Norbu concerns the losses, constraints, and challenges faced by minorities. Tenzin Norbu's sentiments were echoed by Adak Marong Choje and Tsering Wangyal, who lived in the Tibetan Bonpo settlement in Dolanji, Himachal Pradesh, at the time of my interview with them. Tsering Wangyal moved to the Kongpo region from Kham as a young child; he was not certain what village his parents had been born in. He entered India through the border at Missamari in Assam in 1959 and lived in the transit camp for a few months. His two daughters did not survive the heat. Wangyal and his family were making their way toward Manali when he heard there was a community of Bonpos working as road construction laborers. He wanted to live with lamas who could pray for the daughters he had lost, so the family joined that community.

Adak Marong Choje had moved to Dolanji from Ladakh. Tibetans of all Buddhist schools would tell him that they had come from the same place and practiced the same religion. As a follower of the Bon religion, he had disagreed with such pronouncements.

"What does it mean to say there is no difference in our schools? It meant to me that my belief did not matter," he explained.[29]

He indicated that he had been invited to belong, but not as he was. He did not think it was right that other Tibetans nudged him to give up his faith to follow the majority. He had worried then that questioning the definition of unity would make him look like he was against the struggle for Tibetan freedom. He knew the United Party was very powerful but insisted that it was wrong to be asked to give up one's religious affiliation.

He wondered to whom could he have gone, if not to His Holiness the Dalai Lama and the exile government. And if the United Party spoke for the exile government, as he had feared, then what could he have done? The United Party's call for unity was not transparent to Tibetans from Kham for a few reasons, including geography and demographics. The distance from Kham and Amdo to the borders of India and Nepal, in addition to the different policies put in place by the Chinese, had constrained Eastern Tibetans' ability to leave. People from Kham and Amdo had made up the majority in Tibet. Now, in contrast, they were minorities among Tibetans living in exile.

Another factor is religion. Non-Gelug religious communities—such as the followers of Bon and the Nyingma, Sakya, and Kagyu schools, who had lived in Kham and Amdo with relative autonomy or as the dominant power—were now under a Gelug government less accustomed to both their regions and their religious lineages. It was new for them to identify as a minority—a term or experience that might not have been discussed before 1950 or in the same way as currently—with an uncertain relationship to power.

The Dalai Lama, in his role as a Gelug leader, is unmatched in his outreach to non-Gelug Buddhist teachers; he has taken Buddhist initiations and teachings from Nyingma and Sakya lamas and made radical changes within the Gelug society, such as discouraging the practice of propitiating the protector spirit Dolgyal, also known as Dorje Shugden. The Dalai Lama had renounced his practice of Shugden in 1975, recognizing that Dolgyal promoted Gelug supremacy and contributed to religious intolerance.[30] All these initiatives, made after the 1970s, encouraged nonsectarianism in the Buddhist schools and gave the different schools space and recognition within exile society.

Similarly, Dawa T. Norbu's editorial in the September 1976 issue of the *Tibetan Review* attempted to address the silence over the government's Gelug hegemony in the mainstream. In "Toward Sectarian Harmony and National Unity," Dawa Norbu focused on the weaknesses and contradictions in Lamaist politics and their effect on Tibetan independence. He stated that eschewing sectarianism had become a political necessity. There were fundamentally different approaches to Buddhism in the four schools, and Dawa Norbu cautioned Tibetans against ignoring the differences. His proposal for letting each school continue its own traditions without dominating others was a call for unity that embraced difference. He offered a few examples of the government's Gelug hegemony: only Gelugpa abbots were paid salaries; the two tutors of the Dalai Lama were given higher status than the heads of other schools; and Bonpos had no representation in the parliament. He suggested that the dominant Gelug school ought to accept an equal status and make sacrifices for the sake of national unity and religious harmony. Dawa Norbu wrote that the government did not do enough to assuage the feelings of minorities.[31]

The same issue of the *Tibetan Review* carried articles by lamas from the different schools of Kagyu, Nyingma, and Sakya. In an interview, scholar and lama T. G. Dhongthok Tulku tells Dawa Norbu about two causes of sectarianism: doctrinally, Gelugpa scholars in the past had criticized Nyingmapa traditions; and during the Thirteenth Dalai Lama's rule, a well-known Gelugpa scholar, Kyabje Phabong-Kha, had stated that Gelugpa represented the most authentic teachings of the Buddha. Dhongthok Tulku added that the struggle between Kagyu and Gelug lamas for power after the fall of the Sakyas was also a cause of sectarianism. He felt that the solution was for the Dalai Lama to be a nonsectarian lama.[32] Both Dawa Norbu and Dhongthok Tulku acknowledged Gelug dominance in their present moment. Religious skeptics of unity, such as Tenzin Norbu and Tsering Wangyal, could not have predicted these inclusive gestures in the 1960s.

The Thirteen suggested that the emerging discourse of Tibetan unity was borrowed from the CCP, as were the punitive tactics deployed to put unity in place. Jamyang Norbu describes the United Party as having a bit of the Kuomintang Party in its organizing principles, in the way it demanded "unquestioning loyalty" to the leader figure.[33] The organization led the "know your enemy, ally, and leader" campaign launched by the exile government targeting Communist and Nationalist China. Some of the methods initiated by the United Party were similar to the class struggle sessions employed by the CCP. Gyari Rinpoche too acknowledges this irony in his book. He mentions that some "overzealous individuals" in the exile government adopted the ugliest methods of the very government (Chinese) they sought to oppose.[34] Gyari Rinpoche observes that some United Party members might have been similarly overzealous in establishing their policies. Ultimately, he writes, the organization was seen more as a divisive force than as a unifying one.[35]

Drawupon Rinchen Tsering revealed to me that the United Party members pasted character posters around Dharamsala denouncing individuals, organized criticism and self-criticism meetings, and produced news articles emulating the CCP's techniques. He recalled seeing posters on electric poles and walls on the road approaching McLeod Ganj in Dharamsala, vilifying him for his support of Gyen Yeshi, the ousted leader of the Chushi Gangdrug. An employee of the exile government told me that there were cleansing character meetings, where United Party members organized debate or criticisms. Perhaps the United Party hoped to achieve a dual purpose: to purge the exile government of people it deemed a threat and to awaken ordinary Tibetans to politics through such activities. According to a friend and former government official, the criticism and self-criticism group meetings generated alienation and fear among government employees. In Communist China, this technique is generally described as temporary alienation of a single member from the group. One member is critiqued for some deviance by the group, and the member also joins in to self-criticize. The purpose was to correct the individual and strengthen ties within the group.[36] In reality, this technique often served to discipline and control people much more than to bring people together.

"Why did the Thirteen organize as a group?" I asked my friend Yugyal, whom I have known since I was a child. I was a guest in his house in Mainpat in 2015.

"We [the Thirteen] came together because we were heartbroken," my friend replied. He said Gungthang Tsultrim had understood their pain.[37]

GUNGTHANG TSULTRIM

Gungthang Tsultrim stands out as the leading figure even among the Thirteen's striking cast of lamas, kings, and chieftains. He served as the *chanzoe* (bursar) for the famous sixth Gungthang Jigme Tenpai Wangchuk of Labrang Tashikyil, a major Gelug monastery in Amdo, before escaping to India.[38] Gungthang Tsultrim also completed three years as a member of parliament in the Tibetan exile government. Merely two years into life in exile, he formed the Tibetan Amdo Drama Troupe with approximately a hundred people. The troupe produced a show on the life of the seventh-century Tibetan king Songtsen Gampo, based on the drama written by the fifth Jamyang Sheypa Tenpa Gyeltsen of Labrang Monastery in Amdo. The Tibetan Amdo Drama Troupe had performed to packed audiences in Calcutta, Bombay, and Delhi and received high praise for the extravagant show. One review in *The Times of India* on February 16, 1962, remarked that the theatergoing audience in Bombay seldom "felt so wholly transported to another region and clime" as they had upon viewing the performance at K. C. College.

Gungthang Tsultrim was a compelling figure even for lamas who were themselves legendary Buddhist masters in their areas. Ugyen Topgyal Rinpoche was a young man when he witnessed the formal meeting among Gungthang Tsultrim, Khamtrul Rinpoche Dongyu Nyima, and Neten Chokling Rinpoche Pema Gyurme Gyatso. Khamtrul Rinpoche was the eighth in his lineage in the Drukpa Kagyud tradition of Tibetan Buddhism, whose Khampagar Monastery in Lhathog, Kham, was under the patronage of the king of Lhathog (presently in Chamdo prefecture) and the king of

Nangchen. Neten Chokling Rinpoche was the third in his lineage of renowned *tertons* in the Nyingma tradition whose monastery in Tibet fell under the Lhasa government's jurisdiction but was composed of monks from regions of Kham.[39] The two lamas had met Gungthang Tsultrim in passing at the close of 1961 in Delhi when he and the troupe were preparing for their tour.

Gungthang Tsultrim was already a controversial figure when the lamas met him the second time in the winter of 1964 in Delhi. Chokling Rinpoche and Khamtrul Rinpoche had heard Gungthang Tsultrim was aspiring to create a settlement for Tibetans from Amdo. When they met him, he spoke about creating multiple residential *rakors*, or blocks, representing different Tibetan regions or religious schools. Conceptually, Clement Town was to exhibit Tibet's plurality. Gungthang Tsultrim's federation-style settlement appealed to the lamas, who wished to establish monasteries and live with the monks and laypeople from their regions. Gungthang Tsultrim's vision contrasted with the exile government's melting pot model. Aiming to build solidarity among Tibetans and produce a more integrated cultural identity, the government had designed refugee settlements to bring together Tibetans from different regions. The other big difference was that these settlements would be administered by officials selected by the Central Tibetan Administration (CTA), adhering to a centralized system, while the blocks and monasteries in Clement Town were to be (potentially) self-administered.

Khamtrul Rinpoche and Chokling Rinpoche would go to see Gungthang Tsultrim every evening in Ladakh Budh Vihar, a hostel for Ladakhi students and Ladakhi pilgrims passing through Delhi, during their stay. Budh Vihar had become a transit camp for Tibetans in 1962 and a refuge for Tibetans from the border areas during the Sino-Indian War. Some Tibetans, like Gyalrong Trochupon Dorje Pasang, also known as Trochupon, and his people spent much of the year there. The outpost near Kashmere Gate had been established by Bakula Rinpoche, also known as Kushok Bakula, to serve

Ladakhis and provided political representation for Ladakhi interests in the Indian capital. Prime Minister Jawaharlal Nehru had picked Bakula Rinpoche to lead a delegation to Tibet in 1956, and he would become the first member of parliament from Ladakh in the Indian Lok Sabha. Bakula Rinpoche and Gungthang Tsultrim had met through Lobsang Phuntsok Lhalungpa, who had a vast network within the Indian ministries as well as international agencies due to his work as the head of the Tibetan division of All India Radio, India's national news service in New Delhi.

After meeting with Gungthang Tsultrim, as Ugyen Topgyal Rinpoche told me, Chokling Rinpoche and Khamtrul Rinpoche would return to their lodgings every evening with stars in their eyes. Gungthang Tsultrim was an eloquent and inspiring speaker who "could coax the sun out from a gray sky," Ugyen Topgyal Rinpoche said.[40] It was not just his persuasive tongue that impressed the lamas but also his vision, which the lamas recognized.

Gungthang Tsultrim held the opinion that Tibet's independence was some time away. He told the lamas that it would take a while, at least thirty years, for any significant political change. He believed it was important for Tibetans to become self-sufficient in the interim. Gungthang Tsultrim intimated that His Holiness the Dalai Lama had invited all Tibetans to contribute toward building a self-sustaining exile community. Ugyen Topgyal Rinpoche recalled that these ideas had departed from the political optimism shaped by prominent nationalists such as Gyalo Thondup, who had indicated that if Tibetans had fourteen steps left toward independence, then ten had already been taken. Ugyen Topgyal Rinpoche said that many Tibetans had begun prefacing statements about the activities of their present with "when we return to Tibet," as though freedom was palpably waiting around the mountain bend.[41] Gungthang Tsultrim, on the other hand, insisted it would be a while before Tibetans could return home. He encouraged Tibetans to be proactive in keeping their distinct cultures alive and to be self-reliant. He also believed that the

Tibetan government ought to negotiate directly with the Chinese government and not with other parties. Ugyen Topgyal Rinpoche felt that Gungthang Tsultrim was one step ahead of everyone else.

Gungthang Tsultrim had heard about the Bhoodan Movement, the voluntary land distribution and reformation movement in India established by Vinoba Bhave in 1951, which, like the Gandhian principle, was based on people's initiative and collaboration. The movement encouraged individuals to think of themselves as trustees of their properties and to share what they had been given. Landowners donated thousands of acres to benefit landless people. Among Vinobha Bhave's many supporters was Jayaprakash Narayan, an activist and social reformer with a sizable following among Indian socialists. Narayan had joined the movement in 1952 and by 1954 was dedicating his life to the cause. Narayan believed that to bring India closer to a society that was built on equality and without exploitation, (Indian) socialism had to be transformed to bring progress to every individual. He believed that Vinobha Bhave's self-help program and self-government of people in small communities could create new institutions and social life. Gungthang Tsultrim's friends, such as Jinpa, who also served as his driver, believed that Tsultrim had been trying to articulate something similar for Tibetans and had hoped they would become self-reliant while continuing to prepare for a fight to regain Tibet.

Gungthang Tsultrim saw opportunity and hope in the Bhoodan Movement's revolutionary vision. Jinpa recalled that he planned to make his petition for land directly.[42] The duo set off for Mathura to meet Bhave. Gungthang Tsultrim introduced himself as a Tibetan refugee and explained his dream to build a settlement. He informed Bhave of his recently established Nehru Memorial Foundation, named in honor of independent India's first prime minister. Again Gungthang Tsultrim made a strategic move, choosing that name when Jawaharlal Nehru's recent death had cast a pensive mood over the Indian continent.

Bhave consulted Jayaprakash Narayan, who happened to be there at that moment, about availability of land. Gungthang Tsultrim's timing had been perfect, according to Jinpa. The king of Dehra Dun had recently donated some of his hunting land in Clement Town. Under the Bhoodan Movement, ninety acres of this land was provided to Gungthang Tsultrim's Nehru Memorial Foundation to rehabilitate displaced Tibetan refugees. Gungthang Tsultrim's opponents in the United Party doubted he was inspired by the Sarvodaya movement and wanted to build a new society in exile for everyone's well-being. Instead they believed he was for replicating and preserving the hierarchal and hegemonic order of the older Tibetan society. The United Party asserted that Gungthang Tsultrim was only able to acquire the land after the Dalai Lama gave his support for the project to the leaders of the Bhoodan Movement.[43] There are other versions of the story, one of which suggests that it was through Lobsang P. Lhalungpa, who introduced Gungthang Tsultrim to the ideas of the Bhoodan Movement, that the land was acquired.

Members of the Group of Thirteen, such as Yugyal from Mainpat, Jamyang Gyaltsen Choklingtsang from Bir Nangchen, and Drawupon Rinchen Tsering from Kamrao, who were involved in the administrative aspects of running their settlements recall hearing that Jayaprakash Narayan had advised Gungthang Tsultrim to register the land with the Lucknow court. He did so on November 1, 1964. The registration certificate identifies ninety acres "for the rehabilitation of displaced Tibetans residing in India as an Agro-Industrial unit on Israeli pattern of Noshav-Shifufi (individual living and collective working) settlement."[44]

Gungthang Tsultrim's network of contacts already included social reformers such as Jayaprakash Narayan, Bakula Rinpoche, R. K. Dhawan (politician and Indira Gandhi's personal assistant when she was prime minister), S. P. Chauhan (the famous social worker from Karnal), Jagjivan Ram (Indian independence activist, politician, and spokesperson for the Dalit community), and Lama Lobsang (who was running Ladakh Budh Vihar). Through this diverse network, he was introduced to other Indian political figures and, conceivably, to new ideas. Much like Bakula Rinpoche, who was able to get around the politics of his home state of Jammu and Kashmir and appeal directly to Prime Minister Nehru, Gungthang Tsultrim built a network of contacts with political presence within Indian political systems. This meant that he could potentially bypass the exile government and speak directly to Indian leaders if needed. Such developments must have, understandably, added to the exile government's concerns as it worked to establish itself as the representative of the Tibetan people.

Gungthang Tsultrim was not the only Tibetan in 1964 with ambitions to build a community. Namkha Dorje had written a letter to Prime Minister Nehru that year requesting that he and two hundred Tibetans from his *phayul*, in addition to another two hundred Tibetans, be settled in a wintry place. The Indian government gave them land in Mainpat, not far from a settlement that had recently been established by the Tibetan government. Namkha Dorje and his people left for Mainpat from Rewalsar via Mandi in 1965.

Namkha Dorje and Gungthang Tsultrim received land to build their settlements independent of each other. Namkha Dorje was in contact directly with the Indian government and Gungthang Tsultrim with Pat Brewster, a New Zealander who ran an aid organization. The same year, a school with Bonpo teachers was established with support from Ockenden Venture in Surrey, England. These self-reliant initiatives were seen to compete with, not augment, the exile government's efforts to take care of all Tibetans, as was clear from the warnings in *Seven Resolutions and Supporting Documents*, published by the United Party in 1965. Perhaps such can-do boldness was incompatible with a campaign of unity that demanded conformity and integration. In hindsight, in part, it was the texts published by the United Party that brought the Thirteen together.

4

THE SEVEN RESOLUTIONS AND SUPPORTING DOCUMENTS

The Nechung oracle's forecast in early 1965 about obstacles to the Dalai Lama's life mobilized the United Party to organize a meeting in Dharamsala on March 12, 1965. The party presided over a gathering comprising representatives from the government and the community on a scale that until then had been considered the prerogative of the government. The agenda was to fulfill the Nechung's advice to achieve unity and to strategize about how Tibetans, both lay and monastic, might be united in action as well as in speech. The meeting gave the United Party the chance to present itself as an organization that had the capacity to be an agent for the government and the voice for the people. The participants unanimously drew up and passed seven resolutions, which they submitted to the Dalai Lama.[1] The document's authority came from its expressed position as representing the consensus of the Tibetan people's will and desire. A second, lesser-known text pushed for the United Party to set up branch offices in Tibetan settlements. Accordingly, offices were established first in Dalhousie, Orissa, and Bumla, and over time in other places where the exile government settled Tibetan refugees. Whereas the United Party's manifesto of five aims distributed in 1964 was limited to the organization and its members, the *Seven Resolutions and Supporting Documents* of 1965, signed by 180 United Party representatives from India, Bhutan, Nepal, and Sikkim, addressed the entire exile population. The seven resolutions prioritized vigilance and outing of Tibetans suspected of collaborating with Communist China and the KMT. The original handwritten document was printed with the title *Seven Resolutions and Supporting Documents* in 1965 and reprinted in the *Truthful History of the Tibetan United Association* published by the United Party in 2005.

Even as early as April 29, 1959, India's Prime Minister Jawaharlal Nehru told the Rajya Sabha, the upper house of the Indian parliament, that there were spies operating in Kalimpong and that while he supported the Dalai Lama's religious activities, he was not willing to support political activities.[2] Kalimpong and Darjeeling were the centers of the Tibetan resistance movement in exile, and many exile Tibetans worked for the CIA and for Indian agencies such as the Research and Analysis Wing (RAW), Intelligence Bureau (IB), and Indo-Tibetan Border Police (ITBP), according to Jamyang Norbu.[3] He suggests that Tibetans worked for these agencies in part because they hoped that the skills they learned would help them in the Tibetan struggle. The Tibetans I spoke to said there were real spies and fabricated spies. They did not fear real spies as much as they did the United Party's power (attributed to Gyalo Thondup's power as the head of Tibetan intelligence) to potentially label them as such and report them to the Indian government. Fears of retribution for opposing the United Party and exile policies were real and palpable enough for a non-Tibetan aid worker to write to the head office of an international aid agency that he feared for the safety of a particular Thirteen member. The worker said that Amdowas (he might have been conflating Khampas and Amdowas) were routinely disappearing into prisons in Rajasthan for no reason.[4]

Seven Resolutions and Supporting Documents opened with the statement that every Tibetan heart was in anguish after hearing the oracle's warning about potential danger to His Holiness the Dalai Lama's well-being. Tibetans could "neither eat nor sleep," it added. The resolutions, drafted after many days of deliberation, were to be "put to practice" without hypocrisy. They were framed as offering Tibetans the right views and actions they could follow to avert obstacles to the Dalai Lama's health, but the text contained more than just the ideology of unity; it was a manual on the duties of belonging to the new Tibetan polity. It named specific individuals as traitors and directed Tibetans to monitor other Tibetans and to report any untoward behavior to the exile government as well as to the Indian government.

There are several veiled or partial allusions in the resolutions that are harder to interpret today, but Tibetans in the 1960s would have readily figured out the identities of individuals who were either named or hinted at. These individuals were held responsible for putting the precious life of the Dalai Lama and the Tibetan nation in jeopardy. By reading the resolutions closely and considering the context—the dramatic challenges taxing the Tibetan exile community—we can better understand what the United Party hoped to accomplish and also why the resolutions inspired a powerful recoil from those who felt attacked by it, among them individuals who would become the Thirteen.

FIRST RESOLUTION

The first resolution instructs lamas, *khenpos* (religious teachers), monks, and nuns to abide faithfully by the five resolutions passed on November 9, 1963, to promote Buddhist doctrine. The document asserts that doing so would fulfill the wishes of the Dalai Lama and prevent dishonor to Buddhism. No further descriptions or explanations are provided. The brevity of this resolution and to whom it is addressed are noteworthy. Lay Tibetans in 1965 might not have understood the context of the resolutions, but the monastic population most likely would have. In that regard, this first resolution speaks directly to its audience. According to a *khenpo*, it was directed at

Kagyud or Nyingma lamas and their followers. (He guessed it was the Sixteenth Karmapa and Dudjom Rinpoche.) He pointed to the use of the term *khenla* (made up of two words, *khenpo* and "lama"). *Khenpo* is a title given in the Kagyu, Nyingma, and Sakya schools to a religious scholar. The equivalent is *geshe* for the Bon and Gelug schools. "Lama" refers to reincarnate religious leaders of all religious schools.

The first conference of Tibetan Buddhist schools in exile was held in Dharamsala in November 1963 and led by the heads of the four schools: the Dalai Lama and Ling Rinpoche representing the Gelug school; the Karmapa, the Kagyu school; the Sakya Trizin, the Sakya school; and Dudjom Rinpoche, the Nyingma school. The religious leaders discussed five agendas: to spread the Buddha dharma widely; to align the external behavior of lamas and monks with the rules of the *vinaya* (rules for monks set by the Buddha) within the Tibetan Buddhist populations in India, Nepal, Sikkim, and Bhutan; to revive and preserve the texts and teachings of Buddhism in light of the destruction carried out by Communist China; to cultivate harmony (they used the metaphor of mixing milk and water) among the different schools of Buddhism; to create the rules and conditions of a constitution for the future free Tibet that would be uniquely Tibetan; and to build a democracy that cared for both spiritual and civic life.

These resolutions would help them reach their shared goals to spread Buddhist teachings, to preserve Buddhist texts, and to maintain the *vinaya*. They resolved to visit Tibetan settlements and give teachings once a month; provide financial support to lamas and monks for learning the Sanskrit or English languages so they could teach beyond the Tibetan populations; give opportunity to non-Tibetans to study Buddhism at the Buxa school (in West Bengal, near Bhutan's border, set up as a transit camp for refugees who entered India through Bhutan; in August 1959, Buxa Choegar or Buxa Lama Ashram was established for monks to continue their scholarly training);

and start a printing press so that religious texts could be published and preserved.

The leaders of the schools agreed to meet frequently under the leadership of the Dalai Lama to build harmony among the schools and prevent potential conflicts. They would be responsible for maintaining unity within their schools and among the four schools, particularly to ensure that the schools' political representative in the exile parliament would work toward unity. All would work toward a constitution that was democratic and that honored the Buddhist framework. The agreement was signed by all the leaders listed above.[5] The resolution's reference to the meeting among the four Buddhist schools serves, in essence, to remind religious leaders of the pledge they had made.

SECOND RESOLUTION

The second resolution stipulates that all Tibetans living in India, Nepal, and Bhutan are to follow the path of the democratic politico-religious system established by the Dalai Lama and that "whatever action one takes, one should not cross even a single ideal/vision of His Holiness which are stated in many of his speeches." Every Tibetan should attempt to lead a moral life, which meant holding the correct view toward friends, foes, and protectors, as well as practicing the essences of refuge, the law of karma, and the Ten Nonvirtues. Those who acted out of ignorance and broke any of the *ka* (commands) of His Holiness the Dalai Lama would be guided by leaders to prevent repeating such behavior:

> All Tibetans—monks, nuns, old, young, and adult—living in India, Nepal, and Bhutan must follow the path of the democratic politico-religious system established with His Holiness's vision. Whatever action one takes, one should not cross even a single vision expressed by

His Holiness in many of his speeches. Everyone must hold the correct view toward friends, foes, and the protector deity. Everyone from the three provinces should remain united and must practice in action the essences of the *kyab-dro* (refuge), the law of *lay-day* (karma), and the Ten Nonvirtues; and they must keep a strong bond among them and lead a moral life. However, if a few people out of ignorance break any of His Holiness's *ka*, then leaders concerned must guide them. If others knowingly act contrary then, whether one is the head, a monk, a nun, or a layperson, the leaders as well as the general public, without any bias or favoritism, must directly air their opinions, supporting one another in order to avoid such things from happening in the future.[6]

The problem with this resolution, as pointed out to me by Yugyal, was that it was unclear to what extent Tibetans had personal freedom in the new democratic polity if they were bound to pledge never to oppose the Dalai Lama.[7] This resolution was also a concern to some Chushi Gangdrug leaders, who by 1965 had reservations about Gyalo Thondup's leading role in the freedom movement. They feared that challenging Thondup might constitute a violation. I had so many questions for Yugyal: What were Tibetans to do if they disagreed with the policies of the exile government? How were they to know when they were going against the Dalai Lama's wishes? How was it possible for everyone to want the same thing? How was one to discipline all personal and political desires? How was democracy to be practiced if the first rule of society was to strictly follow the wishes of the Dalai Lama, even if he is the ideal leader?

Yugyal nodded as if I had answered my own questions.

THIRD RESOLUTION

The third resolution pointed out that Communist China and the Kuomintang Party were to be considered "foes." Tibetans did not want an additional enemy and had hoped that the Kuomintang would change their policy on Tibet, but the party had continued to plot to destroy unity among Tibetans. Thus, all Tibetans had resolved to oppose the Kuomintang. Tibetans overtly or covertly carrying out harmful actions at the behest of the Kuomintang were to be considered enemies and reported to the exile government and the Indian government. The resolution stated that some government *lay-jey* (officials) were under the influence of the two enemies. These individuals were using differences in religious beliefs, provinces, and class to undermine Tibetan unity. They had created rumors in the UN that Tibet was a part of China and that the Drichu River set the boundary of Tibet.

Although no names are mentioned in the resolution, it was thought to be aimed at the following individuals: Surkhang Wangchen Gelek, Yuthok Tashi Dhondup, Gungthang Tsultrim, and brothers Topgyal and Yamphel Pangdatsang. Lhasa aristocrats Surkhang Wangchen Gelek and Yuthok Tashi Dhondup had held positions in the cabinet of the Tibetan government in Lhasa before 1959 as well as in the new exile government. Gungthang Tsultrim had served as a representative from the Amdo region in the new Tibetan parliament in exile. Topgyal and Yamphel Pangdatsang were from a renowned Khampa trading family covering Lhasa, Markham, and Darjeeling.[8] All these individuals were believed to be targeted by the United Party for their frictions with Gyalo Thondup. It is interesting that the United Party chose to use the word *lay-jey* (following the protocol used in Tibet for cadre) to describe the former Lhasa officials in this group and not *zhung zhab*, as used in exile.[9]

FOURTH RESOLUTION

The fourth resolution is directed toward Tibetans, mostly groups of Khampas who were undecided about moving to the refugee settlements being constructed by the exile government. The resolution states that the Department of Home was making great effort to create lists of people in order to usher them to the new settlements. However, some people were

> making their own list, using schools, factories, and settlements as excuses to go their separate ways without the knowledge of concerned local offices established by our government. This violates *samaya* (religious pledge/bond) and is a source that destroys internal unity. We have hereby resolved that such actions, from individuals both high and low, that destroy the exile government's plans and damage unity should not occur and must be stopped from happening in the future in any way, either overtly or covertly.

There are two important aspects of this resolution: the continuation of the theme of a violation of *samaya* and the relation being drawn between *samaya* and unity. For Buddhist Tibetans, *samaya*, which means a bond between an individual and a spiritual master, is sacred and fiercely guarded. Quite often, this bond is established through vows and commitments given at initiations and empowerments. The resolution indicates that Tibetans who go against the government's initiatives are violating *samaya* with the Dalai Lama because the government is fulfilling the deep vision of His Holiness. The violation of *samaya* was destroying internal unity.

There were many reasons, such as the desire to keep families together or to stay close to their cherished lamas, that may have led some Tibetans to "go their separate ways." The number of Tibetans employed in building roads in India was stated to be 21,000 at its highest. Tibetan road laborers were among the first to be taken to the new settlements. The resolution's reference to Tibetans going their "separate ways" refers to individuals who had formed their own work groups on the road construction sites and those who had taken steps to build their own settlements (Namkha Dorje in Mainpat and Gungthang Tsultrim in Clement Town).

Bongsarpon Namkha Dorje had expressed his desire for a settlement with his people as early as 1962. Joyce Pearce, one of the three founders of a nonprofit organization called Ockenden Venture in Woking, Great Britain, recounts meeting Namkha Dorje in Rewalsar in a report on her visit with Tibetan refugees in April 1963. She writes that Namkha Dorje was renting a house for 500 rupees a year and that his party consisted of 290 people, of whom 182 were able-bodied adults working on building roads.[10] He had expressed his concern about the 57 children and 21 elders in his group and told Pearce that he was working on a plan so that children would not be separated from their parents. He had hoped to resettle his group in one place. Pearce reports that she mentioned Namkha Dorje and his situation to the Dalai Lama in an audience with him. The Dalai Lama, she writes, had no knowledge of the situation and no immediate solutions to offer.

Pema Dorje was in Kathmandu when I met him in 2015. He went to Bylakuppe when camps 2, 3, and 4 were being built, and all the workers lived in tents. He had initially refused to join the Tibetan settlement after a friend who had gone there informed him about his group's struggles getting exile officials to support their wish to have their lamas, who were of the Nyingma and Kagyu traditions, to live with them. Dorje joined the Chushi Gangdrug army in 1965, so he was far away from some of the events he was describing. According to Dorje, an exile official in Bylakuppe suggested that their lamas be encouraged to move to Buxa Choegar instead.

In 1959 there were as many as 1,500 monks in Buxa Choegar. Close to 200 lamas and monks from the Kagyud, Nyingma, and Sakya monasteries studied with 1,300 abbots, teachers, and monks from Sera, Drepung, and Ganden, the three famous Gelug monasteries. The number fluctuated as monks came and left. Nyingma, Sakya, and Kagyu monks and lamas chose to be resettled elsewhere partly because of Buxa's Gelug majority and partly because they found it difficult to adapt to the heat and living conditions of Buxa.[11] Kagyu monks left when the Karmapa, the head of the Kagyu school, established a monastery in Sikkim in 1962. Tashi Namgyal, the Chogyal (ruler) of Sikkim, had offered him seventy-four acres of land. Nyingma lamas also established a monastery in Rewalsar in Himachal Pradesh. By March 1968, many more monks had moved to Sarnath, where a Buddhist college was set up.

Pema Dorje's friends in Bylakuppe suspected that their settlement leader wanted to have just one lama, most likely Gelug, to serve as the spiritual teacher for all Tibetans in the settlement. Pema Dorje heard that the group ignored the order and decided to offer two rupees from their monthly earnings toward supporting their regional lamas. Able-bodied Tibetans were working on constructing homes, building roads, and drilling wells for two rupees per day at that time. Tibetan refugees also received free rations of rice, flour, sugar, oil, milk powder, and grain each month. The camp officer is believed to have refused to give any of this to their lamas, so the community shared their rations. These stories from Bylakuppe, whether imagined or partly true, confirmed Pema Dorje's fears about the government's project to erase regional and religious particularities.[12]

FIFTH RESOLUTION

The fifth resolution stressed that it was solely by the grace of His Holiness the Dalai Lama that Tibetans in India, Nepal, and Bhutan were receiving food and clothing. Aid was distributed fairly and evenly by the Central Relief Committee of the government of India. However, per the resolution, "cunning and deceptive people" were seeking and receiving relief assistance directly from the aid agencies by falsifying their names and disobeying the exile government. The resolution urged that such actions, "harmful to our administration, our unity as well as the welfare of our people, must stop. From now onward, all relief assistance will be received through the channels of our government, and this should not be contradicted."[13]

Independent road workers, also known as *khushi* Khampas, as well as individuals who had succeeded in getting funds to establish their settlements felt the fifth resolution was directed toward them. Namkha Dorje was the first among road workers to protest that exile officials were denying relief aid to him and his group working in Manali around the fall of 1962. His daughter, Tsodi Bongsar, says they never got the aid. It is unclear if money, food rations, and clothing were withheld on purpose; the group refused to accept help from the exile government; or extenuating circumstances made it difficult for the government to send them aid. On the advice of a friend in Kullu—Tsodi calls him Chandra Kanti—Namkha Dorje made his appeal for aid directly to the Indian government. Prime Minister Jawaharlal Nehru was visiting Manali in 1963, and her father handed Mr. Nehru a letter, composed with the help of Chandra Kanti. In it Namkha Dorje said that aid distributors overlooked his people and requested help from the Indian government.[14]

After this intervention, aid packages were mailed directly to him. Tsodi recalls her father advising Khampa acquaintances who also had not received aid or had been denied it to appeal directly to the Indian government or to aid agencies.[15] Ugyen Topgyal Rinpoche clarified that exile government officials had told the monks from his monastery that *khushi* Khampas had forfeited their right to aid because they did not follow the exile government's rules. Frustrated, his father, Chokling Rinpoche, had visited the Tibetan Refugee Programme officer in New Delhi. The officers there had doubted that the government would shun sections of its own people and sent a representative to verify the claims. Ugyen Topgyal Rinpoche remembers that two relief aid workers peeked into their tents in Patlikuhl in Himachal Pradesh. Thereafter, the aid organization mailed parcels addressed to "Mr. Chokling."

Rumors soon circulated that Chokling Rinpoche's *gyashok* was receiving aid from Taiwan, not from relief organizations working with the exile Tibetan and the Indian governments. An elder in Bir remembers exile officials pointing to him and saying: "Look at these people. They are getting aid from Taiwan. See, their clothes are different. Ours is real refugee aid, theirs is from Taiwan." Ugyen Topgyal Rinpoche reasoned that in advocating directly for themselves and bypassing the Tibetan officials, they were seen as undermining the authority of the exile government and consequently colluding with the Kuomintang.

Malcolm Dexter, a teacher running Ockenden School for Tibetans, wrote to Joyce Pearce, the school's founder, in 1966 about his visit to a Bon community after his audience with the Dalai Lama. An incidental reference that Dexter and Sangye Tenzin's (a Bon leader, scholar, and teacher at Ockenden) entry to the camp coincided with the arrival of the group's first ever aid rations suggests that the Bon group living in the Kullu Manali area did not receive any aid intended for refugees until 1966.

The network of charity organizations helping in the distribution of aid was complex, especially since Tibetans were scattered across different parts of India. Pat Brewster, the head of a charity organization in India, wrote about the difficulty and unavoidable discrepancy in distributing funds. In a 1965 report to his supervisor in Geneva, he calculated that fifteen million rupees were spent that year on Tibetan refugees toward education, rations, administration, medical programs, and child welfare. The aid, he reported, was not spread evenly. He thought it possible that Tibetans in the road camps were not getting any of the benefits.[16]

Similarly, George N. Patterson, who had been in Kham in the early 1950s and joined his Khampa friends in exile in India in the 1960s, alleges in his book *Requiem for Tibet* that the Tibetan Relief Organization set up in India was run by a committee of Tibetan officials and Indian associates who misused aid and "sold medicines and old clothing on the black market, and added money to their personal accounts."[17] He states that protests were increasing by Tibetans who were "excluded from benefits" or felt that their fellow Tibetans were losing interest in doing "anything regarding a return to Tibet." Patterson explains that these protests were directed against Gyalo Thondup, who was "prominent in every decision and every delegation" and claimed his "authority from the Dalai Lama."[18] Patterson said he was investigating corruption in the distribution of aid. He was declared a yellow journalist by Mrs. Sucheta Kriplani, the chief minister of Uttar Pradesh in the Indian government, and by international aid agencies such as the United Nations and the Red Cross. He is believed to have left India after receiving complaints against him from these agencies. Patterson does not name the groups who claimed to be discriminated against by exile officials. His charges of misuse of aid were not proven.

Prime Minister Jawaharlal Nehru had put the caretaking of Tibetan refugees under not the Home Ministry but the Ministry of External Affairs, which was directly under him. The Central Relief Committee of India was established in 1959 by the Kripalani Committee to coordinate relief efforts and international humanitarian funds. In a report from December 1965, submitted to the Committee on Relief and Gift Supplies of the National Christian Council of India, Brewster, who is identified as a "Tibetan Officer," reports that there were an estimated 55,000 Tibetan refugees in India: 5,000 in Sikkim; 3,000 in Bhutan; 5,000 in the Darjeeling and Kalimpong area; and 9,000 in agricultural settlements. The remaining refugees were scattered in camps along the "mountainous roads up near the Tibetan border."[19]

The report acknowledged the government of India as the greatest contributor to the Tibetan relief programs. Other organizations are named for providing assistance: the United Nations Organization funded rehabilitation projects; the American Emergency Committee (AECTR), the National Christian Council, and Catholic Relief Services provided food, educational, and rehabilitation projects; the Young Men's Club of America provided personnel and vocational training in the agricultural settlements; Save the Children contributed toward residential nurseries for children in Dharamsala and Shimla; Swiss Aid Abroad helped clear land for agriculture and provided personnel and equipment; Swiss Aid funded childcare, housing, and rehabilitation programs; and the Tibetan Industrial and Rehabilitation Society (TIRS) set up industrial programs and settlements. Other organizations supporting Tibetans were OXFAM, CORSO, Lions Club of Germany, and the Tibet Society.[20]

At the heart of resolutions 4 and 5 are questions of authority, efficiency, and sovereignty. The exile polity was eager to centralize all aid movements, given that welfare entitlements are one of the powerful means that states rely on to promote the idea of national identity or identification with a national community. Although *Seven Resolutions and Supporting Documents* does not explain why individuals should not seek aid directly from international organizations, the exile government was attempting to build significant relationships with a multitude of international aid groups, including intergovernmental organizations. These relations provided a means of authority over its refugee-citizenry while helping to establish its sovereign position as representative of the Tibetan people. Having an organized distribution network also made sense, given the huge task of caring for refugees who were scattered in many locations. However, the United Party did not consider the possibility that Tibetans might have had a reason to seek help directly from the Indian government.

The exile polity's concern over Tibetan individuals or groups initiating their own relationships with international officers and agencies is reasonable. The Thirteen were, after all, in touch with many different representatives from international organizations and influential Indian politicians and social workers, many of whom encouraged their diverse histories, values, and identifications. These connections had the potential to give international officers the idea of competing emergent leaders or discord within the Tibetan refugee society.

SIXTH RESOLUTION

The sixth resolution pushed to rescind travel documents for three individuals: Trochupon Dorje Pasang and "Pomzurs." Pomzurs (possibly a snub) combines the names of two: "Pom" refers to Pangdatsang (also Pomdatsang) Lobzang Yamphel and "Zur" to Surkhang Wangchen Gelek. The resolution states that these individuals had been issued documents to travel abroad and mandates that no applications be accepted for their travel documents, and if submitted, should be blocked. The resolution did not provide any further explanations or reasons for preventing these individuals from leaving India.

All those named were wrangling with Gyalo Thondup. The struggles between Thondup and the group predate their journey to exile. Lobzang Yamphel Pangdatsang, sometimes called Yarphel Pomdatsang, was the second of four brothers from the Pangdatsang family, one of the most successful trading families in early twentieth-century Tibet, as indicated in the Tibetan saying, "Sa Pangda, nam Pangda" (the earth is Pangda's, the sky is Pangda's). They were close to the Thirteenth Dalai Lama's family and to the famous political figure Thupten Kunphel, the Dalai Lama's trusted aide. Yamphel Pangdatsang served as the governor of the Chumbi valley, an important border region in Tibet, and was the official Tibetan trade agent in Kalimpong. He was later made the head of the Commerce and Industries Department of the Preparatory Committee of the TAR.[21] According to Carole McGranahan, each of the four brothers, Nyima, Yamphel, Rapga, and Topgyal, had their own domain of power and interest. Yamphel was rich, famous, and well connected in Kalimpong. McGranahan writes that his "invincible status" altered when Gyalo Thondup arrived.[22] Jamyang Norbu suspects that Yamphel committed "the cardinal sin of disagreeing" with Gyalo Thondup, resulting in their falling out.[23] Yamphel and his brother Rapga Tenzin Pangdatsang had their own political ambitions and kept their distance from Gyalo Thondup's political activities in Kalimpong. Rapga was believed to be working for the Mongolian and Tibetan Office in Nanjing in the 1930s, according to McGranahan. He visited Kalimpong in the late 1930s and established the Tibet Improvement Party there in 1939 with the poet Changlochen Kung Sonam Gyelpo and Thupten Kunphel (both of whom had fled to Kalimpong after the Thirteenth Dalai Lama's death). Rapga was deported from India by the British for violating the Foreigners Act of 1940 and the Registration of Foreigners Act of 1939.[24]

Rapga returned to Kalimpong in the 1950s. He took daily walks through the bazaar and often stopped to chat with Hou Ku Hsiong, also known as N. Son Saab, the owner of the popular N Son shoe store on Main Road, N. Son's leather boots were prized by Tibetan traders, local people, and wealthy Tibetans in Lhasa. On August 25, 1962, while Rapga was chatting with Hou and his wife, Lee Kim Sew, a young Tibetan man in a long coat walked into the store and fired his gun at them. The man hit Lee Kim in the foot and missed Rapga, the intended target.

While at a dinner party in Collegeville, Pennsylvania, in May 2024, I was absently listening to a group of Tibetan and Chinese friends discuss their childhood in Kalimpong when I heard Joseph Hou, whom I had met on previous occasions, describe the day his mother was shot in the foot by a Tibetan man. Joe, it turns out, is the son of the famous N. Son Saab. His father had stated that the man had not pulled the gun out of his pocket but had shot at them from under his coat. Hou and Rapga had been sitting "side by side." Joe described the path of the bullet as going between the two men, "through the wooden counter behind them and through the corrugated steeel wall," to enter his mother's left calf.[25] The bullet had gone through her leg without hitting any bone. The gunman was not identified by the police, but Rapga's family believed Gyalo Thondup to be behind the assassination attempt.[26]

Hou had described the man as an inexperienced gunman to his son. Had he been a good shooter, Joe said, both his father and Rapga would have been killed that day. He recalled his father saying that Rapga was wrongly accused of being a Chinese spy. Joe believed that the people behind the assassination attempt had actually wanted to get Yamphel, but since he had been away at that time, they had targeted Rapga.[27]

The United Party's book, published years after Yamphel left for Tibet, claims that he was deceived by the Communist Chinese government into going to Hong Kong, Beijing, and thereafter to Tibet in 1965. The book says that not only did Yamphel return to Tibet but once there, he made disparaging remarks against the Dalai Lama.[28] Rumors suggest that Gyalo Thondup was behind Yamphel receiving a "Quit India" notice from the Indian government which forced him to return to Tibet in 1965, the same year the United Party's resolutions were written.[29]

Surkhang Wangchen Gelek, from the aristocratic family of Surkhang, held the position of cabinet minister in the Tibetan government before the Chinese invasion and served in the cabinet in the exile government. The *Tibetan Freedom* under Gyalo Thondup published a series of articles criticizing Surkhang for betraying the exile government and for taking money from the Mongolian-Tibetan Affairs Commission. Gyalo Thondup writes in his memoir that Surkhang Wangchen Gelek and Yuthok Tashi Dhondup fled Dharamsala for Taiwan to save face when their unreasonable request for a loan of two hundred million rupees for the exile government's expenses was rejected by Prime Minister Jawaharlal Nehru. Thondup claims that even Prime Minister Nehru had cautioned the Dalai Lama against taking advice from "such" ministers. He believes the two ministers "fell in with Guomindang intelligence" and set up a fake representative office of the exile government in Taiwan.[30]

Surkhang Wangchen Gelek is described in Gyalo Thondup's memoir as an informer "currying Chinese favor" and as a "two-faced official."[31] He is also presented indirectly as being one of the regent Taktra Rinpoche's men. Thondup's animosity toward Surkhang seems to have been linked to the latter's relationship with Taktra Rinpoche. Thondup was close to the regent Reting Rinpoche, who in 1944 was not able to get his regentship back from Taktra Rinpoche, the interim replacement he had chosen. Thondup claims that Taktra Rinpoche and his "faction" of twenty or so "conservative officials" planned to depose his brother, the Fourteenth Dalai Lama, and replace him with their own candidate.[32] Gyalo Thondup hints that they killed his father and Reting Rinpoche. He also refers to the people running Tibet at that time as "absolutely incompetent."[33] This dismissal comes after his reference to Surkhang and Liushar Thupten Tharpa's (the equivalent of foreign minister in Tibet) nonchalance in reassuring the Indian diplomat S. N. Sinha (who replaced Hugh Richardson to become the counsel general in Lhasa in April 1950) that Sinha's concern of an "imminent Chinese attack," was "impossible" because Tibet was protected by its mountains.[34]

Lodi Gyaltsen Gyari's assessment of Surkhang is like Gyalo Thondup's. Gyari Rinpoche uses Surkhang Wangchen Gelek's story as an example of how former officials built "troublesome" alliances with "organs of the KMT government" when they realized their powers were eroding. Gyari Rinpoche writes that Surkhang moved to Taiwan in the early 1970s to "set up a rival, so-called 'Kalon office'" that was viewed by the exile government as a direct challenge to its authority.[35]

Jamyang Norbu provides a different perspective. He suggests that Surkhang Wangchen Gelek and Yuthok Tashi Dhondup communicated with the Dalai Lama and kept him informed of their efforts to raise the issue of Tibet. He suggests that the two men's attempt to get Taiwan's support for an independent Tibet might, in hindsight, be "reinterpreted as a farsighted policy initiative."[36] The Taiwanese government had requested the two former cabinet members to represent the Tibetan people under the Chinese regime. Surkhang and Yuthok opted instead to open a *kalon* (ministerial) office to function more like a cultural center.[37]

Former cabinet member Juchen Thupten Namgyal says in his autobiography that Surkhang Wangchen Gelek and Yuthok Tashi Dhondup might have moved to Taiwan under duress. He felt that instead of being ousted from the community, they should have been stripped of their political responsibilities. He poses a question that in part answers itself: how could they have appointed themselves as cabinet ministers when it was the Dalai Lama who traditionally conferred that position?[38]

Yuthok Tashi Dhondup's son, Jigmie Dorje Yuthok, states that Gyalo Thondup targeted Surkhang, Yuthok, and Pangdatsang because he had disagreed with them on certain policies leading up to the Chinese invasion in 1950. The three men were cabinet members of the Lhasa government and had supported a decree to expel all Chinese nationals from Tibet. Thondup had not done so because his wife was Chinese.[39] Gyalo Thondup was also displeased with them because the Kashag in Lhasa had appointed "trustees to sort out the family's finances," according to Jigmie Yuthok.[40]

While this resolution altered the individual lives of those it targeted, it might have also influenced the mobility of every Tibetan into the future. Even to this day, all Tibetan refugees seeking the travel document known as the Identity Card or Yellow Book issued by the Indian government (because of the color of the cover) have to go through the Tibetan exile government.[41]

SEVENTH RESOLUTION

The seventh and final resolution stressed the importance of electing leaders who held politically correct and righteous views toward "protector, friends, and foes." The Tibetan public was urged to recognize their elected leaders, avoid disputes with them, and abide by rules instead of applying wrong definitions for "democracy" and "freedom." The Tibetan subjects were to obey every wish of His Holiness the

Dalai Lama. The duty of the leaders in the settlements was to observe, correct, and report aberrant behavior.

The United Party stated it would set up branch offices in every Tibetan settlement to ensure that the resolutions were obeyed. In preparation, representatives were asked to educate themselves on the resolutions and announce them to the public. Representatives were to meet once a month to discuss the resolutions and their implementation. They were also asked to broadcast and discuss His Holiness's speech (made on March 15, 1965). "At least one general meeting will be held annually in Dharamsala and when the dates are confirmed, Chigdril Tsogpa [United Party] will send out announcements to all the places from where intelligent and useful *dhon chod* (representatives) must be sent."

During this general meeting, each representative would present a report on the success or failure of their implementation of the seven resolutions. Juchen Thupten writes in his book that the settlement offices in Bylakuppe received instructions from the United Party as though they were *yikcha* (official documents) from the government. Officers complied with the instructions to hold monthly meetings for six hundred people in 1965 that echoed the class struggle methods employed by the Chinese Communist Party.[42] Individuals were divided into ten groups of sixty people each. Each group was asked to complete a form responding to eight questions: if an individual was engaging in regionalism; was practicing sectarianism; opposed Yuthok, Surkhang, and Trochupon Dorje Pasang; was accepting relief assistance from anyone outside the government funds; harbored the desire to start separate settlements; or opposed people who did so.

Thubten explains that the right answer was "no" to practicing regionalism and sectarianism and "yes" to opposing Yuthok, Surkhang, and Trochupon. (Tashi Dhondup Yuthok, like Surkhang, had held the position of cabinet minister in the Lhasa government before the Chinese invasion. Trochupon was accused in a series of articles in the *Tibetan Freedom* of working with the Kuomintang and betraying the Tibetan government, most likely because his son went to Taiwan.) "Yes" to opposing individuals who were setting up their own settlements. Thubten suggests that this last point was a reference to the heads of the Nyingma, Sakya, and Kagyu lineages—Dudjom Rinpoche, Sakya Daktri Rinpoche, and the Gyalwa Karmapa—who had established their own monasteries and settlements, the Karmapa in Rumtek and Dudjom Rinpoche in Orissa.[43]

The settlement officer would send the completed forms to the local United Party office every six months. These documents were used to monitor or identify potential foes. Thus, the United Party was functioning almost like a government and institutionalizing a battle against what it defined as regionalism and sectarianism. The tone of *Seven Resolutions and Supporting Documents* is of an entity confident of its power to eliminate any challenge to its authority. What is striking is that all social agency and social agents are subsumed within the United Party's agenda for unity. Each of the seven resolutions illustrates the paradoxical relationship of the part to the whole. The antinomy created between unity and regionalism also created a new equation between a regional and a Tibetan identity.

The resolutions were distributed in the settlements, according to Drawupon. Even if Tibetans could not read or understand the references and contexts, the documents controlled behavior, stood in for knowledge, and established a way of thinking about difference. The texts came with power and carried the threat of social ostracization. Tibetans realized they could be next to be named in an official document. The resolutions marshaled the oracle's prophecy of the danger to the Dalai Lama's life—a potential devastation that horrified all Tibetans—and the power ascribed to the Tibetan body to prolong his life, to establish a relationship between the Tibetan subject and the government where both private and public life were bound to a religious value.

The Tibetan subject in exile was governable for several reasons, but especially because Tibetans were willing to be led by the Dalai

Lama. From private altars at home to public spaces, the Dalai Lama presided in the fused role of spiritual guru and political leader. The laws of religion ruled the private lives of many. For Buddhist Tibetans, the guru takes precedence over temporal positions. Tibetans were always already in a position of obeisance to the Dalai Lama, and to the exile government by its nearness to him. The routinization of certain practices involving the government could be incorporated alongside existing everyday private spiritual practices. The United Party's *Seven Resolutions and Supporting Documents*' push for a reformed future Tibetan society cemented on existing religious sentiments was an effective calculation.

CITIZENSHIP: A COMMUNITY OF VALUE

Tibetans were forced to shift from the subject position of *nangpa* (insider) to refugee-citizen by the loss of their homeland. They were being asked to prove they were refugees, which entailed a narrative of dispossession, yet they were ushered into refugee citizenship, which involved learning a history of ideas and arguments about what it meant to be a Tibetan national in exile. The multiple levels of internal and external recognition—being dispossessed and having to reconstitute as old members of an upgraded polity— were complicated by history and the historical experience of coming from diverse regions of Tibet.

In *Citizenship and Its Discontents*, the scholar Niraja Gopal Jayal discusses the routinely dashed aspirations of citizens as well as the many ways citizenship is theorized, understood, experienced, and claimed in India. Jayal proposes that what appears as a consensual concept is in practice full of ambivalences and doubts and can emerge in "morally loaded binaries."[44] Binaries such as good and bad, thin and thick, active and passive citizenships are ways the concept of citizenship expresses and establishes normative preferences and desired virtues. But there is much to consider on the border between citizen and migrant and between the formal and normative status of citizenship and immigration. Bridget Anderson, a scholar of migration and citizenship, makes a compelling case that modern states don't present themselves as peoples bound by legal status alone but as "a community of value" of people who share "common ideals and (exemplary) patterns of behavior expressed through ethnicity, religion, culture, or language—that is, its members have shared values."[45] It is through the community of value that states also claim legitimacy.

Citizenship and immigration are ultimately about status in the sense that they are about honor, worth, and membership in a society of value, described by Jayal as being inhabited by good citizens and by Anderson as inhabited by those who "possess and display civic virtues" rather than those who don't. For Anderson, this community manifests values but is also valued and seen to need protection, usually from outsiders. For good citizens—defined as law-abiding and "hard-working members of stable and respectable families"—culture is "extrinsic rather than constitutive, a way of life, not power and rule."[46] Both scholars also point out that community membership is permeable and often associated with the greater good.

It is not too far-fetched to suggest that the United Party's manifesto, *Five Aims of the Tibetan United Association*, published in 1964, and *Seven Resolutions and Supporting Documents*, published in 1965, played a role in simultaneously defining the new Tibetan citizen in exile and reassuring the traditional Tibetan that democracy would not alter a familiar world order. Both texts reiterated familiar Buddhist beliefs as a reference point for the Tibetan identity and the greater good of freedom by suggesting that all Tibetans were already linked to the Dalai Lama under the laws of *samaya*. However, solemnizing of personal religious devotion into political responsibility meant that religious duty would supersede political desires. The message is consistent in all the resolutions: His Holiness the Dalai Lama gave democracy to the Tibetan people, and it is the duty of the people to adhere to his vision by practicing *samaya* and unity.

The criteria for membership provided by the United Party sought the development of faithfulness among Tibetans and expected them to follow the moral and political vision of the new administration; keep the struggle for independence and the greater good of a reformed Tibet as a priority; adhere only to the sanctioned definition of democracy and freedom; and condemn challenges to the Dalai Lama's vision of unity as acts of disunity that hurt national efforts. This meant that Tibetan refugees seeking to belong as refugee-citizens in the territory-less state of the exile government accepted that a sense of collective purpose and obligation would induct them into the new Tibetan citizenry, but not guarantee rights, in the initial stages. There appears little opportunity to negotiate other terms of recognition.[47] On the contrary, within the framework of unity, the norm of assent already precluded recognition of desires and identities upheld by the United Party. Or, to put it in another way, within the framework of unity, the norm of obedience to the "right way" meant that expressions for other desires could be read in two ways: dissent against the Dalai Lama and anti-Tibetan unity.

The United Party's manifesto in 1964 and the resolutions in 1965 indicate that the organization was committed to democracy, but its terms are not recognizably democratic in any conventional sense. The goals of the party as expressed in these documents can be interpreted as an attempt to translate democracy into a new religious contract between the reformed Tibetan subject and the Dalai Lama in which there is no commensurate sense of the people as being crucial other than in a subordinate role. The contradiction made democracy less about participation in a society or community and more about fulfilling a religious duty or obligation. It was a process of the sacralization of democracy and political life. The terms "democracy" and "unity" were not clearly defined by the exile government or the United Party in the early years, but the import of these concepts to the Tibetan dream of freedom was not ambiguous. An elder in Kathmandu told me he thought that the United Party's goal was to create a secular society, but they knew that only His Holiness the Dalai Lama could get Tibetans to be open to change. That is why the party had to use religion to get Tibetans to consent to democracy. But it also meant placing all authority and all responsibility in one leader.

Nationalist sentiment operates most clearly at the level of quotidian life. *Seven Resolutions and Supporting Documents* succeeded in escalating the social death of prominent political figures of the past—such as Wangchen Gelek Surkhang, Tashi Dhondup Yuthok, Yamphel Pangdatsang, and Trochupon Dorje Pasang—by naming and shaming them for their alleged disservice to Tibetan unity. Tashi Dhondup Yuthok and Wangchen G. Surkhang lived in Taiwan for a few years. Yuthok later settled in Canada and died there. Surkhang died in Taiwan. Lobzang Yamphel Pangdatsang, as mentioned earlier, was compelled to leave India. His daughter, Wangmo Pangdatsang, suffered for being part of the Pangdatsang family when she came to Darjeeling to sort out her family estate. The people of Darjeeling and Kalimpong ostracized her and reported on her to the Indian intelligence bureau largely because of their perception of Yamphel Pangdatsang as a Chinese spy.[48] On a visit to Dharamsala to seek an audience with the Dalai Lama on June 22, 1966, she was insulted by groups of Tibetans and her request for an audience was challenged. Likewise, Trochupon Dorje Pasang had to leave India because of the effective campaign against him. The resolutions had the potential to establish identities of individuals as traitors or patriots, which in turn had the power to form a new social status in exile. Such tactics are not uncommon in the process that governments or states employ to cultivate loyalty among citizens.

Tibetan nationalists embraced unity as an inviolable national project, indeed as a national condition to the struggle, and they were suspicious of Tibetans with ideas that contrasted with it. Tibetans also had to be willing to give up their unique and varied ways of feeling the past that corresponded to their individual histories because Tibetan nationalists believed that the right history was one that kept the right vision in place. Alternate representations of the nation were difficult to establish as truthful, and when expressed, came with a price.

In 1966, two teachers in the Ockenden School came under attack for teaching their students what they knew to be true: that certain regions of Kham and Amdo had not been under the Lhasa government in 1950, and that the Bon religion had predated Buddhism. Nationalists were not so concerned that these were historical realities but that the facts upset the narrative of an always united Tibet.

5

AGAINST THE GRAIN OF HISTORY
Mutiny at the Ockenden School

On the last day of April in 1966, thirty students walked out of a school in Dharwar, Karnataka, after accusing two of their teachers of teaching them "wrong history" and attempting to turn them into Bonpos, or adherents of the Bon religion from Tibet. That young students would be stirred to revolt against their teachers and leave the school is uncommon in Tibetan society, given the importance of the teacher in student-teacher relationships in Tibetan Buddhist traditions. That this happened in the early days of exilic life when dissent against authority was disjointed with the needs of the moment was even more surprising. A Bonpo *geshe* brought the event at Ockenden School to my attention in 2013. I was astonished that young schoolboys with no memory of Tibet were wounded listening to facts and historical details that went against what they accepted as history. Rather than focusing on the details of the revolt itself, the *geshe* turned my attention to the students' idealistic projection of Tibetan history and the newspaper *Bhod-mi Rangwang*, or *Tibetan Freedom*'s, representation of an uncustomary response to school lessons as a story of young Tibetans rising up to defend their nation.

I was raised in Tibetan refugee communities where the majority identify themselves as adherents of the Gelug, Kagyu, Nyingma, or Sakya traditions. Even though Bon was recognized by the exile government as the fifth religious tradition of Tibet, I was taught as a child that Bon was a pre-Buddhist religion.[1] Bon was described as an aberration from Buddhism: Bonpos walked around the stupa counterclockwise, believed in magic, and were responsible for the demise of Buddhism in Tibet. I was not taught at home or by the community that Bon is integral to Tibetan identity and history. I wasn't even told that Buddhism and Bon borrow many rituals and practices from each other. Only while writing this book did I come to understand that when Tibetans refer to Bon in exile, they are referring to a distinct religious movement of Yungdrung Bon (Eternal Bon) that emerged in the tenth and eleventh centuries at the same time that Buddhism gained prominence in Tibet. Like Tibetan Buddhism, Yungdrung Bon is an organized religious or monastic system, described by scholars of Bon Per Kvaerne and Dan Martin as both distinct from and "not entirely unrelated" to the non-Buddhist practices of the imperial period.[2] Kvaerne and Martin suggest the study of Bon in four different contexts: one, as a "cluster" of many non-Buddhist religious practices and beliefs that were not yet a religious system during and following the Tibetan Empire (seventh to ninth centuries); two, as beliefs and practices in the tenth to eleventh centuries and documented in texts; three, as post-eleventh century traditions that had become a religion known as Eternal Bon with monastic institutions; and finally, as beliefs and practices from the Himalayan areas that are known as Bon and have affinities with category two, and possibly category three.[3] Regardless of Bon's longevity in Tibet, its marginality in a society dominated by the four schools of Buddhism hardly warranted fear, yet here was an event where young students cared enough about national history to risk their education.

The Ockenden School was set up in 1965 by the Ockenden Venture, a charity organization founded by three schoolteachers from Surrey, England. Established under the 1940 War Charities Act, the organization focused its first humanitarian aid on young Eastern European refugees following World War II. The scope was amended in 1962 to support displaced children beyond Europe after one of its founders, Joyce Pearce, advocated to assist Tibetan refugees in India. Ockenden students were meant to become among the first generation of Tibetan refugees to receive an education and to graduate from school. Ockenden and exile officials hoped this new generation would serve the community as scholars, translators, and liaison officers.

Education was central to the exile government's plan to prepare young Tibetans for a modern future while also grounding them in the Tibetan language and culture. Instead of sending Tibetan children to existing Indian schools, the government created separate Tibetan schools. The dual objective at the heart of the policy motivated the government to do this even though Tibetans had little managerial experience and lacked material resources to run institutions.[4] A customized Tibetan education aimed to help answer questions such as: Who am I? Where have I come from and where did my parents come from?[5]

The exile government's Tibetan School Administration was established under the Ministry of Human Resource Development of the Indian government in 1960, and the first Tibetan school, the Tibetan Refugee Educational Institute, was established in Mussoorie in the state of Uttar Pradesh, now Uttarakhand, on March 3, 1960. By 1962, two more residential schools were built, one in Shimla and the other in Darjeeling. The government also formed a new wing, the Council for Tibetan Education, under the department of education to prepare the curricula for the schools.[6]

The Ockenden school was neither fully under the exile educational administration nor like the makeshift and interim educational options developed for Tibetan children in more remote locations where Tibetans found employment. The school was to be managed by the Ockenden Venture with some input from the education council. Ockenden hired Malcolm Dexter as headmaster, Sangye Tenzin, and a few other instructors to educate the forty-two boys.[7] Sangye Tenzin, who was awarded a *geshe* degree in Tibet, had returned to

India after teaching and studying at the School of Oriental Studies (SOAS) in London.[8] Two additional teachers, Gyaltsen Choden, a Tibetan instructor, and Kelsang Liushar, a steward, had been appointed by the Tibetan education council. The school had relocated from Mussoorie to Dharwar in South India, where it had more space. Prior to relocating, the students had spent three months waiting in Mussoorie with very little to do. Even though the students and teachers had shown small signs of discontentment while waiting, they were upset when they saw their new environs in Dharwar because of the heat and sanitary conditions. Still, the revolt was unexpected and unimaginable for Dexter and Sangye Tenzin.

On April 29, 1966, Dexter and Sangye Tenzin left for a routine excursion to the bazaar and returned in the late afternoon to find they had "a revolt" on their hands.[9] Two days later, thirty students abruptly left the school with their bedding, uniforms, and even textbooks. That day, May 1, Dexter wrote a letter to the school's founder, Joyce Pearce, in Surrey, describing it as the most difficult and important letter he had ever written. "Sangye and I were absolutely heart-broken," he wrote.

In his letter, Dexter revealed that the students had held a meeting to discuss their complaints against the school while the two teachers had gone to the market. Upon their return, several students refused to do their one-hour garden chore. The boys complained that they had come to school to study, not work. Dexter explained that since arriving in Dharwar, the students had been asked to put in one hour's manual labor around the school premises. Some of the students turned violent and threatened to beat Sangye Tenzin. Dexter confessed having spanked some of the younger boys to control them and decided to expel the ringleaders, six students in all. Hinting at the play of complex religious and political machinations, Dexter revealed that it had boiled down to Sangye Tenzin's Bonpo identity. In his letter to the Bureau of the Dalai Lama on May 6, Dexter accused Kelsang Liushar and Gyaltsen Choden of having instigated the boys to revolt.[10] He emphasized that the two teachers had uncharacteristically gone off to see a movie at the height of the hullabaloo.

The story came together to me after consulting four sources: the *Tibetan Freedom* newspaper; letters and testimonials exchanged between Joyce Pearce in Surrey and Malcolm Dexter, the school's headmaster; letters sent by the Bureau of the Dalai Lama to Joyce Pearce; and letters written by third-party observers (friends of Dexter) and volunteer teachers who attempted to make sense of the incident. Although it seems an unsurprising story about students testing authority in school for some, these documents tell a more complex biography of a nation and how it is secured through a process that includes the "contestation, co-option, and marginalization of alternate histories and visions."[11] The afterlife of this event, which lingers within the Bonpo community while leaving barely a trace in the larger exile consciousness, is also an indication of how history is personal and how events are shaped by ordinary people's actions and responses as much as by individuals in power.

LETTERS FROM THE FIELD

In a collective letter to founder Joyce Pearce, twenty-five students explained that they left Ockenden because of their uncongenial relationship with primarily two teachers: Dexter and Sangye Tenzin. They listed twelve reasons for their discontentment, religion being the first and the most grievous. The students complained that the teachers spoke about Bon and neglected the "holy doctrine" of Buddha, which they cherished. The letter writers also accused them of holding negative views of the Tibetan government and a hidden motive of turning Ockenden into a Bonpo center. They ended with a plea to Pearce to replace the teachers.[12]

A follow-up letter to Pearce was signed by thirty boys.[13] The students informed her that they were heading to Dharamsala to report the events to the Dalai Lama.[14] Pearce also received a letter from the Bureau of the Dalai Lama, dated May 5, informing her that the boys had been expelled from Ockenden School and inviting her thoughts on the situation.[15]

In her response to Dexter on May 4, Pearce advised him not to punish the boys for writing to her and foregrounded her understanding of religious sectarian debates as the primary reason for the turmoil. She suggested that Dexter address the matter of religion first.

"Is it not likely that," she wrote, "as you have explained to me, the Bompos [sic] are of a different sect from the Dalai Lama that they may feel Sangye has a different approach in the matter of religious instruction?"[16] She wondered if hiring Mr. Phalla, who had been the head of the Dalai Lama's secretariat in the Tibetan government in Lhasa, would help to keep the balance. Pearce assumed that being of a "different sect," that is, Gelug, Phalla would restore peace.

Dexter's letter to Pearce on May 10 intimated he had read the students' letter but believed the religious reasons unfounded. Indeed, he stated that the complaints were not worth refuting: Sangye Tenzin neither taught the Bonpo doctrine nor made an issue of religion. The "reverse" was true, he said: the students began their day with thirty minutes of prayers to the Dalai Lama and the Buddha. Dexter clarified that both he and Sangye Tenzin preached tolerance in the school and treated students from all religious schools and provinces with equal respect.

Dexter also directed Pearce's attention to the existing careful balance of Tibetan faiths in the school. Both Kelsang Liushar and the "Dharamsala teacher," referring to Gyaltsen Choden, were Buddhists (and Gelug).[17] To clarify for Pearce the range of Tibetan faiths, Dexter indicated he would ask Dr. David. L. Snellgrove, a professor of the Tibetan language at the School of Oriental and African Studies in the University of London, to provide her with essential details regarding the "religious strife" that had complicated political and social life in Tibet for centuries. He hinted that such tensions persisted within the exile community. Snellgrove was among the first Western scholars to study Bon and work with Tibetan Bonpo scholars, including Sangye Tenzin and Samten Gyaltsen Karmay in the 1960s. This new scholarship was not readily accessible to Tibetan refugees in India. Even Western scholars up until the 1960s had viewed Bon the way Tibetans did, as a form of folk religion that preceded Buddhism in Tibet, a religion that developed alongside Buddhism in Tibet, or as a shamanistic practice full of superstitions and divination. These representations were challenged by scholars such as Snellgrove who, unlike Tibetan Buddhists, saw Bon as a form of Buddhism, not its opposite.

"Do we go on? Or do we, abandon the project and cut our losses?" Dexter asked Pearce on May 10.

While the Ockenden administrators were debating the role of religious strife in the revolt, they also turned to the Council for Tibetan Education, who held a different opinion of the reason. Joyce Pearce's tone is tentative in her letter to Tenzin N. Takla, the council's assistant director. She wrote on May 13 that there were always two sides to a question. She surmised that moving from the comfortable mountain climate in Mussoorie to the scorching heat of South India had made the boys unhappy. She wondered why they had waited so long to ask questions on religious pedagogy when they had ample and easier opportunities to do so in Mussoorie.

While Tenzin Takla agreed that there were two sides to the story, he turned away from the issue of weather to more central questions raised by the students. He determined that their admission of leaving the school of their own volition refuted Dexter's accusations against Kelsang Liushar and Gyaltsen Choden.[18] The council, he stated, had closely examined the reports made by the students and concluded that Dexter and Sangye Tenzin carried at heart the intention to "strike discord among Tibetans" and to "disrupt the national pride and cultural values" the students cherished.[19] They had responded defiantly because of their loyalty to the Tibetan culture and nation.

Takla expressed his disappointment; he had regarded the students as potential leaders for the community and nation. He offered two suggestions for the way forward: to dismiss Dexter and Sangye Tenzin and run the school under His Holiness the Dalai Lama's direction, or run it jointly with the Tibetan Schools Society. The event, he repeated, had endangered the community's peace. Takla did not explain how the community was harmed or indicate if the council had spoken to Dexter and Sangye Tenzin to get their point of view.

Takla's response must have alarmed the Ockenden Venture, because it wasn't long before they sent Peter Woodard to investigate the incident.[20] His exhaustive eighty-nine-page analysis, "A Report on the Mutiny at the Ockenden School Dharwar Mysore," contains copies of letters exchanged between different parties involved in the events, transcripts of Woodard's interviews with thirty students and teachers, and minutes of his meetings with the Dalai Lama and government officials. The contents of the interviews echo the sentiments expressed in the testimonies made public to Tibetan refugees in the newspaper *Tibetan Freedom*.

Woodard's meeting with the Dalai Lama, Tenzin N. Takla, and the Dalai Lama's private secretary, T. C. Tara, on June 1, 1966, at Swarg Ashram in Dharamsala did not go well, judging by the written minutes: two sides were formed and two outcomes embraced. Woodard refused to accept the council's decision that Dexter and Sangye Tenzin had deliberately sowed dissension. Instead, he insinuated the revolt was a plot hatched by the Tibetan teachers under instructions from Gyalo Thondup but didn't explain how he arrived at his conclusion. The two parties—the representative of the Ockenden Venture and the Tibetan exile establishment—stood behind the respective teachers each had hired for the school. Woodard suggested the school retain Dexter and Sangye Tenzin with closer input from the council, while the council suggested the school continue without the two teachers. Woodard implied that it was important to make the right decision because European donors were watching this incident unfold, and a big appeal for Tibetans had been planned in Europe. Takla retorted that it was equally important as a "matter of principle" for Tibetans. He reiterated that Sangye Tenzin and Dexter had deliberately undermined Tibetan authority figures and religion.

In a follow-up letter to Pearce on June 5, T. C. Tara expressed his disappointment about the "unhappy incident" as well as Woodard's allegation that Gyalo Thondup was behind it.[21] He felt that Woodard's unwillingness to fire Dexter and Sangye Tenzin left the Bureau of the Dalai Lama with no other option but to shut down the school. Support for the Bonpo teachers was also waning among the school's founders. Pearce wrote to Dexter that he had been unwise in handling the situation. She explained in a letter on June 16 that his relationship with the students had broken down because he had been accused of beating them, and because the boys had felt the "external society" would support them.[22] She admitted that Ockenden was not prepared to be involved in Tibetan politics and intrigues. She felt the exile government was justified in looking into Ockenden's intentions if they felt the school was not supporting the Dalai Lama's policies.

Pearce is equally direct with Woodard in a letter dated June 17, expressing her concern that he had accused Gyalo Thondup of orchestrating the incident without any evidence. She included this in a letter to a colleague in the Tibetan Refugee Aid Society in Canada and shared that the Ockenden School could only stay open if it was to be run by the exile government. She wondered if the conflict was the outcome of trying to bring a Western education system in line with Tibetan culture, perhaps analogous to the experience progressive thinkers of the Middle Ages faced when they offended the Church. She concluded that a school seeking to align Tibetan education with Western requirements while preserving fundamental elements of Tibetan faith would have to move forward carefully if it aimed to succeed in both goals. Per Pearce's assessment, teaching alternate histories came into conflict with traditional authority.

The decision made by the exile government prevailed, and the thirty students never returned to Ockenden. The school was shuttered. Letters sent by volunteer teachers at Ockenden to Joyce Pearce admit sadly that Tibetan authorities had no intention to conduct a fair investigation and did not try to reach a solution that would be acceptable to all. Even if the school were to reopen, they felt it would be destined to fail.

RIGHT AND WRONG HISTORY

Readers of *Tibetan Freedom* learned about the Ockenden school incident from articles written between June 1 and June 8, 1966. These tell a very specific history of the revolt that counters Woodard's belief of a plot hatched by anti-Bonpo teachers. Yet it offers no alternative perspective. Although the timing of the articles coincided with Woodard's private meeting with the Dalai Lama, the author of the first one was a teacher at the school, but not present at the meeting. That article on the boys' revolt, "A Report by Gyaltsen Choden, a Tibetan language teacher at Ockenden School," was published on June 2, 1966.[23] Prior to Ockenden, Choden had served as an education secretary for the exile government in 1964. He had also worked for Gyalo Thondup and helped to establish the *Tibetan Freedom* press, and thus he had ties to both the education department and Gyalo Thondup.[24]

Writing in the first person and in the Tibetan language, Gyaltsen Choden describes Dexter's and Sangye Tenzin's teaching pedagogy as oscillating between playfulness and harshness. He found their relationship with the students to be disrespectful in addition to inconsistent. For example, they would beat students and call them names such as "wild Tibetans" and "pigs." Gyaltsen Choden accused the two teachers of advising him to follow their strict disciplinary methods with the pupils. He portrayed himself as someone who preferred maintaining discipline through guidance and advice. He explains:

I knew the reasons for these beatings, i.e., because the students did not agree to engage in studying Bon religion. Buddhism, monks, and lamas were disparaged and they [the teachers] stated that the Tibetan government did not exist. The students did not follow their erroneous paths to break the bond between His Holiness and the Tibetan people by criticizing Tibetan government officers and stating that eastern Tibet was not a part of Tibet.[25]

In Gyaltsen Choden's version of events, Dexter and Sangye Tenzin were engaged in activities that undermined the achievements of the Tibetan exile community in religion and politics. Gyaltsen Choden also was offended by the two teachers' use of Chinese terms, such as chopsticks, in front of foreign and Indian dignitaries; this gave the impression that Chinese and Tibetan traditions were similar. He felt that the two teachers were manipulating His Holiness the Dalai Lama's name and diminishing the goodwill that donors and sponsors held toward Tibet.

Gyaltsen Choden interpreted Dexter's and Sangye Tenzin's ordinary and individual actions in relation to their service or disservice to the nation. He had been so troubled by their behavior that he had written to the department of education threatening to leave the school if the two were not dismissed. He also admitted having sent a letter to Ockenden but didn't provide the date.

A second employee, Kelsang Liushar, gave testimony published on June 6, under the title "The Reason Why Kelsang Left Ockenden," that similarly pointed to Dexter's and Sangye Tenzin's disruptive teaching styles. Liushar also speculated that moving the school from Mussoorie to the remote location of Dharwar made it possible for the two teachers to turn the students away from Buddhism and create discord among them. He accused Dexter and Sangye Tenzin of favoring Bonpo students.

The *Tibetan Freedom* continued their exploration of the Ockenden incident by turning to students' own first-person accounts. On

June 7 the paper published testimonies by five students on their reasons for leaving the school, and on June 8 it published three more. A fourteen-year-old student stated that he was compelled to revolt because he felt the teachers intended to do away with Buddhism and wanted to convert the students to Bon. Another student testified that although he had been at Ockenden for only two weeks, he had witnessed the two teachers make disparaging remarks against Buddhism and the exile government. He wrote that Sangye Tenzin referred to there being two distinct dialects in Tibet. Additional testimonies from six other students were printed on June 7 and 8.[26] Read together, the complaints circle three recurring topics: Amdo and Kham's political status; representation of the controversial forty-first King of Tibet, Lang Darma; and the Tibetan script.

First, many students pointed to the political affiliations and alleged statements of their teachers as causing discord at the school. The students expressed in different ways that Dexter and Sangye Tenzin emphasized Amdo and Kham's political autonomy from the Tibetan government in Lhasa. One student singled out Sangye Tenzin for saying his birthplace in Gyalrong was fully independent and did not pay any taxes to the Lhasa government.[27] Another emphasized that Amdo *was* one of the three provinces of Tibet and that he was shocked at being taught otherwise.

The students similarly disdained the teachers' relationship to the last king of a unified Tibetan empire, complaining that the teachers idealized Lang Darma, Tibet's most vilified king, commonly held responsible for the persecution of Buddhism in Tibet. This was one reason they suspected that the teachers wanted to promote Bon in the school and convert the younger students.

Finally, many of the students alleged that Dexter and Tenzin emphasized in class that Thonmi Sambhota was not the inventor of the Tibetan script and that a script had existed in Tibet before his time. This contradicted what they held as the established fact about the first Tibetan script.

The testimonies published in the *Tibetan Freedom* indicate that the students were hurt because the teachers challenged the narratives they held as truth. These complaints are also expressed in their letter to Joyce Pearce. Tibetan songs, operas, and stories determine that Lang Darma is a villain, that Thonmi Sambhota transformed Tibetans from barbarians into modern people even though literacy was mostly concentrated in the monasteries and among the elite, and that Tibet comprises the regions of U-Tsang, Kham, and Amdo. Their confusion, even anger, is both palpable in their letters and understandable as a form of frustration about what they received as unfamiliar and threatening historical retellings. However, the power the students gave to alternative historical narratives (such as those related to Bon or their mis/interpretation of these narratives as challenging the Tibetan government and creating disharmony among Tibetans) is instructive. The questions raised allow insights into what was thought to constitute history and shape collective identity, and the worldviews creating this narrative. They allow us to see how history was fit into Tibetan education, storytelling, and nationalism by Tibetan educators, administrators, and nationalists—those with power to make decisions.

The *Tibetan Freedom* did not present Dexter's or Sangye Tenzin's side of the story or analyze the "untruths" that Tenzin was alleged to have taught. Nor did it inform the public that the Dalai Lama knew Sangye Tenzin and had encouraged him to teach and support Bon education in exile. Instead, the articles emphasized that the two teachers had concocted historical lies, undermined the Dalai Lama's position, impaired unity among Tibetans, and hurt national sentiments. The publication of the testimonials in *Tibetan Freedom* was significant. The paper's goal was primarily to inform Tibetans of national and international events related to the Tibetan struggle, and it had traction at a time when media sources were exiguous in the community.

While the story was circulating for days in the newspaper, possibly solidifying anti-Bon sentiment, the thirty of the forty-two students who had left Ockenden were sent to schools run by the exile government. The letters do not mention what happened to the remaining students.

Western aid organizations were watching the event closely and offering one another their own readings. Pat Brewster, who worked on several rehabilitation projects in his capacity as the director of the Tibetan Refugee Programme of the National Christian Council of India, wrote to his colleague in Geneva on June 2 that he had spoken with Dexter and with the students as well as with administrators in Dharamsala and believed that Tibetans suspected Dexter and Sangye Tenzin were teaching ideas that contradicted dominant religious and national feelings. He feared the matter could not be "patched up."[28]

Brewster was convinced "religion and politics" had come into the matter, and he thought it had been silly to get a Bonpo lama to be the chief teacher at the school in the first place.[29] His comment indicates that Sangye Tenzin's Bon background might have been an issue for Tibetan Buddhists. In 1966, the year of the incident, Bonpo Tibetans did not have representation in the Tibetan parliament. Bon practitioners, who were a minority in exile, did not fit into any existing Buddhist group or fall into collectives that were built around geographical regions. They were at the margins of the community.[30] Given that all other schools run by the exile government probably didn't have much, if any, mention of Bon religion or history in the curricula, the significance placed on Ockenden teachers mentioning Bon suggests that there might have been more in question for exile officials than history lessons for forty-two young students.

Looking back, the Thirteen members I spoke to think it was not just the lessons that were a problem, it was the fact that the school was not under the direct supervision of the exile government. They pointed out that 1966 was also the year when Tibetans of the Bonpo faith had received help from the Catholic Relief Agency to buy land in Dolanji in Himachal Pradesh. They had plans to build a settlement where they could live together. This momentous achievement for the Bonpos meant something else for exile officials. The United Party had in fact cautioned Tibetans against building their own settlements and schools. Thus, the school was part of a wider campaign that the party was conducting against actions found to be falling outside the exile government's control.

BON AND BUDDHISM

While letters and the *Tibetan Freedom* constitute one important kind of historical archive for understanding the Ockenden revolt, another less documented but historically urgent archive also exists. I visited the Bonpo settlement in Dolanji in 2015. The Menri Monastery sits on the summit of the hill on which the settlement is built. I came across young monks playing soccer during a break from their studies on my visit to the main chapel. The strip of blue piping on their yellow cotton vests pronounced they were Bon. A young monk hoisted his robe above his knees before kicking the ball. The ball flew over the heads of the three players who ran backward, their faces turned up to the sky, and vanished over the short wall. We all followed with our eyes as it rolled down the hillside.

I could see small patches of fields, moss green in the early summer light, twinkling at the bottom of the hill. There were trees studded with unripe plum, pomegranate, and apricot fruits. I spotted the farm of the eighty-seven-year-old man I'd spoken to the previous day. Tsering Wangyal had been among the first group of seventy Bonpo families to move to the settlement in 1967. Each had been given a piece of land corresponding to the size of their family. He still farmed a portion of his land with help from his sister and his late wife's brothers. Six elders lived and farmed together. He said to me that all of them were slowed down by age. He had entered India through Assam in 1960 with his wife, two daughters, and nine other family members. His daughters, unable to tolerate the heat, had fallen ill and died within their first year in India. He had not found a Bonpo lama to offer prayers for them. He narrated his story to me, the names of the dead populating his entry into exile. His fingers slipped over his prayer beads. Together we had counted the many names for despair.

"We have come a long way," he said.[31]

"*We*, as in the Tibetan society in exile?" I asked.

He gestured with his chin in the direction of the monastery.

Khedup Gyamtso was twenty-one years old when he was a student at Ockenden. We spoke briefly about the school during my visit to Dolanji. In a follow-up phone conversation in July 2024, he explained that they had moved from Mussoorie to Dharwar with the hope of expanding the school. The students had wanted a playground. They were told by the teachers that if they wanted one, they would have to build it. He remembered clearing trees and brush from the land. The students had complained to the teachers that it was difficult to work in the heat. That was how the incident began, he said.[32]

There were ten students, including him, who were older. Ten students with the highest grades from the Tibetan Homes school in Mussoorie had been selected to join Ockenden. All in all, there were forty-two students. I asked him to describe a day in his school life. They began their morning with prayers to His Holiness, followed by Buddhist mantras, then classes for the different groups. The older students took lessons in English, Hindi, Tibetan, history, geography, civics, and mathematics. They had not been in Dharwar for very long, he said.

"What do you make of the students' complaints in their letters to Joyce Pearce that they were being turned into Bonpos?" I asked.

They studied from textbooks published by the Council for Tibetan Education. He couldn't recall if the texts mentioned Bon. Most of the students were young adults raised in the Tibetan school system or within the Buddhist community. They didn't recite any Bon mantras in school or read any Bon texts, he recalled. Khedup Gyamtso is a Bonpo.

What would have been the purpose of converting twenty Tibetan students to Bon? he asked. What would the teachers have gained from that?[33]

Gyaltsen Choden and Kelsang Liushar had left with the thirty students. Khedup Gyamtso had remained in Dharwar until the school was shut down. He later joined the vocational training program in Clement Town. He recalled that the Bon community had worried for Sangye Tenzin's safety. I told him that letters from the volunteer teachers to Joyce Pearce expressed their concern that the Tibetan community might physically harm Sangye Tenzin because of the allegations against him.

The next day, I requested an audience with Lungtok Tenpai Nyima, the 33rd Menri Trizin of the Bon school. He was recognized as the head of the Yungdrung Bon tradition by the exile government in 1978. Lungtok Tenpai Nyima Rinpoche has served as the leader of exiled Bonpos as well as the spiritual head of Bon monasteries in Tibet and Nepal for over twenty years.

In 1968, he was still known as Sangye Tenzin. I tentatively raised the name of Ockenden. He nodded kindly but said nothing. I did not press further.

From Dolanji I made my way to Dharamsala, where I asked a few Tibetan officials working for the exile government if they had heard about the Ockenden school. They had not. One official said he did remember something; it had to do with students revolting.

"Those were the dark days of our exile history," he said. "We have come a long way."

I asked what the event meant to him.

"What purpose does this story serve?" he asked.

"It is an important part of exile history," I said.

He stated as if I should already know: "It depends."

I am not the first one, of course, to have walked away with these questions. Ugyan Choedup, a historian and scholar of Tibet, first encountered the story of the Ockenden incident during a trip to Dolanji in 2017. Like me, he had never heard it mentioned outside of the Bonpo community. He analyzes the two ways the event is remembered by comparing its fleeting mention in Gyaltsen Choden's autobiography to the story's haunting life in the hearts of exiled Bonpos. In Gyaltsen Choden's book the incident is an uncomplicated case of "students revolting against the unrestrained harsh corporal punishment" by school authorities.[34] For Bonpos the revolt is an early example of "the marginalization of Bonpos from the exile Tibetan (Buddhist) national order" and the exile leadership's effort to control the story of the nation.[35] Choedup reads the Ockenden event as an example of a "fragmentary and forgotten episode" from the exile past that speaks of "differential" histories and worldviews.[36]

David L. Snellgrove, the scholar appealed to by Dexter back in the 1960s, came to a similar analysis of the situation at Ockenden and of history in his letter to Pearce, dated May 26, 1966. Snellgrove explained that Western interpretation of Tibetan history was based on critical evaluation and differed in some respects from the history that Tibetans were accustomed to. While new scholarship did not undermine Tibetan belief in Buddhism, Tibetans were understandably reacting against new ideas as antitraditional. This included studies on Bon and the military success of pre-Buddhist Tibet. Snellgrove felt that talking about religion with Tibetans from different religious orders was a delicate problem.[37] It was hard to avoid conflicts with traditional attitudes; he did not think this was unique to Tibetans. He pointed to the disputes in India over choosing between Indian traditional history and history as understood by the West.

Both Choedup's and Snellgrove's analyses of the events at Ockenden show its entanglement with the broader political processes of building the nation in exile, in which the writing of national history demands amnesia about certain events and people. The *Tibetan Freedom's* reinforcement of the sanctity of the official biography of the nation in its representation of the events and the measures taken by exile officials confirms that the Tibetan leadership was enlisting history to serve the idea of the nation. A closer examination of three areas of concern will help elucidate how the Ockenden event might have been perceived as disrupting the story of the nation that was being realized at that moment.

No one is more maligned in Tibetan history than the ninth-century monarch Lang Darma, in popular culture and canonical texts. Tibetan Buddhists still resist an unoffending depiction of him. Tsepon Shakabpa's *Tibet: A Political History* (1984) was among the first available published political accounts of Tibet written in a somewhat contemporary-style format of history and translated into English. His was also among the only available history books written in English covering the events of the Chinese invasion in 1950 until Tsering Shakya wrote his important account of modern Tibet. Shakabpa, who was the finance minister in the Lhasa government as well as a scholar, wrote that Lang Darma was put on the throne around 838 by ministers who leaned toward Bon, and that they designed laws to destroy Buddhism in Tibet.[38] Darma's ministers sealed up Buddhist temples and ordered Buddhist monks to either marry, take up arms, become huntsmen, or convert to Bon. Individuals who refused were killed.[39] Similarly, Geshe Lhundup Sopa's Tibetan language text, *Lectures on Tibetan Religious Culture*, a popular book used to teach Tibetan to new learners, mentions that Lang Darma managed to destroy the teaching of the *vinaya* in Central Tibet during his brief reign.[40] Lang Darma's association with Bon meant that Bon became synonymous with the decline of the Tibetan empire and the persecution of Buddhism.

This historiographical portrait of Lang Darma, according to Samten Gyaltsen Karmay, has rarely been questioned by ordinary Buddhist Tibetans.[41] Samten G. Karmay challenges sources that gave the impression that the king was a follower of the Bon religion, proposing that the conflict that led to the persecution of Buddhism during the reign of Lang Darma could have been related to political struggles between the ecclesiastical leaders and the secular authority, and not necessarily a "struggle between the two religious establishments."[42] Matthew Kapstein agrees with Karmay that early sources do not establish that Lang Darma's persecution of Buddhism ever took place.[43] Later Buddhist sources responsible for this king's image neglect the Tibetan military administration of the territories under his control and focus instead on depicting the king in a "degrading manner."[44]

In offering an alternate view of Lang Darma, the teachers at Ockenden had challenged not just the accepted reason for the end of the Tibetan empire but also the very basis of a certain Tibetan historical consciousness. Recasting Lang Darma as an important historical figure undercut a fundamental plot and periodization of Tibetan history that was formulated on the rise and fall of Buddhism.[45]

Similarly, Tibetan historical accounts narrate the invention of the Tibetan script by Thonmi Sambhota as having brought light to the benighted land. In most Tibetan texts, the decision of the thirty-third king, Songtsen Gampo, to send his minister Thonmi Sambhota to study Buddhism in India, which also resulted in the importation of the Gupta script that was used to draft the Tibetan alphabet, is identified as among the most significant events in Tibetan history. Bonpos believe that transmission of Bon came from and flourished in a place known as Zhangzhung that existed in what is now Western Tibet, before or at the beginning of the Tibetan imperial period. The language spoken in Zhangzhung is believed to have been a Tibeto-Burman language, replaced by Tibetan by the eleventh century.[46] In a recent analysis of Zhangzhung and Bon, scholar Per Kvaerne observes that narratives suggesting that Bon flourished in Zhangzhung for centuries before reaching Tibet arose in the tenth or eleventh centuries, long after the events described. He also suggests that the narrative of Zhangzhung's importance to Asian civilization as well as to Bon gained its fullness in India when Tibetan Bonpos felt they "needed to assert their identity" in a radically altered space of exile.[47]

Kvaerne sees this shift as a result of two trends: a "cultural development" to glorify the Tibetan past and downplay Indian influence and the emergence of a Bonpo effort to give Bon "the same kind of factual, historical basis and prestigious status" that Tibetan Buddhists hold for Buddhism.[48]

Thus, suggesting that Thonmi Sambhota was not the first to invent the Tibetan script challenged the role of Tibetan culture and identity based on a shared language and tradition. It contemplated an alternate source for culture: Zhangzhung, not India. Ongoing study of Bonpo manuscripts might reveal more about the first and second centuries of indigenous Tibetan history.[49] But that would entail shifting hegemonic views and narratives of Tibet, Tibetan Buddhism, and Tibetan identity.

Lastly, to admit that sections of Kham and Amdo had not been under the direct political authority of the Tibetan government in Lhasa at the time of the Chinese invasion risked endangering the national goal of Tibetan independence from Chinese rule in addition to undermining the sovereignty of the exile government.

The tension in the Ockenden story is not so much between Western education and traditional Tibetan education—an attractive option for a postcolonial world lens—as about controlling narratives about Tibet. The incident took place at a crucial moment when Tibetan exile officials, cultural institutions of society, and community members were beginning the work of creating, preserving, and promoting a stable narrative about Tibetan history. The construction of an official historical narrative, here as elsewhere, is a social, cultural, and political process.[50] It legitimizes selective events or versions of events over others as being acceptable or true, which can further shift perspectives on the past and alter the meaning of concepts such as nation and identity.[51] As a result, certain people, events, and cultures belong to the official history of place while others are elided.[52]

The Tibetan exilic consciousness was defined by terms compounded largely from the deep and long history of Buddhism, and by the feeling of being "permanently at risk" because the majority of Tibetans were under Chinese colonial rule.[53] In other words, the Tibetan exile effort was directed to bringing diverse groups of Tibetan people together in a unique stateless polity to create a cohesive and united nation whose identity was both cultural and political. The need for a unified narrative meant that dissenting or controversial voices were dispelled. This has been expressed, for example, by veterans of the Chushi Gangdrug who feel their histories are not yet fully acknowledged or accepted into the official history in exile.

More than two decades ago, Tsering Shakya noted that the autobiographies published by the Information and Publicity Office and the Library of Tibetan Works and Archives (LTWA) of the exile government provided little important information as sources of history largely due to the reluctance of the writers to engage in controversy and confrontation. In other words, details that compromised the national narrative were "glanced" over in the drive to tell the "truth" of the nation.[54] Even as the LTWA gathered valuable information in the interviews recorded with important political figures who had served in the Lhasa government like Phala Thupten Woeden (lord chamberlain), Liushar Thupten Tharpa (foreign secretary), and Kundeling Woeser Gyaltsen (senior official also called Kundeling *Dzasa*), they were not published in books because the exile government "felt that some of these accounts compromised the official versions of history."[55]

Nobody with voice in the community questioned why Dexter and Sangye Tenzin were not given the chance to present their side of the story. Nor did anyone consider the possibility that the "untruths" they were critiqued for teaching were, in fact, historically relevant and necessary to an education in Tibetan history and identity. The reality is that the government shut down a much-needed school and dismissed two accomplished and trained scholars at a time when there were only a handful available.

Tibetans from the Thirteen who were observing closely concluded the revolt was yet more evidence of the United Party's power within the exile community. The event confirmed for them that the *Seven Resolutions and Supporting Documents* was not merely a text, it was a warning. Individuals mentioned in it became keenly aware of being stripped of their past and renamed as traitors. Individuals named in the document also became aware of one another.

6

THE CONVERGENCE OF THE THIRTEEN LEADERS

In the spring of 1965, Gungthang Tsultrim invited Chokling Rinpoche to visit Clement Town, where a few families had already settled into their new homes. Construction had begun for a primary school; Tsultrim had plans to build a monastery next. Chokling Rinpoche found himself in Clement Town in a conclave with Khamtrul Rinpoche, Kathok Ontrul Rinpoche, and Tobga Yugyal, the nephew of the sixteenth Karmapa. Drawupon told me that Gungthang Tsultrim had also invited him, Trochupon Dorje Pasang, and Lingtsang Yarling Wangyal to visit the settlement. Drawupon had considered asking the Gawa people (from the Kyekudo area in the kingdom of Nangchen, where he had served as the chieftain) scattered across India if they would consider joining him in a Gawa *rakor* in Clement Town. Drawupon would later establish the Kamrao settlement at the encouragement of the Dalai Lama.

Gungthang Tsultrim's confidence and his project emboldened Khamtrul Rinpoche and Chokling Rinpoche. The United Party's warnings to Tibetans against building their own settlements and schools were not something the lamas took lightly, and Khamtrul Rinpoche's monks, scarred from their previous clashes with United Party supporters, certainly did not either. Given the party's popularity, Tsultrim's undertaking seemed impossibly courageous.

The group met a second time that year, in Delhi, where they were joined by Trochupon Dorje Pasang (who by then had sent his sons to Taiwan and had been vilified in the *Seven Resolutions and Supporting Documents*) and Palyul Dzongnang Rinpoche, a well-regarded Nyingma lama who had relocated from Rewalsar to build his monastery in Clement Town. Dzongnang Rinpoche and Gungthang Tsultrim had met during their terms in parliament in Dharamsala and had become good friends. Tsultrim had once casually mentioned to Dzongnang Rinpoche that he hoped to build a settlement. Dzongnang Rinpoche had responded that he'd be interested in living there, according to Jinpa, Tsultrim's aide and friend. Gungthang Tsultrim had contacted Dzongnang Rinpoche once the land and the funds had been secured to build Dhondupling Tibetan Colony in Clement Town. The Mindrolling Monastery was established in the settlement in January 1965 under the guidance of Dzongnang Rinpoche and Khochhen Rinpoche.

According to a monk who was at the meeting as Chokling Rinpoche's attendant, the participants in this second meeting bonded over their concern about the United Party's scapegoating tactics and methods of social ostracism of individuals they marked as opponents to their project of unity. Those targeted in the *Seven Resolutions and Supporting Documents* felt they had come to an impasse: they could not express their fear of the United Party to government officials, the majority of whom they believed to be supporters of the party and already disposed to assume the worst about them. Some Khampas had been told by exile officials they were too emotional, difficult, and too quick to take offense. The need of the hour was to focus on national concerns, the big picture, not smaller, private, or communal concerns. The company of men agreed that like-minded individuals who were viewed as challenging the government might benefit from consulting and helping one another: Gungthang Tsultrim had seemed like the obvious leader. It also helped that he was an Amdowa (like the Dalai Lama and Gyalo Thondup) and Gelug.

Some individuals were wary of crossing paths with the United Party. In the early 1960s, Chushi Gangdrug members had approached Khamtrul Rinpoche's monks asking for their signatures in a campaign against Martham Thoesum, also referred to as Marnang Thoesum, a Chushi Gangdrug veteran who had accused Chushi Gangdrug elite leaders of misusing funds allocated for the resistance movement. The monks had refused to sign the document, explaining they didn't want to get involved in politics. This refusal to sign a public denouncement of Thoesum and his friends, effectively a statement of support for Chushi Gangdrug leaders, including Gyalo Thondup, had drawn criticism from Kalimpong and Darjeeling Tibetans.[1] This was one of the reasons Khamtrul Rinpoche and his monks moved to Banuri in Himachal Pradesh, and from there to Dalhousie. In Dalhousie, they established a wood-block printing press and a thangka painting workshop. Yet again they were asked to sign a petition, this time to join the United Party.

One of the senior monks, the Tibetan instructor for young monks, was adamant against taking the pledge to join the United Party primarily because he didn't want to take a vow. Other monks feared that by refusing to join they would be drawing attention to themselves. The monastery declined to sign the petition despite their concerns about retribution. In refusing to pledge their allegiance to the United Party, the monks said, they were cast as opponents of the project of Tibetan unity. Gungthang Tsultrim had understood the desires and fears of the Khampa chieftains and lamas and provided a solution: he would help them build their own settlements and live with their clan if they didn't want to live in Clement Town.[2] He promised to introduce them to Pat Brewster, who had helped Tsultrim get funds from Swiss Aid to Tibetans to construct one hundred homes in Clement Town in January 1965. Gungthang Tsultrim and Pat Brewster were introduced to each other by Tsultrim's close friend Lobsang Phuntsok Lhalungpa.

Pat Brewster and his wife, Dorothy, had sold their farm in Kuri Bush, near Dunedin in New Zealand, to pay their way to India when

Brewster got the job to run the refugee department at CORAGS (Co-ordinating Relief Agency of the National Christian Council of India). He had applied to three overseas positions and accepted the first offer he received. Brewster was thirty-nine, and he and Dorothy moved to Delhi with their four children under the ages of seven. "I set out for India full of confidence," he writes in a personal narrative, *Life history of Gibbon Brewster (Pat)*.[3]

The Clement Town pioneering project was important for Gungthang Tsultrim, his Tibetan admirers, and those funding the project. Brewster wrote in glowing terms of the final plans for the settlement in letters to Swiss Aid to Tibetans in Geneva. On March 9, 1965, Brewster reported that the Dalai Lama's bureau, the engineer hired for the project, and Gungthang Tsultrim's Tibetan partners were very pleased with the master plan. He described the windows and doors as peculiar to Tibetan architecture and predicted that such designs might well be the future of Tibetan housing in India. He stressed the importance of this pioneering project that created "characteristically Tibetan design at low cost."[4] Brewster's letters to the project's donor indicate that the initial plan of building seventy housing units for "Amdos" needed to be reevaluated. On March 25, 1965, Brewster wrote that more "Amdo families" had come to Clement Town seeking housing. Brewster could be using "Amdo" to describe all Tibetans at the settlement at this juncture. He also provided a glimpse into the kind of community Gungthang Tsultrim was hoping to create. For example, one housing unit for the elderly would be attached to every eight family units. Tsultrim didn't want elders to be segregated in a special home and instead hoped they would live with the rest of the community. Brewster writes, "We can leave that to the Tibetans to work out, but the idea is for the old people to be merged completely in the living community, not in a separate Old People's Home."[5] In his personal notes, he mentions that Clement Town was a "big success." The project convinced him that "successful rehabilitation was possible on a massive scale," with money. He decided to establish the Tibetan

Industrial Rehabilitation Society (TIRS), which would be a little different from other relief organizations of the time.[6]

Brewster's reports and letters to the head office of the World Council of Churches, one of the main funders of the project, provide a glimpse into his personal vision for the rehabilitation of Tibetan refugees in India. In his report to the National Christian Council of India (NCC) in December 1965, he envisions the NCC taking the role of using small and strategic funds to work directly with and through the project partners like the one he was involved with in Clement Town, and to buy land for Tibetan groups and establish industries. In his letter to the NCC on February 21, 1966, Brewster advocated for resettling Tibetan refugees living in the road camps into small settlements. He explains that even though Tibetans did not have the skills for light industry, it was important to keep the communities together in "small groups to preserve as far as possible their cultural and religious cohesion" and implies that he could do this work.

Brewster introduced the TIRS as a registered Charitable Society, and therefore not subject to income tax, that would channel funds from overseas agencies, prepare projects for donor agencies, and oversee the implementation of Tibetan projects in India under the sponsorship of the Dalai Lama. The objective was to rehabilitate more than 4,000 Tibetans working in Himachal Pradesh. The capital for TIRS's overhead costs in the first year was provided by the Dalai Lama (Rs. 20,000); Swiss Aid to Tibetans (Rs. 15,000); and the National Christian Council of India (Rs. 15,000). The chair of the TIRS committee in 1966 was a member of the Indian parliament. The first committee members included several members proposed by the Tibetan exile government, including the Dalai Lama, Brewster, and a member of the Central Relief Committee. By 1966, Brewster was involved in several exile government projects. In addition to his work with TIRS and the NCC, he was the coordinator of development programs in Bylakuppe funded by various voluntary agencies and the Delhi coordinator for a settlement near Dharwar in Mysore.

The TIRS's strategy was to fund programs that would drive Tibetans toward self-sufficiency. Brewster indicates that he would be working directly with project partners. The TIRS team consisted of Brewster as a consultant, William (Bill) Davinson as the field director (referred to by Thirteen members as "Captain Davinson"), and Mervyn Bobb as the general officer. It is clear from the letters and reports that Brewster and Davinson were personally involved in appraising and purchasing the land for the settlements. Brewster mentions in his letter on August 11, 1966, to Dr. Ernest Wiederkehr at Swiss Aid to Tibetans that he and Davinson had gone to see a tea estate in Bir a week earlier, and that Davinson had checked out a limestone quarry in Himachal Pradesh as potential settlement locations for Tibetans. Ugyen Topgyal Rinpoche remembers that Davinson had been at a dinner gathering when he heard about the availability of a property in Bir and had left for Bir immediately. The Nangchen division of the Tibetan Khampa Industrial Society was established in Bir and the Taopan Gapa Welfare Society in Kamrao after TIRS purchased the two businesses. Brewster raised over a million dollars for TIRS in four years.[7]

The older Thirteen members remember Brewster as willing to help them find solutions to the struggles they faced, whether identifying how to increase sales or fixing faulty machines in their various small industries.

Chanzoe Ngawang Tenpa, a leader of the United Party, suspected that Brewster was responsible for teaching the Thirteen leaders to organize themselves and might have filled the Thirteen's "stomachs" against the exile government.[8] Chanzoe Tenpa suggested to me that the Thirteen had doubts about the government and Brewster might have been able to build on them. Although that scenario gives too much agency to Brewster and none to the Thirteen leaders, it is clear from Brewster's correspondences to his supervisors that he sympathized with the Khampa leaders' interest in building their settlements and championed Tibetans to become economically self-reliant.[9]

Brewster mentioned in his reports to his funders as early as December 1965 that Tibetans at the road camps were being overlooked by relief efforts and needed to be settled. He believed in supporting small groups. He also reported that most relief agencies were moving toward economic rehabilitation and education and suggested that future efforts be aimed at hastening "toward independence and self-help."[10] He thought he could play a strategic role in working directly on such projects and proposed buying land and settling the refugees, citing Clement Town as a model. Brewster appears to already have had groups in mind for his future projects.

In a report on Tibetan refugee aid programs in India in November 1966, Brewster suggests that building a self-supporting Tibetan community depended on undertaking projects on a larger financial scale. He also suggests that the officers in charge (perhaps referring to himself) be given greater freedom to make financial and operational decisions. Brewster's association with Gungthang Tsultrim and the Thirteen brought him unwanted attention, not just from the United Party but also from local and international organizations. In his personal notes he writes that he was tired of his responsibilities by mid-1969. He had worked for six years with only one "home-leave." He felt used and exploited and weary of speculations about why he was in India at all. A Tibetan student who had received a scholarship to study in the United States had mentioned to Brewster that he had been "grilled" by people he suspected of being in the CIA with questions such as: "Who is this Brewster?" "What is he there for?" "Who is paying him?"[11]

Gungthang Tsultrim and Brewster introduced the lamas and chiefs to an Indian government official named Mr. Nag. The Thirteen believe he was the Under Secretary of External Affairs. Nag assured the leaders and lamas that they were not breaking protocol in India by advocating for direct assistance from aid agencies. Gungthang Tsultrim also introduced the leaders of the groups to Lobsang Phuntsok Lhalungpa. Lhalungpa's correspondence with the Tibet

Society of the United Kingdom indicates he helped some of the Thirteen get funding for their projects. In a draft of a report dated June 19, 1996, he describes the Thirteen as "religious minorities" who speak the same dialect and share religious affinity and spiritual allegiance to their own schools.[12] Lhalungpa explains the groups aimed to "preserve their own tradition in all its distinctive forms" by living together.[13] They had sought the blessing of the Dalai Lama to do so and were hoping to find patrons to help them buy land for their "resettlement as craft communities." Lhalungpa introduces Tibetans in Clement Town as the "Amdo community" and mentions that they have already started workshops for a laundry business, making leather goods, and a "noodle producing factory." He writes that Khamtrul Rinpoche's community in Dalhousie included refugees from different areas of Kham who were attempting to set up weaving, knitting, carpentry, wood carving, ritual dance, and sculpting training workshops.

Lhalungpa mentions that a Bonpo group under Lopon Tenzing Namdak was in Manali, and that eighty of the three hundred people were engaged in spinning yarn for the Khadi Commission. Lhalungpa describes these groups as being led by "responsible and devoted" leaders. The groups had expected "moral support and guidance" from Tibetan officials but were not able to obtain it. Despite this and other difficulties they faced, they were doing their best to "maintain good relations with Dharamsala." It is unclear what Lhalungpa means by "difficulties" they were encountering, but he does reveal that "certain elements in Darjeeling started at Dharamsala, a campaign of vilification against all the groups and individuals working for their resettlement."[14] "Certain elements" is a reference to the United Party, which was based in Darjeeling in the early days. He mentions that Namkha Dorje's group had clashed with Tibetan officials. Receipts for funds accepted, signed by Chokling Rinpoche, Khamtrul Rinpoche, Sakya Trizin Rinpoche, and Lopon Tenzin Namdak Rinpoche in July 1965, indicate that Lobsang Lhalungpa was successful in getting financial support for the groups from the Tibet Society of the United Kingdom.

Brewster's reports to Swiss Aid to Tibetans provide a timeline of the establishment of TIRS's industrial settlements: Tibetan Taopon Gapa Welfare Society with a lime quarry at Kumrao, Himachal Pradesh, in 1966, funded by Catholic Relief Services (CRS);[15] Kham Kathok Tibetan Society with a hydrated lime plant in Sataun, Himachal Pradesh, in 1966, also funded by CRS; Tibetan Khampa Industrial Society (Nangchen and Derge) settlements in Bir, Himachal Pradesh, in 1966, with a woolen mill (funded by Swiss Aid to Tibetans) and a tea garden (funded by the Norwegian Refugee Council).[16] The last was Kham Lingtsang settlement in Munduwala, Uttarakhand, established on twenty-five acres of land in 1974. There were 150 people from Lingtsang kingdom in Kham who moved there under the leadership of Yarling Dorje Wangyal, a minister of the king of Lingtsang, and later of the Lingtsang king, Jigme Wangdu.

By mid-September 1967, about forty Tibetans were being trained in weaving at Panipat. A hundred homes were almost completed in Bir for those picking tea leaves at the tea garden. The lime quarry was producing first-grade limestone in Kamrao, and a hundred homes were planned for the families living there. The factory at the hydrated lime plant in Sataun was near completion. The TIRS, as indicated in their reports, was working with the Tibetan government to establish these settlements. Even if the United Party or officials from the exile government disapproved of the Thirteen settlements with traditional nonelected leaders at the helm instead of exile officials, intervening directly to stop them would have meant revealing internal strife to Indian and foreign benefactors. The Thirteen were equally dependent on the exile government's cooperation since some international aid organizations were hesitant to fund them without the government's approval. Contrary to claims that the Thirteen had formed settlements without the knowledge of the exile government, they were funded by TIRS, which included government representatives. TIRS also helped establish the Tibetan Cholsum Industrial Institute in Paonta Saheb in 1967, the Sakya Tibetan Society in Puruwala in 1968, and the Bir Tibetan Society, and it funded many other projects directly run by the exile government.

The settlements would come to be known as the Thirteen settlements, but only twelve of them were completed. Trochupon Dorje Pasang had left India after the United Party's shunning campaign against him. Trochupon, according to Sodam from Kamrao, had hoped to settle in Rumtek. After he left India, a group of Tibetans from Nangchen, who perhaps had hoped to settle with Trochupon, were taken by Sodam to one of the settlements in Mungod, Karnataka, instead. All settlements except the Tibetan Bonpo settlement in Dolanji and the Nangchen settlement in Mainpat were funded by the TIRS. At that time, Lopon Tenzin Namdak was the chief tutor of Menri Monastery and led the work to build a Bonpo refugee settlement. He and Pon Sangye Namgyal were able to get funds from Catholic Relief Services to buy land and build homes for followers of Bon in Dolanji. Lopon Tenzin Namdak had been introduced to Gungthang Tsultrim by Lhalungpa. He had personally traveled to as many as nineteen potential settlement sites, including a few at Sataun and Chauntra, recommended by Brewster. He described the long trips as arduous during my audience with him in Kathmandu in 2015. He had found the locations too small for the Bonpo community, who also expressed their desire to be in the mountains. Dolanji had felt right.

Namkha Dorje had sent Karma Tsultrim and another clan member to decide if the land in Mainpat would be suitable when it was allocated to them by the Indian government. The duo reached Mainpat in early autumn. They were thrilled with the lushness of the place and met indigenous communities who lived there and had cattle. The two men reported to Namkha Dorje that Mainpat had reminded them of their *phayul* in Tibet: the land was green and the weather was pleasant. The Bongsar clan and two hundred *khushi* Khampas who had worked with them on the road sites moved to Mainpat in 1965. The Indian government built them homes of bamboo and gave them hundreds of sheep. Tsodi and Yugyal both admitted that not one sheep survived their first summer. The elders suffered just as much. Yugyal said wistfully that the two men would not have been fooled if they had visited Mainpat in the summer.[17] Over time these Tibetan nomads in Mainpat learned to farm. Most were growing buckwheat and potatoes on their land when I visited in 2015. Tiny shoots of buckwheat were visible in long neat rows. Many of the farms had been leased to local Indians, including Yugyal's land.

Thus, each settlement had taken their own initiative toward fulfilling their dream of being with their clan, people from their area, or the lamas from their ancestral lands. The formal establishment of the Thirteen came much later, and after each group had their settlement. Rumors spread within the exile communities that the settlements had been created with funding from Taiwan's Mongolian and Tibetan Affairs Commission (MTAC) or Chinese Communist Party agents or both. Exile officials and the United Party knew the Thirteen were funded by relief organizations known to the government, yet never challenged the misconceptions. The community's treatment of the settlements as taboo outposts in exile was also shrugged away. The Thirteen felt they had been pushed to the edges of the margin in exile.

A FEDERATION OF THIRTEEN

The first formal meeting of the Thirteen leaders took place in April 1966 in a house owned by an Indian industrialist named Ashoka from Calcutta. Juchen Thupten Namgyal, a lifelong politician and Chushi Gangdrug veteran, who served in the Tibetan parliament and the cabinet, claims to have attended a few subsequent meetings.

Most of the settlements had been built. The leaders focused on identifying the goals and key players of the United Party in this first meeting. They were in consensus that the United Party had used Khampas as well as the sentiments of democracy and unity to settle Gyalo Thondup's personal scores with Lhasa aristocrats. They speculated that the party's next step would be to sever the traditional ties and allegiances that had secured religious and clan systems for Khampas and suspected the party hoped to put a new elite, loyal to Gyalo Thondup, in place. They agreed to oppose the United Party on all fronts by securing their individual religious institutions and settlements. The group discussed practical strategies to protect themselves from accusations of antigovernment practices. Juchen Thupten writes that both the Chushi Gangdrug and the United Party were led by Gyalo Thondup at this point, and the United Party was very powerful.[18]

The second formal meeting of the Thirteen leaders was held in Delhi in the same year. This was also the year Sangye Tenzin was vilified for teaching the "wrong history" at Ockenden School. At this meeting, the leaders discussed the need to legally register themselves as individual nongovernmental associations, and in addition, to register collectively as a single cooperative society with the Indian government. They thought that consolidating their energy and securing legal protection would shield them from the United Party.

However, this was risky. The exile government discouraged Tibetans from forming social and political organizations outside of those it sanctioned. The Dalai Lama himself had stressed he was against the establishment of institutions that directly or indirectly promoted conflicts among Tibetans or fostered regional or local interests at the expense of the national.[19] The group decided to ask the Karmapa, the head of the Kagyu school, to be their patron. This decision may have been both personal and strategic, in addition to following a practice that was in the realm of tradition. Monasteries, as key institutions of these polities, provided a range of services. Monastic hierarchs often served as advisors to nomadic leaders and as mediators within and outside their borders. In some regions, the chief was also the lama of the area's largest monastery. For example, until the early nineteenth century the Derge king was the abbot, head of the famous Derge Gonchen (which was of the Sakya school), and still maintained close relations with key Nyingma and Kagyu monasteries in the region.[20] Yudru Tsomu mentions that the Derge kingdom is often described as "the alliance between secular and religious powers."[21] Likewise, the Nangchen kings are extolled in oral accounts for their piety, and Nangchen is esteemed as a place of meditators. Monasteries also gave ordinary nomads access to storage centers to protect their produce and provided shelter for the destitute. Thus, these communities had reasons for maintaining close ties to their chiefs and lamas.

Almost all the Thirteen leaders were members of nomadic, semi-pastoral, or settled communities organized politically into self-governing societies.[22] Among them were hegemonic and hereditary leaders referred to as *gyelpo* (king), *ponpo* (leader), and by other *tusi* titles bestowed by the Qing, such as *behu* (leader of one hundred households) and *bechang* (leader of fifty people). They came from political or social units that had lived with fluid borders.[23]

Many of the leaders of the Thirteen had known each other in Tibet. For example, Khamtrul Rinpoche and Chokling Rinpoche were close friends. They were also already acquainted with Bongsarpon Namkha Dorje and Drawupon Rinchen Tsering, from Nangchen, besides Drubwang Pema Norbu Rinpoche from Payul and Kathok Ontrul Rinpoche and Jagoetsang Namgyal Dorje from Derge. Others had crossed paths in exile. Lopon Tenzin Namdak Rinpoche had met Gungthang Tsultrim via Lobsang Lhalungpa. Namkha Dorje had met Gungthang Tsultrim in the winter of 1961 in what was then the Sri Lankan Dharamshala (Lanka Dharamshala to Tibetans) near the central railway station in Delhi that provided accommodations for Sri Lankan Buddhist pilgrims. Namkha Dorje's daughter, Tsodi, remembers that the guesthouse had a huge dorm with rows of beds. Gungthang Tsultrim and his performers had been staying there too.

It is possible the Thirteen leaders thought the Karmapa would be sympathetic to their desires. He had, after all, moved with his monastic community to Sikkim in 1961 to establish Tsurphu Monastery. The monastery in Rumtek was completed in 1966. The Karmapa's position as a prominent Buddhist leader was not limited to the Eastern Tibetan community but extended to the Buddhist communities in the mountain regions of Nepal, India, and the Kingdom of Bhutan. The Karmapa was not present at the meetings, but he had sent a representative. He declined the offer to serve as their patron.

The third meeting took place in Delhi with the following individuals: Khamtrul Rinpoche and Dorzong Rinpoche from Tashi Jong, Chokling Rinpoche from the Nangchen settlement in Bir, Dzongnang Rinpoche from Mindrolling Monastery in Clement Town, Jagoetsang Namgyal Dorjee and Barchungpontsang Thutop Gonpo from the Derge settlement in Bir, Drawupon Rinchen Tsering from Taopon settlement in Kamrao, Pon Sangye Namgyal from the Bonpo settlement in Dolanji, and Gungthang Tsultrim from Clement Town. Everyone reconfirmed their desire to form a cooperative society. They sought the Karmapa's support a second time. To their surprise and relief, the Karmapa traveled to Dharamsala to meet the Dalai Lama and was assured that he had no problem with the organization if the Karmapa was to be their patron. Upon his arrival in Delhi, the Karmapa and as many as seventy individuals from the collective convened at the Lodhi Hotel. The Karmapa explained to the group that the Dalai Lama had given his consent. (A press release issued by the Information and Publicity Office of His Holiness the Dalai Lama on August 9, 1978, confirms that the Karmapa's appointment as the head of the organization in the 1960s was approved by the Dalai Lama.)[24]

Sodam, an eighty-three-year-old family friend of mine, whose root guru is the Karmapa, recalled that everyone at that gathering had rejoiced.[25] The Karmapa had stated that the task of the collective was to preserve Tibet's spiritual traditions. With that, the Bhod Dedon Tsogpa, the Tibetan Welfare Association, was formally established as a cultural and social welfare organization.

At this meeting the members voted for a standing committee. As patron, the Karmapa was automatically made the president; the remaining committee members were appointed or agreed upon: the Eighth Khamtrul Rinpoche Dongyu Nyima and the Third Chokling Rinpoche Pema Gyurme as vice presidents; Gungthang Tsultrim and Yongdzin Lopon Tenzin Namdak as general secretaries; Jagoetsang Namgyal Dorjee and Pon Sangye Namgyal as treasurers. The other founding members were Bongsarpon Namkha Dorje, Chanzo Damchoe Yongdue (the general secretary of the Karmapa), Drawupon Rinchen Tsering, Drubwang Pema Norbu Rinpoche (Penor Rinpoche), Kathok Ontrul Rinpoche, Nangchen Lharge, Palyul Dzongnang Rinpoche, Trochupon Dorje Pasang, and Yarling Wangyal. The organization's head office was to be in Jangpura, Delhi. The Karmapa offered several thousand rupees toward their first operating funds. He also offered them the gifts he had received from his devotees on his visit to Bir and Dharamsala. The committee drafted practical standing rules, for example, permitting members to stay for free in the office at E-28 Jangpura in New Delhi.

The Tibetan Welfare Association brought together illustrious lamas of Bon and the Drukpa Kagyud, Kagyud, Nyingma, and Sakya lineages: the sixteenth Karmapa, Yongdzin Lopon Tenzin Namdak Rinpoche, Drubwang Penor Rinpoche, Kathok Ontrul Rinpoche, Khamtrul Rinpoche, Dorzong Rinpoche, Neten Chokling Rinpoche, and Palyul Dzongnang Rinpoche.

It also brought together prominent families of Kham that had ruled in a variety of ways since the fourteenth century: Jagoetsang Namgyal Dorjee, the steward of the famous clan leader Jagoetsang Topden, one of the four main chieftains under the Derge king in Kham; Barchungpontsang Thutop Gompo, also among the

FIGURE 6.1 Tsokhag Chusum/Group of Thirteen leaders and members with Prime Minister Indira Gandhi, 1976, New Delhi. Standing, left to right: Gungthang Ngodup, Tsodi Bongsar, Prime Minister Indira Gandhi. Seated second row, left to right: Kathok Phurpa, Chime Luthoktsang, Chunphel, Jamyang Gyaltsen Choklingtsang, unknown, Karma Thutop, Tenpa Gyaltsen, unknown, unknown, Sonam Damdul, unknown, Lingtsang Sey Jigme, (others unknown). Seated front row, left to right: Congress member, Kathok Phurpa, Drawupon Rinchen Tsering, Gunthang Tsultrim, Dorzong Rinpoche, Khamtrul Rinpoche, Amdo Phuntsok, Bongsarpon Namkha Dorjee, Sonam Topgyal, Pon Sangye Namgyal, Gungthang Tsultrim's aide

Tibetan Welfare Association

Jagoetsang clan in Derge, and the chieftain of Barchung in the kingdom of Derge; Pon Sangye Namgyal, the chieftain of Sogh Geimar in the Nagchu region in Kham;[26] Lingtsang Choegyal Jigmey Wangdu, the king of Lingtsang in Kham (Yarling Dorje Wangyal was a minister of the kingdom who had brought the camp

FIGURE 6.2 Tsokhag Chusum/Group of Thirteen leaders with Pat Brewster. Front row seated, left to right: Yugyal, Dzongnang Rinpoche, Gungthang Tsultrim, unknown, Zasep Nganglo, Pon Sangye Namgyal, Karma Tsultrim, Kuche Tenzing. Middle row, left to right: Drawupon Rinchen Tsering, Trochupon Dorje Pasang, Captain Davinson, George, Pat Brewster, Khamtrul Rinpoche, Chokling Rinpoche, Domang Gyatrul Rinpoche, Lingtsang Yarling Dorje Wangyal. Standing third row, left to right: Jinpa (first left), Akhu Tselo (fourth left), Khamo (fifth left), Bongsarpon Namkha Dorje (second man standing with hat), Ngushel Khen Rinpoche, unknown, Bongpa Lama, Phurko, Lingtsang Jigme, Gungthang Ngodup

Tibetan Welfare Association

together and asked Jigme Lingtsang to join them); Bongsarpon Namkha Dorje, the chieftain of Bongsar in the kingdom of Nangchen in Kham; Trochupon Dorje Pasang, the chieftain of Trochu and Choktse in the kingdom of Gyarong in Amdo; Pon Lhagel, the chieftain of upper Drongpa in the kingdom of Nangchen in Kham; Pon Sonam Dakpa, the chieftain of Lhutri in upper Drongpa in the kingdom of Nangchen; Drawupon Rinchen Tsering, the chieftain of Ga Kyekundo in the kingdom of Nangchen. Such a diverse gathering

FIGURE 6.3 Small group with Prime Minister Indira Gandhi. Front, seated: Prime Minister Indira Gandhi. Standing, left to right: Chogyal Rinpoche, Dorzong Rinpoche, Khamtrul Rinpoche, Jagoetsang Namgyal Dorjee, Chokling Rinpoche, Secretary of Bhoodan Movement, Gungthang Tsultrim, Dzongnang Rinpoche

Tibetan Welfare Association

of chieftains, kings, and lamas was perhaps unprecedented in modern Tibetan history, as was the project that brought them together.[27]

Each settlement had its own blueprint. The settlements led by erstwhile regional chieftains (the Nangchen settlement in Mainpat, the Lingtsang settlement in Manduwala, the Kathok settlement in Sataun) comprised Tibetans mostly from the same clan and area. Many of the settlements led by lamas, in particular the Bonpo settlement, drew Tibetans from all regions to live together. Drawupon's settlement in Kamrao attracted people from his region, but because there were fewer of them in exile, the settlement was open to any Tibetan who wished to live in Kamrao. The Nangchen camp in Bir drew people from different areas of Nangchen, such as Pon Lhagel and Pon Sonam Dakpa and their clans. Similarly, of the 110 families

FIGURE 6.4 Group with Pat Brewster. Left to right: Pon Sangye Namgyal, Jagoetsang Namgyal Dorjee, Dzongnang Rinpoche, Trochupon Dorje Pasang, Chokling Rinpoche (hidden), Khamtrul Rinpoche, Pema Dhondup, Pat Brewster, Akhu Tselo, Jhanag, Zoepa, Topga, Yugyal, Penor Rinpoche, Kathok Bonpo Tulku, Gungthang Tsultrim, Tsurphu Nhorma, Gyaltsur, Karma Singye

Tibetan Welfare Association

who settled in the Derge division in Bir, 90 were from different parts of Derge and the rest from Kongpo, Litang, Gonjo, Lingtsang, Chamdo, and Central Tibet. Gungthang Tsultrim had suggested that Chokling Rinpoche work with Jagoetsang Namgyal Dorjee to invite families from Derge to the Bir camp. The Derge and Nangchen divisions in Bir were registered in 1966 and were administered together, with Chokling Rinpoche as president and Jagoetsang Namgyal Dorjee as vice president. The land in Chauntra was purchased later, and people from Nangchen and Derge, or those who didn't get a house in Bir, moved there. After the deaths of both leaders, the two divisions were administered separately, but they continue to be registered as one society.[28]

Why did a discrete group of Tibetans feel they needed to form a collective in order to protect themselves from their own people?

"It just happened; it wasn't planned," Jadurtsang Sonam Zangpo, in Dolanji said. They suddenly found themselves accused of not living under the rule of the exile government. He had served as the chief justice commissioner and as a member of the Tibetan parliament.

"We didn't want to rebel against anyone, least of all the exile government. It was just a desire to protect our own faith and our community," he continued. He felt the pain of having to explain himself all the time, even to this day.[29]

Another elder said that the Thirteen were made the enemy. He said the accusations that they took money from Taiwan wounded him deeply.

My friend Yugyal from Mainpat explained his dream in simple terms: he fled his *phayul* with his people, and he dreamed of returning to Nangchen with them. How could that dream have posed a threat to Tibetan unity? His group of five hundred people arrived in Mainpat and settled in camp 2. They were asked to accept the representative in the existing camp number 1 as their leader. They insisted, in turn, upon Namkha Dorje serving as their camp leader. They argued that they had approached Prime Minister Nehru precisely because they had wished to live with a leader who had led their people for generations. Rumors were spread that Tibetans in camp 2 were pro-Chinese and receiving funds from the Kuomintang Party. Elders in Mainpat told me that when they decorated their camp to mark events related to religious protectors specific to their practices, Tibetans from camp 1 would provoke them by saying they were putting up Taiwan's national flag.[30]

The elders said they learned to ignore the constant taunts from Tibetans in camp 1, but it was a lot harder to keep their cattle alive. They were afraid they would not be able to support themselves through the second year. Namkha Dorje requested help from the Karmapa, who suggested they move to Bhutan. The community of five hundred Tibetans left Mainpat to go to Bhutan but were held back by the Indian government in Ambikapur for four months. The Indian government convinced them to return to Mainpat by promising them better homes and more financial support.

Asi Lama was visiting Mainpat when I spoke to him on November 2, 2023. He told me over WhatsApp that they kept to themselves and brushed off the rumors and the frequent character smears.[31] It was harder to tolerate the backlash that came in the form of restrictions on their children's access to Tibetan schools. In 1967 or 1968, Wangdu Dorjee visited Mainpat, and during his public address he mentioned that there were two paths available to Tibetans: the "white path" and the wrong "black" path. He advised Tibetans to listen to the Dalai Lama and take the right path. He held those in camp 2 to be examples of dishonorable people on the wrong path. The home minister's message perturbed at least a hundred Tibetans (none from the clan), who decided to join camp 1. They later confessed to their friends in camp 2 that they had left because they were afraid to be known as anti-Dalai Lama or antigovernment.[32]

Like all Tibetans, the Thirteen leaders and their people had to adjust to the new realities in exile. For the leaders, this meant reevaluating their identity as lineage holders and guardians of people they had once ruled. Perhaps they realized that the DNA of the social organizations and systems that held their clans and their people together was not seen as compatible with the operative logic of the social mobilization of a Tibetan national movement. They had left their homeland just as the Chinese government had brought changes to their traditional roles. The transformation to equal citizens called for something similar. Forgetting was crucial in both contexts.[33]

At the heart of the Thirteen's struggle against the United Party, as I understand it, and by extension what they saw as the assimilationist tendencies of the exile society, lay the fear that they were hounded by the United Party and unprotected by the exile government. Their fear of being asked to leave their clan and their chiefs at a time when their company was crucial, and of being asked to give up their religious traditions in favor of what they assumed to be a reformed Buddhist practice that might include nationalizing one kind of Buddhism over others, was real. They understood the oaths and offerings by Tibetans in exile to the Dalai Lama as metonymic acts attempting to create communion and solidarity with one another. They also understood the other possibility, that oaths established a narrow code of conduct. All members of the Thirteen I spoke to had accepted the exile government as the nerve center of the polity in exile. They thought that creating opportunities in exile to continue their religious education was fulfilling their role as religious teachers as well as the government's priority to preserve Tibetan identity and culture. They also hadn't imagined that caring for their clan and religious communities, which they accepted as their duty, conflicted or interfered with the exile government's work.

Even if the Thirteen leaders had no political ambitions, as they claimed, their photos with Prime Minister Indira Gandhi indicate their presence was known to Indian leaders. They had gathered an eclectic group of contacts. The act of forming or making a group public endows it with the power to speak in its members' name but also presents problems.[34] The exile government's disapproval of the Thirteen was never made public, but officials' descriptions of the group as having split from the exile community indicate that the Thirteen's organization was seen as a maneuver to form something like a microregional space. The Thirteen's refusal to accept representatives from the exile government in their settlements made such conclusions available. They were using their group rights to resist the exile government's centralizing goals, revealing to some extent the porousness and flexibility of the exile polity operating in a liminal space.

Minutes of meetings held by exile administrators to discuss relations between the United Party and the Thirteen indicate the polity was aware of the tensions between the two groups. As early as 1967, the Thirteen reached out to exile administrators to express their concern about the United Party's role in the annual government meetings. The administrators did not address the concerns raised and reasoned instead that the Thirteen's lack of faith in the government was the root of the problem. Perhaps they were more concerned that certain international relief leaders and Indian government administrators would think that the Thirteen were behaving like autonomous bodies beyond the rule of the exile government. The exile administrators in 1967 were hoping to squash rumors before they became a larger political problem for a government that was still securing its authority.[35]

One former exile official described the Thirteen to me as a kind of counterhegemonic civil society led by Khampa elites who championed the right to practice democracy without clearly exhibiting what a democratic structure would look like within their own organization. He said that the United Party members he had known believed that the Thirteen leaders sought to challenge the antinomies of Tibetan democracy, but to also use it to their advantage—that is, they were using democracy to prolong their traditional hegemonic positions as chiefs and lamas. He recalled that party members took the position that the Thirteen wanted only the benefits of belonging to the exile government and used one or two incidences of conflict to build an argument about systemic prejudice against Khampas.

Powers held by the Thirteen leaders could survive because of the belief that authority emanated from chieftains and lamas, not from the people. The Thirteen was an organization led by men—as was the United Party—who were not voted democratically into prominence but had been born into positions of power and into a long lineage of privilege. The leaders ran the organization much like they had presided over their remote nomadic clans, with flexible rules and with some impunity. Loyalty to the clan and the ability to care for it were the guiding principles crucial to the identity and honor of the leaders and their members. There was less room or opportunity in such company for "ordinary" men and for women to make their opinions known. The assistants to the chiefs and lamas didn't feel that they had the liberty of speech in the presence of their superiors. Lobsang Gyatso, who was a Bonpo and from Central Tibet, said that he was a minority within the Thirteen, and men like him often felt ignored during meetings.

Women were not participants in these meetings. The only woman I know to have attended a few meetings is Tsodi Bongsar, the daughter of Bongsar Namkha Dorje and Demtso. She often accompanied her father to meetings with Indian officials to serve as translator for English and Hindi, and she remembers attending some of the informal meetings with other Thirteen members in restaurants in Delhi. She did not speak when the Thirteen met but recalls Gungthang Tsultrim inviting everyone, including her, to share their perspective. The perspective of men dominates this narrative of the Thirteen, but it was the women—wives, mothers, daughters, and sisters—who labored to financially support their families, maintain their homes, and send children to schools or to monasteries. It was women who maintained order in the domestic sphere and in the settlements while the men occupied themselves with the community. When I visited Yugyal in 2015, he admitted to me that he had been an absent father. Tseten Palmo, his wife, had to raise their children and handle the farm. She agreed that he gave more time to the community than to his own family.

Women and children who were part of the Thirteen allow a different glimpse of the group's leaders. They understand the sacrifices made in service to the nation in a different way because it intimately shaped their private and public lives. Tsodi remembers her father, Pon Namkha Dorje, was beset with financial problems after reaching Mainpat and after every single sheep had died. The aid supplied by the Indian government was barely sufficient for their people. They had nobody to turn to. She recalls accompanying her father to

Clement Town to ask Gungthang Tsultrim to help them obtain a bank loan. When they were unsuccessful in getting a loan, they traveled to Dharamsala, where my mother was a member of the Tibetan parliament. She was able to arrange Rs. 5,000 for them. Namkha Dorje felt responsible for members of his clan and community. The financial problems never went away, Tsodi remembers. They had to sell their family valuables to meet the needs of the extended family.

Dorjee Lhamo Barchungtsang, who was married to Barchungpon Thutop Gombo, said she had to sell her jewelry piece by piece to feed the family and send their daughters to school in Kalimpong. Barchungpon's commitment to the nation left very little time and resources for the family. Similarly, in a message over WhatsApp on June 22, 2023, Tseten Drawutsang shared that she doesn't have many memories of Drawupon, her father, as a child because he was away serving the government in his capacity as a member of parliament and as a member of the Chushi Gangdrug. His salary as a parliament member was about Rs. 75 a month. Her mother and her uncle, who was a monk, supported the family. Tsomo Yangchen, Drawupon's wife, made ends meet by knitting sweaters under the streetlamps to sell to Khadi Bhandari. She also sold her jewelry to meet school-related expenses for her three children. She told me that her husband was accused of receiving money from the MTAC. She said she never saw the dollars supposedly from the Chinese. All she saw was struggle.

Gungthang Sonam Wangyal, the grandson of Gungthang Tsultrim, who lives in Toronto, Canada, remembers seeing his grandmother Khamo cry every night from the time he was three years old until he was seventeen. "I never had the opportunity to grow up with my grandfather," he said to me over the phone.[36] He is reminded of what he never had by strangers as well as by his loved ones who knew and admired Gungthang Tsultrim. Over the years he learned that Gungthang Tsultrim always carried his prayer beads in his hands and chanted his prayers out loud when he was home; he was a joyful man; he had simple needs, he drank a cup of milk in the morning and after that only had hot water; he wore the Tibetan *chuba* whether he was relaxing at home or attending to business. Sonam Gungthang hears often from people who knew his grandfather that he had vision: for example, he set up vocational training opportunities for Tibetans in Clement Town at the same time that he planned for a primary school.

The United Party and the Thirteen have a few things in common: they were committed to a Tibetan future; they had devoted and dynamic members; many of their protagonists were also leaders within the Chushi Gangdrug; and members of both groups feel misunderstood. However, the United Party had power and access to funds and the government's support. They came to be seen as representing the interests of all Tibetans and as being progressive, and the Thirteen were represented as protecting the interests of Eastern Tibetans. While a narrative of the Thirteen's Buddhist-centric worldview and clan culture and the United Party's Western-looking view was also easily within reach, the Thirteen were presented as dissidents and members of the United Party as patriots. More than a few members of the Thirteen said to me that the United Party was responsible for designating them as antigovernment.

That some traditions came to be privileged and normalized as a shared Tibetan identity does not suggest that there existed truer or more stable traditions, simply that the adoption of Central Tibetan as well as Gelug traditions in the early years of exile was partly practical (Central Tibetans comprised the majority of the exile population) and partly strategic (the exile government was led initially by old Lhasa aristocrats and government officials, who were mostly Gelug). The fear of a hegemonic standard did produce competing options and desires because the exile Tibetan population was composed of a more diverse group of Tibetans than had prevailed under the Tibetan government before 1959.

Several elders stated to me that it had been difficult to know how to navigate politics in exile in those early days. Hadn't His Holiness the Dalai Lama on several occasions asked Tibetans to be self-sufficient and assist him in building the exile community? They felt that on the one hand, His Holiness was encouraging Tibetans to question and investigate all policies in the spirit of democracy and the principles of Tibetan Buddhism, and on the other hand, government officials and the United Party instructed them that following unquestioningly the wishes of the Dalai Lama was the foremost duty of all Tibetans.

Members of the Thirteen also stated that they wished to know why the United Party had so much power within exile politics. They wanted to believe the exile government existed for all Tibetans. They found an ally in Gungthang Tsultrim. As a Gelug and an Amdowa, he seemed a safe and likely leader for an unlikely project of a motley group.

7

A POLITICS OF SORROW

Tibetan refugees first noticed Gungthang Tsultrim when he formed an Amdo drama troupe around 1960 or 1961. Sonam Tobden, an eighty-three-year-old man living in Clement Town, suggested to me in 2022, as Jinpa had in 2015, that Tsultrim had unintentionally upstaged the exile government's Academy of Tibetan Music, Dance, and Drama, which had been formed with twenty-six members on August 11, 1959, in Kalimpong. In their book, the United Party criticized Gungthang Tsultrim for overreaching. They faulted him for creating a performance group on purpose—to disrupt the exile community.[1]

Both Tobden and Jinpa had performed with the Amdo troupe in Delhi, Calcutta, and Bombay, but they recall their performance for the Dalai Lama in 1963 as the most meaningful one. In an audience with the artists afterward, the Dalai Lama had encouraged Gungthang Tsultrim to help the government by establishing a settlement for Tibetans. Tsultrim took His Holiness's words to heart, recalled Jinpa. Perhaps Tsultrim's fault was his audacity to do what most Tibetans thought was exclusively the government's mandate.

There was, moreover, a bigger transgression. Tobden thought that Gungthang Tsultrim was bold in not deferring to Gyalo Thondup's wishes. Tsultrim parted ways with the majority of Amdowas in exile. He followed his own vision, and in doing so was seen as causing a tear in the Amdo community over which Gyalo Thondup otherwise held sway.

In the pamphlet *The Assasination* [sic] *of Gungthang Tsultrim*, also referred to as *Pasang Nagpo (The Black Friday)*, Gungthang Tsultrim's supporters describe him as a "gem of a man." The pamphlet praises him for having "a most pleasant disposition" and a personality that attracted everyone. He had "a very cool temperament and was always seen smiling. He was loved and admired, not only by the Tibetans but by his numerous Indian friends as well. He did not have even one personal enemy. Then why would anyone want to kill him?"[2]

Of course, many Tibetans in Clement Town had an answer to that rhetorical question. Gungthang Tsultrim, after all, had been at the center of much national debate since 1962. Residents knew that he had been guarded by his supporters for several years precisely because they feared he would be killed. A previous attempt had been made.

Gungthang Tsultrim's personal communications indicate he feared for his life long before he was assassinated. On April 22, 1971, he wrote a petition to the secretary of the Ministry of Home Affairs of the government of India seeking Indian citizenship. He expresses concern about the restrictions imposed on members of the Thirteen under the 1946 Foreigners Act, which gives the central government the power to regulate or restrict the entry or presence of "foreigners" or non-Indian citizens in India, suggesting they were unjust and being used as a form of harassment against those who criticized Gyalo Thondup. He intimates that Gyalo Thondup's power was unchallenged by exile officials and that the Thirteen's only recourse for protection was to become Indian citizens.

In a letter to Prime Minister Indira Gandhi on June 23, 1971, Gungthang Tsultrim addressed the "split" among Tibetans living in India as an effect of what he described as Gyalo Thondup's project to "safeguard his own supremacy." He argues that Gyalo Thondup's personal agenda interrupted the implementation of His Holiness the Dalai Lama's democratic policies. Gungthang Tsultrim claims he is being punished and harassed by Gyalo Thondup's supporters for having sent a previous letter (on April 4, 1970) to the prime minister. These persecuting tactics, he states, compelled 20,000 Tibetans from the Thirteen settlements to seek Indian citizenship. He explains that they only made the decision after confirming that it did not contradict the Dalai Lama's wishes. Tsultrim pledges his loyalty to His Holiness the Dalai Lama more than once in the letter.

The Thirteen's decision to seek Indian citizenship was not received well by the exile government. In his letter to Prime Minister Gandhi, Gungthang Tsultrim notes that "malicious propaganda" about the Thirteen working against the Dalai Lama is being spread in the Tibetan community. Exile officials had visited the settlements to talk to the Thirteen. Some of the settlements—Tsultrim mentions Bir—had retaliated by insulting these officials. Gungthang Tsultrim mentions that a man was killed in Clement Town. He calls the murder "an ugly and unfortunate incident" but skips over the details.[3] He ends the letter on an ominous note, stating he lives in "constant danger to my person," and notes, "all efforts by this group will be made to eliminate me physically."[4]

Gungthang Tsultrim was most likely referring to the United Party, not the exile government, as "this group." The "ugly and unfortunate incident" was the murder of Gawa Zamkhen Tashi Yarphel, who was stoned to death by a group of Clement Town Tibetans. An elder in Clement Town said that Zamkhen Tashi had sent a petition to the Tibetan government asking for their intervention in the goings-on regarding applications for Indian citizenship. The security minister, Kalon Tsewang Tamdin, and member of parliament Alak Jigme Rinpoche had come to address Tibetans in Clement Town.[5] Town elders describe Gungthang Tsultrim as having been "ambushed" by Yarphel that day and say that he almost died. The United Party writes in *Truthful History of the Tibetan United Association* that Amdo Phende, Tselo, and Gawa [Zamkhen] Tashi, all from Clement Town, were critical of Tsultrim's activities. The party states that a group of people from Clement Town went to Zamkhen Tashi's house and killed him by pelting him with stones, sticks, and knives because they feared he would reveal "Tsultrim's relations" with Taiwan's Mongolian and Tibetan Affairs Commission.[6]

Although Gungthang Tsultrim did not mention the harassment the Thirteen experienced in his letter to Prime Minister Gandhi, he wrote about it in his letter to the secretary of home affairs, claiming that the Thirteen members were targeted, not because they were a threat to India's security but because they had voiced their "protests against their internal problems in general" and against Gyalo Thondup in particular. Tsultrim wrote that Gyalo Thondup's position in both Tibetan and Indian political circles empowered him to punish Tibetans who opposed his ideas. Gungthang Tsultrim pledged his loyalty to the Dalai Lama and revealed it had become impossible to "submit to the private regime of Mr. Thondup," whom he identified as at the center of the campaign against him and the members of the Thirteen by the exile government, the United Party, and private individuals. The only way for the Thirteen to escape Gyalo Thondup's indiscriminate use of Indian laws against them, Gungthang Tsultrim concluded, was for them to seek Indian citizenship.

Gungthang Tsultrim's description of the exile society as the "private regime" of Gyalo Thondup expresses a view held by many members of the Thirteen. Thondup's power appeared phantasmagorical and unbounded to them; he towered over the average Tibetan. The Thirteen members do not dispute his contributions to the Tibetan exile community, but they also do not accept his undertakings and use of power as irreproachable. Gyari Rinpoche, who was close to Gyalo Thondup, describes him as an "extremely influential, highly controversial," and also a "very much misunderstood" person. He was an "institution far larger than any individual."[7] Gyari Rinpoche admits he was "not the easiest person to work with and a bit unpredictable" and not very inclusive in his "undertakings."[8] His "parallel activities" had "unintentionally undermined Dharamsala's authority," and Gyari Rinpoche suggests that Dharamsala and Gyalo Thondup mistrusted each other.⁹ He lists Gyalo Thondup's many contributions to the Tibetan society in his book. Gungthang Tsultrim painstakingly kept his critique of Gyalo Thondup separate from his loyalty to the Dalai Lama in his letters to the Indian government. While emphasizing that he appealed for Indian citizenship only after confirming that it would not go against the Dalai Lama's wishes, Tsultrim cites the Dalai Lama's interview with Arbind Mulla published on April 18, 1971, in the *Times Weekly* as evidence.¹⁰ In the interview the Dalai Lama was asked for his view on Tibetans adopting Indian nationality. The Dalai Lama responded that there was nothing wrong in doing so, and that it should be up to individual people to decide. He added, however, that Tibetans ought not to forget their distinct Tibetan culture and habits. The interview was republished in the May 1971 issue of the *Tibetan Review* under the title "The Dalai Lama Speaks Out."

The Thirteen's petition for Indian citizenship generated interest from the Indian media. On August 4, 1971, the *Times of India* printed an article, "Tibetan refugees seek Indian citizenship," reporting that a group was seeking Indian citizenship because they seemed "to have lost all hope of being able to return to their homeland." The article elaborated:

> The refugees are split into two groups—one led by Gyalo Thondup, elder brother of the Dalai Lama, and the other by Gonthong Tsultrim [*sic*]. These groups have been indulging in mutual recriminations which sometimes culminate in violence, creating a law and order problem. However, both factions owe allegiance to the Dalai Lama. It is learned that nine prominent leaders belonging to different Tibetan refugee settlements have jointly submitted a memorandum to the Union Home Minister, demanding a curb on the activities of Mrs. Thondup, wife of the Dalai Lama's brother.

Mrs. Thondup was most likely mentioned as a tactic to draw attention to her Chinese identity; the Sino-Indian War of 1962 had not faded from memory. Gungthang Tsultrim and Gyalo Thondup, both charismatic leaders from Amdo who had ties with the Kuomintang Party (KMT) from their days in Tibet, elicited extreme feelings from Tibetans: either unquestioned loyalty or deep skepticism. They had come to represent competing visions for Tibetan governance and identity in exile. Given his status as the chief of security for his brother, the Dalai Lama, and as the person in charge of foreign affairs and the head of Tibetan intelligence, Gyalo Thondup's words reverberated with authority. In its book, the United Party did not hold back in describing Gungthang Tsultrim as someone whose every action was aimed at disrupting Tibetan unity. In the chapter "About the Gungthang Tsultrim Incident," the party intimated Tsultrim was in contact with the KMT and was running an office funded by the MTAC.

Exile officials revealed their real position on Gungthang Tsultrim in unexpected places. In the "Readers' View" section of the *Times of India* on June 10, 1971, parliament members "Ven. Jigme Rinpoche, Phagpa Tshering, and (Mrs.) Gha Yondon" challenged a prior *Times of India* article reporting a split in the Tibetan exile community.[11] Alak Jigme Rinpoche, Choney Phagpa Tsering, and Taktser Gawa Yangdon served in the fourth commission of the exile government from 1969 to 1972. They denounced the *Times*'s report of discord within the community as baseless and stressed that all Tibetans were united and were "obediently" following the exile leadership. The published article had referred to Gungthang Tsultrim as a leader from "Amdo province" who was seeking Indian citizenship. The Tibetan parliamentarians took offense at this. They maintained, "In fact, he was not even a village headman. Since Mr. Tsulthim's [*sic*] arrival in India, he has been indulging in various activities to undermine the unity of the Tibetan community in exile."

The letter further confirmed something that had not yet been made public: Tsultrim's official expulsion. It stated that elected parliament members from the Amdo region, joined by other leaders, had submitted a memorandum to the Tibetan cabinet in 1965 opposing Gungthang Tsultrim's activities. As a consequence, "He was disowned and expelled from the Tibetan community. A follow-up of the above-mentioned memorandum was submitted in 1967 to the Tibetan Cabinet and to all the various departments concerned."

The letter confirmed what the exile government had not made explicit for over a decade: Gungthang Tsultrim's outsider position in the Tibetan exile community. Writing about this in the Indian newspaper made his banishment official. The message seemed to be that Tsultrim was a traitor tearing people apart and unworthy of belonging. By contrast, the letter lauded Gyalo Thondup as an exemplary Tibetan patriot holding the nation together and "a man who had on a number of occasions led our delegations abroad to plead Tibet's case in the UN."

It is ironic that the parliamentarians relied on examples of censure from "regional" communities to support their repudiation of Gungthang Tsultrim's regionalism. Members of the Tibetan parliament revealed that they felt it necessary to respond publicly to the *Times of India* to unequivocally reject Tsultrim. The word "disown" can be read to mean "to reject," "to abandon," or "to refuse to recognize." However, an act of banishment highlights that Gungthang Tsultrim was, in fact, a significant member of the Tibetan community, albeit as a threat to the establishment. The letter also reveals the importance accorded to the idea of unity within the government.

While inclusion into the Tibetan polity was informal and private, the act of exclusion, as indicated in the oath taken in Bodh Gaya as well as in the pamphlets distributed by the United Party, was public, and a power wielded by the government. Exclusion took de facto and de jure forms of social ostracism, such as the parliamentary letter and the resolutions passed by the United Party, as well as lack of access to education, health, and refugee aid. Exclusion also came in punitive and legal ways, such as mobility restrictions under the Foreigners Act of 1946 imposed upon Pon Namkha Dorje and Yugyal. Cheme Jagoetsang, who was in Bir at the time of our meeting in 2022, recalled that Jagoetsang Namgyal Dorjee, the leader of the Derge settlement in Bir, was arrested in Calcutta along with Sadhutshang Lo Nyendrak in 1970 and imprisoned for two weeks. He also recalled seeing a copy of a notice stating that his father was a threat to India's national security. Cheme suspected that many of the Thirteen leaders received a similar notice.[12] Tibetans expressed their goal as to advocate for emancipation, for a political reality different from that offered by the Chinese, but also ended up tormenting those who did not embrace the dominant views of the exile government.

Gungthang Tsultrim concluded that Indian citizenship would give the Thirteen new avenues of protection, including a judicial system with legal safeguards. He had expressed to the Thirteen leaders, according to Yugyal, that their best option for equality and self-representation as Tibetans was to become Indian nationals. However, in the 1960s and 1970s, to do so was read as a disavowal of the Tibetan movement. By contrast, Tibetans in Europe and America were viewed as having no choice but to become citizens. Gungthang Tsultrim and the rest of the Thirteen were in a predicament: publicly targeted and disowned by the exile establishment but also criticized for seeking protection from the Indian government. Even within the condition of statelessness, there was a division between those who belonged and those who did not. The Thirteen's project to seek Indian citizenship quietly fizzled out. Yugyal thought it was because the exile government had put pressure on the Indian government to reject their petition.

Gyari Rinpoche confirms in his memoir that the exile government was able to convince the Indian government "not to accede to the Tsokhag Chusum's request for blanket citizenship for all its members."[13] He believed that had a large group of Tibetans been granted Indian citizenship, it would have caused further divisions within the community in addition to undermining the exile government. In a press release from the Information and Publicity Office on August 9, 1978, the exile government stated that although no Tibetan individuals were prevented from taking Indian citizenship, the 1971 attempt by the Thirteen to seek citizenship en masse was objectionable because it "was tantamount to killing the Tibetan issue."[14] The release suggests that the matter had been resolved through discussions. Members of the Thirteen do not recall such a discussion, but it is possible a meeting had taken place between select leaders.

The next serious charge against Gungthang Tsultrim came a few years later, over his alleged role as the secret head of the MTAC. An article published on May 18, 1977, in the *Young Army Journal*, a minor newspaper in Taiwan, alleged that Tsui Shi Yan, the official head of the MTAC, had commented that the agency was working closely with the Thirteen.[15] The secretary of the Information and Publicity Office of the exile government, Namgyal Dorjee, was sent to the settlements of Bir, Tashi Jong, Sataun, Munduwala, and Clement Town with a copy of the article in Chinese and its Tibetan translation. The government asked each of the Thirteen settlements to respond.

On January 14, 1978, Gungthang Tsultrim sent a letter to the secretary stating that the news report was "lies fabricated" to destroy the Thirteen. Tsultrim called the allegations of ties with Taiwan "bogus" and indicated he knew who was behind them.[16] He states that the Thirteen was formed to:

> Create a stable livelihood for our people, to promote and spread Buddhist schools of thought, to protect Tibet's ancient culture and to protect our people. Other than these, unless there are opportunities to bring benefits to our struggle for freedom, we have no intention whatsoever to build relationships with any country, including Taiwan.

However, our association is unable to say whether individuals have associations of any kind. As you know this is happening with Tibetans, both ordinary and higher-ups.

Gungthang Tsultrim distinguishes between the decisions made by the Thirteen as an organization and those made by private individuals. He states that he only speaks for the Thirteen as an organization. This leaves open the interpretation of there being individuals within who might have had relations with Taiwan. Tsultrim never clarifies his own personal position. The ambiguity is important. Accusations made against Tsultrim or other members of the Thirteen were also accusations against the collective. Surviving members insist that the Thirteen as an organization did not receive funds from Taiwan. In the same letter, Gungthang Tsultrim stresses that "ordinary" Tibetans within the society as well as "higher-ups" within the government had relations with Taiwan and that exile government officials knew this very well. (The government's own ties with Taiwan would be revealed later.)

Gungthang Tsultrim asked the cabinet to send a letter to other exile ministers declaring his and the Thirteen's innocence, and also to communicate this to the exile community. The Bonpo community in Dolanji, one of the Thirteen settlements, also protested the accusations against them in a letter to the Tibetan cabinet. They point out that Gungthang Tsultrim had already clarified that the Thirteen had not taken any funds from Taiwan and express their willingness to take an oath in person to prove their innocence. In response, the cabinet reassured the Thirteen members that they suspected Taiwan to be behind the publication of the article, not the Thirteen. They requested that each of the thirteen settlements write a letter confirming that the allegation made by Taiwan was baseless.

Gungthang Tsultrim responded that he would provide a clear answer after conducting his own investigation into the matter. The exchanges with the exile leaders reveal that the Thirteen placed importance on having the government's trust. Their repeated requests to clear their name within the Tibetan society indicate they understood the government's authority over the people, and that they valued how it and the Tibetan people viewed them.

The Tibetan public's feelings of rage toward the Thirteen had not yet abated when a second scandal erupted on February 6, 1978. The *Tung-yang Nyin-rai Sar-Shok*, a newspaper from Calcutta produced by the MTAC, printed a Tibetan New Year greeting in Chinese bearing felicitations to the MTAC from the Thirteen. The Information and Publicity Office sent a letter of inquiry about this to the Thirteen on March 7, 1978, with a copy of the advertisement.

Gungthang Tsultrim denied the Thirteen's hand in this sponsored publication. In his reply on March 17, 1978, he suggests their innocence could be proved by confirming who had paid for the advertisement. Given that the leaders of the Thirteen settlements did not always consult one another about their activities, it is possible that one of them paid without seeking consensus from the others. It is equally possible, as Tsultrim expresses to the exile government, that individuals who wanted to harm him and the Thirteen paid using the Thirteen's name. His point was that either way, the government could not accuse him personally, or the Thirteen as an organization, without proof. The two elected representatives from Kham, Rinchen Tsering and Tsering Choden Dhompa, are believed to have also pushed exile officials to refrain from accusing the Thirteen without providing evidence and without hearing them out.

Many United Party supporters accused Gungthang Tsultrim of receiving money from Taiwan. The party believed that Tsultrim had even used money from the MTAC to pay for expenses related to the Dalai Lama's visit to Clement Town in 1965. Likewise, Amdo Dhondup, the same man identified by Tsultrim as being behind his murder, claims in his memoir, published in 2019, that it was public knowledge that Tsultrim took money from Taiwan as early as 1960, after he was elected to the Tibetan parliament. Dhondup accuses him of receiving money from the Taiwan Kalon Office, later run by Surkhang Wangchen Gelek and Yuthok Tashi Dhondup. He states that Tsultrim was good friends with the two men.[17]

Gyari Rinpoche explains the logic behind these supposed relations. He writes that some Tibetans from Amdo and Kham, who had close ties with the Nationalist government in the pre-Communist era, did not share the view that the KMT was an enemy like the CCP. They believed that the KMT was an ally. He suggests that chieftains and religious leaders whose regions had not fallen under the Lhasa government had hoped to retain their traditional influences and their titles under the new exile government. When that turned out not to be the case, they felt pushed aside. These Khampa leaders, Gyari Rinpoche writes, might have understood the significance of a "united front" to confront the Chinese Communist Party, but they didn't "fully appreciate" the process. He suggests that resentment led some to form alliances with offshoots of the KMT government.[18] Gyari Rinpoche does not explain further. Such comments attempt to shed light on the way historical legacies worked with politics, but they also establish who was and was not aligned with the policies of the government: for example, to suggest that Khampa leaders were driven to their politics out of resentment, unlike Gyari Rinpoche (and his father), devoted to the process of national unity.

Regardless of their veracity, the allegations that the Thirteen colluded with the MTAC proved harmful to Gungthang Tsultrim. The published news articles were accepted by many Tibetan refugees as evidence. These scandals were brought to the public by the United Party, as well as groups such as the Tibetan Youth Organization and the Tibetan Women's Organization, which were established in the 1970s. A group of Amdowas living in the refugee settlement in Hunsur, Karnataka, wrote a letter to "Mr. Tsulti Yen," head of the MTAC bureau in Taiwan, on October 28, 1977, and published it in that month's issue of the *Tibetan Review*. The letter reveals the general attitude of Tibetans in the settlement toward Taiwan, the People's Republic of

China, and Tibetans deemed to have ties with them. The Amdowas of Hunsur charge the Taiwanese government with creating discord among Tibetans by suggesting all Amdowas and Khampas maintained ties to it. Such statements, the authors of the letter point out, promote "false impression among our people." They continue: "as for Mr. Tsultrim, we have always regarded him as a shameful element within our community right from the time we came as refugees in India in 1959."

For the authors, Gungthang Tsultrim's activities from the onset of Tibetan exile made him "nothing more than a traitor to our cause for which we express our continued intolerance." The group sought to stress their disassociation from the Thirteen, both as people from the Amdo region and as Tibetans.

> We would like to make it very clear that we strongly deny the accusation of our having maintained any relationship and taking aid from Taiwan and the so-called Mongol Organisation. We have neither wish nor reason to place ourselves into such harmful acts of betrayal. Leave aside taking any aid, it is something we cannot even think of. Any association with this very name is detrimental to our cause and makes us shamefully mad.

The exile government never cleared the names of the Thirteen leaders as requested by them. The government did not publicize the reassurances it had communicated in letters to the leaders, and the cabinet decided not to issue clarifications. And just as the Thirteen feared, the government's silence paved the way for the Tibetan public to focus on the Taiwan issue. The *Young Army Journal* article was the hottest topic during the annual gathering of Tibetan administrators in March 1978. Many Tibetans declared that the Thirteen did not follow the Dalai Lama's leadership. There was a suppurating conviction in that room that if Communist China was the external enemy of Tibet, then the Thirteen was the internal enemy. As emotions rose, Kasur Jetsun Pema, a much-loved civic leader and the Dalai Lama's younger sister, is alleged to have asked the public in attendance, "Who is Tsokhag Chusum [Group of Thirteen]?" and "Who is its head?" She is said to have followed with a remark that the head of the organization should be identified and banished from society. The Thirteen described this scene to exile officials in a letter as well as during a face-to-face meeting with members of the government.

In a letter on April 17, 1978, the Thirteen asked the exile government why it had not publicly cleared their names during the annual gathering as promised. The letter, signed by the leaders, expresses their hope that the government will not betray their trust. In a letter sent to the Thirteen earlier, on April 10, 1978, the government had stated that writing back and forth would only complicate matters. They suggested representatives of the Thirteen meet face-to-face with the exile government to air out matters on July 9.[19] The exile government reassured the Thirteen that they would let the Tibetan public know they were blameless and said it had not wanted to draw attention to these small problems. Given that they had identified Taiwan and the People's Republic of China as enemies and that parliamentarians had publicly denounced Gungthang Tsultrim as a traitor, the downplaying of these accusations exemplifies the forms of control that kept the Thirteen unfairly fixed in the public imagination as the internal enemies of Tibet.

The proposed meeting on July 9 never took place. Instead, on June 16, 1978, the news that Akhu Tsultrim had been shot rippled through the Thirteen settlements. Members of the Thirteen were so devastated that they remember where they were when they heard it. Jamyang Gyaltsen recalled that a man named Tseja flew into Bir on a motorbike to relay the news. Jamyang Gyaltsen left for Clement Town immediately with Sey Dhonyo from the Derge Bir division. Drawupon's daughter Tseten was visiting her father in Dharamsala when Tsering Choden Dhompa rushed into their quarters with the news. She remembers her father and my mother, both representatives of Kham in the parliament, sitting in silence for a while. Then they made plans to leave for Clement Town. Tsodi Bongsar thinks her father, Namkha Dorje, got the word through a telegram. He immediately sent Asi Lama and Tashi Topgay from Mainpat to Clement Town. Asi recalls everyone there being sad and afraid.

THE ASSASSINATION OF GUNGTHANG TSULTRIM

On the evening of June 16, 1978, Gungthang Tsultrim complained of a headache, and forgoing the meal prepared for him, opted instead for yogurt. After eating, he retreated to the backyard to finish his evening prayers. Tsultrim's driver and trusted aide, Jinpa, who lived next door, was finishing his dinner with his family when the sound of four gunshots punctured the evening's stillness. Jinpa said he rushed toward Tsultrim's house. Tsultrim's wife, Khamo, had also rushed to the backyard. They found Tsultrim on the ground. He had been shot in the back.

Jinpa recalls Gungthang Tsultrim often sitting in the backyard on warm summer evenings. That day, he had circled his neck with a wet towel to hasten the cooling process. Summer evenings were special. People would linger in their yards when the sun was not so punishing and there was sometimes the additional comfort of a breeze. The year had been going well: half of the people in Clement Town had turned into actors for Tsultrim's film, and there were talks underway of building more houses in the settlement. Gungthang Tsultrim had been shot on a day that was significant to many residents: June 16, the day the Chushi Gangdrug was formally established in Lhoka, Tibet.

The details of Gungthang Tsultrim's death were circulated in English and Tibetan in the pamphlet *The Assasination* [sic] *of Gungthang Tsultrim*, written by members of the "Tibetan Welfare Association, a confederation of Thirteen Amdo and Khampa settlements in India," and distributed in Clement Town a few days afterward. Khamo and Jinpa are quoted in the pamphlet as saying they had glimpsed the back of a man fleeing into the jungle when they reached Tsultrim's side. There were no fences separating the homes, and the back doors opened onto what they referred to then as the jungle. Jinpa had conducted a search of the surroundings with two other men from the settlement. They found a pair of spectacles that they attributed to the assassin. They suspected he had gotten away through the jungle and toward the new highway.[20] Gungthang Tsultrim was taken to Peshin Hospital in Dehra Dun and was pronounced dead on June 18 in the early morning.

Clement Town was abuzz with rumors that the bullets retrieved from the premises were the kind used by the Tibetan resistance army's 22 Unit in Chakrata. They suspected the gun was procured from the unit. Individuals professed to knowing such facts, unrelated to their quotidian lives in the settlement, because many of them had friends or family members in the unit, situated half a day's journey by bus from Clement Town.

From his hospital bed, Gungthang Tsultrim accused three men—Wangdu Dorjee, Phakte, and Amdo Dhondup—of plotting his murder. All three men were Tibetan and were known to have opposed Tsultrim's plans to expand the Clement Town settlement. Phakte had been known as an active member of the United Party's local chapter.

At the time of his death, Gungthang Tsultrim was buoyant about the success of the feature film he had directed and produced. *Roof of the World*, filmed in Himachal Pradesh and Spiti, was the first film by a Tibetan refugee with actors from the Clement Town settlement. The film had had a successful screening in Dehra Dun with many of its actors in attendance. According to Jinpa, who also acted in the film, the event was boisterous. He remarked how surprised he had been seeing himself and others magnified on the screen. Everyone had looked different from what they imagined themselves to be. It was the first time Tibetans had seen a film in which every actor was known to them as friend, neighbor, uncle, or mother. Jinpa recalled how they were teased and celebrated simultaneously! Tsultrim had been happy that night. He had expressed his wish to show the movie in theaters throughout India. According to the film's promotional flyer distributed in 1978, the film was screened for the President of India, Neelam Sanjiva Reddy, on June 23, at the Rashtrapati Bhavan, the presidential palace, in Delhi.

At the time of his death, Gungthang Tsultrim had also been promised funding to build more homes in Clement Town by MYRADA, a nonprofit organization in Bangalore, but the expansion project had been momentarily stalled due to objections from Tibetans living in the vicinity and, the Thirteen suspected, from some exile officials. Letters sent from Tibetans in Mussoorie and Rajpur to local Indian officials indicated they wished to live in a government-run settlement, not in Tsultrim's settlement.

Longtime Clement Town residents such as Jinpa and Sonam Tobden believed that Gungthang Tsultrim's plans to expand upset many local Tibetans, who accused Tsultrim of diverting funds they believed should have gone to the exile government.[21] A letter from Gungthang Ngodup, Tsultrim's brother, to the district magistrate in Dehra Dun on June 27, 1979, indicates that the struggle continued after Tsultrim's death. Ngodup writes that some Tibetans were instigated to write to the local government and to the exile Tibetan leaders with "false accusations" against Clement Town residents.

Not too long before his death, Gungthang Tsultrim had remarked to some of the younger men in Clement Town that the Thirteen had accomplished what it had set out to do. The goal of establishing diverse monasteries and settlements had been achieved. Luthoktsang Chime, who lived in Kathmandu when I spoke to him in 2015, had spent a few months in Clement Town in the 1970s. His friends had been itching to organize a Dokham (Amdo and Kham) youth group with programs advocating for Tibetan independence. Gungthang Tsultrim had advised them to first avail themselves of the opportunities in the settlement; he pointed out that they could study their diverse cultural practices. Tsultrim had felt the organization had reached a new phase of peaceful coexistence with the exile government. It had been a year or so since he had dismissed his bodyguards. "He had lost his fear of being killed by fellow Tibetans," Chime explained. Tsultrim had convinced Chime and his friends that the times had changed. He believed the exile government finally understood the Thirteen's goals and had even hoped to request the Dalai Lama to inaugurate the Gelug monastery in Clement Town.[22] Gungthang Tsultrim's murder was deeply personal for men like Luthok Chime, who looked up to him. Even after three decades, talking about it moved Chime to sadness.

By the mid-1970s, the Thirteen leaders met rarely, if at all. They were busy tending to their own growing pains. Kamrao, Mainpat, and Dolanji were not easily accessible by road. Neither did they have access to phones; messages had to be exchanged via telegrams. In addition to material difficulties, the settlements were struggling to keep their industries afloat. A report from Sonam Rapten, the director of Tibetan Industrial Rehabilitation (TIRS), to John Conway at the Tibetan Refugee Aid Society in Vancouver, Canada, on December 8, 1971, indicates that many of the agency's projects suffered losses due to mismanagement.[23] Dawa T. Norbu made the same observation in an editorial with a telling title, "TIRS: Not a Success Story," in the July 1973 issue of the *Tibetan Review*. Dawa Norbu stated that the small-scale industries established by the TIRS in the settlements run by the Thirteen "flopped." He dismissed the argument by TIRS that the incompatibility between the nomadic backgrounds of the Tibetans and the complex industrial setting made success difficult and pointed out that some of the industries did not need workers with special skills. He suggested that the problem was bad relations between Indian managers and Tibetan leaders, stating that individual interests had taken over the businesses.

Dawa Norbu's summary did not consider the unexpected challenges that beset the different settlements. For example, the Tibetan Khampa Industrial Society in Bir running the tea estate and factory was hampered in its production of tea in part because of old tea rollers, dilapidated factory buildings, and lack of shade-furnishing trees in the tea garden. They suffered heavy losses from 1971 to 1972. By 1975, it was futile to continue. Jamyang Gyaltsen Choklingtsang, then in his early twenties, recalled that Tibetans in Bir put an incredible amount of effort into the tea garden, but it had been impossible to break into the competitive tea market with their technology. Brewster had left in 1971, and the new TIRS administrators were less receptive to appeals for new equipment or operating funds from the Thirteen settlements. A TIRS report in June 1975 mentioned that the Nangchen and Kathok settlements had weak leaders, and the director suggested holding off funding new projects until competent leaders or external administrators took over.

In October 1972, Kalyan Singh Gupta, the general secretary of the Central Relief Committee of India led by J. B. Kripalani, toured the Thirteen settlements run by the TIRS. In his report sent to John S. Conway in Vancouver, Gupta advised transforming the settlements into agriculturally based communities supported by handicrafts. He saw little future in the industries set up in the previous decade by TIRS. He wrote that the lime kilns in the Kham Kathok settlement had been "silent" since March 1972, and the "settlers are unemployed." He mentioned that "Lama Shingkyong was not there" despite being informed about his visit. Gupta reported that the lime quarry in Kamrao too had been closed for the past year, and that many of the Tibetans had gone to sell sweaters for additional income. Gupta is not the only one to complain about Shingkyong Rinpoche's mismanagement of the settlement's funds. Tibetan elders in Sataun told me during my visit that the lime business would have been very profitable had Rinpoche invested the gains into the business instead of using the community's money to support his lavish lifestyle.

Gupta had more favorable impressions of the Derge Division in Bir and of Tashi Jong. He mentioned that the Derge Division had a good crop of soybeans and that Tibetans were producing carpets, shoulder bags, and shawls for sale. He described Khamtrul Rinpoche and Dorzong Rinpoche in the Tashi Jong settlement as actively dedicated to developing the settlement. Gupta wrote, "It won't be wrong to say that this settlement is near to self-sufficiency due to the far-sighted policies of Rev. Khamtul Rinpoche. Khamtul Rinpoche is greatly loved and respected by his own people. In the real sense it is a Craft Community."[24]

Pat Brewster had foreseen the need for trained administrators to help run the settlement businesses from the start. In his personal notes he mentions it was a huge task to find skilled and honest administrators (managers, accountants) to help the traditional leaders. Even if good administrators existed, he could not convince them to move to live "rough in a settlement in the depths of the country," when they could find better-paying jobs elsewhere.[25] He emphasized the need to train young Tibetans in basic administrative skills, and Dorothy, his wife, made that a reality. She created a live-in course in administration for fifteen young Tibetan men in Delhi. She taught basic arithmetic, bookkeeping, and English, and a Peace Corps volunteer gave typing lessons. The program was successful: thirteen of the fifteen young men trained that first year returned to assist their leaders in the settlements.

However, conditions that Brewster could not have predicted contributed to the businesses failing. He had envisioned that light industry would support wage earners and their dependents in the settlements, but two years after their establishment, he realized that many young men were missing. He found out that they had been recruited by the Indo-Tibetan Border Police, the CIA, and other organizations that offered more money. He writes, "Also, older men seemed scarce in the TIRS settlements for a large part of the time, especially in the summer," because they were working in the mountains building roads. Brewster realized the settlements "were a kind of home-base and dormitory with older, inactive men, women and children." He had hoped to end the exploitative roadwork that gave "no protection for families," but it still offered more wages than what the settlements could afford to pay.[26]

Brewster's personal papers indicate the many challenges of working in India in the 1960s. Raising money for the projects was hard, but the disbursement of the funds and the administration of TIRS was "a much more difficult job." There were corruption and bribery to contend with. He had kept a no-bribes policy for one and a half years, until a shipment of streptomycin promised for TB hospitals run by the church was held up in Calcutta. The port controller wouldn't release the medicine unless he got a "little something." Brewster writes that he refused to bribe the employee and sought high-level officers in the Indian government to help him. The medicine was eventually released, but it took time that he realized patients didn't have. This event made him evaluate his "sacred principles against someone's life," especially when they depended on him to help them.[27]

Cultural differences also complicated fundraising. For example, he writes that Tibetans expected TIRS to help them build a "lavish temple" in each settlement "out of funds given by Christian groups in the West." He could see the merit in the proposal—"the temple was more important to the Tibetans than a school"—but admits it placed him in a tricky position of explaining the situation to donors. In addition, there was "a lot of conspicuous expenditure going on among the Tibetan nobility in Delhi." He thought some of that money could have been diverted to building the temples.[28]

It was not just industries run by the Thirteen that were struggling in the 1970s. The TIRS projects run by the exile government had also shut down. For example, the woolen mill run by the Bir Tibetan Society (BTS) suffered heavy losses and had to sell off its machinery.

Many of its employees went back to road construction. Similarly, the fiberglass factory in Paonta Sahib had closed, and the blanket factory established afterward also ran into losses.

Contrary to rumors that Taiwan funded the Thirteen, the reports reveal the obstacles that the Thirteen faced. Brewster's letters indicate that international aid agencies had to choose between TIRS projects and those requested by the exile government, which often resulted in the postponement of much-needed help for the Thirteen. Letters and reports also indicate that Tibetans in the Thirteen settlements, like Tibetans elsewhere, were doing their best to learn to be self-sufficient, including reorganizing themselves into agricultural settlements when the small industries did not yield any profit. Loss of leadership made a huge difference in the spirit and well-being of the community. The Nangchen settlement in Bir and Kathok settlement in Sataun suffered a devastating loss in spiritual and civic leadership when Chokling Rinpoche and Kathok Ontrul Rinpoche passed away in the mid-1970s. The Nangchen settlement in Bir became the first among the Thirteen settlements to be run by the exile government in 1976 at the suggestion of Juchen Thupten Namgyal, then minister of the Information and Publicity Office.[29] The settlement remained part of the Thirteen despite its new relationship with the government. There is no evidence that the other settlements objected to their decision. The Thirteen's varying relationships with the exile government exemplify their individual autonomy within the organization.

Leaders of the Thirteen also made independent decisions regarding the Tibetan movement. In 1972, the group Bhod Rangwang Denpai Legul (Righteous Tibetan Freedom Movement), formed by politician and scholar Kalon Tripa Samdhong Rinpoche, introduced a resolution for all Tibetan refugees to make a nominal monthly contribution called the Freedom Seed Money toward running the exile government. In return, they would be given a document called the

Rangzen Lagtheb (Freedom Handbook), more commonly known as the green book.

Mimicking a passport, the green book still serves as the basis for claiming rights from the exile government but also for securing Tibetan citizenship in the future. The book symbolizes its holder's acknowledgment of the exile government as their legitimate government. Some groups within the Thirteen refused to apply for it. Some individuals in Mainpat applied but were denied by exile officials because they were seen to be on the "wrong path." Gungthang Tsultrim's attitude regarding the green book is clear in a letter to Namkha Dorje in January 1978. He stated that it was up to individuals in the Thirteen to do as they pleased, but he personally felt that Tibetans should pay their dues as much as possible. He was upset at rumors that the Karmapa had advised the Thirteen not to. Tsultrim believed these rumors were spread by people who wanted to disturb the good bond between the Dalai Lama and the Karmapa.

For some members of the Thirteen the green book was an opportunity to protest against their exclusion; for some it was a way to make peace and to represent themselves. Lobsang Gyatso from the Bon settlement in Dolanji told me that he had wanted to pay dues to support the Tibetan movement. He had believed it was part of the practice of democracy. He felt the Bon community had achieved their goal of building a place where they were safe to practice their faith. The government had also acknowledged Bon formally. In 1977, a Bon religious representative was elected to the sixth assembly of the Tibetan parliament alongside representatives from the Gelug, Kagyu, Nyingma, and Sakya schools.[30] This was monumental for Gyatso. In 1975 when the Bon community had first petitioned for representation in the parliament, there had been only one vote in their favor from a total of fifteen legislators. That vote had come from a single mother representing Kham. That, I was to learn from Bonpo *khenpos* in 2015, was Tsering Choden Dhompa, my mother.

Bon representation in the Tibetan parliament in 1977 had meaning for those of the Bon faith. It also gave some hope to the Thirteen that the government was beginning to see them a little differently. Gungthang Tsultrim's assassination shattered the brief feeling of acceptance. Tsultrim had been murdered by a fellow Amdowa who had friends in Clement Town. Sonam Tobden in Clement Town said he had known Tenzin, the alleged assassin. They had first met in camp 2 in Bylakuppe around 1962. At eighty-three, Tobden had a sharp memory and equally astounding energy. When we met in 2022, I had to interrupt him a few times during the interview to ask if he needed to rest or to drink some tea.

Tobden said that he and Tenzin had worked together, side by side in Bylakuppe. Tobden had left his job as soon as he received Gungthang Tsultrim's invitation to live in Clement Town. He was given a house in Amdo *rakor*, where he still lives. In 1977, he ran into Tenzin in Clement Town, who told him that he was in Rajpur learning to be a mechanic and to get a license to drive trucks. Tenzin had visited Clement Town a second time to ask Gungthang Tsultrim to write him a letter of support for his intended course. Tobden had invited Tenzin to his house, and while chatting, he noticed Tenzin's spectacles. "They had a peculiar arm," he said to me, attempting to draw a picture.[31] Tobden said he had remarked on this odd feature, and Tenzin had replied that he was wearing glasses to protect his eyes while riding the motorbike. Tenzin didn't have an eyesight problem. Tobden did not immediately recognize the spectacles when they were recovered near Tsultrim's house on the night of his murder, but by and by, he remembered them from his conversation with Tenzin. The following day, Tobden went to Mussoorie, where Tenzin's wife worked, pretending to have a package for her. Tenzin's wife informed him that Tenzin was away in Ludhiana for work and hadn't been home for a week.

"Are these his glasses?" Tobden had asked, extending the pair of spectacles toward her.

"Yes," she confirmed.

Tobden returned to Clement Town with the confirmation he needed. Tsultrim's friends had conducted a search for Tenzin, but by then he had disappeared. They heard he had left for Nepal. Tenzin was found in Kathmandu, arrested, and brought back to India, and was released in June 1983 after serving a few years in jail. "He was received as a hero in Dharamsala," Tobden said.[32]

Tenzin's side of the story was published in the June–July issue of the *Tibetan Review* in 1983. He insisted he was innocent, had been framed by the Thirteen, and received an unfair trial. He admitted to having been in Clement Town and asking Tsultrim for a reference letter, but asserted that he had left in May 1978 after completing his course. He stated he had been in Kollegal in South India at the time of Tsultrim's murder.[33]

BLACK FRIDAY

The day of Gungthang Tsultrim's assassination is denoted as "The Black Friday" in the pamphlet *The Assasination [sic] of Gungthang Tsultrim*. Written in Tibetan and English, the text makes a direct appeal to the government of India for protection and to the Indian press for support. It suggests that Gungthang Tsultrim's death triggered fear among those who shared his ideas of meeting the same fate—being "eliminated" under similar circumstances.

The pamphlet's significance today is different. In 1978, there was a great deal at stake for its authors. The English version is printed while the Tibetan version is handwritten. Tibetans outside Clement Town saw the English version reproduced in the *Tibetan Review* in August 1978, two months after Gungthang Tsultrim's death. The Thirteen members living outside did not know of the authors. Two elders I spoke to suspected that Gungthang Ngodup, Tsultrim's brother, had written it. Some others think there was a young Western man in Clement Town who might have helped write the English version.[34]

The Assasination [sic] of Gungthang Tsultrim, referred to in Tibetan texts and minutes of meetings as *Pasang Nakpo* (*The Black Friday*), hailed Gungthang Tsultrim as a beloved Tibetan leader who died as a martyr for "his Amdo and Khampa brethern [sic]." The pamphlet extended Tsultrim's appeal to a monolithic group of people, Amdowas and Khampas, when in reality a smaller number of people from the regions looked up to him as a leader. The pamphlet indicated that "Mr. Tsultrim" was from "Amdo province," a region where people viewed themselves as politically "free." Tsultrim had dared object to exile government administrators who neglected minority groups and had no "love or regard" for Amdowas and Khampas. According to the pamphlet, he had established the Tibetan Welfare Association keeping only the "welfare of Amdos and Khampas in view." The pamphlet mentions His Holiness the Dalai Lama was also from Amdo and that the administrators had made him an "ornamental head." It was trying to establish that the Dalai Lama's power was curtailed by certain administrators, as is believed to have been the case with previous Dalai Lamas in Tibet.

The vilification of the "ministers" of the Dalai Lama's government is not unique in Tibetan history. The Dalai Lama himself has been critical of the old system, and Gyalo Thondup writes in his memoir that there was no law and justice in old Tibet.[35] However, *The Black Friday* was critiquing a reformed polity that was put in place by the Fourteenth Dalai Lama.

The pamphlet suggested that the Lhasa government had exercised "effective" control only over one province, thus upsetting the national narrative that stressed the primacy of the three regions of Tibet. History texts in the present acknowledge that in 1950 many territories in Kham and Amdo fell outside the political mandate of the Tibetan government in Lhasa, but during the early years in exile, this historical fact was not publicly stated out of concern that it could be marshaled to support Chinese assertions of suzerainty and sovereignty over regions of Kham and Amdo.[36] The pamphlet furthermore indicated the formation of an emergent, newly configured minority political subject.

While Tibetan journals were slow to write about Gungthang Tsultrim's murder, Indian newspapers did not shy away from the mysterious event. On July 22, 1978, a month after Tsultrim's assassination, *The Current*, a Bombay weekly, published an article under the sensational headline, "Dalai Lama Aide Strikes to Kill." This article reported that Gungthang Tsultrim's death was "rocking" the Tibetan community. It suggested that the issue at the heart of the "cloak and dagger story of intrigue and death" was Tsultrim's opposition to the "Dalai Lama's Golden" coterie.[37] Tsultrim had also angered them because of his effort to "Indianize" his community by petitioning for Indian citizenship in 1971.

The newsweekly *Vanguard* from Dehra Dun ran a story introducing the fifty-three-year-old Gungthang Tsultrim as a man respected in Tibetan circles. The paper suggested that Tibetans close to the Dalai Lama looked unfavorably upon Tsultrim's ideas to "integrate" in India. It stated that Gungthang Tsultrim's influence with foreign donors was another reason for the tension between him and Tibetan exile leaders. These devastating details of Tibetan internal strife were new to the Indian public and painful to the Tibetan community. On July 26, 1978, the *Deccan Herald* reported that over four hundred Tibetans in Bangalore protested the slanderous and malicious report against the Dalai Lama published in "a Bombay weekly." The protest march was organized by the Tibetan Youth Congress, who accused the Thirteen's *Black Friday* and the article by *The Current* of "defaming" the Dalai Lama and disintegrating the solidarity of Tibetans. The *Tibetan Review* and *Rangzen (Freedom)* magazines published numerous letters by Tibetans who sought to rectify the supposedly slanderous historical untruths in the pamphlet and to rule out any official conspiracy in Gungthang Tsultrim's death. One letter in the

Rangzen summer issue as well as in the *Tibetan Review* stated that although Dokham—Amdo and Kham—were far from the Tibetan capital, the pamphlet's assertion that "Dokham people considered themselves always free is misleading which at the moment can only be called a historical myth."[38] The Regional Working Committee of the Tibetan Youth Congress in Bangalore wrote in the *Tibetan Review*, "There is no account in the Tibetan History, where Dokham people enjoyed independent status."[39]

The letters reveal what Tibetans outside those regions understood of history and how Tibetans saw any form of critique of the exile government as being anti-Tibet. They also point to the incommensurability between the decentralized and flexible features of Eastern Tibetan polities, built over generations of relations between tightly knitted clans, and the modern Tibetan state, held together by concepts over which Tibetans were not totally in control.

The Thirteen members sent a letter to the editor at *The Current* on September 20, 1978, informing them that the published article had caused "considerable anger" in the community. The Thirteen criticized the story's format as misleading and "quite unjustifiable." The photograph of the Dalai Lama had been placed in the top corner, alongside the sensational headline. The Thirteen asked *The Current* to publish an apology, and the editors of the newspaper issued one clarifying that they had published the article in good faith.[40]

The Thirteen also wrote to the cabinet of the exile government asking for a meeting to speak about their leader Gungthang Tsultrim's murder, as well as to discuss their place in the Tibetan society. Tsultrim had not been able to meet with the government to discuss the allegations written in the Taiwanese *Young Army Journal*. The Thirteen leaders now intended to seek justice for his murder, in addition to clarifying a list of seven agenda items with the exile government. These seven items appear banal, even petty, today, but the goal then was to seek recognition and accountability from the exile government. A meeting between the Thirteen and the government, represented by the Standing Committee of Assembly, a few members of parliament, and cabinet members, was scheduled for eight days from July 26 through August 1, 1978. This would be the first face-to-face meeting between the two parties.

Members of the Thirteen expressed to me that for years they had asked for the chance to present their point of view, if not to His Holiness the Dalai Lama, then to those close to him. The question "Who is the Thirteen?" that had echoed through the meeting hall of Tibetans in early 1978 had been more than rhetorical. The Thirteen wanted to give answers in person.

8

THE PEOPLE'S GOVERNMENT

Tremors of mild agitation shook Dharamsala on July 25, 1978, when many members of the Thirteen arrived in town. The *Tibetan Review* reported that the exile government had invited one representative from each of the settlements to the meeting. Instead of thirteen, as agreed upon, 150 individuals had shown up to discuss their "complaints." Each person had paid their own way and found their own accommodation with friends, relatives, or at a hotel in lower Dharamsala. A dozen men took the bumpy bus ride from Kamrao to Clement Town, and from there to Dharamsala. It took a few days for Yugyal and his friends to get from Mainpat to Dharamsala. Bir and Tashi Jong were represented in larger numbers, as they only had a short bus ride.

The Tibetans from the meeting who were alive when I interviewed them in 2015 and again in 2022 provided vivid memories, as though the event was printed on every new layer of epidermal skin in their body. The details, including quoted speech, bore a striking faithfulness to the minutes of the meetings kept by the cabinet and captured in cassette recordings. By contrast, a note-taker for the meeting who was my mother's colleague and friend said that he could not recall any exchanges, only that government officials had been nervous and worried for their safety. They had discussed how to exit the room if the situation got out of hand. The Thirteen members sat in rows of chairs facing the Tibetan government representatives, who sat behind one large table. Member of Parliament Tsering Choden Dhompa, my mother, was among the officials. The tone of the first meeting was emotional. Even the minutes written by the official note-taker indicates that the Thirteen expressed great sorrow.

I once overheard my mother describe the meetings as being "tense and sad" to a lama in Boudhanath in Kathmandu. She had felt both protective of the Thirteen members, who had come with their emotions drawn out like handkerchiefs, and ill at ease, recognizing that the intensity of their emotions could be misunderstood. She had not spoken much during the meetings, Yugyal recalled. He had stated that my mother's presence had been comforting to him and other members who knew her. He had not said much at the meeting either. Members of the Thirteen were speaking "all at once."[1]

On the first day, the representatives of the exile government assured attendees that they trusted the Thirteen's disassociation from Taiwan.[2] Finance Minister Tsering Dorjee acknowledged it was important to clear the matter officially because the story published in the *Young Army Journal* had caused a great deal of anxiety within the exile community. He invited the Thirteen to share their thoughts.

In his opening address, Dzongnang Rinpoche from Clement Town stated that the meeting was not an outcome of a happy occasion but of sadness and hopelessness. The Thirteen were meeting face to face with exile officials to clear rumors about their alleged relationship with the MTAC. He confessed he was afraid to speak up. Nevertheless, he indicated the Thirteen were present to offer their opinion, as befitted the democracy initiated by His Holiness the Dalai Lama. Dzongnang Rinpoche assured the government that the Thirteen had not opposed His Holiness. On the contrary, they had endeavored to follow his instructions to assist the exile establishment and to be less of a burden. Tibetans had fled their country to preserve Buddhism and their culture, and the Thirteen had stayed true to this commitment. Dzongnang Rinpoche asserted that the exile government had many accomplished and dedicated employees, but not one person had surpassed Gungthang Tsultrim's capabilities. Tsultrim had shrugged off warnings from many people that his life was in danger. He had believed he had done nothing to harm the government and had no fear of retribution. He pointed out the paradox: Tsultrim had escaped being killed by the Chinese, only to die at the hands of fellow Tibetans.

Members of the Thirteen had neither "horns on their head nor tails on their behinds," Dzongnang Rinpoche asserted: they were not the devil and had not brought disgrace to Tibet.[3] He said he was thinking and speaking like a frog in a small pond and expressed the Thirteen's disappointment in Jetsun Pema for denouncing them as the internal enemy at a public gathering of Tibetan officials and community members. He pointed out that she was not an ordinary person, implying that her condemnation of the Thirteen carried weight.

Dorzong Rinpoche from Tashi Jong, who had succeeded Gungthang Tsultrim as the Thirteen's general secretary, echoed these sentiments. He assured exile representatives that members of the Thirteen had come to smooth relations with the government. They hoped to find a way to live in the Tibetan society without discrimination. He pointed to the government's one-sided receptivity to public excoriations against the Thirteen, while ignoring their repeated pleas to speak on their behalf or to give them fair representation. He stated that the government's silence and their reluctance to adjudicate on behalf of the Thirteen bolstered accusations that they were not obeying His Holiness the Dalai Lama and were a threat to Tibet's freedom. Dorzong Rinpoche explained that the Thirteen had been established to protect Kham and Amdo languages and culture, not to create disharmony in the community.

Did the government need the Thirteen? Did they intend to abandon and cast the Thirteen aside from the 80,000 Tibetans in exile? Dzongnang Rinpoche asked. The suggestion made during the general meeting that the Thirteen should be banished implied that both the public and the government considered them harmful members of the community. The Thirteen were in Dharamsala to receive the government's honest responses.[4]

Ugyen Topgyal Rinpoche from Bir said that Thirteen members feared meeting the same fate as Gungthang Tsultrim. Despite being guiltless, they had been made to look guilty. He expressed his disappointment in exile administrators for their willingness to believe the rumors without the benefit of evidence. He pointed out that private verbal and written assurances to the Thirteen that they were not opposing the government furnished by some exile officials were contradicted by public expulsions by other officials.

Members of the Thirteen asked which of their actions constituted being antigovernment. Various members shared their experiences living on the social margins of the exile Tibetan society. Amdo Tenpa, who had traveled from Clement Town, stated that His Holiness had said becoming self-reliant was one way to help the Tibetan cause. He revealed he had been told by Home Minister Wangdu Dorjee: "If you stay in Clement Town, you have gone against His Holiness the Dalai Lama. If you stay in Rajpur, you're following him." Such statements made those living in Clement Town feel like orphans. He said the cabinet was "the one we have to whom we can express our grief," and he pleaded that the cabinet should either take care of them or allow them to live in Clement Town, where they felt cared for.[5]

Jamyang Gyaltsen, who had come from Bir, asked how it had come to be that the Thirteen were so maligned. What activities had the Thirteen initiated that destroyed the Tibetan community's religion and politics?

"Did we accept money [salary] from Taiwan? Who gave us the money? Tell us clearly," he pleaded, and noted, "We gave our blood and flesh to bring His Holiness to India." "We" refers to the Chushi Gangdrug members who escorted the Dalai Lama from Tibet to India. Many members of the Thirteen had family who had served in the Chushi Gangdrug in India or had fought in their local resistance armies in Tibet. They had sacrificed their lives for the nation. The Thirteen had built settlements and established monasteries. "What have we done that is against His wishes?" Jamyang Gyaltsen inquired.[6]

Tsewang Tashi expressed his loss of faith in the exile government. Gungthang Tsultrim's murder had devastated him.

"Go ahead, do whatever you want with us," he declared. "Be transparent if you intend to expel us," he repeated.

Gungthang Tsultrim was valuable to Tibet, yet he was murdered.

"As for useless and unwanted men like me, give me permission to leave the community," he added. Tsewang Tashi indicated that the Thirteen had no official power.[7]

During the course of the meeting, the Thirteen repeatedly pressed the government to state its position on Jetsun Pema's indictment of them on a public platform. They asked if Jetsun Pema had been speaking on behalf of the government. If she had expressed a personal opinion, as Alak Jigme Rinpoche, the speaker, had intimated, then why had the government remained silent? How was it that the Thirteen were not allowed to express their own personal opinions in public? Was it the Kashag's or the speaker's point of view that the Thirteen were not following the leadership of His Holiness the Dalai Lama? Far from a minor matter, their concerted attempt to get cabinet members and exile officials to respond to parliament member Alak Jigme Rinpoche's and Jetsun Pema's public condemnation had profound implications for the fledgling project of Tibetan nationalism and democracy in exile. At stake was the question of who had permission to speak in Tibetan society and to represent the people. They were also indirectly asking who wielded power behind the scenes. Did the United Party's exceptional place in the Tibetan community have something to do with Gyalo Thondup?

For over a decade, the Thirteen had been questioning the United Party's privilege of place in Tibetan exile politics. The party was permitted to participate in the annual meetings held by the government, to organize official meetings, and to speak on behalf of the people as well as, it seemed, the government. Why was the party not bound to the same rules and standards as other organizations? What accounted for its exceptionality? How was it, they asked, that the Thirteen was criticized for taking matters into their own hands and not following the government when members of the United Party did whatever they wanted? The Thirteen's questions were prompted by their concern that challenging the United Party came with potential backlash from the community because it also meant critiquing members of the *yabshi* (family members of the Dalai Lama), whom they viewed as supporting the United Party.

The cabinet minister Tsering Dorjee encouraged the Thirteen to speak their minds, as appropriate in the democratic system the exiled community had adopted. He stated that if officials representing the government had made mistakes, then the government would be happy to respond to clear up the confusion.

The discussions regarding the *Young Army Journal* article ended on a conciliatory note by the end of the second day. The Thirteen requested all exile officials to raise their hands if they found them to be blameless, and all the officials present did so. Likewise, the officials asked the Thirteen if they agreed to produce a press release rejecting the allegations in the *Young Army Journal* about relations between the Thirteen and the MTAC, and the Thirteen members too raised their hands. They requested the cabinet to clear the organization's name by publicly recognizing their innocence at the next general meeting. They reiterated that the government's silence only served to condone the lies spread about them. The officials gave their assent.

Once the Thirteen members were assured of the government's support, they returned to the question about belonging. On the third day of the meeting, Dorzong Rinpoche asked if the government would permit the Thirteen to leave the exile political community if they saw the Thirteen as going against the government. They did not wish to continue to be seen as troublemakers. He explained that they wanted unity and peace just as much as the exile government did. In response, a cabinet minister stated that the Tibetan government was a people's government, alluding to the difficulty of responding to a request from the people to opt out of being members. But, responded Dzongnang Rinpoche, hadn't exile leaders already publicly expelled the Thirteen from the society?[8]

Drawupon Rinchen Tsering, who was a member of the Tibetan parliament as well as one of the Thirteen leaders, suggested that the Thirteen members should be permitted to express their grief and the cabinet should be willing to listen to them. He pointed to the stalemate before them: the Thirteen were asking to leave the community and the cabinet had no response. He concluded that the people need the government, and the government needs its people.

Dorzong Rinpoche persisted, restating his question in more pointed terms: "Are we needed in the society or not? Are we needed in the fight for Tibet's freedom? Thus far, if you think we have done anything for Tibet's freedom, will you acknowledge it, will you let the rest of the community know your position?"[9]

The discussion had moved back to the concerns expressed on the first day, about the Thirteen's place in the community. Even as members repeatedly sought to convey the harm they had suffered at the hands of the United Party, whose authority seemed to overlap with that of the government, the government representatives appeared not to comprehend how fully the Thirteen had felt abandoned. Instead, the officials explained that abandoning members of a community because it found fault with them was not a democratic practice. Having failed to clarify the United Party's relationship to government authority, they reiterated that the government did not support the denunciations of the Thirteen. They stated that all Tibetans were needed to achieve the goal of Tibetan independence and it was not permissible for the Thirteen to leave the community.

Like Drawupon, Dzongnang Rinpoche pointed out the impasse at hand: the Thirteen could not get permission from the government to leave the community, and yet elected administrators, civic leaders, and ordinary citizens had the authority to repeatedly banish the Thirteen from Tibetan society. He stated that his hope of finding someone who would listen to their pain had been dashed and there was not one person in the government who could address their sorrowful predicament.

Members of the Thirteen returned to the question of belonging, framing it in multiple ways over the many days: "Are we valued by the government? Will you speak up for us? Are we needed in this struggle?" These questions indicate how crucial recognition from the government, which also meant recognition from His Holiness the Dalai Lama, was to the Thirteen. And perhaps this is what it came down to in the end: Tibetans seek recognition from the Dalai Lama because his approval has meaning to them and defines their place in Tibetan exile society. Or, to put it in another way, Tibetans' relationship to the Dalai Lama shapes how Tibetans feel and are remembered.[10]

In a briefing on the early days of the meeting, the *Tibetan Review* described the Thirteen members as having shown animosity and contempt for the Tibetan government. Members of the settlements who had attended admitted they had been unruly. Some of them gave long impassioned speeches, some had angry outbursts, and some even threatened to harm officials. Shingkyong Tulku from Sataun, for example, banged on the table, preventing the parliament's deputy speaker from speaking. The men stomped their feet to create a drumming echo to drown out the words of exile representatives.

They had lived with pain for so long, and they wanted to hear answers face to face.

"We behaved badly," a friend admitted, and added that it was the photograph of His Holiness in the room that curbed their emotions a bit.

As bumpy as the discussions were, the two parties had settled into a form of reconciliation by the fourth day. Then everything turned upside down on July 30, the sixth day of the talks. Government representatives indicated that His Holiness the Dalai Lama had expressed concern over the pamphlet *The Assasination [sic] of Gungthang Tsultrim*.[11] He believed it challenged the government's twenty years of effort to take care of Tibetans in exile. On the night of August 2, 1978, the leaders of the Thirteen were called to an urgent meeting with members of the cabinet and parliament in a restaurant in lower Dharamsala to discuss this new development.[12] Exile officials, including my mother, stated they understood that the pamphlet had not been written with everyone's approval and input but disapproved of it for a number of reasons. It went against Tibetan policy. It obstructed and went against His Holiness's work to unite all Tibetans. The regional focus implied that one region didn't like the other, which was sad given that inside Tibet, Tibetans from all regions rebelled against the Chinese. And the statement that His Holiness the Dalai Lama was an ornamental head was faulty and harmful, as it intimated he had no power. The brochure provided material the Chinese would delight in and had the potential to disappoint Tibetans inside Tibet.

Exile officials remarked that the Thirteen had no right to speak on behalf of the people of Kham and Amdo. They reminded the Thirteen that it was a welfare organization, not meant to play a role in national politics. The officials concluded that the doubts and suspicions on both sides could not be surmounted overnight after all; future meetings would have to be held to clear up the misunderstandings between the government and the Thirteen members.[13]

The tenor of the meeting had shifted by that sixth day. Knowledge of the Dalai Lama's displeasure weakened the Thirteen's resolve. The position of exile officials had also shifted from more receptive to proscriptive. Now the Thirteen were under fire to answer questions regarding their loyalty. Dorzong Rinpoche stated that the Thirteen had affirmed they had no intentions of hurting the government. The members acknowledged that while the pamphlet offered a different perspective, it contained some mistakes. They chose to accept responsibility instead of blaming a few members for producing it. They agreed that if His Holiness felt the pamphlet was problematic and harmful to the community, they would issue a statement of clarification. Ten exile representatives and a few members of the Thirteen formed a smaller conclave to discuss the language for this statement. The officials found the first draft prepared by the Thirteen members inadequate and asked the Thirteen to revise, which they did. They were instructed to get signatures from representatives of each of the settlements. Then this statement was to be made available to the Tibetan public.

In return, and yet again, the Thirteen requested the cabinet to publicly announce support for them in a press release or at the next annual meeting of Tibetan administrators. Once again, the officials agreed to do so. The meeting concluded with the clarification statement, in the form of a press release in English, being signed by twenty members of the Thirteen. It was in essence an apology.

The statement was published on September 20, 1978, under the title "Declaration of the Association of Thirteen Groups." It declared that the pamphlet on the "assassination of Mr. Gungthang Tsultrim" was not written by a Tibetan and that it contained "certain inaccuracies." The statement clarified, first, that "Lhasa is the capital city of Tibet. Kham, Amdo, and U-Tsang, the three provinces, have constituted the one nation of Tibet with the central government at Lhasa." Second, His Holiness the Dalai Lama had always enjoyed "full authority and decision-making powers." Third, the government-in-exile led by His Holiness the Dalai Lama was the only "true and legitimate Government of Tibet," and all the "people of the three Provinces of Tibet recognize this Government and they all enjoy equal rights." The document focused on proving the legitimacy of the exile government, both historically and in exile. The twenty men who signed were aware of the political relationships they did or did not have with the Lhasa government prior to the Chinese invasion of Tibet.[14] The turn in the attitude of the officials as well as of the Thirteen revealed that while the desire for reconciliation might have guided the meeting, ultimately their decision was based on guessing what might least hurt the Tibetan movement and the Dalai Lama.

Juchen Thupten, who was the minister of information at that time, and Drawupon Rinchen Tsering and Tsering Choden Dhompa, parliamentary representatives of Kham, met with the Dalai Lama to discuss the *Black Friday* pamphlet. Following that meeting, they advised the Thirteen to return to their settlements. Members who were present at the meeting recall that Juchen Thupten promised he would follow up on the government's agreement to clear the Thirteen's name to the Tibetan public. The Thirteen trusted that he would be able to make good on his promise.

Dorzong Rinpoche informed the Thirteen that His Holiness was disappointed with them and there was nothing more to be done. They had hoped for a chance to express their pain to His Holiness the Dalai Lama and had not intended to upset him. They felt they had achieved the opposite of their desires and had nobody to turn to.

When I met Yugyal in Mainpat in 2015, he said that it still hurt to think about the meeting. Everything had been going well and then had turned in the other direction because of *The Black Friday*.

The night before the sixth day of the meeting, Home Minister and chair of the cabinet Kalon Wangdu Dorjee had banged at the gate to the Dalai Lama's private office, asking to be let in. He expressed his fear that the Thirteen would harm him and asked to take shelter inside the private office. Ugyen Topgyal Rinpoche from Bir had heard that Wangdu Dorjee slept on a table there.[15] The next morning he is believed to have met the Dalai Lama by chance and explained why he was in the office. His Holiness is believed to have first heard of the pamphlet at that moment.

Although the meeting was unsatisfactory to both parties, that discussions of this nature took place is noteworthy. The event provides a glimpse into the attempts by the two parties to discuss the rights and duties of Tibetans in their precarious positions as refugee-citizens.

The Thirteen members' grievances of being subjected to moral policing and social ostracization by groups in power and their insistence that the government hear them out also speaks volumes about the challenges the Tibetan exile administration faced in its unusual task of having to unite its people and build a community of value that had no unified territory or territorial right. The Thirteen had reached out to the government several times, informing them of small and large acts of discrimination against them by the United Party and government officials. They had also offered alternate ways of working with the government that might have helped strengthen the community's bonds. Letters from the Kashag to the Thirteen also convey that the government was attempting to do its best to clear the rumors about the Thirteen within the community. Contrary to Lodi Gyaltsen Gyari's opinion, Yugyal and other elders in Mainpat believed deeply that the Thirteen had been driven to form their settlements not by resentment but by care for their clan members and hope of recognition and acceptance from their government.

The Thirteen members' despair is evident in the letter they sent to the Tibetan cabinet on August 2, 1978. The letter expresses concern about the lack of response from the government on the seven points the members had attempted to raise over the course of the year and during their meetings in Dharamsala. Instead, the writers state, they had discussed "other things," and the exile government's understanding had been "upside down," since nothing had come of the exchanges between the two groups.[16] The Thirteen compared their hope for a dialogue with the government with that of an individual returning empty-handed from the spring or tap for water. They concluded on a note of resignation that there was nothing left for the people to do, and nothing to hope for.

Government minutes of the meetings state that all parties lost the opportunity for dialogue because of the emotional state of the Thirteen members. However, the exile government's actions afterward reveal that something else might have been afoot. The government did not explicitly exonerate the Thirteen of the charges as it had promised to do more than once during the meeting. Instead, it published a press release in English titled, "In reply to Allegations Contained in the Pamphlet 'The Assassination of Gungthang Tsultrim,'" which obliquely implicated the group even as it declared upfront that members of the Tibetan Welfare Association (the Thirteen's registered name) had indicated the pamphlet was conceived by a "well-connected Indian" and was "issued by a few Tibetans" in their name.[17] The press release came out from the exile government's Information and Publicity Office on August 9, 1978. It is a remarkable document that states its intention and authority to offer the truth on Tibetan history and polity. In disproving the contents of *The Black Friday*, the government reveals its idea of historical or national truth.

The government's press release pointed out the following harmful "untruths": first, it described discussions about Kham and Amdo's autonomy from the Tibetan government as "baseless" and "a very un-Tibetan notion, first invented by the Chinese with the aim of dividing Tibetans so that when the Tibetan fight for independence is won, the Chinese will have to give up only one or two regions of Tibet. All Tibetans are aware of the Chinese policy of Divide and Rule."[18] In truth, the authors of the pamphlet were circumspect in describing the relations among the three regions, illustrating that they understood the sensitivity around it. What the pamphlet had actually stated was that due to the distance of Amdo and Kham from Lhasa (the journey took six months on horseback), the Lhasa government "exercised their effective authority only over one province, i.e. Lhasa."[19] The pamphlet continued that the people of Kham and Amdo considered themselves free. However, all Tibetans, including those from Kham and Amdo, had the "greatest respect and love for His Holiness the Dalai Lama" and considered him "The God-Incarnate."

Next, the press release stated that allegations of His Holiness the Dalai Lama being a "prisoner" and merely an "ornamental head" were objectionable because they attempted to "belittle the sacred person of

His Holiness the Dalai Lama." Such actions only benefited "a non-Tibetan." Lastly, the press release objected to the pamphlet's descriptions of the exile government being run by "monied people from Lhasa," who discriminated against Amdos and Khampas, preventing them from being granted an audience with the Dalai Lama.

The press release offered the following facts to correct the pamphlet's allegations: the Tibetan administration offered financial support to many of the Thirteen settlements and was not against the Thirteen, nor did it oppose the "so-called 'rising popularity of the late Mr. Tsultrim'"[20]; exile officials were not responsible for Tsultrim's death; sixteen of the twenty-nine members of the highest decision-making body of the exile government were from the Amdo and Kham regions, which disproved the pamphlet's allegation that the government was controlled by wealthy "Lhasans" who were "deadly against" Tibetans from Kham and Amdo; all who wished to seek an audience with His Holiness must go through the same office and process; and all Tibetans enjoyed "equal rights" and representation under the Constitution of Tibet written in exile. It explained, "In our own office, six out of nine are from Kham and Amdo," and, furthermore, "everyone who does not deal in falsehood" knew that the Tibetan Welfare Association was composed of Khampas, Amdowas, and a large number of Tibetans from U-Tsang.[21] In other words, the organization was not established just for Amdowas and Khampas as indicated in the pamphlet. The government's press release also highlighted that the Amdowas and Khampas in the organization made up a small portion of the total Amdowas and Khampas in exile.

This official statement attempted to set the record straight on "baseless" allegations but provided very few historical facts of its own. It also set out to explain the "self-contradictory" statements in the pamphlet, which do exist, with contradictory remarks of its own. In doing so, the official statement revealed the exile government's positions:

1) It established the ideological character of Tibetan nationalism as having been constituted to oppose Communist China.
2) It identified history's task as to serve the project of Tibetan unity.
3) It stated that the pamphlet contradicted the "most obvious fact," that "His Holiness the Dalai Lama, as the head of the Tibetan Government-in-exile, is the indisputable temporal and religious leader of the Tibetan people and His decisions are final and binding and His pronouncements the final authority on any question."[22]

The press release confirmed what the United Party had been insisting on in its documents and most Tibetans accepted: that unity among Tibetans was crucial; the policies laid out by the government were to be followed; and both China and Taiwan were the enemies of Tibet. The writers of the brochure, described as "writer/agents/provocateurs," had intended to deceive the public and cause disunity among Tibetans. Their work was viewed as "un-Tibetan." The meaning of "un-Tibetan" is unclear. It seems to be linked to acts that might benefit the Chinese, but it can also be interpreted as linked to speech and acts that oppose or contradict the Dalai Lama or the exile government. For example, the authors of the pamphlet are described as "un-Tibetan" for writing that Kham and Amdo were not "somehow part of Tibet." The pamphlet's nod to a past political reality, their authors' reality, was seen to have served China's claims to sovereignty more than it did the struggle for Tibetan independence.

Likewise, belittling the "sacred person" of His Holiness the Dalai Lama by labeling him a mere ornamental head and alleging that Kham and Amdo people were neglected by the exile government are also described as "non-Tibetan" actions because they were not seen to benefit any Tibetan.

The exile government also responded to other contradictions in the *Black Friday* pamphlet. For example, it objected to the stand that the exile government had been against the Thirteen from its inception in light of the fact that the appointment of the Karmapa as the Thirteen's "head" had been "approved by His Holiness the Dalai Lama." In addition, it stated that delegates of the Thirteen had representation in the annual general conference.[23] It pointed out that the pamphlet's mention of Gungthang Tsultrim's opposition to the exile ministers as well as his reverence for the Dalai Lama was "self-contradictory" because the ministers were appointed by His Holiness and "any Tibetan who esteemed Him should also respect the Tibetan Government-in-Exile."[24] Undoubtedly, the press release conflated the two—the exile ministers and the Dalai Lama—leaving little to no room for criticizing the actions of the former. It did not mention that the organization had written a forthcoming public statement to clarify the details about the pamphlet, in collaboration with exile government officials.

After refuting the pamphlet's "provocative, baseless and malignant allegations," the concluding paragraph indicated that the "false and fratricidal provocations" were not composed by patriotic Amdowas and Khampas or by the general members of the Thirteen. Thus, the press release relayed the Thirteen's insistence that they owed no allegiance to the "treacherous" KMT regime without directly vouching for them.[25]

National consciousness, whether it is defined as the recognition of shared characteristics among members of a nation—and their difference from people of other nations—or as a recognition of being products of a shared history, is a critical force in independence struggles. Austrian thinker and politician Otto Bauer explains that it "becomes a determinant basis of human action" in its linkage to the national sentiment or the ability to see the specifics of one's nation and its difference from others.[26] Bauer calls this a "national sentiment."[27] National sentiments can give rise to methods of evaluation, whereby others' positive reception of things associated with one's nation is pleasurable and good while criticism is seen as a reproach. Bauer's analysis of difference is helpful in evaluating how challenging it can be to have an honest community dialogue if the very act of expressing opinions different from those held by the Dalai Lama or the government is in danger of being judged by fellow Tibetans as un-Tibetan and unpatriotic.

The Tibetan exile government's decision to publish and distribute the press release, after protracted meetings between the two parties had taken place and intimations that the conversations would continue at a later time, shows that protecting the Thirteen as members of the Tibetan community was not among the government's chief concerns. Indeed, the press release reinforced popular negative notions about the Thirteen. The August 1978 issue of the *Tibetan Review*—still the most popular journal in English at that time devoted to Tibetan affairs—also printed it.

The underlying message of *The Black Friday*—that perceived dissent against the government was not tolerated—was illustrated through the ensuing public denouncements, issued by both the government and fellow Tibetans. The cabinet sent a letter to the Chief Secretary of the Government of Uttar Pradesh on August 16, 1978, to clarify that the "leaflet" contained "a great deal of factual inaccuracies."[28]

Eric Hobsbawm, pointing to the difficulty of knowing how the nation is viewed "from below" in reasonably stable and experienced democratic systems, observes that there is little evidence of national consciousness's even or synchronous development among a people. In other words, it is hard to know how ordinary people, who are often at the receiving end of policies and propaganda of governments, spokesmen, and activists of nationalist or non-nationalist movements, actually see the nation.[29] While opinions expressed by the United Party and other political organizations, such as the Tibetan Youth Congress and the Tibetan Women's Association, indicated that they voiced the will of the people, these organizations were also closely aligned with the exile government. Albeit adjacent to the seat of power, they played a critical functionary role in vocalizing government policies and desires. At the same time, the people's effort to discredit the Thirteen was used by exile officials and functionaries to argue that their official ideologies democratically expressed the views of the Tibetan people.

One of the difficulties in writing about these past events has been considering how time has affected stories, characters, and what is agreed upon as being true or unfaithful to history. By attending to modes of historical expression that range from texts and written accounts to oral storytelling and the ephemera of community memory, this retelling of events does not seek to establish the supremacy of textual narrative but follows the styles in which the story of nation has been told from the margins.

All the odds were against the Thirteen, members say, even as they retell their story.

CONCLUSION
A Statement of Real Truth

Modern states are understood as heterogenous communities of people held together by a shared legal status and fixed in place through territorial sovereignty. But it is also through shared values that states claim legitimacy, as Bridget Anderson has written. A community of values signifies people who agree on common ideals and behavior. Those who are seen as breaking with the values, or as failing to be good citizens, are viewed as a disappointment and a threat to the local community as well as to the nation. These individuals are regarded as failed citizens from inside the community of values.

People who fall into this category of failed or not-quite-good-enough citizens become "tolerated" subjects who, according to Anderson, must "endlessly prove themselves" to have the right values.[1] The category includes rioters, criminals, and often the poor. It can extend to anyone seen as incapable of living up to the liberal ideals exhibited by the law-abiding and "hardworking good" citizen. In other words, the failed citizen is seen to lack both values and value. Like the noncitizens who exist outside the community of values, failed citizens exist in a conundrum: they do not have rights because they are believed to lack the values and do not have values because they lack rights. Banishment from a geographical territory places an individual outside the borders of physically demarcated space. Banishment from a community of values, by contrast, can be invisible, emotional, and internal.

The Thirteen felt that the exile government had made them outcasts by allowing the United Party to dictate terms of membership in the Tibetan society. Operating within the unbounded space of the Tibetan exile nation and being banished from the community of values meant perpetual alienation, which was enforced by public shaming, defamation of character, and campaigns of exclusion.[2] The Thirteen looked to the Tibetan government to officially absolve them of accusations of colluding with Taiwan. They were not willing to be tolerated as problems, much less excluded, without the chance to represent themselves. Their insistence on clarity with regard to their standing in the Tibetan society was born out of their experience of exclusion.

The Thirteen had never questioned the government's legitimacy, but the narrative suggesting otherwise was reinforced in part because of the press release issued by the government on August 9, 1978, condemning *The Assasination [sic] of Gungthang Tsultrim* pamphlet. Two letters written shortly after the government's press release illustrate the depth and breadth of the paranoia it elicited. In a letter addressed to the Indian Prime Minister Moraji Desai on August 13, 1978, about one hundred Khampas from Dharamsala questioned the Thirteen's authority to speak for Khampas and Amdowas. They emphasized that the Thirteen represented a small portion of the total number of Khampas in exile. In contrast, the letter writers professed to be living amicably with their "brothers" from the "U-Tsang and Amdo provinces" of Tibet. They named the exile government as the "only true and legitimate" government and stated that they faced no discrimination for being Khampas.[3] Although the letter does not reference *The Black Friday*, their arguments respond to its contents. The letter implies that the Thirteen were not committed to living amicably with their brothers and did not recognize the exile government as legitimate. The *Tibetan Review* reported that Amdowas from

Dharamsala had also sent a letter to Prime Minister Moraji Desai (and the Tibetan cabinet) on August 18, 1978, declaring they did not identify with the Thirteen's divisive regional politics.

The Kham Amdo Youth Organization from Bylakuppe wrote directly to the Thirteen denouncing them as followers of the Chinese Communist Party and labeling them "wolves in lamb's clothing." They described Dzongnang Rinpoche and Gungthang Ngodup as "Chinese spies." In a letter to the Kashag (cabinet) on September 20, the Thirteen stated that in the letter, the youth organization shamed them for stating in *The Black Friday* that Kham and Amdo were independent regions. Not a single Tibetan, the writers had claimed, accepted the views of the Thirteen, whose work had split the community and obstructed Tibetan freedom. The letter stressed that all of Tibet was one nation, one race, and one people. They warned the Thirteen to stay silent: "If you don't, then we have decided that there is nothing left to do but kill you."[14] The Thirteen wrote to the Kashag that they had done their best to stay devoted to the government and didn't want to publicly display these letters because it would hurt many Tibetans. They asked the government to pay heed to the death threats and to take responsibility, pointing out that Tibetans sending letters of denouncement were responding to the government's press release published in the *Tibetan Review* as well as the *Sheja* (a monthly journal in Tibetan published by the CTA). Lost in the details was the fact that the Thirteen had revised and published clarification on *The Black Friday*, with the government's help.

On September 28, 1978, representatives of the Amdo community in Dharamsala sought an audience with the Dalai Lama. This meeting is an example of the many roles the Dalai Lama has had to fulfill for the Tibetan people since he was fifteen. He has an impossible job and has carried it out with care toward the Tibetan people. Given the place that he holds in their hearts and the meaning they give to his every word, it is inevitable that there will always be Tibetans who will be interpreted as having disappointed him. In that meeting, the

Dalai Lama explained to the audience that independence for a united Tibet was a Tibetan objective, and it was not to be given up. He stated that the practice of democracy means making room for different ideas. He also indicated that the present moment was not the time for people from Kham and Amdo to speak as if their regions had not been under the Tibetan government. Tibetans had not been able to unite under a single government in the past, and the government in Lhasa had not catered to people in Amdo. However, the government-in-exile was ensuring equal representation for all regions and religious schools. Everyone, he reminded them, had suffered. All Tibetans had protested equally against the Chinese. He comforted the audience, saying that Tibetans should keep courage; they had truth on their side. They would have to face challenges with faith, even those challenges that arose within the community.

Referring to recent conflicts—most likely Gungthang Tsultrim's murder—the Dalai Lama stated there were bound to be conflicts in any society and Tibetans would have to face and challenge them, not avoid them. He thought it was good that the Thirteen had spoken face to face with the government and felt that some obstacles had been cleared and indicated there would be another opportunity for dialogue after some people's anger cooled down. This could be a reference to some members of the Thirteen, although he did not mention them by name. The Dalai Lama also assured the audience that if exile officials had made mistakes and there was no reasonable explanation for them, the government would apologize. He further stated that if the United Party and its officials had carried out activities without the government's knowledge, then they would be expected to apologize too. He was confident that doubts and misgivings would clear like the sky without clouds once people talked calmly with one another. He expressed doubt that people with "crooked horns" existed in the Tibetan community, but if there were people who misinterpreted facts and fell under other influences, a line would be drawn between "us" and "them," per both Buddhist karma and civil law.[5]

The Dalai Lama concluded that Gungthang Tsultrim's behavior was regrettable for Tibet in general, and for Amdo people and for Gelugpa in particular. Given the ambiguity around Gungthang Tsultrim's alleged offenses, it is difficult to know if the Dalai Lama was extending compassion toward Gungthang Tsultrim or confirming Gungthang Tsultrim as a disappointment. He did not elaborate on the regrettable activities Tsultrim had been involved with but stated that his death was awful and sad for everyone.

In his closing remarks, the Dalai Lama said that "we" are disappointed with the whole episode. It is not clear who "we" stands for—those in the room, the whole of the Tibetan community, or the Tibetan policy makers. His Holiness stated that the government condemned the murder and had nothing to do with it. He expressed his shock that a few people felt the government was responsible and explained that the accusation must have been made out of anger. He ended his address by stating that it was important to think logically and to be careful. Just because some Amdowas and Khampas had done something wrong, it was not good to shout *ki ho ho* (a victory cry or warrior's shout) and desire revenge; it was time to be peaceful instead.[6]

The Thirteen had expressed several times during their meeting with government officials that they had come to make peace. They had asked several times over many correspondences and in face-to-face meetings for the government to shield them from wrongful injuries by speaking the truth about them. The members of the Thirteen I knew well—and who would show their vulnerability by telling me how they felt—are no longer alive. They loved Tibet more than any other place in the world, and they understood their work to be to fight for it without evading the complexity of what that meant, living under very different conditions from the homeland they had left.

Carole McGranahan observes in her book *Arrested Histories: Tibet, the CIA, and Memories of a Forgotten War* that Chushi Gangdrug veterans want their resistance history to be socially known as well as to be part of national history, not forgotten. The veterans also recognize that for their history to be national history, the Dalai Lama would need to acknowledge the Chushi Gangdrug's contributions to Tibetan social and political life. There is pain in waiting for that acknowledgment; there is pain in wanting this recognition; and there is pain living with the nation's amnesia. Many of the members of the Thirteen who are also Chushi Gangdrug veterans understand this well. McGranahan translates their hearts' desire: "What they seek is not memory (they have that) but recognition" from the community, from the exile government, and most of all, from the Dalai Lama.[7]

During their face-to-face meeting with the exile officials in Dharamsala, members of the Thirteen had asked: Are we needed by the government? Have we done anything for the struggle?

Recognition, not revenge, is at the heart of these questions and of the politics of sorrow.

The desire for peace and the desire for recognition are related. For Tibetans, both are seen to emanate from the Dalai Lama. Without the opportunity to speak directly to him, without the Dalai Lama's recognition of their place in the society, the Thirteen probably felt their questions would remain unanswered. Why did the Thirteen never have an audience with the Dalai Lama? Was it because their petitions or requests for an audience never made it beyond government officials, as they suggested in *The Black Friday*? Or did they never make such a request, assuming they would not be granted one? These questions are vital not just because of the Dalai Lama's centrality to Tibetan society but also because of his unparalleled power to shape the Tibetan historical narrative. The regard Tibetans hold for the Dalai Lama is also sometimes manifested in their attempts to predict or interpret his thoughts and words about people and events to benefit themselves or discredit others.

The campaigns against the Thirteen continued to build after a group from Dharamsala called the Cholsum Mimang or the United People submitted a letter to the Tibetan cabinet on November 13, 1978.

The letter stated that the Thirteen's criticism of exile officials was disrespectful and had angered His Holiness the Dalai Lama. It also suggested that Palyul Dzongnang Rinpoche in Clement Town was "selling" Tibet and harming the government of India and that a petition be sent to the government of India to put him under observation. This was followed by a letter signed by sixty-eight Tibetans in Shillong on November 26, 1978, accusing Dzongnang Rinpoche of trying to separate the head (the exile government) from the body (the people of Tibet) by using religion and regionalism. It charged that Dzongnang Rinnpoche had slandered His Holiness, harmed the exile government, and offended Gyalo Thondup and Jetsun Pema. The letter praised Gyalo Thondup for his work for the exile government and suggested that he be recognized for his contributions to society.

Similarly, Tibetans from the settlement in Walung, Nepal, sent a letter to the cabinet stating that men like Dzongnang Rinpoche were thorns to the heart. Others took a more confrontational approach. Tibetans from Kollegal sent a letter directly to the Thirteen in Clement Town and to other settlements, warning them of consequences if they continued their "disgraceful" work. They expressed their happiness at Gungthang Tsultrim's death and advised members of the Thirteen to think carefully, because if they continued to take money from the Kuomintang, they would meet the same end. The letter stressed that Gungthang Tsultrim was not a "clean" Tibetan.

Many of the letters targeted Dzongnang Rinpoche by name because of a misinterpretation of a statement he made during the eight-day-meeting with the exile government. The official transcribers and note-takers appear to have had difficulty understanding a metaphor as well as the dialect he had used, causing people to misunderstand one of his remarks as an insulting characterization of the Dalai Lama. Dzongnang Rinpoche had stated that Tibetans had accused the Thirteen of not following the leadership of the Dalai Lama; Tibetans had also labeled the Thirteen as a source of harm to the struggle for freedom. Dzongnang Rinpoche had asked exile parliamentarians in the room to use their own wisdom to differentiate between right and wrong—and not to behave like their head lama and "crazy leader." He was referring to Alak Jigme Rinpoche, who was the parliament chair. Alak Jigme Rinpoche was also a lama. Many Tibetans interpreted "head lama" to be a reference to the Dalai Lama instead.

Sodam, who was at the meeting, explained that when Dzongnang Rinpoche referred to the "lama," he was discussing Alak Jigme Rinpoche's role in raising the issue of the Thirteen at the annual general meeting. But word spread through the community that Dzongnang Rinpoche had insulted the Dalai Lama.

In the sea of letters castigating the Thirteen, the only letter of support came from a Derge group in Nepal. They asked the government to curb the rumors spread by an unnamed cabinet member who was creating discord between Khampas and Amdowas. They predicted that the government's silence and reluctance to defend the Thirteen against untruths would lead to an irreparable rift between the community and the government.

It is possible that the exile government had evidence that put the loyalty of the Thirteen in question. If that was the case, the government's actions can be interpreted as compassionate and as shielding the Thirteen instead of exposing them to the full wrath of the people. However, the repeated promises that the government found no fault with them also suggest that the exile government chose, repeatedly, to do very little to protect the Thirteen from the propaganda against them. Tashi Namgyal, a relative who was living in Kathmandu when I reconnected with him in 2015, was in his early twenties when he worked in the office of the Dorpatan settlement in Nepal. He recalled receiving a letter from Dharamsala asking Tibetans, even those in remote settlements without access to a paved road, to write letters to the Kashag denouncing the deceased Gungthang Tsultrim and the Thirteen.

"The Thirteen never had a fair chance," he said.[8] He felt the Thirteen members were targeted because they disagreed with dominant ideas about what Tibet meant to Tibetans.

With Gungthang Tsultrim portrayed as a man who had supposedly broken his *samaya*, his religious pledge, his supporters were not able to grieve properly for him. Even their grief had been turned into an act of treason. Gungthang Tsultrim, as remembered by his friends, had unwavering spiritual devotion to the Dalai Lama. He was a critic of the United Party and Gyalo Thondup. Yugyal described him as a leader who listened. Sodam described him as a man who lived simply and thought majestically. Members of the Thirteen respected and liked him. He was a storyteller, they say. He had a sense of humor. He had vision. He brought people together. He would have accomplished a lot for Tibet had he lived more years, they say. His friends mourn the life he could not have.

To develop a Tibetan identity that unites not only Tibet's many regions but also its far-flung diaspora is a worthy aspiration. Yet in practice, transcending differences based on region and religious school is easier said than done. The community's repeated denunciations of the Thirteen also help to reveal forms of violence inherent in the politics of unity. The fallout after Gungthang Tsultrim's murder strengthened the stereotype of Khampas as people to be feared. It also made acceptable the idea that when Khampas disagree with a policy, they are motivated by "regionalism," not expressing a difference in opinion or an alternate point of view. Khampas may feel that the burden of taking a different view is their responsibility. These feelings have solidified over the many decades.

Yossi Shain, a political scientist, observes that no ruling government or nonruling group commands absolute loyalty. He is referring to nation-states, but his analysis of the ways loyalty is induced is pertinent to understanding loyalty, what it is, and how it works within states and also in communities aspiring to be states. Shain writes that every group in power convinces its citizens it is the most authentic entity to represent the state. Positioned to frame their interests as universal, groups in power often identify loyalty to themselves with loyalty to the nation.[9] To that end, they tend to regard challenges to national missions as acts of "national disloyalty" and consequently "derogate political opponents as being linked to alien interests."[10] They also impose psychological and "material penalty," such as defamation and excommunication, on citizens who reject their authority.[11]

National loyalty is often defined by locating its negation: acts that are defined as disloyal or shameful. No member in a "national community," Shain writes, extends support to those "not in power" without thinking of whether this will be seen as disloyalty to the government.[12] This concern is heightened in an exile community where individuals struggle to create a sense of what can be understood as a normal life. For exiles, being in accord with the community is psychologically necessary.

If the letters written by Tibetans against the Thirteen were meant to express the values of the Tibetan national community and national consciousness, then they also reveal that this consciousness was governed by an ideology with very little room for opposition, creativity, or alternate ideas. There was no place for diversity in its model of unity or genuine inquiry or constructive criticism in its appropriated model of democracy. For example, the primary objection in the letter sent by the Khampa Youth Organization on August 20, 1978, was to the alleged statement in *The Black Friday* that Kham and Amdo were "independent." The group stated that all Tibetans rejected this view and knew Tibet as one nation. To say otherwise was to split the community. The letter writers ignored the explanation provided in the pamphlet regarding the Lhasa government's limited control over Kham and Amdo as well as the historical reality, issuing a punishing denouncement of members of the Thirteen as "Chinese spies," revealing in this example how arbitrarily the Thirteen were labeled as the enemy. These letters reveal the strength of the Tibetan people, not lost in all these years of life in exile: our faith, expectations, and hope for Tibet. They also show our vulnerability, what we have yet to learn: the ability to hold two opposing ideas about belonging, to accept that different opinions are important for our future, and to be courageous and fair in using our faith, expectations, and hope in each other. Love for country is a strange kind of love.

Tibetans making the public denouncements were attempting to showcase their commitment to the nation and its leaders. Their words were barbs. Dzongnang Rinpoche and many members from Clement Town ultimately were unable to continue to live in India. Heartbroken and cast out, they had no recourse but to return to their old hometowns in Amdo and Kham, where only a few at the time of writing this book are still alive.

A STATEMENT OF THE REAL TRUTH

The booklet *Ngo yoe denpay sel dag* or *A Statement of the Real Truth*, published in Tashi Jong on December 7, 1978, offers the Thirteen's interpretation of their eight-day-long meeting with the government. Handwritten in Tibetan script, the text reminds readers that the Tibetan society in exile had been established with the goal of preserving Tibet's "ancient culture and religion."[13] As they sought to clarify, the Thirteen had been formed on the basis of their commitment to do just that. The text corrected falsehoods established by the United Party by providing the Thirteen's truth, as suggested in the title. The "real truth" is a cry from an embattled group; it too has its blind spots. The booklet attempts to respond to the letters sent by community members claiming to tell true history as well as to the government's press release regarding *The Black Friday*. The Thirteen state that they did not come together out of self-interest or fear of losing their traditional authority and privilege. Neither had they sought luxurious lives, nor spread rumors and baseless accusations using politics and

256   CONCLUSION: A STATEMENT OF REAL TRUTH

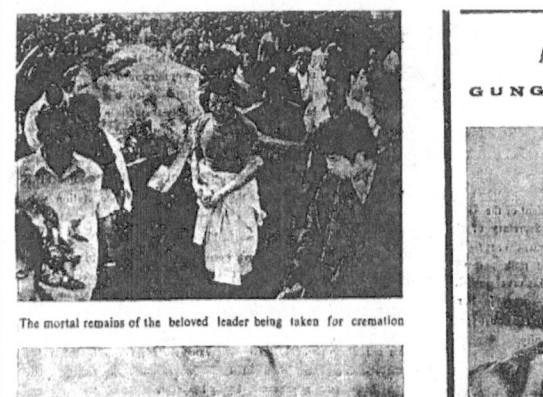

FIGURE CON.1   *The Assasination [sic] of Gungthang Tsultrim: Black Friday*, published by the Tibetan Welfare Association in 1978.

Tibetan Welfare Association

dharma to malign their critics. The Thirteen was meant to uphold generations of carefully preserved knowledge and a civilization more precious than their lives. As the booklet's authors wrote, the group was formed to preserve not just one person's lineage but the many lineages of the individuals in the collective.

The Thirteen members objected to the rumors spread and the petitions organized against them. They had drafted the statement to use the freedom of expression and equality of all before the law and to put an end to rumors about them. The text expressed their pain in

FIGURE CON.2 *A Statement of the Real Truth*, published by the Tibetan Welfare Association (the Thirteen) in 1979.

Tibetan Welfare Association

being lambasted as harmful to the Tibetan cause. It stated that the campaign against them was the work of a few people under the "material influence of Gyalo Thondup" and insisted that absent thorough investigation, the allegations would "bring discord and bring disharmony" to the Tibetan cause.[14]

The statement clarified that the Thirteen's critique of five Tibetans (Wangdu Dorjee, Alak Jigme Rinpoche, Amdo Dhondup, Gyalo Thondup, and Jetsun Pema) did not automatically extend to the entire exile government.[15] Here, the Thirteen asked that the government make the five individuals accountable instead of implicitly defending them. The statement called for Tibetans to change with the times. It suggested that denouncing and criticizing individuals who held different opinions and writing letters without first seeking to know the facts was a mistake that only showed Tibetans were meeting new situations with hidebound methods inadequate to the practice of democracy.[16] Such actions didn't exhibit even a faint whiff of democracy.

A Statement of the Real Truth was the last public document produced by the collective.

The tension between the Thirteen and the exile government lingered for over a decade, but little about their relationship surfaced as meaningful public discourses in the one or two commentaries in the *Tibetan Review*. The elders living in the Thirteen settlements said they tried to keep to themselves so as not to be seen as causing trouble. Every now and then the Thirteen were mentioned in a footnote to illustrate an oppositional voice, or in a story about regionalists blotting an otherwise model refugee society. Many of the members who labored to build the settlements are not alive today. The Thirteen settlements are run by the department of home of the exile government, with relations to members mutually arrived at. Some settlements maintain their own leaders in addition to the representatives assigned by the government. Decades ago, this is what Namkha Dorje had hoped for.

Carole McGranahan writes that although the relationship between the government and the Thirteen was eventually mended, the scars remain in the "disputes between those who consider themselves beyond and those who consider themselves bound to regional and sectarian affiliations."[17] I think my friend Yugyal lived within a paradox that demanded great acceptance: he had to keep alive the feeling of being with his clan and his people, despite its own inequalities, and to fight to free his land within a national movement that was silent about his history and doubted his love for the nation. He fought hard for both his clan and his nation; they were inextricably linked for him. He accepted that the bond he shared with his clan from Tibet would not transfer to the next generation, born in exile. His children would not perceive themselves as the *de*, the "people" of Bongsar, as he did. Yugyal and those of his generation were loyal to Namkha Dorje as their *pon*, "chief," and not just because the connection between their families and the chief had been maintained for generations. This structure would loosen over time; it was inevitable and necessary, Yugyal said. He felt that for his lifetime he was comforted being with his people.

What some interpreted as harmful regionalism was for Yugyal a means to preserve the idea of home in the absence of homeland. How could that manifest in the same way for all Tibetans when their experiences and realities were not uniform? What to the Khampas in the 1960s and 1970s seemed traditionally "Tibetan" and worth preservation—such as their own languages and social structure—was perhaps too particular, hierarchical, and regional in the exile government's idea of a reformed and egalitarian future Tibet. That is to say, being a Khampa, something that was central and unremarkable to Khampa identities, had the potential to be conspicuous in the larger society and a threat to Tibetan unity. Strangely, that perspective lingers even as the Tibetan society organizes itself differently today. For example, Tibetans identify themselves in a number of ways: with the refugee settlement they lived in, the Tibetan school system they were part of, and/or as members of the various social or political organizations in the diaspora. Their relation to the places their parents came from is unstable and continues to change as Tibetans make yet another journey from the settlements in India and Nepal toward the West.

The words "regions" and "regionalism" mean something different to the generation born inside and outside the Tibetan refugee settlements. The Tibetan use of "regionalism" includes a wide range of references: individuals identifying themselves as belonging to the regions of U-Tsang, Kham, and Amdo; organizing themselves into social and cultural groups based on their regions; or forming political groups that seek to prioritize the interests of their regions. Most often, regionalism is still associated with Khampas and to a lesser degree with Amdowas, in the sense that assertions of Khampa identity or interests, or deep filiation with their respective regions in Kham, are held as a form of regionalism in the way that U-Tsang identity, normalized as "Tibetan," may not be.

The fact that the Thirteen had managed to build settlements within ten years in exile without burdening the exile government could have been a cause of celebration and been cited as an example of the strength of refugees as well as the accommodations made to the people by the exile government. Although the politics of sorrow relegated the Thirteen to footnote status in Tibet's history of exile, the elders I know in the settlements live with a sense of achievement that they contributed to creating a vibrant Tibetan community in exile.

In 2015, I asked Marong Choeje during my visit to Dolanji why the Thirteen had diminished over time. I had meant to ask when the Thirteen felt they no longer needed to be protected or stopped being known as "the Thirteen." Lacking the appropriate word, I had settled for what translated into Tibetan as "Why did the Thirteen diminish?"

"There is no diminishment," he responded.[18]

He suggested I ask instead: How are the Thirteen living today? What do Tibetans know of their history?

He recalled the difficulties the Bonpo community faced in establishing the settlement in Dolanji. Each individual worked hard to build the settlement, brick by brick, tree by tree. He was proud of what they had accomplished.

When he came into exile, Tibetan Buddhists would say to him, "Poor thing, you are a Bonpo." He had no problem being a Bonpo. He felt the problem was that Bonpos were seen as woeful. People he lived with and worked alongside thought this identity was a reason to pity him. He was grateful he could be with a community where he could study, practice Bon, and live as a Bonpo.

"Without the Thirteen it would have been difficult for people to know us, to acknowledge us at that time," he said. "Over time, Tibetans got to know about Bon and Bonpos." To say things have diminished is to suggest otherwise, as he explained to me.

"We don't have to lose heart," he said.

In his conversation with me in 2015, Yugyal noted that the Thirteen's pursuit of living with their clans and preserving their particular religious and regional practices had come at a cost, but it had been the only way. I had asked him how he had endured the travel bans and the condemnations from Tibetans in the settlements surrounding their camp in Mainpat. "We got used to it," he responded. The Tibetans in the Thirteen settlements had each other. They maintained their devotion to His Holiness and to the lamas of their schools. They guarded their memories, choosing to remember, not to forget. "We are still here," he said.

They had even dedicated the highest spot in their settlement to the protector deity of Bongsar. For the duration of his life in exile, Yugyal was able to be with people whose forebears had lived on the same nomadic land for generations. They also kept in close touch with their relatives and friends, who continue to live on their ancestral land of Bongsar in Nangchen. Yugyal and I would speak every now and then on the phone. We had spoken a few days before his sudden death, while he was on pilgrimage in Bodh Gaya. He had sounded happy. We always spoke to each other in the Nangchen dialect. He wanted to know how the book was progressing. I understood him to be proud of his life's work, what his community had endured, and what they had accomplished as Tibetans despite the ongoing dislocation.

Likewise, the elders in Bir pointed out that they are still working for Tibet's future and the Tibetan exile community. Their children speak the dialects and they have grown old with Tibetans as they had hoped to. They have been faithful to a dream of cherishing Tibet.

On my most recent visit to Clement Town in June 2022, I asked Tenkyab, a monk in his late sixties, about his feelings about the Thirteen. He was born in Gangtok and brought to the settlement as a young child. Clement Town is home to him. We were sitting in a café owned by a Tibetan woman who has lived in Clement Town as long as Tenkyab has. He was drinking cold coffee, I was having hot chai.

He waved his arms around. "Look at what the leaders and people of the Thirteen built," he said.

Tenkyab thinks of Clement Town as a space where all religious schools of Tibetan Buddhism can flourish and where people from all parts of Tibet can maintain their particularities. The land they live on belongs to Tibetans. He used his fingers to count the Thirteen's accomplishments: the Lingtsang settlement is esteemed for its handicraft industry, in particular for their metal crafts of Tibetan Buddhist religious items; Bir and Chauntra settlements draw scholars and Buddhists from all over the world to study at Palpung Monastery, which is a re-creation of Palpung of Tibet, and at the Dzongsar Khyentse Chokyi Lodro Institute. The Palpung complex has a monastic university, school, nunnery, health center, and library. Likewise, the Dzongsar Shedra (monastic college) at Chauntra graduates Buddhist teacher-scholars fluent in Tibetan, English and Chinese. The Khampagar Monastery established by Khamtrul Rinpoche in Tashi Jong is one of the few places outside Tibet supporting a special yogic and meditation practice. More than 120 monks and nuns have received their *geshe* degree, equivalent to a doctoral degree, from the Bon Dialectic School in Dolanji. The Mindrolling Monastery in Clement Town, established by Dzongnang Rinpoche, and the Namdroling Monastery in Bylakuppe, established by Penor Rinpoche, are Buddhist education centers and tourist highlights in the Indian states of Karnataka and Uttarakhand respectively. Tenkyab also listed the Tibetan schools run by the exile government and innumerable small-scale businesses in each of the settlements. He sees these institutions and private enterprises as contributions made by the Thirteen to the preservation of a Tibetan future. From his perspective, such contributions are goals that complement, not contradict, those held by the Tibetan administration and its leaders.

For a moment, I saw the view before us as he did. The evening light cast a soft glow on the statue of the Buddha towering above the houses remodeled in recent years. A row of Indian tourists bustled toward the public park and the golden Buddha. They overtook two Tibetan elders who walked swaying to the swing of the pendulating prayer beads in their hands. Three teenage girls walked past us with their arms linked in a chain, their shorts and sneakers dusty from the football game they had just finished in the school's playground. They were singing a popular Tibetan song from Tibet. As if on cue, the gongs went off in the Mindrolling Monastery.

ACKNOWLEDGMENTS

This book belongs to the people of the Thirteen settlements, those I knew as a child and those who continue to live there. I am deeply grateful to them for opening their hearts and homes to me. I'm still leaning on their stories to understand what it means to resist, to endure, and most of all, to build community and home, over and over. While I cannot write the names of every individual in the twelve settlements, I thank the following in their place: Lama Achu, Lama Asi, Lama Drubju Tenzin, Cheme Dorjee Jagoetsang, Chime Luthoktsang, Choyang Dorje, Drawupon Rinchen Tsering, Dicky Wongmo Choklingtsang, Dorjee Lhamo Barchungtsang, Gungthang Sonam Wangyal, Jadur Sonam Zangpo, Jamyang Gyaltsen Choklingtsang, Jinpa, Kalzang Norbu, Khargi Choklingtsang, Khedup Gyamtso, Lama Tenkyab, Lingtsang Kushe Tenzing, Lobsang Gyatso, Marong Choeje, Metok Lhantso, Ugyen Topgyal Rinpoche, Pema Dorje, Sherap Tharchin, Sonam Damdul, Sonam Tobden, Tashi Topgay, Tashi Togyal, Tendhar, Tenpa, Tenzin Norbu, Lama Tsering Phuntsok, Tsering Wangyal, Tseten Drawutsang, Tsodi Bongsar, Thupa Gyaltsen, Ugyen Jigme, and Yugyal. I am grateful to the Thirty-Third Menri Trizin Lungtok Tenpai Nyima Rinpoche, and to Yongdzin Lopon Tenzin Namdak Rinpoche for the audience with them.

I could not have reached the details of the story without Ugyen Topgyal Rinpoche and Chentse Yeshe Rinpoche. Chentse Rinpoche was patient and kind, even when I asked the same questions over many years. He introduced me to many individuals in Bir, Tashi Jong, and Clement Town. Ugyen Topgyal Rinpoche's memory, his experience, and his history with many of the founding leaders were extraordinarily important to telling this story. Likewise, I am deeply grateful to my dear friends Sonam Damdul (Sodam) and Yugyal, who spent days with me perusing documents and allowed me to dig into their memories. They were young men when they dedicated their efforts to help build the settlements of Kamrao and Mainpat, respectively.

I thank the following for sharing their experience and knowledge on several topics, including the Chigdril Tsogpa, Chushi Gangdrug, Tibetan politics, and Tibetan nationalism: Chanzoe Ngawang Tenpa, Dege Cheme Dorjee, Genyen Chodon, Jamyang Norbu, His Eminence Professor Samdhong Rinpoche, Juchen Kunchok Chodon, Kasur Tashi Wangdi, Khenpo Chodak Gyatso, Kongpo Thubten Dimmedtenkar, Rinchen Norbu, Tashi Namgyal Drayabtsang, Tashi Tsering Josayma, Tashi Topgyal, Tenzin Chhodak, and Trindu Pon. Carole McGranahan and I shared many conversations on exile and Chushi Gangdruk that helped me tremendously, as her book *Arrested Histories* does, on belonging.

I'm grateful to Chris Connery, Christine Hong, Rob Wilson, and Wlad Godzich at the University of California, Santa Cruz, and to Tsering Shakya at the University of British Columbia, Vancouver, for their guidance and their support as I made my way through my research and writing, and years later, to this book. Christine, my brilliant mentor, would take walks with me and help me think through the project when I was in graduate school. I'm grateful for her guidance, then and now. My gratitude to Bhuchung D. Sonam for translating many of the texts into English and for his honest responses every time I reached out to him for his opinion on my interpretation of events.

The following institutions funded my research between 2014 and 2022 in India and Nepal: Research Center for the Americas (previously Chicano Latino Research Center) at UCSC with research funds and the Non-citizenship 2016–17 Andrew W. Mellon Foundation John E. Sawyer Fellowship; Villanova University with a Faculty Research grant as well as a summer grant; and the English Department at Villanova University. My gratitude to the Vice Provost for Research and Falvey Library at Villanova University for their support toward the index and a sensitivity editor in the publication of this book through the Subvention of Publication Program. A big thank you to Tsering Wangyal Shawa for the two beautiful maps.

My gratitude to the following individuals, institutes, and offices for their help in my research: the Library of Tibetan Works and Archives (LTWA) in Dharamsala; the Kashag Cabinet Secretariat in Dharamsala; the Surrey History Centre in Woking, UK; the World Council of Churches, Geneva Archives, in Geneva, Switzerland; the wonderful librarians in the Rare Books and Special Collections libraries at the University of British Columbia in Vancouver, Canada; and Deborah Brewster for allowing me to read her father's (Pat Brewster) personal notes. Special thanks to the librarians in the Foreign Language Reference Department in the LTWA archives in Dharamsala: Yeshi Tashi, Tenzin Choesang, and Dolma Tsering.

I am indebted to the following scholars whose work has contributed to my education in writing this book: Anne Frechette, Bridget Anderson, Bryan J. Cuevas, Carole McGranahan, Catherine S. Ramirez, Dan Martin, Dawa Norbu, Dibyesh Anand, Elliot Sperling, Emily Mitchell-Eaton, Eveline Washul, Fiona McConnell, Gray Tuttle, Jamyang Norbu, Janet Gyatso, Juan E. Poblete, Katia Buffetrille, Kesang Tseten, Kurtis R. Schaeffer, Lobsang Sangay, Maria Turek, Matthew T. Kapstein, Melvyn C. Goldstein, Per Kvaerne, Samten G. Karmay, Stéphane Gros, Sylvanna M. Falcon, Tsering Shakya, Trine Brox, Ugyan Choedup, Yudru Tsomu, and many more.

The support I received from many colleagues and friends provided me with a deep sense of confidence and comfort in this otherwise solitary task. They offered their time and labor to read a section, a chapter of the manuscript, or the entire book over these many years. Their comments, critiques, and suggestions are all in its pages. I thank Adrienne Perry, Alan Drew, Barbara Weyermann, Chentse Yeshe Rinpoche, Claudia Lopez, Dechen Pemba, Eva Herzer, Geshe Monlam Tharchin, Jamyang Phuntsok, Jean Lutes, Kabir M. Heimsath, Kara Hisatake, Karma Gyaltsen Neyratsang, Nyima Woser Choekhortshang Rinpoche, Tsering Yangzom Lama, Mary Mullen, M. G. Srinivasan, Megan Quigley, Sarah Papazoglakis, Per Kvaerne, Tsering Wangchuk, Ugyan Choedup, Valerie Melvin, and Yumi Lee. My deepest gratitude to Shelly Bhoil for the countless days she spent editing the entire manuscript; to Christine Hong and Marilyn Seaton for reading the final manuscript and for helping me think through thorny parts; and to Adam Riekstins for invaluable editorial assistance and Cynthia Col for the index.

Kading Che to Gray Tuttle, Ariana King, and the Weatherhead East Asian Institute at Columbia University for seeing this book.

I am grateful to Caelyn Cobb, Leslie Kriesel, and Monique Laban at Columbia University Press.

LIST OF THIRTEEN FOUNDERS AND SETTLEMENTS

Some dates correspond to when the land was obtained and some to when the settlements were registered.

1. The Sixteenth Gyalwang Karmapa, Rumtek Monastery, Rumtek, Sikkim, 1962.
2. Pema Norbu Rinpoche, Namdroling Monastery, Bylakuppe, Karnataka, 1963.
3. Gungthang Tsultrim, Dhondupling Tibetan Colony, Clement Town, Uttarakhand, 1964.
4. Dzongnang Rinpoche, Mindrolling Monastery, Dhondupling Tibetan Colony, Clement Town, Uttarakhand, 1964.
5. Bongsartsang Namkha Dorje, Nangchen Settlement, Mainpat, Chattisgarh, 1965.
6. Kathok Ontrul Rinpoche, Kham Kathok Tibetan Society, Sataun, Himachal Pradesh, 1966.
7. Jagoetsang Namgyal Dorjee, Tibetan Khampa Industrial Society, Dege Division, Bir and Chauntra, Himachal Pradesh, 1966.
8. The Third Neten Chokling Rinpoche, Tibetan Khampa Industrial Society, Nangchen Division, Bir and Chauntra, Himachal Pradesh, 1966.
9. Drawutsang Rinchen Tsering, Tibetan Taopon Gapa Welfare Society, Kamrao, Himachal Pradesh, 1966.

10. Lopon Tenzin Namdak Rinpoche, Tibetan Bonpo Foundation, Dolanji, Himachal Pradesh, 1966.
11. The Eighth Khamtrul Rinpoche, Khampagar Tashi Jong Tibetan Settlement, Tashi Jong, Jekhli Beth, Himachal Pradesh, 1969.
12. Sey Jigme and Yarling Dorje Wangyal, Kham Lingtsang Settlement, Munduwala, Uttarakhand, 1974.
13. Trochupon (Trochu Dorje Pasang) settlement, never built.

Appendix

WHO'S WHO

Andrugtsang Gompo Tashi	The founder of the Chushi Gangdrug.
Baba Yeshi/Gyen Yeshi	General of the Chushi Gangdrug force in Mustang.
Barchungtsang Thutop Gompo	Chieftain of the Barchung clan in Derge; Thirteen founding member; Chushi Gangdrug leader.
Drawutsang Rinchen Tsering	Chieftain of Ga Kyekudo (Nangchen); Member of Parliament in exile; Thirteen founding member; founder of the Taopon setttlement in Kamrao; Chushi Gangdrug leader.
Juchen Thupten Namgyal	Kalon Tripa in exile; Minister of Information in the Tibetan cabinet; Member of Parliament in exile; Chushi Gangdrug leader.
Neten Chokling (Pema Gyurme) Rinpoche	The third incarnation of the great terton Chogyur Lingpa of the Nyingma school; Thirteen founding member; founder of the Nangchen settlement in Bir.
Gungthang Tsultrim	Head administrator for Gungthang Rinpoche in Labrang Tashikhyil in Amdo, Tibet; Member of Parliament in exile; Thirteen founding member; founder of the Clement Town settlement; Chushi Gangdrug leader. Also known as Akhu Tsultrim.

Kasur Gyalo Thondup	Elder brother of the Fourteenth Dalai Lama; Foreign Minister in the Tibetan cabinet in exile; coordinator of the Chushi Gangdrug and CIA relations; head of security for the Dalai Lama; presumed leader of the United Party.
Gyaritsang Lodi Gyaltsen Rinpoche	Reincarnation of Khenchen Jampal Dewe Nyima of the Nyingma lineage; Foreign Minister in the Tibetan cabinet in exile; Envoy of the Dalai Lama; Member of Parliament in exile. Also known to Tibetans as Gyari Rinpoche.
Jagoetsang Namgyal Dorjee	Steward of the clan leader Jagoetsang Topden, one of the four main chieftains under the Derge King in Kham; Member of Parliament in exile; Thirteen founding member; founder of the Derge settlement in Bir; Chushi Gangdrug leader.
Kasur Jetsun Pema	Younger sister of the Fourteenth Dalai Lama; Minister of Education in the Tibetan cabinet; President of the Tibetan Children's Village (TCV).
Jinpa	Friend and associate of Gungthang Tsultrim.
Khamtrul Rinpoche Dongyu Nyima	The eighth incarnation of Khampa Karma Tenphel, a Drukpa Kagyu lineage master; Thirteen founding member; founder of the Khampagar Monastery and settlement in Tashi Jong.
Kathok Ontrul Rinpoche	The head lama of Kathok Monastery, founded in Palyul, Derge; Thirteen founding member; founder of the Kathok settlement in Sataun.
Lungtok Tenpai Nyima Rinpoche, the 33rd Menri Trizin (formerly known as Sangye Tenzin Jongdong)	The thirty-third spiritual head of the Bon Community worldwide and abbot of Menri Monastery; Thirteen founding member; teacher at Ockenden School.

APPENDIX: WHO'S WHO ⌘ 273

Ugyen Topgyal Rinpoche	Incarnation of Taksham Nuden Dorje of the Nyingma lineage; Member of Parliament in exile; son of Chokling Rinpoche.
Patrul Jampal Lodroe Dzongnang Rinpoche	The second incarnation of a lineage within the Nyingma Palyul system; Member of Parliament in exile; Thirteen founding member; cofounder (with Khochhen Rinpoche) of Mindrolling Monastery in Dhondup Ling Tibetan Settlement in Clement Town.
Pema Norbu Rinpoche (Penor Rinpoche)	The eleventh incarnation of a lineage within the Nyingma Palyul system; served as head of the Nyingpa lineage; Thirteen founding member; founder of Namdroling Monastery in Bylakuppe.
Bongsartsang Namkha Dorje	Chieftain of the Bongsar clan in Nangchen; Thirteen founding member; founder of the settlement in Mainpat.
Sonam Damdul (Sodam)	Member of Parliament in exile; representative of Kumrao Settlement in the Thirteen.
Tsongkha Lhamo Tsering	Assistant to Gyalo Thondup; headed the Tibetan section of the intelligence operations of the Chushi Gangdrug. Known to Tibetans as *Dronyik* or Secretary Lhamo Tsering.
Tsodi Bongsar	Translator for Namkha Dorje; daughter of Namkha Dorje.
Wangdu Dorjee	Minister of Home Affairs in exile.
Yugyal	Served as representative and aide to Namkha Dorje of Mainpat Settlement.
Lobsang Phuntsok Lhalungpa	Scholar; writer; official of the Tibetan government in Lhasa; head of the Tibetan division of the Indian national news service *All India Radio* in 1956.

NOTES

PREFACE

1. Carole McGranahan, *Arrested Histories: Tibet, the CIA, and Memories of a Forgotten War* (Durham, NC: Duke University Press, 2010), 4.
2. McGranahan, *Arrested Histories*, 4.

INTRODUCTION

1. Tibetan Welfare Association, *The Assasination [sic] of Gungthang Tsultrim* (Self-pub., June 1978), 4–5. Referred to in texts and cabinet minutes as *The Black Friday*.
2. "The Murder of Gungthang Tsultrim," *The Tibetan Review* XII, no. 7 (July 1978): 9. The newspaper's first edition was printed in April–May 1967 as *The Voice of Tibet* in Darjeeling. The price for one copy was 30 paisa.
3. "The Murder of Gungthang Tsultrim," *The Tibetan Review*, 9–10.
4. "Gungthang Tsultrim—A Political Victim?" *Tibetan Review* XIII, no. 8 (August 1978): 6.
5. Tibetan Welfare Association, *The Assasination [sic] of Gungthang Tsultrim*, 6.
6. Tibetan Welfare Association, *The Assasination [sic] of Gungthang Tsultrim*, 5.
7. Tsering Wangyal, "Politics of Sorrow," *Tibetan Review* III, no. 8 (August 1978): 3.
8. Wangyal, "Politics of Sorrow," 3.
9. Wangyal, "Politics of Sorrow," 20.
10. "Tsultrim Murderer Apprehended," *Tibetan Review* XVI, no. 9 (September 1978): 8.
11. Samten Gyaltsen Karmay, "Who are the Amdowas: Letters," *Tibetan Review* XIII, no. 9 (September 1978): 27.
12. Matthew T. Kapstein, *The Tibetans* (Malden, MA: Blackwell, 2006), 84.
13. Kapstein, *The Tibetans*, 114.
14. Kapstein, *The Tibetans*, 133.

15. Kapstein, *The Tibetans*, 137.
16. Tsering Shakya, *The Dragon in the Land of Snows* (New York: Penguin, 1999), xxix.
17. Melvyn C. Goldstein, *A History of Modern Tibet, Volume 3* (Berkeley: University of California Press, 2014), 80; Kenneth Knaus, *Orphans of the Cold War* (New York: PublicAffairs, 1999), 4; Dawa Norbu, *China's Tibet Policy* (Surrey: Curzon Press, 2001), 147. Dawa Norbu contests China's claim that Tibet was officially incorporated into China during the Yuan Dynasty by pointing out that Tibet was one of nineteen countries that made up the Mongol global conquest of Asia. Unlike the others, Tibet was saved in 1207 by submitting to Chingghis Khan and in 1240 by the Sakya Pandita's appeal to the Godan. This means Tibet became a special or indirect part of Chingghis Khan's empire seventy-two years before his sons or grandsons conquered China in 1279.
18. Dawa Norbu, "The 1959 Tibetan Rebellion: An Interpretation," *The China Quarterly* 77 (March 1979): 80.
19. Norbu, "The 1959 Tibetan Rebellion," 80.
20. Stéphane Gros, "Frontier Tibet: Trade and Boundaries of Authority in Kham," *Cross-Currents: East Asian History and Culture Review* 19 (June 2016): 11.
21. Gros, "Frontier Tibet," 4.
22. Stéphane Gros, "Frontier (of) Experience," in *Frontier Tibet: Patterns of Change in the Sino-Tibetan Borderlands*, ed. Stéphane Gros (Amsterdam: Amsterdam University Press), 44.
23. Dawa Norbu, *Tibet: The Road Ahead* (London: Rider, 1998), 97.
24. Dawa Norbu, "Han Hegemony and Tibetan Ethnicity," *International Studies* 32, no. 3 (1995): 299.
25. Maria Turek, "Return of the Good King," in *Frontier Tibet: Patterns of Change in the Sino-Tibetan Borderlands*, ed. Stéphane Gros (Amsterdam: Amsterdam University Press, 2019), 461.
26. Edward W. Said, *Culture and Imperialism* (New York: Vintage, 1994), 209.
27. Said, *Culture and Imperialism*, 209.
28. Tibetan Welfare Association, *Ngo yoe Denpay Sel dag* (*A Statement of Real Truth*) (Self-pub., Tashi Jong, 1979).
29. Lodi Gyaltsen Gyari, *The Dalai Lama's Special Envoy: Memoirs of a Lifetime in Pursuit of A Reunited Tibet* (New York: Columbia University Press, 2022), 142–43.
30. Gyari, *The Dalai Lama's Special Envoy*, 143.
31. Jadur Sonam Zangpo, interview by author, Dolanji, July 27, 2015.
32. Tibetan United Association, *Cholsum Chigdril Tsogpai Logyue Ngoeden Jhungrim Debther Drangsong Gyepae Choetin She Jawa Shugso* (*Truthful History of the Tibetan United Association*) (Dharamsala: Tibetan United Association, 2005), 30.
33. Benedict Anderson, "Introduction," in *Mapping the Nation*, ed. Gopal Balakrishanan (London: Verso, 1996), 1.
34. Sonam Damdul, interview with author, Dharamsala, India, July 16 and Clement Town, August 4, 2015; Clement Town, June 2–3, 2022.
35. Tenzin Norbu, interview with author, Bir, India, July 20, 2015.

1. A GOVERNMENT IN EXILE ᛞ 277

36. Chime Luthoktsang, interview with author, Kathmandu, Nepal, November 17, 2015.
37. Tenzin Gyatso, the 14th Dalai Lama of Tibet, *Freedom in Exile* (New York: HarperCollins, 1990), 12, 56.
38. Melvyn C. Goldstein, *A History of Modern Tibet, 1913–1951: The Demise of the Lamaist State* (Berkeley: University of California Press, 1989), 91.
39. Tsering Shakya, *The Dragon in the Land of Snows*, 132.
40. Department of Information and International Relations, *Tibet and the Tibetan Struggle: 10 March Statements of His Holiness the Dalai Lama (1961–2005)* (Dharamsala: Central Tibetan Administration, 2005), 10.
41. Tenzin Gyatso, the 14th Dalai Lama of Tibet, *My Land and My People*, (New York: Hachette Book Group, 1997), 193.
42. Department of Information and International Relations, *Tibet and the Tibetan Struggle*, 2.
43. Trine Brox, *Tibetan Democracy: Governance, Leadership and Conflict in Exile* (London: I. B. Tauris, 2016), 55.
44. Jigme Yeshe Lama, "Exile Tibetans and the Dance of Democracy," in *Tibetan Subjectivities on the Global Stage: Negotiating Dispossession*, ed. Shelly Bhoil and Enrique Galvan-Alvarez (New York: Lexington Books, 2018), 176.
45. Trine Brox, *Tibetan Democracy*, 266.
46. Dawa Norbu, *Culture and the Politics of Third World Nationalism* (New York: Taylor & Francis, 1992), 214–215; Eric Hobsbawm, "Ethnicity and Nationalism in Europe Today," in *Mapping the Nation*, ed. Gopal Balakrishnan (New York: Verso, 2012).
47. Frantz Fanon, *The Wretched of the Earth* (New York: Grove Press, 2004), 145.
48. Prasenjit Duara, "De-Constructing the Chinese Nation," *The Australian Journal of Chinese Affairs* 30 (July 1993): 2.
49. Duara, "De-Constructing the Chinese Nation," 14.
50. Duara, "De-Constructing the Chinese Nation," 20.
51. Prasenjit Duara, *The Global and Regional in China's Nation-Formation* (Oxon: Routledge, 2009), 61–62.
52. Clifford Geertz, *Interpretation of Culture* (New York: Basic Books, 1973), 258.
53. Geertz, *Interpretation of Culture*, 243.
54. Geertz, *Interpretation of Culture*, 261.
55. Geertz, *Interpretation of Culture*, 261.
56. David Lloyd, *Anomalous States: Irish Writing and the Post-Colonial Moment* (Durham, NC: Duke University Press, 1993), 5.
57. Lloyd, *Anomalous States*, 4.

1. A GOVERNMENT IN EXILE

1. Heinrich Harrer, "Flight in a Sandstorm: A Miraculous Escape," *Life Magazine*, May 4, 1959, 30.

2. Jamyang Norbu, *Echoes from Forgotten Mountains* (Gurugram: Penguin Random House, 2023), 543.
3. Tenzin Gyatso, the 14th Dalai Lama of Tibet, *My Land and My People* (New York: Warner Books, 1977), 178.
4. Gyalo Thondup and Anne F. Thurston, *The Noodle Maker of Kalimpong* (New York: PublicAffairs, 2015), 196.
5. Tenzin Gyatso, the 14th Dalai Lama of Tibet, *Speeches of His Holiness the XIVth Dalai Lama (1959–1989)*, trans. Sonam Gyatso (Dharamsala: Library of Tibetan Works and Archives, 2011), 1.
6. Tenzin Gyatso, the 14th Dalai Lama of Tibet, *Speeches of His Holiness the XIVth Dalai Lama*, 6.
7. Many changes to the parliament have been made over the decades, such as enforcing that some seats be reserved for women, increasing to forty-six members (1991), and extending terms to five years (1985).
8. John F. Avedon, *In Exile from the Land of Snows* (New York: Knopf, 1984), 107.
9. Avedon, *In Exile from the Land of Snows*, 106.
10. Central Tibetan Administration. *The Constitution of Tibet*. Dharamsala, 1963.
11. Tenzin Gyatso, the 14th Dalai Lama of Tibet, *Freedom in Exile* (New York: HarperCollins, 1990), 170.
12. Dawa Norbu, "The 1959 Tibetan Rebellion: An Interpretation," *The China Quarterly* 77 (March 1979): 74.
13. Avedon, *In Exile from the Land of Snows*, 107.
14. Hugh Richardson, *High Peaks, Pure Earth* (London: Serindia, 1998), 1–2.
15. Melvyn C. Goldstein, *A History of Modern Tibet, Volume 3* (Berkeley: University of California Press, 2014), 80. The convention was signed by Great Britain and Tibet. China did not sign the agreement and does not recognize it.
16. Stéphane Gros, "Frontier (of) Experience Introduction and Prolegomenon," in *Frontier Tibet: Patterns of Change in the Sino-Tibetan Borderlands*, ed. Stéphane Gros (Amsterdam: Amsterdam University Press, 2019), 41–84. Gros suggests that Central Tibet is what the Chinese refer to as Xizang. Xikang is the term used for Kham in early 1900 Chinese texts. Xizang is also used to indicate "Tibetan" culture or an individual. According to Rongxing Guo (*China's Regional Development and Tibet* [Singapore: Springer, 2016]), *xi* (west) and *zang* refers to Tibetan people or culture in any of the three regions. He believes Xizang came into use since the middle of the Qing dynasty (1644–1911).
17. Tsering Shakya, *The Dragon in the Land of Snows: A History of Modern Tibet Since 1947* (New York: Penguin, 1999), 40. Tsering Shakya writes that the Communist Chinese needed to win over the Khampas in order to penetrate Central Tibet and were able to influence some. According to Robert Ford, who ran the radio and communications systems in Tibet, Tibetan soldiers "feared the Khampas more than the PLA."
18. Yudru Tsomu, "Taming the Khampas: The Republican Construction of Eastern Tibet," *Modern China* 39, no. 3 (May 2013): 319–344.

1. A GOVERNMENT IN EXILE ⚙ 279

19. Yudru Tsomu, "The Rise of a Political Strongman in Derge in the Early Twentieth Century: The Story of Jago Topden," in *Frontier Tibet: Patterns of Change in the Sino-Tibetan Borderlands*, ed. Stéphane Gros (Amsterdam: Amsterdam University Press, 2020), 368.
20. Maria Turek, "Return of the Good King," in *Frontier Tibet: Patterns of Change in the Sino-Tibetan Borderlands*, ed. Stéphane Gros (Amsterdam: Amsterdam University Press, 2020), 469.
21. Mark E. Frank, "Planting and Its Discontents: Or How Nomads Produced Spaces of Resistance in China's Erstwhile Xikang Province," *Resilience: A Journal of the Environmental Humanities* 3 (Winter/Spring/Fall 2015–16): 126.
22. Frank, "Planting and Its Discontents," 115.
23. Frank, "Planting and Its Discontents," 126
24. Frank. "Planting and Its Discontents," 125.
25. From conversations with Drawupon and elders from pastoral nomadic communities. Robert B. Ekvall, "Law and the Individual among the Tibetan Nomads," *American Anthropologist*, New Series, 66, no. 5 (October 1964): 1114.
26. Frank, "Planting and Its Discontents," 134.
27. Carole McGranahan, *Arrested Histories* (Durham, NC: Duke University Press, 2010), 68, 172.
28. Tenzin Gyatso, the 14th Dalai Lama of Tibet, *My Land and My People*, 65.
29. Melvyn C. Goldstein, *A History of Modern Tibet, 1913–1951: The Demise of the Lamaist State* (Berkeley: University of California Press, 1989), 62.
30. Cheme Dorjee, interview with author, December 7, 2020. Dege Cheme served briefly as an assistant to Palpung Ontul Karma Dechen, the representative for Sakya, Kagyu, and Nyingma monks at Buxa Chogar.
31. Cheme Dorjee, interview with author, December 7, 2020.
32. Discussed as *"ghur serpo"* later in this chapter.
33. Avedon, *In Exile from the Land of Snows*, 81; Lodi Gyaltsen Gyari, "Status and Position of the Tibetan Youth Congress," *Tibetan Political Review*, October 5, 2014. Lodi Gyaltsen Gyari, *The Dalai Lama's Special Envoy: Memoirs of a Lifetime in Pursuit of a Reunited Tibet* (New York: Columbia University Press, 2022), 222.
34. Dawa Norbu, "The 1959 Tibetan Rebellion," 80.
35. Dawa Norbu, "Han Hegemony and Tibetan Ethnicity," *International Studies* 32, no. 3 (1995): 309–310.
36. Dawa Norbu, *Culture and the Politics of Third World Nationalism* (London: Routledge, 1992), 213.
37. Norbu, "Han Hegemony and Tibetan Ethnicity," 309.
38. Shakya, *The Dragon in the Land of Snows*, 191–192.
39. Tenzin Gyatso, the 14th Dalai Lama of Tibet, *Speeches of His Holiness the XIVth Dalai Lama*, 14. In a speech to a select group of government officials on September 9, 1960, the Dalai Lama expressed he didn't have faith in written oaths and that he believed in action.
40. Gyari, *The Dalai Lama's Special Envoy*, 115.
41. Gyari, *The Dalai Lama's Special Envoy*, 117.

42. Juchen Thupten Namgyal, *Juchen Thupten gyi kutse logyue*/Ju chen thub bstan gyi sku tshe'i lo rgyus (*Autobiography of Juchen Thupten*), 21 vols. (Chauntra, District Mandi, H.P, India: Juchentsang, 2014), 5: 342–343. Juchen Thupten lists the following individuals as representing their various organizations, monastic institutions, and government institutions: Lobpon Pema Gyaltsen of Loseling, representative of Drepung; Lobpon Lobsang Dhonyoe, representative of Sera Thekchen Ling; Shartse Lobpon, Lobsang Choephel, representative of Ganden Monastery; Ngawang Lekden, representative of Gyutoe and Gyumey; Palpung Ontul Karma Dechen, representative of Sakya, Kagyu, and Nyingma; Khenpo Ngawang Jinpa, representative of Tharpa Choeling in Kalimpong; Jinpa Gyatso, representative of Phelgye Ling Monastery in Bodh Gaya; Khenchung Ngawang Dhondup; Tsepon Namling Paljor Jigme; Rupon Sonam Tashi, representative of Utsang Magkar; Amdo Choedak and Jagoe Namgyal Dorjee, representatives of the Chushi Gangdrug, Amdo, Golok, and Lang; representative Lobsang Dorjee; representative Amdo Gyatong; Pesur Dorjee Norbu, representative of Tsang; representative Tsering Topgyal; representative Wangdu Dorjee; representative Sonam Tenzin; representative Chogye Sherab; representative Tsetan Namgyal; representative Marnang Pema Tsewang; representative Lhawang Tsering; representative Markham Sonam; representative Sonam Tsewang; representative Aphur; representative Jigme Namgyal; Thubten Jungnye; representative Zoepa; Nyandak; Atra; Phurbu; Akhu; Yeshi Tsering.
43. Translated by Bhuchung D. Sonam based on the oath printed in Tibetan in Juchen Thupten's autobiography. The oath is also printed in full in Gyari, *The Dalai Lama's Special Envoy*, appendix A, 641.
44. Jacob P. Dalton, "Foundational Violence," in *The Taming of the Demons* (New Haven, CT: Yale University Press, 2013), 124–125. Dalton uses "self-demonizing rhetoric" to describe how Tibetans wrote about themselves as responsible for the age of fragmentation in Tibet. He suggests the self-demonizing went with the concept of the pure place that India held for Tibetans. Tibetans didn't feel they could "get Buddhism right" without help from India (124). Attributing the Chinese occupation of Tibet to faults in the Tibetan people seems to echo the ways the age of fragmentation is also attributed to the lowly character of the Tibetan people.
45. Dawa Norbu, "The 1959 Tibetan Rebellion," 80.
46. Namgyal, *Juchen Thupten gyi kutse logyue*, 5: 340–342.
47. Namgyal, Juchen *Thupten gyi kutse logyue*, 5: 340–343.
48. Cheme Dorjee, interview with author, December 2020.
49. Gyari, *The Dalai Lama's Special Envoy*, 114.
50. Gyari, *The Dalai Lama's Special Envoy*, 114.
51. Dawa Norbu, "The 1959 Tibetan Rebellion," 81.
52. Norbu, "The 1959 Tibetan Rebellion," 81.
53. Norbu, "The 1959 Tibetan Rebellion," 92.
54. Romila Thapar, *The Past as Present* (London: Seagull Books, 2019), 127.
55. Tenzin Gyatso, the 14th Dalai Lama of Tibet, *Freedom in Exile*, 157.

56. Michael L. Walter, *The Political and Religious Culture of Early Tibet* (Leiden: Brill, 2009), 27. Walter describes a set of oaths as being the glue that held together the religious and internal politics in the courts of the early Tibetan kings.
57. Norbu, *Echoes from Forgotten Mountains*, 161.
58. In his address to a group of Amdowas after Gungthang Tsultrim's death on September 28, 1978, ("His Holiness the Dalai Lama's Speech to the Representatives of *Domey* Meeting Held on 28 September 1978," published by CTA, Dharamsala, September 28, 1978), the Dalai Lama explains that the old Lhasa government had been like a private house administering the government because it was associated with the Gelug tradition. The exile government, in contrast, was a new polity where all *tsampa*-eaters were equal and had the same rights. This speech is also published in *Cholsum Chigdril Tsogpai logyue ngoeden jhungrim debther drangsong gyepae choetin she jawa shugso/Chol gsum chig bsgril tshogs pa'i lo rgyus dngos bden byung rim deb ther drang srong dgyes pa'i mchod sprin zhes bya ba bzhugs so* (*Truthful History of the Tibetan United Association*) (Dharamsala: Tibetan United Association, 2005), 107–114.
59. Eveline Yang, "Tracing the *Chol kha gsum*: Reexamining a Sa skya-Yuan Period Administrative Geography," *Revue d'Etudes Tibetaines* 37 (December 2016): 551–568. The *colga* was a geo-administrative unit of decimal structures used by the Mongols to determine its population. The Sakya did not control areas of Kham and Amdo.
60. Gros, "Frontier (of) Experience Introduction and Prolegomenon," 45.
61. Namgyal, *Juchen Thupten gyi kutse logyue*, 5: 344. Trochupon is also written as Trichupon.
62. Namgyal, *Juchen Thupten gyi kutse logyue*, 5: 344.
63. Ann-Marie Blondeau, "How does the Chinese government value the idea of a 'greater Tibetan autonomous region' suggested by some people around the Dalai Lama," in *Authenticating Tibet: Answers to China's 100 Questions*, ed. Ann-Marie Blondeau and Katia Buffetrille (Berkeley: University of California Press, 2008), 124.
64. Prasenjit Duara, "Civilization and Realpolitik," *India International Centre Quarterly* 3/4 (Winter 2009–Spring 2010): 20–33/20.
65. Prasenjit Duara, *The Global and Regional in China's Nation-Formation* (Oxon: Routledge, 2009),190.
66. Duara, *The Global and Regional*, 190.
67. Duara, *The Global and Regional*, 190.
68. Eliott Sperling, "The Yuan Dynasty," in *Authenticating Tibet: Answers to China's 100 Questions*, ed. Ann-Marie Blondeau and Katia Buffetrille (Berkeley: University of California Press, 2008), 14–17/12; Wang Hui, *The Politics of Imagining Asia* (Cambridge, MA: Harvard University Press, 2011), 84. In Sperling's words, frontier people were seen as "incapable of true nationhood on their own." This claim echoed older imperial Chinese worldviews that looked on frontier peoples as "subnational" (12). Such an interpretation of the new national territory of

China elided the incommensurability between the old relations and the modern ideas of sovereignty.

69. Yudru Tsomu, *The Rise of Gonpo Namgyel in Kham: The Blind Warrior of Nyarong* (Lanham, MD: Lexington Books, 2016). In her study of the kingdom of Nyarong in Kham, Yudru Tsomu shows how the integration strategies (or what might be considered revisionist strategies) adopted by the government of Republican China toward the Kham frontier were shaped by the efforts of the new Chinese intellectuals of the Republican period to reimagine a new geospace where frontier peoples were made conationals. This was also an attempt to counter the Thirteenth Dalai Lama's declaration of Tibet's independence in 1913 and his effort to claim sovereignty over Kham.

    Fabienne Jagou, "The Dispute between Sichuan and Xikang over the Tibetan Kingdom of Trokyab (1930s–1940s)," in *Patterns of Change in the Sino-Tibetan Borderlands*, ed. Stéphane Gros, 344. Jagou suggests that the kingdoms of Kham were viewed as "a no man's land" by the Nationalist government.

    Prasenjit Duara, "History and Globalization in China's Long Twentieth Century," *Modern China, The Nature of the Chinese State: Dialogues Among Western and Chinese Scholars* 34, no. 1 (January 2008): 152–164. The citizens of frontier races had little relationship, direct or indirect, with Chinese rulers. Duara writes that the nation form relies on a "homogenized" and a fairly direct relationship "between citizen and state" (154).

70. Jian Chen, "The Chinese Communist 'Liberation' of Tibet, 1949–51," in *Dilemmas of Victory*, ed. Jeremy Brown and Paul Pickowicz (Cambridge, MA: Harvard University Press, 2008), 138. This program of a China federation disappeared from the party's official discourse in 1949. In its place came "a grand plan of pursuing a unified socialist China incorporating Xinjiang, Inner Mongolia, and Tibet" (131). Chen explains that this new plan rested on the myth of the unity of the five nationalities (*wuzu gonghe*: Hans, Manchus, Mongolians, Hui Muslims, and Tibetans) created by the nationalist government. The new China did not come about by destroying the old, but rather by continuing some very salient features of the Nationalist Party that the Chinese Communist Party (CCP) had initially repudiated as concealing "its policy of national oppression" (132). Until the 1940s the CCP favored giving the regions of Xinjiang, Mongolia, and Tibet full autonomy. Plus, the decision whether they would form a federation with China and the Han people was to be guided by the principles of national self-determination. This shift from national self-determination to "uniting all nationalities into a big family" seemed to have gone unnoticed by most other party members.

71. Wang Hui, *China from Empire to Nation* (Cambridge, MA: Harvard University Press, 2014), 4. Wang Hui suggests that the opposition between the narratives of empire and nation-state is linked to narratives of European nationalism.

72. Wang Hui, *China from Empire to Nation-State*, 129–130.

73. Wang Hui, *China from Empire to Nation-State*, 132–133.

74. Wang Hui, *China from Empire to Nation-State*, 133–134.
75. Wang Hui, *China from Empire to Nation-State*, 136.
76. Wang Hui, *China From Empire to Nation-State*, 136.
77. Alex Gardner, "Khams pa histories: Visions of People, Place and Authority," *The Tibet Journal* 28, no. 3 (2000): 69.
78. Stéphane Gros, "Introduction," in *Frontier Tibet: Patterns of Change in the Sino-Tibetan Borderlands*, ed. Stéphane Gros (Amsterdam: Amsterdam University Press), 3.
79. Goldstein, *A History of Modern Tibet, Volume 3*, 81. Alex Gardner, "Khams pa Histories: Visions of People, Place and Authority," *The Tibet Journal* 28, no. 3 (2000): 72. Gardner mentions that not all these ranks were *tusi* because there was also the *tuguan*, the imperial policy. Most Khampa local rulers were *tuguan* according to Gardner. But he also writes that it is difficult to say which states were *tusi* and which *tuguan*.
80. Gros, "Introduction," in *Frontier Tibet*, 37.
81. Dilgo Khyentse Rinpoche, *Brilliant Moon: The Autobiography of Dilgo Khyentse* (Boston: Shambhala, 2008), 3.
82. Homi K. Bhabha, ed., *Nation and Narration* (New York: Routledge, 1990), 5.
83. Prasenjit Duara, "De-Constructing the Chinese Nation," *The Australian Journal of Chinese Affairs* 30 (July 1993): 25.

2. UNITY IN EXILE

1. Tsodi Bongsar, *Nangchen Sremo: The Story of Tsodi Bongsar from Nangchen* (Self-pub., India, 2023, digital copy), 12–13.
2. Jamyang Norbu, *Echoes from Forgotten Mountains* (Gurugram: Penguin Random House, 2023), 278.
3. In a progress report on February 21, 1966, to The World Council of Churches, Geneva, G. Brewster, known as Pat Brewster, then director of the Tibetan Refugee Programme of the National Christian Council of India, wrote there were about 20,000 Tibetans working on the roads and "living in temporary roadside shelters which are often tents."
4. Tenzin Gyatso, the 14th Dalai Lama of Tibet, *Freedom in Exile* (New York: HarperCollins, 1990), 158.
5. Yugyal, interviews with author, Mainpat, India, September 17–19, 2015.
6. Yugyal, interviews with author, Mainpat, India, September 17–19, 2015.
7. Yugyal, interviews with author, Mainpat, India, September 17–19, 2015.
8. Rajesh Kharat, "Gainers of a Stalemate: The Tibetans in India," in *Refugees and the State: Practices of Asylum and Care in India, 1947–2000*, ed. Ranabir Samaddar (New Delhi: Sage Publications, 2003), 289. Kharat writes that 3,000 refugees were settled in Bylakuppe on more than 3,000 acres of land leased for 99 years by Nijalingappa, then chief minister of Mysore, in December 1960 (five years difference from Phuntso). In 1963, Switzerland resettled 1,000 Tibetan refugees. Tibetans building roads and living in the transit camps near

their work sites in Himachal Pradesh, Arunachal Pradesh, Kalimpong, and Sikkim were among the initial refugees resettled in Bylakuppe.
9. One of Namkha Dorje's assistants thought that it was Lama Lobsang who introduced Namkha Dorje to Prime Minister Nehru.
10. Asi Lama, interview with author, phone call, November 2, 2023.
11. Tenzin Gyatso, the 14th Dalai Lama of Tibet, *Freedom in Exile*, 212.
12. Tenzin Gyatso, the 14th Dalai Lama of Tibet, *Freedom in Exile*, 212. The Nechung oracle is the human host or medium to the protector deity Pehar Gyelpo, also known as Dorje Drakden, one of many spirits subdued by Padmasambhava and committed under oath to defend Buddhist Tibet.
13. Tenzin Gyatso, the 14th Dalai Lama of Tibet, *Freedom in Exile*, 211.
14. Lodi Gyaltsen Gyari, *The Dalai Lama's Special Envoy: Memoirs of a Lifetime in Pursuit of a Reunited Tibet* (New York: Columbia University Press, 2022), 135. Gyalo Thondup is believed to have encouraged people to work for unity as early as 1961 in Darjeeling. TUA was also believed to be a revival or built upon the framework of Dedhon Tsokpa or the Welfare Association, established in Kalimpong in 1959, which had decided to hand over responsibilities to the new exile government.
15. Carole McGranahan, *Arrested Histories: Tibet, the CIA, and Memories of a Forgotten War* (Durham, NC: Duke University Press, 2010), 146.
16. Chanzoe Ngawang Tenpa, interview with author, Dharamsala, India, July 13, 2015.
17. Ugyen Topgyal Rinpoche, interviews with author, Bir, India, June 12–14, 2022.
18. Gyari, *The Dalai Lama's Special Envoy*, 136.
19. Drawupon Rinchen Tsering, interviews with author, Kamrao, India, August 8–12, 2015.
20. Gyalo Thondup and Anne F. Thurston, *The Noodle Maker of Kalimpong* (New York: Public Affairs, 2015), 212.
21. Tibetan United Association, *Cholsum Chigdril Tsogpai logyue ngoeden jhungrim debther drangsong gyepae choetin she jawa shugso/Chol gsum chig bsgril tshogs pa'i lo rgyus dngos bden byung rim deb ther drang srong dgyes pa'i mchod sprin zhes bya ba bzhugs so* (*Truthful History of the Tibetan United Association*) (Dharamsala: Tibetan United Association, 2005), 14. The book mentions that the former secretary of the department of security, Phenpo Tsedung Lobsang Yeshi; Tehor Tsewang Trinley from Darjeeling; Nyarong Pon Nyima Gyaltsen; Nangra Gendun Zoepa; Bawa Chakzoe Kalsang Tashi; Kirti Chakzoe Lobsang Sangey; Gyangtse Langpa Pasang Gyalpo; Labrang Pema Dorje; Shelkar Tsering Wangdu, and other patriots realized the importance of uniting the people of the three provinces to build Tibet's movement and to fulfill the Dalai Lama's wishes and the visions of the exile government. The United Party was following the great oath to be like a solid mountain of iron.
22. Tibetan United Association, *Cholsum Chigdril*, 14–15. The standing committee members from the religious schools are said to have been in name only and attended only the annual general meeting. Nine members from the three

provinces and four religious schools were elected: Taklung Nyima Sangpo (Nyingma); Dhondup Gyalpo (Kagyu); Lopon Tashi Tenzin (Sakya); Dromo Dungon Rinzin Choedar (Gelug); Karze Tsega Dorjee (Kham); Tenzin Namdo (Rongpo Rabten Gon, Kham); Litang Lobsang (Kham); Labrang Sonam Gyal (Amdo); Gyarong Ngaro Ignyen (Kham); Chone Passang Tsering (Amdo); Tsennyer Nyima Wangyal (U-Tsang); Drashi Gyapon Dorjee (U-Tsang); Shelkar Drungyik Tsering Wangdu (U-Tsang). Many Chushi Gangdrug members signed the pact to follow the aims of the United Party. As some party members put it: Khampas who later turned against the United Party had been early members.

23. Gyari, *The Dalai Lama's Special Envoy*, 136–137.
24. Prasenjit Duara, *Rescuing History from the Nation* (Chicago: University of Chicago Press, 1995), 5, 27. Duara finds twentieth-century China to be an interesting study because of the hold of modern nationalism as well as the narrative of History. New vocabulary, such as "feudalism," "revolution," and so on came to the Chinese language via the Japanese language. For Tibetans, many of these words were translated from the Chinese.
25. There are two terms for democracy in Tibetan. From 1959 to 2007 two different spellings with slightly different meanings were used: *dmangs gtso* and *mang gtso*. The first was less often used by the Dalai Lama after 1992, and the government-in-exile standardized the spelling to *mang gtso*. The people, however, don't seem to differentiate between them, according to Trine Brox in "Democracy in the Words of the Dalai Lama," *The Tibet Journal* 33, no. 2 (Summer 2008): 65–90.
26. Tibetan United Association, *Bhod Cholsum Chigdril Tsogpae mig yul dontsen gna/ Bhod Chol gsum chig sdril tsogs pa'i dmigs yul don tshen lgna* (*Five Aims of the Tibetan United Association*), Darjeeling, India: Tibetan United Association, April 23, 1964, 8. *Cholsum Chigdril Tsogpai logyue ngoeden jhungrim debther drangsong gyepae choetin she jawa shugso/Chol gsum chig bsgril tshogs pa'i lo rgyus dngos bden byung rim deb ther drang srong dgyes pa'i mchod sprin zhes bya ba bzhugs so* (*Truthful History of the Tibetan United Association*), Dharamsala: Tibetan United Association, 2005), 171–175.
27. Tibetan United Association, *Five Aims of the Tibetan United Association*, 1–15.
28. Tibetan United Association, *Five Aims of the Tibetan United Association*, 13.
29. Tenzin Gyatso, the 14th Dalai Lama of Tibet, *Speeches of His Holiness the XIV Dalai Lama (1959–1989) vol. 1*, trans. Sonam Gyatso (Dharamsala: Library of Tibetan Works and Archives, 2011), 115.
30. Ugyen Topgyal Rinpoche, interview with author, Bir, India, June 11, 2022.
31. Ugyen Topgyal Rinpoche, interview with author, Bir, India, June 11, 2022.
32. Juchen Thupten Namgyal, *Juchen Thupten gyi kutse logyue/ Ju chen thub bstan gyi sku tshe'i lo rgyus* (*Autobiography of Juchen Thupten)*, (Chauntra, District Mandi, H.P, India: Juchentsang, 2014), 6: 59.
33. Tenzin Gyatso, the 14th Dalai Lama of Tibet, *Speeches of His Holiness the XIV Dalai Lama*, 50–51. The Dalai Lama cautions Tibetans against misinterpreting democracy as being a "lawless system" in a speech to exile officials in

October 1964. He states the importance of balancing "democratic representation and bureaucratic implementation"—democracy and centralization.

34. Chanzoe Ngawang Tenpa, interview with author, Dharamsala, India, July 13, 2015.
35. Chanzoe Ngawang Tenpa, interview with author, Dharamsala, India, July 13, 2015.
36. Ugyen Topgyal Rinpoche, story narrated to the author on WhatsApp, June 19, 2022.
37. Carole McGranahan, "Tibet's Cold War," *Journal of Cold War Studies* 8, no. 3 (2006): 116.
38. Thondup, *The Noodle Maker of Kalimpong*, 188.
39. Thondup, *The Noodle Maker of Kalimpong*, 188.
40. Chamberlain Phala Thupten Woeden, one of the most powerful politicians in Tibet and in exile, was from U-Tsang; he had gone to Taiwan, as had Gyalo Thondup, and nothing was made of their relations with Taiwan. Martham Thoesam, a former monk, was very active within the Chushi Gangdrug community in Kalimpong and Darjeeling. He was one of the founders of a political association, Mimang (the people) established in exile in 1961, according to Jamyang Norbu in *Shadow Tibet*. Other founders were Lithang Tseta Lobsang Tashi, Trehor Gara Lama, Tsakhalo Lhazoe Gyaltsen, Tungsun Jhola, and Manang Abo Pema Tsewang. Manang Abo was a member in Lhasa before 1960. When the controversy over the misuse of CIA funds reached its peak in 1962–1963, Thoesam and his friends distributed pamphlets suggesting that Gyalo Thondup be investigated for misusing funds meant for the warriors. It was not long before Thoesam, Manang Abo, and others were denounced as Chinese spies. Abo was held under house arrest in Calcutta and Thoesam was arrested by Indian intelligence and held in Calcutta. He was accused of having ties to Communist China and was transferred to the Deoli Internment Camp in Rajasthan, where many Chinese residents of India were also held. Thoesam was told that he would be released after two to three years. Khamtrul Rinpoche's monks refused to sign a document renouncing Thoesum because they knew him well and believed the accusations against him to be false. Thoesam was held in prison for ten years according to them. He lost his property and his relations, and was not permitted to return to his home in Darjeeling. He maintained his innocence until his death.
41. Namgyal, *Juchen Thupten gyi kutse logyue*, 6: 217–218.
42. Writer, interview with author.
43. Cheme Dorjee, phone messages on WhatsApp, 2022.
44. Rinchen Norbu, interview with author, Gangtok, India, September 6, 2015. Rinchen Norbu worked for the *Ranwang Parkhang* for sixteen years. He stated that the funder and founder were from the Chushi Gangdrug but was never certain where the funds came from. Whether from the Chushi Gangdrug or from the exile government, it was assumed the money was obtained by Gyalo

Thondup. All of the Chushi Gangdrug leaders were involved then with Gyalo Thondup; they felt he had the skills to communicate with both Western and Indian leaders, which many of the Chushi Gangdrug leaders lacked. Gyari Rinpoche was helping as a translator while he was in the seventh grade at Mount Hermon school. Rinchen Norbu was the only Khampa working with five *kudaks* (aristocrats) in *Ranwang Parkhang* for a while. He recalled them saying: What is a *khamtuk* (kid from Kham) doing in the midst of *kudaks*? Around 1965, the newspaper was given over to Chigdril Tsogpa, the United Party. Dorjee Lhamo Barchungtsang, interview with author, Kathmandu, Nepal, November 16, 2015.

45. The divide between Lithang and Batang troops added to this tension.
46. George N. Patterson, *Requiem for Tibet* (London: Aurum Press, 1990), 181. In 1950 Tsepon Shakabpa purchased gold bullion in the United States; this was put under the Sikkim Chogyal's protection. In 1950 additional gold from the Dalai Lama's treasury was also placed for safekeeping in Sikkim. The sale of the gold never worked out.

    Thondup, *The Noodle Maker of Kalimpong*, 215. Gyalo Thondup blames Dundul Namgyal Tsarong (George Tsarong) for "mismanagement" and for losing the money. Tsarong's family refutes these charges with countercharges insisting Gyalo Thondup was involved in making the decisions.
47. Central Tibetan Administration, "Kashag's statement to all Tibetans on the recent conflicts in Lo," August 28, 1971; Kenneth John Knaus, *Orphans of the Cold War* (New York: PublicAffairs, 1999), 293.
48. Thondup, *The Noodle Maker of Kalimpong*, 232.
49. Ann Frechette, *Tibetans in Nepal: The Dynamics of International Assistance among a Community in Exile* (New York: Berghahn Books, 2002), 18.
50. McGranahan, "Tibet's Cold War," 116.
51. Namgyal, *Juchen Thupten gyi kutse logyue*, 6: 284. Juchen Thupten writes about the arrest and death of Amdo Dolma Kyab on August 14, 1970. Thupten claims Kyab was arrested on February 6, 1970, on his way to Pokhara, Nepal, by order of Lhamo Tsering. Lhamo Tsering claimed Kyab had charged into their compound saying he would destroy the establishment in Lo Manthang. Thupten writes that on February 21, 1970, Lhamo Tsering ordered 400 soldiers under Dhargon Pedor to fire at 32 people under Gayang or Markham, Tsepak of Karze Choeden, Asang, and A-Thinley of the third, ninth, and eleventh companies who went to ask about Kyab's arrest, resulting in the death of 12 people and 16 horses (288). The Kashag's statement in 1971 states that Kyab died by suicide.
52. Central Tibetan Administration, "Kashag's statement to all Tibetans on the recent conflicts in Lo," August 28, 1971.
53. Central Tibetan Administration, "Kashag's statement to all Tibetans on the recent conflicts in Lo," August 28, 1971. The official statement accused Gyen Geshe of embezzlement, killing "a number of our own people," and robbing Tibetans.

Frechette, *Tibetans in Nepal*, 71. Gyen Yeshi stated in personal communications with Ann Frechette that he had been "kicked" out by the exile government.
54. Tenzin Gyatso, the 14th Dalai Lama of Tibet, *Speeches of His Holiness the XIV Dalai Lama*, 71.
55. Tenzin Gyatso, the 14th Dalai Lama of Tibet, *Freedom in Exile*, 193.
56. McGranahan, *Arrested Histories*, 146–147.
57. McGranahan, *Arrested Histories*, 147.
58. Gyari, *The Dalai Lama's Special Envoy*, 144.
59. Sonam Damdul, interviews with author, Dharamsala, India, July 16; Clement Town, India, August 16, 2015; Clement Town, June 2–3, 2022.
60. Tashi Gelek Dorjee Damdul and Tashi Dhondup, *Resistance and Unity: The Chinese Invasion, Makchi Shangri Lhagyal, and a History of Tibet (1947–1959)*, ed. Carole McGranahan (Chennai: Notion Press, 2019), 285.

3. THE GROUP OF THIRTEEN

1. Tenzin Norbu, interview with author, Bir, India, July 20, 2015.
2. Tenzin Norbu, interview with author, Bir, India, July 20, 2015.
3. Janet Gyatso, "Down with the Demoness: Reflections on a Feminine Ground in Tibet," *The Tibet Journal* xii, no. 4, "A Special Issue on Women and Tibet" (Winter 1987): 34–46. Gyatso reflects on the significance of the *Srin-mo* (female evil spirit) in Tibetan histories that perceives the planet as a living being, feminine but not beneficent and where demoness is a threat to goodness.
4. Tenzin Norbu, interview with author, Bir, India, July 20, 2015.
5. Lodi Gyaltsen Gyari, *The Dalai Lama's Special Envoy: Memoirs of a Lifetime in Pursuit of a Reunited Tibet* (New York: Columbia University Press, 2022), 146.
6. Tenzin Norbu, interview with author, Bir, India, July 20, 2015.
7. Department of Information and International Relations, DIIR, *Tibet and the Tibetan Struggle: 10 March Statements of His Holiness the Dalai Lama 1961–2005* (Dharamsala: Central Tibetan Administration, 2005), 20–21.
8. Department of Information and International Relations, DIIR, *Tibet and the Tibetan Struggle: 10 March Statements of His Holiness the Dalai Lama*, 21.
9. Tenzin Norbu, interview with author, Bir, India, July 20, 2015.
10. Some accounts suggest this arrest took place in 1962 and others in 1963.
11. Khenpo Tsewang Dongyal Rinpoche, *Light of Fearless Indestructible Wisdom: The Life and Legacy of His Holiness Dudjom Rinpoche* (Boston: Snow Lion, 2008), 129.
12. Dongyal Rinpoche, *Light of Fearless Indestructible Wisdom*, 129–130.
13. Tenzin Norbu, interview with author, Bir, India, July 20, 2015.
14. Jamyang Norbu, "Untangling a Mess of Petrified Noodles II," September 13, 2016, https://www.jamyangnorbu.com/blog/2016/09/13/untangling-a-mess-of-petrified-noodles-ii/.

15. Jamyang Norbu, "Untangling a Mess of Petrified Noodles II," September 13, 2016, https://www.jamyangnorbu.com/blog/2016/09/13/untangling-a-mess-of-petrified-noodles-ii/.
16. Gyalo Thondup and Anne F. Thurston, *The Noodle Maker of Kalimpong* (New York: PublicAffairs, 2015), 212.
17. Gyari, *The Dalai Lama's Special Envoy*, 153.
18. Gyari, *The Dalai Lama's Special Envoy*, 141.
19. The Defense of India Act, 1962. Legislative department, Government of India.
20. Jamyang Norbu, "Untangling a Mess of Petrified Noodles II," September 13, 2016. https://www.jamyangnorbu.com/blog/2016/09/13/untangling-a-mess-of-petrified-noodles-ii/.
21. Mei-hua Lan, "From Lifanyuan to the Mongolian and Tibetan Affairs Commission," in *Managing Frontiers in Qing China: The Lifanyuan and Libu Revisited*, ed. Dittmar Scholrkowitz and Ning Chia (Leiden: Koninklijke Brill, 2017). The MTAC was formed along the lines of the Qing dynasty's establishment of the Mongol Office to symbolize that Inner Mongols were now under Manchu rule. That office took care of Qing and Mongol relations and was renamed Lifanyuan in 1638. The new office added relations with Tibet and Muslim polities in the far west to its duties. In 1906 it was renamed Lifanbu. When the Republic of China took over from the Qing in 1911, both Mongolia and Tibet declared their independence. Sun Yat-sen's concept of the Republic of Five Nationalities (Han-Chinese, Manchus, Mongols, Muslims, and Tibetans) supposed a principle of equality. The Lifanyan ended in 1912 and the Office of Mongolian and Tibetan Affairs established under the Interior Ministry to reflect a shift in China's attitude toward Mongolia and Tibet. The ROC's continuation of the office is a continuation of imperial ideology and practice, of seeing Tibet as part of China.
22. Jamyang Norbu, *Echoes from Forgotten Mountains* (Gurugram: Penguin Random House, 2023), 94.
23. Gyari, *The Dalai Lama's Special Envoy*, 137.
24. Gyari, *The Dalai Lama's Special Envoy*, 144.
25. Gyari, *The Dalai Lama's Special Envoy*, 139.
26. Gyari, *The Dalai Lama's Special Envoy*, 137.
27. Gyari, *The Dalai Lama's Special Envoy*, 146–147.
28. According to minutes of the meeting, the individual accused of breaking up Kathok Ontrul's prayer stated that he did not tell Rinpoche to join the Gelug monks. He indicated that Ontrul Rinpoche had been willing to join them.
29. Marong Adak Choje, interview with author, Dolanji, India, July 28, 2015.
30. Community leaders approached Tibetans living in the settlements, as well as those living in Nepal, Sikkim, and in the West, to sign a letter or take a vow to prove that they were not following Shugden. The community's response, ostracizing and punishing Tibetans who did not comply, is further evidence

of its tendency to shun those who don't follow the Dalai Lama's instructions or wishes.
31. Dawa Norbu, "Editorial: Toward Sectarian Harmony and National Unity," *Tibetan Review* xi, no. 9 (September 1976): 3–4.
32. Dawa Norbu, "Four Rivers Have the Same Water," interview with T. G. Dhongthok, *Tibetan Review*, vol. xi, no. 9 (September 1976): 29. Rinpoche states that in his personal view the Dalai Lama was a *rime* practitioner but that in public he taught mostly Gelugpa teachings (24–25).
33. Jamyang Norbu, "Untangling a Mess of Petrified Noodles II," September 13, 2016. https://www.jamyangnorbu.com/blog/2016/09/13/untangling-a-mess-of-petrified-noodles-ii/.
34. Gyari, *The Dalai Lama's Special Envoy*, 138.
35. Gyari, *The Dalai Lama's Special Envoy*, 137.
36. H. F. Schurmann, "Organization and Response in Communist China," *The Annals of the American Academy of Political and Social Science*, vol. 321, *Contemporary China and the Chinese* (January 1959): 57. Schurmann writes that these strategies also led to deep alienation.
37. Yugyal, interviews with the author, Mainpat, India, September 17–19, 2015.
38. Labrang Tashikhyil was founded by the First Jamyang Zhepa, Jamyang Zhepai Dorje, in 1709. The Qoshot Mongols provided the land and paid for its construction, according to *The Treasury of Lives* (https://treasuryoflives.org/institution/Labrang-Tashikhyil). Jamyang Zhepa, Amdo Zhamar, and Gungthang incarnations had seats in Labrang. Gungthang Jigme Tenpai Wangchuk (1926–2000) became the throne holder of Labrang Tashikhyil in 1954 and served for three years. He was imprisoned and accused of leading and plotting protests against the Communist government of China. He was also punished for refusing invitations to visit Beijing and accept administrative positions in the government. He was in prison from 1958 until 1979 and died in 2000.
39. Khamtrul Rinpoche was the son of a chieftain in Nangchen. Chokling Rinpoche was from Derge.
40. Ugyen Topgyal Rinpoche, interviews with author, Delhi, India, November 10–11, 2015.
41. Ugyen Topgyal Rinpoche, interviews with author, Delhi, India, November 10–11, 2015, Bir, India, and on September 6, 2017.
42. Jinpa, interviews with author, Clement Town, India, July 30–August 1, 2015.
43. Tibetan United Association, *Cholsum Chigdril Tsogpai logyue ngoeden jhungrim debther drangsong gyepae choetin she jawa shugso/Chol gsum chig bsgril tshogs pa'i lo rgyus dngos bden byung rim deb ther drang srong dgyes pa'i mchod sprin zhes bya ba bzhugs so* (*Truthful History of the Tibetan United Association*) (Dharamsala: Tibetan United Association, 2005), 99.
44. The document is signed by Sri. Kant Singh Chouhan, the Chief Officer of Land Distribution in the U.P. Bhoodan Yagna Committee in Lucknow.

4. THE SEVEN RESOLUTIONS AND SUPPORTING DOCUMENTS

1. Tibetan United Association, *Drochoe dhon tsen dun dh'e gyab non chey jhugs so/gros chod don tshan bdun dang de'i rgyab gnon bcas bzhugs so* (*Seven Resolutions and Supporting Documents*) (Darjeeling, India: Tibetan United Association, 1965).
2. "Freedom Given Only for Religious Activities," *Times of India*, April 21, 1959.
3. Jamyang Norbu, *Echoes from Forgotten Mountains* (Gurugram: Penguin Random House, 2023), 765.
4. Diana Maclehose, Letter to Joyce Pearce, July 31, 1966, Files on the Ockenden International, SHC Reference 7155/8/1/12.
5. "The Resolution of the Conference of the Four Major Sects of Tibetan Buddhism and Bon: the first to the eleventh conference," published by the Department of Religion and Culture, CTA.
6. Translated by Bhuchung D. Sonam.
7. Yugyal, interviews with author, Mainpat, India, September 17–19, 2015.
8. Surkhang Wangchen Gelek was chair of the first Kashag (ministers of the cabinet) in exile.
9. As pointed out by Tsering Shakya in a private text message.
10. Joyce Pearce, "Report on visit to Tibetan Refugees in India. April 16th–May 18th, 1963." Courtesy Prof. Tsering Shakya, private collection (his private archive).
11. Ontol Rinpoche, for example, moved from Buxa to Darjeeling because he was unable to adapt to the heat. Kagyud lamas such as Zurmang Trungpa Rinpoche, Drukpa Kagyud Chongon Rinpoche, and Drushey Rinpoche were there briefly and then left to establish their own monasteries elsewhere. Some monks from Trangu Monastery (Kagyud) were there too. There were about twenty-seven Sakya monks.
12. Pema Dorje, interview with author, Kathmandu, Nepal, November 24, 2015.
13. Tibetan United Association, *Seven Resolutions and Supporting Documents*, 1965.
14. Tsodi Bongsar, interview with author, Toronto, Canada, 2019; phone conversation, June 20, 2022.
15. Tsodi Bongsar, interview with author, phone conversation, June 20, 2022.
16. Pat Brewster (Committee on Relief and Gift Supplies, National Christian Council of India), "Review of the Tibetan Refugee Programme," December 1965.
17. George N. Patterson, *Requiem for Tibet* (London: Aurum Press, 1990), 181.
18. Patterson, *Requiem for Tibet*, 182.
19. Brewster, "Review of the Tibetan Refugee Programme," December 1965, 1.
20. Brewster, "Review of The Tibetan Refugee Programme," December, 1965, 2.
21. The Pangdatsang family established themselves as important figures in Lhasa, rising to the ranks of aristocracy in society and government. Rapga Pangdatsang, the middle brother, founded the Tibetan Improvement Party in

1939. Based in Kalimpong, this is viewed as the first political party in Tibet and was not well received by the Tibetan government, as its goal was to create a democratic and modern political system. Carole McGranahan has more on Rapga's political activities: "In Rapga's Library: The Texts and Times of a Rebel Tibetan Intellectual," *Cahiers d'Extreme-Asie* 15 (2005): 253–274. Topgyal and Ragpa revolted against the Tibetan government's army in 1943 on account of what Jamyang Norbu describes as Lhasa politics in his book *Echoes from the Forgotten Mountains*, as well as against the Kuomintang and the Communists. Rapga was accused of being an agent for the Chinese. Jamyang Norbu writes that Topgyal Pangdatsang didn't rise against the Communist Chinese government in 1956 like other Eastern Tibetan leaders. Heather Stoddard's work on the Pangdatsang is important in understanding their contributions and their role in Tibetan history.

22. Carole McGranahan, *Arrested Histories: Tibet, The CIA, and Memories of a Forgotton War* (Durham, NC: Duke University Press, 2010), 144–145. Also see more on Pangdatsang in McGranahan's book, and the biography of Rapga Pangdatsang on *The Treasury of Lives*, https://treasuryoflives.org/biographies/view/Rapga-Pangdatsang/P1KT1.

23. Jamyang Norbu, "Untangling a Mess of Petrified Noodles II," *Shadow Tibet*, September 13, 2016, https://www.jamyangnorbu.com/blog/2016/09/13/untangling-a-mess-of-petrified-noodles-ii/.

24. Carole McGranahan, "Rapga Pangdatsang," *Treasury of Lives*, https://treasuryoflives.org/biographies/view/Rapga-Pangdatsang/13521.

25. Joseph Hou, conversations and texts with the author, Collegeville, Pennsylvania, U.S.A., May 18 and July 15, 2024.

26. McGranahan, "Rapga Pangdatsang."

27. Joseph Hou, interviews and texts with the author, May 18 and July 15, 2024.

28. Tibetan United Association, *Cholsum Chigdril Tsogpai logyue ngoeden jhungrim debther drangsong gyepae choetin she jawa shugso/Chol gsum chig bsgril tshogs pa'i lo rgyus dngos bden byung rim deb ther drang srong dgyes pa'i mchod sprin zhes bya ba bzhugs so* (*Truthful History of the Tibetan United Association*) (Dharamsala: Tibetan United Association, 2005), 84–85, under the section "About Pomda Wangmo." The book claims that on June 22, 1966, Wangmo came with "Guomintang employee Tsepakh Dorjee and his wife" and that Dharamsala Tibetans and government employees protested against her being there. They threatened that they would not take responsibility if something happened to her. They also protested against her seeing the Dalai Lama. Wangmo had clarified that her only reason for being in Darjeeling was to sort out the family estate and to seek an audience with the Dalai Lama.

29. Jamyang Norbu writes in his blog *Shadow Tibet* that an American scholar claims that the Indian government took this action on Gyalo Thondup's advice. https://www.jamyangnorbu.com/blog/2016/09/13/untangling-a-mess-of-petrified-noodles-ii/.

30. Gyalo Thondup and Anne F. Thurston, *The Noodle Maker of Kalimpong* (New York: PublicAffairs, 2015), 213–214. Gyalo Thondup calls the move to Taiwan

a "defection." For more on Gyalo Thondup and Yuthok see Jamyang Norbu, https://www.jamyangnorbu.com/blog/2016/09/13/untangling-a-mess-of-petrified-noodles-ii/.
31. Thondup, *The Noodle Maker of Kalimpong*, 135.
32. Thondup, *The Noodle Maker of Kalimpong*, 65.
33. Thondup, *The Noodle Maker of Kalimpong*, 97.
34. Thondup, *The Noodle Maker of Kalimpong*, 97.
35. Lodi Gyaltsen Gyari, *The Dalai Lama's Special Envoy: Memoirs of a Lifetime in Pursuit of a Reunited Tibet* (New York: Columbia University Press, 2022), 124.
36. Jamyang Norbu, https://www.jamyangnorbu.com/blog/2016/09/13/untangling-a-mess-of-petrified-noodles-ii/.
37. https://treasuryoflives.org/biographies/view/Surkhang-Wangchen-Gelek/2423.
38. Juchen Thupten Namgyal, *Juchen Thupten gyi kutse logyue/Ju chen thub bstan gyi sku tshe'i lo rgyus (Autobiography of Juchen Thupten)*, 21 vols. (Chauntra, District Mandi, H.P, India: Juchentsang, 2014), 6:131.
39. Jigmie Dorji Yuthok, "Yuthok's Rejoinder to the Noodle Maker," *Tibetan Political Review*, July 30, 2016. Now removed from the internet.
40. Jigmie Yuthok, "Yuthok's Rejoinder to the Noodle Maker."
41. Tsering Shakya, email to author, February 2, 2022.
42. Namgyal, *Juchen Thupten gyi kutse logyue*, 6: 59. Gyari, *The Dalai Lama's Special Envoy*, 138.
43. Namgyal, *Juchen Thupten gyi kutse logyue*, 6: 59.
44. Niraja Gopal Jayal, *Citizenship and Its Discontents* (Cambridge, MA: Harvard University Press, 2013), 3.
45. Bridget Anderson, *Us and Them? The Dangerous Politics of Immigration Control* (Oxford: Oxford University Press, 2013), 2.
46. Anderson, *Us and Them?* 3.
47. Tariq Modood, "A Basis for and Two Obstacles in the Way of a Multiculturalist Tradition," *British Journal of Sociology* 59, no. 1 (2008): 49. Modood writes that "To be a citizen, no less than to have just become a citizen, is to have a right to not just be recognized but to debate the terms of recognition."
48. Drawupon Rinchen Tsering, phone interview with author, August 2023. Jigme Yuthok had also requested an audience and had not been granted one. Both Wangmo Pangdatsang and Jigme Yuthok's request are discussed in a joint Kashag and parliament official meeting in 1977.

5. AGAINST THE GRAIN OF HISTORY: MUTINY IN OCKENDEN SCHOOL

1. Per Kvaerne and Dan Martin, *Drenpa's Proclamation: The Rise and Decline of the Bon Religion in Tibet* (Kathmandu: Vajra Books 2023), 2.
2. Kvaerne and Martin, *Drenpa's Proclamation*, 9.
3. Kvaerne and Martin, *Drenpa's Proclamation*, 6.

4. Tsepak Rigzin, "The Tibetan Schools in the Diaspora," in *Exile as Challenge: The Tibetan Diaspora*, ed. Dagmar Bernstorff and Hubertus von Welck (Hyderabad: Orient Longman Private Ltd., 2004), 367.
5. *The Spirit of Tibet: Universal Heritage. Selected Speeches and Writings of HH The Dalai Lama XIV*, ed. A. A. Shiromany and Tibetan Parliamentary and Policy Research Center (New Delhi: Allied Publishers Ltd., 1995), 317.
6. Tibet Documentation, *Exile: A Photo Journal (1959–1989)* (Dharamsala: Tibet Documentation, 2017), 87. The council had formed a publication section, a team of renowned religious teachers—Dudjom Rinpoche, Zemey Rinpoche, and Ngor Thartse Rinpoche—to help write textbooks for the schools. Tibetan children were also being sent to Europe. The Pestalozzi Children's Village in Trogen, Switzerland, was established in October 1960 to resettle children in Switzerland. In addition, about 200 Tibetan children were adopted by Swiss families. Three years later, the Pestalozzi International Children's Village in Sussex, England, admitted twenty-two Tibetan children, followed by another batch of twenty-eight. By the early 1970s, there were as many as 600 Tibetan children studying or living in Europe.
7. According to Dexter's and Dr. Snellgrove's respective letters on May 29, 1966, Tenzin and Dexter had met with the Dalai Lama before accepting the job at the school.
8. All documents related to Ockenden refer to Geshe Sangye Tenzin Jongdong as Sangye Tenzin. He was already an acclaimed scholar, teacher, and practitioner at the time of this incident. In 1968, as the thirty-third abbot of Menri, he was named Lungtok Tenpai Nyima Rinpoche.
9. Malcolm Dexter, letter to Joyce Pearce, May 1, 1966.
10. In his letter to the Bureau of the Dalai Lama on May 6, 1966, Dexter explains that Kelsang Liushar and Choden had gone to see a movie at the height of events.
11. Ugyan Choedup, "Competing visions: schooling the nation and the 'revolt' at the Ockenden Tibetan school," *International Journal of Asian Studies* 20 (2023): 501.
12. Peter Woodard, "A Report on the Mutiny at the Ockenden School," 1. Files on the Ockenden International, SHC Reference 7155/8/1/11–14.
13. Perhaps those who wrote the first letter to Pearce were reunited with five of the younger students from the school who had been escorted by Gyaltsen Choden.
14. Woodard, "A Report on the Mutiny at the Ockenden School," 4. Thirty boys signed the letter. It is not dated.
15. T. C. Tara, letter to Joyce Pearce, May 4.
16. Joyce Pearce, letter to Malcolm Dexter, May 4, 1966, pp. 1–2, Files on the Ockenden International, SHC Reference 7155/8/1/11.
17. Malcolm Dexter, letter to Joyce Pearce, May 10, 1966, pp. 1–2, Files on the Ockenden International, Reference, 7155/8/1/13, Ref. no. MRWD/DM. Dexter also expresses this suspicion in his letters to Gyalo Thondup on

May 5, and to Mrs. Taring, who was running the Tibetan Homes Foundation in Mussoorie, on May 7. Letters to Pearce written by Diana Maclehose and Per Kvaerne, both working as teachers in Ockenden, also express their suspicion about the role the two Tibetan teachers played in organizing the revolt and mention that the students threatened to physically harm Dexter and Tenzin.

18. T. N. Takla, letter to Joyce Pearce, May 25, 1966, Files on the Ockenden International, SHC Reference 7155/8/1/Thirteen, Ref. no. MRWD/DM.
19. T. N. Takla correspondence, May 25, Files on the Ockenden International, 3.
20. He was rumored to be Pearce's boyfriend.
21. T. C. Tara, letter to Joyce Pearce, June 5, 1966, pp. 1–7, Files on the Ockenden International, SHC Reference 7155/8/1/13.
22. Joyce Pearce, letter to Malcolm Dexter, May 13, 1966, Files on the Ockenden International, SHC Reference 7155/8/1/13.
23. Gyaltsen Choden, *Bhod kyi gyalrab dang drel we mitsei logue dentam drimed sersun tseg pe lhunpo/Bod kyi rgyal rabs dang 'brel ba'i tshe'i lo rgyus bden gtam dri med gser gzhun brtsegs pa'i lhun po* (*Tibet: A History of Tibet and a Stainless Truthful Biography*) (Self-pub., Karnataka, India, 2016), 368. Gyaltsen Choden writes that he worked briefly for the newspaper *Tibetan Freedom* around 1960 at the invitation of Gyalo Thondup. He recalls that he had refused to sign a letter with the decision to expel ten students and suggested instead they be sent to a training course. His suggestion was dismissed, the students were beaten, and all but five rebelled against Dexter (368).
24. Gyaltsen Choden, *Bhod kyi gyalrab dang drel we mitsei logyue dentam drimed sershun tseg pe lhunpo*, 365–370.
25. Translated from the Tibetan by Bhuchung D. Sonam.
26. These six students were Ugyen, Tsering Dorjee, Penpa, Jamdak, Wangdu, and Tsering.
27. Lungtok Tenpai Nyima, the 33rd Menri Trizin, or Sangye Tenzin was born in 1927 in the village of Kyongtsang in the far eastern province of Amdo. He visited Gyalrong at the age of 26.
28. Pat Brewster, letter to Wiederkehr, June 2, 1966, 1.
29. Pat Brewster, letter to Wiederkehr, 3.
30. Another volunteer working with Gungthang Tsultrim to build the settlement in Clement Town expresses his suspicion about an "underground turbulence" spreading across the Tibetan political body in a letter to Pearce dated July 23, 1966. He refers to similar crises in places such as Mainpat, Rajpur, and Dalhousie, where members of the Thirteen were living and were named "running dogs" of the Chinese.
31. Tsering Wangyal, interview with author, Dolanji, India, July 28, 2015.
32. Khedup Gyamtso, phone interview with author, July 24, 2024.
33. Khedup Gyamtso, phone interview with author, July 24, 2024.
34. Choedup, "Competing visions," 501.
35. Choedup, "Competing visions," 500.

36. Choedup, "Competing visions," 501.
37. Woodard, "A Report on the Mutiny at the Ockenden School," 1–89.
38. W. D. Shakabpa, *Tibet: A Political History* (New Delhi: Potala Publications, 1967), 51.
39. Shakabpa, *Tibet: A Political History*, 52.
40. Geshe Lhundup Sopa, *Lectures on Tibetan Religious Culture*, vol. 1 (Delhi: Library of Tibetan Works and Archives, 1983), 129.
41. Samten Gyaltsen Karmay, "King Glang Dar-ma and His Rule," In *The Arrow and the Spindle: Studies in History, Myths, Rituals and Beliefs in Tibet, Vol. II*, ed. Samten G. Karmay (Kathmandu: Mandala Publications, 2005), 15.
42. Karmay, "King Gland Dar-ma," 28.
43. Matthew T. Kapstein, *The Tibetans* (Malden, MA: Blackwell Publishing, 2006), 80.
44. Karmay, "King Gland Dar-ma," 24.
45. For more on periodization, see Bryan J. Cuevas, "Some Reflections on the Periodization of Tibetan History," in *The Tibetan History Reader*, ed. Gray Tuttle and Kurtis R. Schaeffer (New York: Columbia University Press, 2013), 67–78.
46. Kvaerne and Martin, *Drenpa's Proclamation*, 13.
47. Per Kvaerne, "Zhangzhung, Bon, and China: The Construction of an Alternative Tibetan Historical Narrative," in *Tibetan Subjectivities on the Global Stage*, ed. Shelly Bhoil and Enrique Galvan-Alvarez (Lanham, MD: Lexington Books, 2018), 7.
48. Kvaerne, "Zhangzhung, Bon, and China," 7.
49. Namkhai Norbu and K. Dhondup, "Tibetan Culture," *The Tibet Journal* 3, no. 3 (Autumn 1978): 39–40.
50. Carole McGranahan, *Arrested Histories: Tibet, the CIA, and Memories of a Forgotten War* (Durham, NC: Duke University Press, 2010), 3.
51. McGranahan, *Arrested Histories*, 3.
52. Prasenjit Duara, *Rescuing History from the Nation* (Chicago: University of Chicago Press, 1995), 5. In his analysis of the relationship between the nation-state and nationalism and the linear "evolutionary history" in early twentieth-century China, Duara suggests that national history secures "the nation as a subject of History." It transforms views of the past as well as the meaning of the nation and the world, particularly by establishing "which peoples and cultures belonged to the time of History and who and what had to be eliminated" (5).
53. Jonathan Boyarin and Daniel Boyarin, *Powers of Diaspora: Two Essays on the Relevance of Jewish Culture* (Minneapolis: University of Minnesota Press, 2002), 4. The Boyarins use the term "permanently at risk" to explain the diasporic consciousness as composed of "contingency and genealogy."
54. Tsering Shakya, *The Dragon in the Land of Snows* (New York: Penguin, 1999), xxxiii.
55. Shakya, *The Dragon in the Land of Snows*, xxxiii.

6. THE CONVERGENCE OF THE THIRTEEN LEADERS

1. Achu Lama, interview with author, Tashi Jong, India, July 22, 2015.
2. Dorje Pasang did spend some time in a section called Gyarong Rokor, and the Lingtsang group in Lingtsang Rokor. The people of Lingtsang had escaped together from Tibet under the guidance of Yarling Wangyal, a minister in the Kingdom of Lingtsang. They had first lived in Gangtok, then moved to Rajpur in the late 1960s, where they lived for five years. After Yarling Wangyal's death, Sey Jigme, who had been in Kalimpong, came to Rajpur at the request of the people of Lingtsang. They eventually established their own settlement in Munduwala, near Dehra Dun, with Gungthang Tsultrim's help.
3. Pat Brewster, *Life History of Gibbon Brewster (Pat)*, Personal papers, 43. Self-published, n.d. Courtesy of Deborah Brewster and the Brewster family. Read at Deborah Brewster's home, New York, July 26, 2024.
4. G. (Pat) Brewster, Letter to Swiss Aid to Tibetans, March 9, 1965, Ref. 008786. Some of Pat Brewster's letters are signed "G. Brewster."
5. G. (Pat) Brewster, Letter to Mr. Ernest Wiederkehr, Swiss Aid, March 25, 1965.
6. Brewster, *Life History of Gibbon Brewster (Pat)*, Personal papers, 45.
7. Brewster, *Life History of Gibbon Brewster (Pat)*, Personal papers, 49.
8. Chanzoe Ngawang Tempa, personal interview, July 13, 2015, Dharamsala. He thought the Thirteen formed with a good goal but took the wrong path because the leaders were arrogant.
9. Pat Brewster, "Letter to Dr. Ernest Wiederkehr," August 11, 1966, Ref. 012085: 2.
10. Pat Brewster, "Review," December 1965, 2.
11. Brewster, *Life History of Gibbon Brewster (Pat)*, Personal papers, 57.
12. Lobsang Phuntsok Lhalungpa, "A Brief Report," June 19, 1965. Draft of a report with notes. Permission from Samphe Lhalungpa, draft of report dated June 19, 1965, with handwritten revisions by Lobsang Phuntsok Lhalungpa.
13. Lhalungpa, "A Brief Report," 1.
14. Lhalungpa, "A Brief Report," 3.
15. Drawupon Rinchen Tsering, personal interview, Kamrao. He was asked by the Private Office of the Dalai Lama to lead the settlement. Drawupon met Brewster in Sataun, where TIRS had purchased land for a smaller settlement; from there they traveled to Kamrao, a remote hill. It had seemed an impossible site; the closest neighbors were in the village tucked in the distant mountains. Drawupon signed the documents for both camps. Kathok Ontrul Rinpoche would settle in Sataun with members of his monastery and people.
16. By October 1966, Brewster's letters were being sent on letterhead of the organization Sharan (Christian Agency for Refugees), which indicates that the organization's name had changed or the funds were being sent through this different organization. In his letter to Weiderkehr on November 3, 1966, Brewster writes that there was a change in the organizational structure and that the

Tibetan Refugee work was being conducted through Sharan. This organization was a joint program of the World Council of Churches and the National Christian Council of India. So it was a separate entity from CORAGS, the organization that had hired him to work in India.

17. Tibetans from Mainpat's camp 1 made life difficult for Namkha Dorje's clan by telling the larger society that the Khampa camp was pro-Chinese and receiving funds from the Kuomintang party.
18. Juchen Thupten Namgyal, *Juchen Thupten gyi kutse logyue/Ju chen thub bstan gyi sku tshe'i lo rgyus (Autobiography of Juchen Thupten)*, 21 vols. (Chauntra, District Mandi, H.P, India: Juchentsang, 2014), 6: 216–217. Thupten writes that the United Party had spread rumors that Penor Rinpoche was receiving money from Taiwan. Thupten was living in Bylakuppe at this point.
19. Tenzin Gyatso, the 14th Dalai Lama of Tibet, *My Land and My People* (New York: Hachette Book Group, 1997), 194. As recent as the Dalai Lama's eightieth birthday the cabinet urged all Tibetans to "engage in acts that are consistent with the wishes of His Holiness the Dalai Lama and at the same time endeavor ceaselessly in preserving, promoting and acting upon traditional Tibetan values."
20. Yudru Tsomu, "The Rise of a Political Strongman in Derge in the Early Twentieth Century: The Story of Jago Topden," in *Frontier Tibet: Patterns of Change in the Sino-Tibetan Borderlands*, ed. Stéphane Gros (Amsterdam: Amsterdam University Press, 2019), 370.
21. Tsomu, "The Rise of a Political Strongman," 370.
22. Even within this group, the differences exist in their political formations and history.
23. Richard Tapper, *Frontier Nomads of Iran: A Political and Social History of the Shahsevan* (Cambridge: Cambridge University Press, 1997), 8. Dawa Norbu, *Tibet: The Road Ahead* (London: Rider, 1998), 97. Tribes are not specifically referring to nomads, as there were semipastoralists referred to as tribes. For Richard Tapper the coincidence between nomads and tribes is not so much causal as it is a function of their relations with the state. He suggests that states developed from military forces that drew from nomadic tribes' armed groups. Rulers sometimes created tribes and tribal chiefs, and nomadism was a strategy (8).
24. "In Reply to Allegations Contained in the Pamphlet 'The Assassination of Gungthang Tsultrim,'" published by the exile government in Dharamsala, August 9, 1978.
25. Lodi Gyaltsen Gyari, *The Dalai Lama's Special Envoy: Memoirs of a Lifetime in Pursuit of a Reunited Tibet* (New York: Columbia University Press, 2022), 143–145. Gyari Rinpoche writes that the Karmapa only agreed to be the head of the Thirteen after "influential Khampa leaders convinced him that the future of the Dharma was at great risk." Members of the Thirteen reminded me that the Karmapa was affiliated with their monasteries in Kham and was their root guru, so it was natural for them to turn to him.

6. THE CONVERGENCE OF THE THIRTEEN LEADERS ⚜ 299

26. "Sogh" stood for the river Soghde, which ran through the region, and "Geimar" for the low hidden valley. There were thirty-nine chiefs in Hor, and Sogh Geimar was one of the regions of which Sangye Namgyal was chief.
27. The gathering helped bridge old feuds. For example, Drawupon Rinchen Tsering and Jagoetsang Namgyal Dorjee held unresolved bad blood over the battle in Yushu in the mid-1950s. They had formally reconciled their differences when they got to India. Drawupon said in a voice message to me that six Chushi Gangdrug members took an oath (*nagyen*) when the Chushi Gangdrug was regrouped in Mustang to work in harmony and toward their goal of freedom. Andrugtsang Gompo Tashi and Gyen Yeshi were on one side and Drawupon Rinchen Tsering and Jagoe Namgyal Dorjee on the other. Drawupon spoke of his great affection for Jagoe Namgyal Dorjee and their close friendship.
28. The Woollen Factory was established by the exile government, and a group from lower Drunpga settled there. The settlement was viewed as being established by the exile government to keep track of the Thirteen settlements.
29. Jadurtsang Sonam Zangpo, interview with author, Dolanji, India, July 2, 2015.
30. Drubju and Asi Lama, phone interview with author, November 2, 2023.
31. Asi Lama, interview with author, November 2, 2023.
32. Drubju and Asi Lama, interview with author, November 2, 2023.
33. Ernest Renan, "What is a Nation?" in *Nation and Narration*, ed. Homi Bhabha (London: Routledge, 1990), 11. Renan writes that forgetting is crucial to the creation of a nation: "Unity is always effected by means of brutality." The essence of a nation is that "all individuals have many things in common, and also that they have forgotten many things." Eric Hobsbawm points out that the kind of history nations seek is partly built on myths ("Ethnicity and Nationalism in Europe Today," in *Mapping the Nation*, ed. Gopal Balakrishnan [New York: Verso, 2012], 255). The past, also a construction, relies on remembering as well as forgetting. Hobsbawm echoes Renan that historical error is a crucial factor in the nation's makeup.
34. Engin F. Isin and Patricia K. Wood, *Citizenship and Identity* (London: Sage Publications, 1999), 37–38.
35. Minutes of the Kashag meeting regarding the United Party and the Thirteen held on July 20, 1977. Attendees included members of the cabinet and the parliament: Kesang Damdul, Lodoe Tharchin, Lobsang Khenrap, Lobsang Singye, Lo Nyendrak, Tsering Wangdu, Tsering Choden Dhompa, Dechen Dolma, Thupten Dawa, Gyurme Woeser Gyantse, Jampa Wangdu, Gyantse, Thupten Sangye, Tenzin Dhondup. In this meeting Lobsang Yeshi, representing the United Party, stated that the party followed the Dalai Lama and worked under him. The United Party didn't aim to be bigger than the exile government but to help the government.
36. Gungthang Sonam Wangyal, phone interview with author, August 19, 2023.

7. A POLITICS OF SORROW

1. Tibetan United Association, *Cholsum Chigdril Tsogpai logyue ngoeden jhungrim debther drangsong gyepae choetin she jawa shugso/Chol gsum chig bsgril tshogs pa'i lo rgyus dngos bden byung rim deb ther drang srong dgyes pa'i mchod sprin zhes bya ba bzhugs so* (*Truthful History of the Tibetan United Association*) (Dharamsala: Tibetan United Association, 2005), 98. Years later the Academy of Dance was renamed the Tibetan Institute of Performing Arts or TIPA.
2. Tibetan Welfare Association, *The Assasination* [sic] *of Gungthang Tsultrim* (Self-pub, June 1978), 4–5. Referred to more popularly as *The Black Friday*.
3. On June 17, 1971, exile representatives who visited Clement Town were met with resistance, and one Tibetan man who opposed Tsultrim was killed when fellow Tibetans from the camp threw stones at him. Gyari Rinpoche writes in his autobiography that the Thirteen sought Indian citizenship "with the intention of making a clean break with the CTA" (143).
4. Letter from Gungthang Tsultrim to PM Indira Gandhi, June 23, 1971.
5. Amdo Dhondup, *Gyal khab Sum Gyi Mangmi/Rgyal khab gsum gyi dmag mi* (*A Soldier of Three Nations*), New Delhi: Denrab Tsomrig Tsogchung, 2019, 302–303.
6. Tibetan United Association, *Cholsum Chigdril Tsogpai Logyue Ngoeden Jhungrim Debther Drangsong Gyepae Choetin She Jawa Shugso* (*Truthful History of the Tibetan United Association*), 2005, 98–114.
7. Lodi Gyaltsen Gyari, *The Dalai Lama's Special Envoy: Memoirs of a Lifetime in Pursuit of a Reunited Tibet* (New York: Columbia University Press, 2022), 149.
8. Gyari, *The Dalai Lama's Special Envoy*, 150.
9. Gyari, *The Dalai Lama's Special Envoy*, 151, 269.
10. Gungthang Tsultrim, letter to Mrs. Gandhi, June 23, 1971. Copies were forwarded to Shri K. C. Pant, the Minister of State for Home Affairs; the secretary of Home Affairs; the district magistrate; and the superintendent of police in Dehra Dun.
11. The first article on the Thirteen's citizenship application appeared before June 1971.
12. Cheme Dorjee Jagoetsang, email correspondence, October 7, 2020.
13. Gyari, *The Dalai Lama's Special Envoy*, 143.
14. Central Tibetan Administration, "In Reply to Allegations Contained in the Pamphlet 'The Assassination of Gungthang Tsultrim,'" Dharamsala, August 9, 1978, 6.
15. "13-Groups Deny Taiwanese Connection," *Tibetan Review* XIII, no. 10 (October 1978): 6.
16. Minutes of the Kalon's visit to the Thirteen settlements mention that Gungthang Tsultrim sent a response to the secretary of the Information and Publicity Office on November 11, 1977, saying that Bawa Kalsang Choephel had given this information to the Chinese reporter, who then published the news in a small private-run newspaper.

17. Amdo Dhondup, *Gyalkhab Sum Gyi Mangmi/Rgyal khab gsum gyi dmag mi* (*A Soldier of Three Nations*) (New Delhi: Denrab Tsomrig Tsogchung, 2019), 301–302.
18. Gyari, *The Dalai Lama's Special Envoy*, 12Brewster, *Life History of Gibbon Brewster (Pat)*, Personal papers, 51.25.
19. The Kashag Cabinet Secretariat, Letter to the Thirteen, April 10, 1978, Dedon File no 68, 1978, Ref. b (*kha* 37). The following Thirteen members were to attend the meeting, according to a letter from Gungthang Tsultrim to the exile government on January 3, 1978: Chodak from Rumtek; Sey Dhonyo and Kunchok Ngudup from the Derge Bir settlement; Jamyang Gyaltsen and Pema Losel from Nangchen Bir settlement; Dorzong Rinpoche and Genam from Tashi Jong; Gungthang Tsultrim and Lobsang from Clement Town; Dzongnang Rinpoche and Khorchen Tulku from Clement Town; Jinchong Tulku, Dongen, and Anam from Sataun; Sodam from Kamrao; Sey Jigme from Lingtsang settlement; Pon Namkha Dorje and Yugyal from Mainpat; and Yongdzin Lopon Tenzin Namdak Rinpoche and Namkha Tenzin from Dolanji settlement.
20. *The Black Friday* states that Kesang Gosar and Kesang joined Jinpa to look for the assassin. He was caught in Nepal, possibly with help from Gen Yeshe. The Thirteen raised Rs. 10,000 from the settlements toward legal fees to file a case against the apprehended suspect.
21. The Dalai Lama had also inaugurated the Tibetan Woollen Mill in Bir in April 1968.
22. "Director's Report on the Present Activities and Future Plans of the Seven Settlements Under TIRS," from the director, Sonam Rapten, to John Conway at the Tibetan Refugee Aid Society in Vancouver, Canada, December 9, 1971.
23. University of British Columbia Library Archives, RBSC-ARC-1554-4-13.
24. Elders from the Thirteen also state that Juchen Thupten, who was from Kham, was trusted by many of the Thirteen leaders and that he ultimately tricked them into reconciling with and joining the CTA for his own political gains.
25. Pat Brewster, *Life History of Gibbon Brewster (Pat)*, Personal papers, 43. Self-published, n.d. Courtesy of Deborah Brewster and the Brewster family. Read at Deborah Brewster's home, New York, July 26, 2024.
26. Brewster, *Life History of Gibbon Brewster (Pat)*, Personal papers, 48.
27. Brewster, *Life History of Gibbon Brewster (Pat)*, Personal papers, 51.
28. Brewster, *Life History of Gibbon Brewster (Pat)*, Personal papers, 53–54.
29. Yungdrung Namgyal served as the first Bon representative.
30. Sonam Tobden, interview with author, June 2, 2022.
31. Sonam Tobden, interview with author, June 2, 2022.
32. Sonam Tobden, interview with author, June 2, 2022.
33. In 2022, I met a writer from Amdo who said his cousin had been hired to transport Tenzin from India to Kathmandu after the murder took place. His cousin had been upset, the writer said, because he was never paid the fees he had been promised.

34. Gungthang Ngodup returned to Tibet after Gungthang Tsultrim's death. He was in Lhasa when I spoke to him in December 2020. He could not recall much of the past and said his memory was failing. He said there was little sense returning to the stories of the past. The leaders were no longer alive, so it was not possible to tell the truth of the story.
35. Gyalo Thondup and Anne F. Thurston, *The Noodle Maker of Kalimpong* (New York: PublicAffairs, 2015), 87.
36. The Dalai Lama's *My Land and My People* states that the northeastern part of Tibet (Amdo) was under "Chinese control" at the time he lived there with his family. Tenzin Gyatso, the 14th Dalai Lama of Tibet. *My Land and My People* (New York: Hachette Book Group, 1997), 11.
37. *Tibetan Review* XIII, no. 8 (August 1978): 22. *The Current* uses the word "horle." After asking many of the older Tibetans, I decided to use "coterie." Nobody knew what "horle" stood for. They thought it referred to the inner circle.
38. Karma Gyatsho, "Putting the Record Straight," *Rangzen* III, no. 2 (Summer 1978): 7–8.
39. Regional Working Committee, Tibetan Youth Congress, "Blasphemy Against Buddhism," *Tibetan Review*, letters, XIII, no. 8 (August 1978): 4–5.
40. The *Tibetan Review* mentions that *The Current* editor apologizes in that paper's September 1978 issue.

8. THE PEOPLE'S GOVERNMENT

1. Yugyal, interview with author, Mainpat, India, September 17–19, 2015.
2. Exile officials attending the meeting were: Drawupon Rinchen Tsering (MP), Tsering Choden Dhompa (MP), Losang Tenzin, Tsering Gyamtsen, Thupten Jungney, Jampa Kanden (secretary of the department of security), Sonam Topgyal (secretary to the cabinet), Tashi Togpay (secretary to the department of home), and Tenpa Tsering (secretary to the department of communications).
3. The Kashag Cabinet Secretariat, "Important Points from the Minutes of the second day of meeting," July 27, 1978, Dedon File no. 68, 1978, Ref. b (*kha*), 390–389, pp. 1–2. Also interviews with Ugyen Topgyal Rinpoche, Jamyang Gyantse, Drawupon, Yujay, and Sodam.
4. The Kashag Cabinet Secretariat, "Important Points from the Minutes of the second day of meeting." Also interviews with Ugyen Topgyal Rinpoche, Jamyang Gyaltsen, Jadur Sonam Zangpo, Drawupon Rinchen Tsering, Yujay, and Sodam.
5. The Kashag Cabinet Secretariat, "Important Points from the Minutes of the second day of meeting." Also interviews with Ugyen Topgyal Rinpoche, Jamyang Gyaltsen, Jadur Sonam Zangpo, Drawupon Rinchen Tsering, Yujay, and Sodam.
6. The Kashag Cabinet Secretariat, Dharamsala, Central Tibetan Administration, Dedon File no. 68, 1978. Also interviews with Ugyen Topgyal Rinpoche,

8. THE PEOPLE'S GOVERNMENT ⋒ 303

Jamyang Gyaltsen, Jadur Sonam Zangpo, Drawupon Rinchen Tsering, Yujay, and Sodam.
7. The Kashag Cabinet Secretariat, Dharamsala, Central Tibetan Administration, Dedon File no. 68, 1978.
8. The Kashag Cabinet Secretariat, "Important Points from the Minutes of the second day of meeting." Also interviews with Ugyen Topgyal Rinpoche, Jamyang Gyaltsen, Jadur Sonam Zangpo, Drawupon Rinchen Tsering, Yujay, and Sodam.
9. The Kashag Cabinet Secretariat, "Important Points from the Minutes of the second day of meeting."
10. Carole McGranahan, *Arrested Histories: Tibet, the CIA, and Memories of a Forgotten War* (Durham, NC: Duke University Press, 2010), 13. McGranahan shifts dominant views of the Chushi Gangdrug to explain that recognition of the resistance, not revenge, drives Chushi Gangdrug veterans.
11. Exile officials at this meeting were: Juchen Thupten (Minister of Communications); Drawupon Rinchen Tsering (MP); Tsering Choden Dhompa (MP); Tsejar (MP, Nyingma); Youdon Namgyal (MP, Bon).
12. The Kashag Cabinet Secretariat, "Night meeting in Dharamsala restaurant with Thirteen leaders," August 2, 1978, Dedon File no. 68, 1978, Ref. b (*kha*), 385–371. Exile government officials at this meeting included Rinchen Tsering Drawupon (MP), Tsering Choden Dhompa (MP), Lozang Tenzin, Tsering Gyaltsen (MP, Nyingma), Thupten Jungney (MP), Jampa Kanden (security secretary), Sonam Topgay (cabinet secretary), Tashi Togpay (home secretary), and Tenpa Tsering (communications secretary). Also interviews with Ugyen Topgyal Rinpoche, Jamyang Gyaltsen, Jadur Sonam Zangpo, Drawupon Rinchen Tsering, Yujay, and Sodam.
13. Per interviews with Ugyen Topgyal Rinpoche, Jamyang Gyaltsen, Jadur Sonam Zangpo, Drawupon Rinchen Tsering, Yujay, and Sodam.
14. "We the members of the Tibetan Welfare Association hereby state that the pamphlet in English concerning the assassination of Mr. Gungthang Tsultrim which was issued from Clement Town in the name of the Tibetan Welfare Association was not written by a Tibetan. The contents of the pamphlet contains certain inaccuracies. We would like to clarify a few major points as under:

> 1. On page 5 of the said pamphlet it was stated that the three provinces of Tibet are Kham, Amdo, and Lhasa. We would like to state clearly that Lhasa is the capital city of Tibet. Kham, Amdo, and U-Tsang, the three Provinces, have constituted the one nation of Tibet with the central Government in Lhasa.
>
> 2. His Holiness the Dalai Lama is the supreme religious and temporal head of all the people of Tibet and has always had full authority and decision-making powers.

> 3. Although it is stated in the said pamphlet that the late Mr. Gungthang Tsultrim has always opposed the so called Ministers of the Dalai Lama's administration, we wish to state clearly here that there is only one true and legitimate Government of Tibet, and that at present is the Government-in-Exile headed by His Holiness the Dalai Lama. All the people of the three Provinces of Tibet recognize this Government and they all enjoy equal rights."

> The press release was signed by the leaders Dorzong Rinpoche (Tashi Jong), Dzongnang Rinpoche (Clement Town), Kathok Drimed Shingkyong Rinpoche (Sataun), Chokling Rinpoche Ugyen Dorje (Bir Nangchen), Thonyon Jagoetsang (Bir Derge), Jigme Lingtsang (Lingstang Settlement), Sodam (Kamrao), Tashi Topgyal (Mainpat), Tempa Phuntsog (Dolanji), Pema Gyalpo Tulku (Ngedon Gatsel Ling Monastery), and Karma Tsewang (camp. no. 4, Mysore). Additional signatures from "People's Representatives" were Geleg Namgyal (Tashi Jong), Shitro Tharge (Derge Bir), Jamyang Gyaltsen (Bir Nangchen), Yeshey Dorje (Lingtsang), Soenam (Kathok Sataun), Janga (Kamrao), Lobsang Phuntsog (Clement Town), Thakpo Tulku (Ngedon Gatsel Ling Monastery), and Rinchen Gyaltsen (Dolanji).

15. Ugyen Topgyal Rinpoche, interview with author, Bir, India, June 11, 2022.
16. According to a letter sent by the Thirteen to the Kashag on July 27, 1978, the seven points the Thirteen wished to raise with the exile government were to discuss the question and statement Jetsun Pema had made during the general annual meeting and Alak Jigme Rinpoche's remarks against the Thirteen at the same meeting (Jigme Rinpoche was a member of parliament representing Amdo) The Thirteen wished for him to apologize; for Wangdu Dorjee to step down from his position as home minister, as Gungthang Tsultrim had alleged he was one of the four people responsible for killing him; for the government to investigate all of Gyalo Thondup's activities; to ask why the minister of religion had asked the Karmapa not to go to Taiwan when the Karmapa had been going to Europe; to look into false accusations and posters defaming Drawupon Rinchen Tsering in Dharamsala; and to discuss Gungthang Tsultrim's murder.
17. Central Tibetan Administration, The Information Office, "In Reply to Allegations Contained in the Pamphlet," Dharamsala, 1978, 2.
18. Central Tibetan Administration, "In Reply to Allegations Contained in the Pamphlet," 2.
19. Tibetan Welfare Association, *The Assasination [sic] of Gungthang Tsultrim* (Self-pub., June 1978), 5.
20. Central Tibetan Administration, The Information Office, "In Reply to Allegations Contained in the Pamphlet," Dharamsala, 1978, 3.
21. Central Tibetan Administration, "In Reply to Allegations Contained in the Pamphlet," 4-7.
22. Central Tibetan Administration, "In Reply to Allegations Contained in the Pamphlet," 2.

23. Central Tibetan Administration, The Information Office, "In Reply to Allegations Contained in the Pamphlet," Dharamsala, 1978, 2.
24. Central Tibetan Administration, "In Reply to Allegations Contained in the Pamphlet," 3.
25. Central Tibetan Administration, "In Reply to Allegations Contained in the Pamphlet," 6.
26. Otto Bauer, *The Question of Nationalities and Social Democracy* (Minneapolis: University of Minnesota Press, 2000), 120–121.
27. Bauer, *The Question of Nationalities*, 121.
28. The letter indicates that it was being brought personally by Deputy Secretary for Home Affairs Tashi Tobgye.
29. Eric Hobsbawm, *Nations and Nationalisms since 1780*, 2nd ed. (Cambridge: Cambridge University Press, 1990), 11.

CONCLUSION

1. Bridget Anderson, *Us and Them? The Dangerous Politics of Immigration Control* (Oxford: Oxford University Press, 2013), 5.
2. See Carole McGranahan, *Arrested Histories: Tibet, the CIA, and Memories of a Forgotten War* (Durham, NC: Duke University Press, 2010).
3. "STOP PRESS," *Tibetan Review*, August, 1978, 9. The letter follows the article on Tsultrim's murder as well as the press release from the government. The *Review* indicates that Amdos of Dharamsala sent a similar letter on August 18.
4. Letter from Dotoe Khampa Youth Organization, August 20, 1978. Also mentioned in a letter from Dorzong Rinpoche to the Kashag on September 20, 1978. The Kashag Cabinet Secretariat, Dharamsala, Central Tibetan Administration, Dedon File no. 68, 1978; and in private collections of Thirteen members.
5. Tibetan United Association, *Cholsum Chigdril Tsogpai logyue ngoeden jhungrim debther drangsong gyepae choetin she jawa shugso/Chol gsum chig bsgril tshogs pa'i lo rgyus dngos bden byung rim deb ther drang srong dgyes pa'i mchod sprin zhes bya ba bzhugs so* (*Truthful History of the Tibetan United Association*) (Dharamsala: Tibetan United Association, 2005), 112–113.
6. Tibetan United Association, *Truthful History of the Tibetan United Association*, 114.
7. McGranahan, *Arrested Histories*, 13.
8. Tashi Namgyal Drayabtsang, interviews with the author, Kathmandu, Nepal, November 16, 2015 and September 4, 2017.
9. Yossi Shain, *The Frontiers of Loyalty* (Middletown, CT: Wesleyan University Press, 1989), 20.
10. Shain, *The Frontiers of Loyalty*, 20.
11. Shain, *The Frontiers of Loyalty*, 20.

12. Shain, *The Frontiers of Loyalty*, 22.
13. Tibetan Welfare Association, *Ngo yoe denpay sel dag/Dngos yod bden pa'i gsal bsgrags* (*A Statement of the Real Truth*) (N.p.: Tashijong, 1979), 1.
14. Tibetan Welfare Association, *A Statement of the Real Truth*, 11–14.
15. Tibetan Welfare Association, *A Statement of the Real Truth*, 11–14.
16. The texts suggests that the methods practiced in the seventh century cannot be used in the present moment because they would not work or be relevant—in other words, that the United Party was using orthodox forms of coercion that would not be suitable for the democracy they purported to champion.
17. McGranahan, *Arrested Histories*, 148.
18. Marong Choeje, interview with author, Dolanji, India, July 28, 2015.

BIBLIOGRAPHY

SPEECHES AND STATEMENTS

Central Tibetan Administration. Information and Publicity Office of His Holiness the Dalai Lama. Press Release. "In Reply to Allegations Contained in the Pamphlet 'The Assassination of Gungthang Tsultrim.'" Dharamsala, August 9, 1978.
——. Kashag Cabinet Secretariat. "Statement to all Tibetans on the recent conflict in Lo (Mustang)." Dharamsala, August 28, 1971.
"His Holiness the Dalai Lama's Speech to the Representatives of *Domey* Meeting Held on 28 September 1978." Dharamsala, September 28, 1978, published in a booklet in Dharamsala. Reprinted in Tibetan United Association, *Cholsum Chigdril Tsogpai logyue ngoeden jhungrim debther drangsong gyepae choetin she jawa shugso/Chol gsum chig bsgril tshogs pa'i lo rgyus dngos bden byung rim deb ther drang srong dgyes pa'i mchod sprin zhes bya ba bzhugs so* (*Truthful History of the Tibetan United Association*). Dharamsala: Tibetan United Association, 2005, 107–114.

MINUTES

Central Tibetan Administration, Kashag Cabinet Secretariat. Dedon File no. 68, 1978.
——. Assembly of Tibetan People's Deputies. "Minutes of the Extra Session of the Standing Committee." Dharamsala, October 17, 1975, n.p. (7-page handwritten document).
——. Kashag Cabinet Secretariat. "During the Meeting" (*Ngo zom nangwai kab*). Handwritten notes. Dedon File no. 68, 1978, Ref. b (*kha*), 533–515, pp. 1–18.
——. Kashag Cabinet Secretariat. "Important Points from the Minutes of the Second Day of Meeting, July 27, 1978." Dedon File no. 68, 1978, Ref. b (*kha*), 390–389, pp. 1–2.
——. Kashag Cabinet Secretariat. "Minutes of Meeting on August 3, 1978, in Dharamsala between Representatives from Thirteen Group and Deputy Speaker

308 BIBLIOGRAPHY

Lobsang Dhargyal and Cabinet Sec. Sonam Topgyal." Dedon File no. 68, 1978, Ref. b (*kha*), 448–443, pp. 1–6.

———. Kashag Cabinet Secretariat. "Minutes of the Meeting on July 30, 1978 held in Lower Dharamsala." Dedon File no. 68, 1978, Ref. b (*kha*), 417–414, pp. 18–22.

LETTERS AND REPORTS

Bonpo Monastic Center. Letter to the Kashag. December 27, 1977. Dedon File no. 68, 1978, Ref. b (*kha*), 37/128, Dharamsala.

Central Tibetan Administration. Information Office. Letter to the Thirteen from the Kashag. April 17, 1978. Dedon File no. 68, 1978, Ref. b (*kha*), 37.

———. Kashag Cabinet Secretariat. Draft of Letter from the Kashag to Branch Settlements of Tibetans. April 1978. Dedon File no. 68, 1978, Ref. b (*kha*), 37/95, Dharamsala.

Dege Welfare Association. Correspondent, letter to the Kashag, Dedon File no. 68, 1978.

Dharamsala People's United (Dharamsala Cholsum Mimang). Letter to the Kashag. November 13, 1978. Dedon File no. 68, 1978, Ref. b (*kha*), 37/265, pp. 1–5.

Dhomey Amdo. Correspondent, letter to Tsulti Yen. October 28, 1977. Dedon File no. 68, 1978, Ref. b (*kha*), 37/41.

Gungthang, Tsultrim. Correspondent, letter to the Kashag. Reached CTA March 1, 1978. Dedon File no. 68, 1978, Ref. b (*kha*), 37.

———. Correspondent, letter to Prime Minister Indira Gandhi. July 23, 1971. Private collection.

Gungthang Tsultrim/Tibetan Welfare Association. Correspondent, letter to the Kashag. April 10, 1978. Dedon File no. 68, 1978, Ref. b (*kha*), 37.

Kham Amdo Youth Organization. Correspondent, letter to the Kashag. August 20, 1978. Dedon File no. 68, 1978, Ref. 498.

Kollegal Settlement. Correspondent, letter to the Thirteen. N.d. Dedon File no. 68, 1978, Ref. b (*kha*), 37/257.

Lhalungpa, Phuntsok Lobsang. Correspondent, draft of report on the Thirteen. July 19, 1965. Private collection of Samphel Lhalunpga.

Pearce, Joyce. "Report on visit to Tibetan Refugees in India, April 16–May 18, 1963." Private collection of Tsering Shakya.

Tibetan Welfare Association. Correspondent, letter to the Kashag. August 2, 1978. Dedon File no. 68, 1978, Ref. b (*kha*), 37.

———. Correspondent, letter to the Kashag. September 29, 1978. Dedon File no. 68, 1978, Ref. b (*kha*), 37.

Shillong Tibetans. Correspondent, letter to the Kashag. November 26, 1978. Dedon File no. 68, 1978.

Walung Settlement. Correspondent, letter to the Kashag. December 9, 1978. Dedon File no. 68, 1978.

DOCUMENTS RELATED TO THE OCKENDEN VENTURE SCHOOL AT DHARWAR, MYSORE STATE, INDIA, IN SURREY HISTORY CENTRE, WOKING

Files on the Ockenden International, Formerly the Ockenden Venture, Refugee Charity of Woking: Records, including papers of Joyce Pearce OBE (1915–1985), Founder, SHC Reference 7155/8/1/11–14, Surrey History Centre, Woking, Surrey.

Boe, W. S. Correspondent, letter to Joyce Pearce, July 11, 1966, pp. 1–3. Files on the Ockenden International, SHC Reference 7155/8/1/13.

Dexter, Malcolm. Correspondent, letter to the Council for Tibetan Education, May 3, 1966. Files on the Ockenden International, SHC Reference 7155/8/1/13, Ref. no. MRWD/DM.

———. Correspondent, letter to Joyce Pearce, May 13, 1965. Files on the Ockenden International, SHC Reference 7155/8/1/12.

———. Correspondent, letter to Joyce Pearce, May 1, 1966, pp. 1–4. Files on the Ockenden International, Reference 7155/8/1/11, MRWD/DM.

———. Correspondent, letter to Joyce Pearce, May 10, 1966, pp. 1–2. Files on the Ockenden International, Reference 7155/8/1/13, Ref. no. MRWD/DM.

Hardy, John W. Correspondent, letter to Joyce Pearce, August 20, 1966, pp. 1–4. Files on the Ockenden International, SHC Reference, 7155/8/1/13.

Kvaerne, Per. Correspondent, letter to Joyce Pearce, May 3, 1966. Files on the Ockenden International, SHC Reference 7155/8/1/13.

Maclehose, Diana. Correspondent, letter to Joyce Pearce, November 24, 1965. Files on the Ockenden International, SHC Reference 7155/8/1/12.

———. Correspondent, letter to Joyce Pearce, May 3, 1966. Files on the Ockenden International, SHC Reference 7155/8/1/12.

———. Correspondent, letter to Joyce Pearce, May 4, 1966, pp. 1–3. Files on the Ockenden International, SHC Reference 7155/8/1/12.

Pearce, Joyce. Correspondent, letter to His Holiness the Dalai Lama, May 11, 1966. Files on the Ockenden International, SHC Reference 7155/8/1/13.

———. Correspondent, letter to G. Woodcock, June 21, 1966. Files on the Ockenden International, SHC Reference 7155/8/1/13.

———. Correspondent, letter to Peter Woodard, June 17, 1966. Files on the Ockenden International, SHC Reference 7155/8/1/13.

———. Correspondent, letter to Tenzin N. Takla, May 13, 1966. Files on the Ockenden International, SHC Reference 7155/8/1/13.

———. Correspondent, letter to Malcolm Dexter, May 4, 1966, pp. 1–2. Files on the Ockenden International, SHC Reference 7155/8/1/11.

Snellgrove, D. L. Correspondent, letter to Joyce Pearce, May 26, 1966, pp. 1–3. Files on the Ockenden International, SHC Reference 7155/8/1/13.

———. Correspondent, letter to Joyce Pearce, May 29, 1966. Files on the Ockenden International, SHC Reference 7155/8/1/13.

Student. Correspondent, letter to Joyce Pearce,. n.d., pp. 1–5. Files on the Ockenden International, SHC Reference 7155/8/1/11.
Student 1. Correspondent, letter to Joyce Pearce, n.d., pp. 1–5. Files on the Ockenden International, SHC Reference 7155/8/1/11.
Student 2. Correspondent. letter to Joyce Pearce, n.d., pp. 1–5. Files on the Ockenden International, SHC Reference 7155/8/1/11.
Takla, T. N. Correspondent, letter to Joyce Pearce, May 25, 1966. Files on the Ockenden International, SHC Reference 7155/8/1/Thirteen, Ref. no. MRWD/DM.
Tara, T. C. Correspondent, letter to Joyce Pearce, May 13, 1966. Files on the Ockenden International, SHC Reference 7155/8/1/12.
———. Correspondent, letter to Joyce Pearce, June 5, 1966, pp. 1–7. Files on the Ockenden International, SHC Reference 7155/8/1/13.
———. Correspondent, letter to Joyce Pearce, n.d. Files on the Ockenden International, SHC Reference 7155/8/1/12.
Tennant, Mark. Correspondent, letter to Joyce Pearce, June 9, 1966. Files on the Ockenden International, SHC Reference 7155/8/1/13.
The Dalai Lama. (Sgd). Correspondent, letter to Joyce Pearce, May 21, 1966. Files on the Ockenden International, SHC Reference 7155/8/1/12.
Umadevi. Correspondent, letter to Joyce Pearce, May 19, 1966, pp. 1–2. Files on the Ockenden International, SHC Reference 7155/8/1/13.
Unknown. Correspondent, letter to Joyce Pearce, July 23, 1966. Files on the Ockenden International, SHC Reference 7155/8/1/13.
Unknown. Correspondent, letter to Joyce Pearce from volunteer teacher, June 30, 1966. Files on the Ockenden International, SHC Reference 7155/8/1/13.
Wiederkehr et al. Correspondent, letter to His Holiness the Dalai Lama, June 3, 1966. Files on the Ockenden International, SHC Reference 7155/8/1/13.
Woodard, Peter. "A Report on the Mutiny at the Ockenden School," pp. 1–89. Files on the Ockenden International, SHC Reference 7155/8/1/11–14.

WORLD COUNCIL OF CHURCHES, GENEVA ARCHIVES, GENEVA, SWITZERLAND

Brewster, G. Committee on Relief & Gift Supplies National Christian Council of India. "Review of the Tibetan Refugee Programme," December 1965.
———. Correspondent, letter to Dr. Ernest Wiederkehr, Swiss Aid to Tibetans, June 2, 1966. Ref. 012085.
———. Correspondent, letter to Dr. Ernest Wiederkehr, August 11, 1966. Ref. 028092.
———. Correspondent, letter to Swiss Aid to Tibetans, March 9, 1965. Ref. 008786.
———. Correspondent, letter to Swiss Aid to Tibetans, June 2, 1966. Ref. 012085.
———. "General Description of Resettlement Work being carried out by Mr. G. Brewster, Director of the Tibetan Refugee programme of the National Christian Council of India," February 21, 1966. Ref. ICA/As/66/10.

BIBLIOGRAPHY ᘂ 311

———. "Progress Report on the Projects initiated by TIRS Up to 15th September 1967." Report to World Council of Churches, September 21, 1967. World Council of Churches, Geneva archives, Geneva, Switzerland.
———."Tibetan Refugee Programme in India." Report to World Council of Churches, November 1966.

OTHER LETTERS AND REPORTS

Brewster, Pat. *Life History of Gibbon Brewster (Pat)*. Self-published, n.d.
Pearce, Joyce. "Report on visit to Tibetan Refugees in India. April 16–May 18, 1963." Courtesy Prof. Tsering Shakya. Private collection.
Rapten, Sonam. Correspondent, letter to John Conway, "Director's Report on the Present Activities and Future Plans of the Seven Settlements Under TIRS," December 9, 1971. Ref. RBSC—ARC—1554-2-29, University of British Columbia Library Rare Books and Special Collections, Vancouver, Canada.

PERSONAL INTERVIEWS

Achu Lama. Personal interview, Tashi Jong, India, July 22, 2015.
Barchungtsang, Dorjee Lhamo. Personal interview, Kathmandu, Nepal, November 16, 2015.
Bongsar, Tsodi. Personal interviews, Toronto, Canada, 2019, 2022.
Chentse Yeshe Rinpoche. Personal interview, Bir, India, September 3, 2015.
Choeje, Marong. Personal interview, Dolanji, India, July 28, 2015.
Choklingtsang, Jamyang Gyaltsen. Personal interviews, Bir, India, July 10–11, 2015.
Damdul, Sonam. Personal interviews, Dharamsala, India. July 16 and August 4, 2015.
Dorje, Choyang. Personal interview, Clement Town, India, July 29, 2015.
Dorje, Pema. Personal interview, Kathmandu, Nepal, November 24, 2015.
Dorjee, (Dege) Cheme. Personal interviews, WhatsApp, December 14–22, 2020; February 2023.
Drawupon, Rinchen Tsering. Personal interviews, Kamrao, India, August 8–12, 2015.
Drayabtsang, Tashi Namgyal. Personal interviews, Kathmandu, Nepal, November 16, 2015; September 4, 2017.
Drubju, Lama. Phone interview, November 3, 2023.
Gungthang, Sonam Wangyal. Phone interview, August 19, 2023.
Gyamtse, Thupa. Personal interview, Bir, India, July 22, 2015.
Gyamtso, Khedup. Personal interview, Dolanji, India, July 21, 2015, and phone interview on July 24, 2024.
Gyatso, Khenpo Chodak. Personal interview, Toronto, Canada, August 12, 2016.
Gyatso, Lobsang. Personal interview, Dolanji, India, July 21, 2015.
Jadur, Sonam Zangpo. Personal interviews, Dolanji India, July 27–28, 2015.

Jagoetsang, Cheme Dorjee. Personal interview, Bir, India, June 13, 2022.
Jigme, Ugyen. Personal interview Clement Town, India, June 1, 2022.
Jinpa. Personal interviews, Clement Town, India, July 30 and August 1, 2015.
Samdhong Rinpoche. Personal interview, Dharamsala, India, September 3, 2017.
Lama. Personal interview, Dolanji, India, July 27, 2015.
Lama Asi. Phone interview, November 3, 2023.
Lama Tenkyab. Personal interview, Clement Town, India, June 2, 2022.
Lungtok Tenpei Nyima Pal Zangpo Rinpoche, the 33rd Abbot of Menri Monastery. Dolanji, India, July 27, 2015.
Luthoktsang, Chime. Personal interview, Kathmandu, Nepal, November 17, 2015.
Norbu, Kalzang. Personal interview, Bir, India, July 20, 2015.
Norbu, Rinchen. Personal interview, Gangtok, India, September 6, 2015.
Phuntsok, Tsering. Personal interview, Bylakuppe, India, September 2015.
Tendhar. Personal interview, Mainpat, India, September 18, 2015.
Tenpa, Chanzoe Ngawang. Personal interview. Dharamsala, India, July 13, 2015.
Tenzin, Norbu. Personal interview, Bir, India, July 20, 2015.
Tenzing, Kushe. Personal interview, Manduwala, India, August 2, 2015.
Tharchin, Geshe Monlam. Personal interview, Dharamsala, India, July 2015.
Tharchin, Sherap. Personal interview, Sataun, India, August 12, 2015.
Tobden, Sonam. Personal interview Clement Town, India, June 2, 2022.
Tobgay, Tashi. Personal interview, Scarborough, Canada, August 19, 2016.
Topgyal, Tashi. Personal interview, Toronto, Canada, August 12, 2016.
Trindu Pon. Phone interview, November 2016.
Tsering, Tashi. Personal interview, Dharamsala, India, July, August 2017.
Tsering, Wangchuk. Personal interview, Toronto, Canada, August 11, 2016.
Ugyen Topgyal Rinpoche. Personal interviews, Delhi, November 10–11, 2015; September 6, 2017; June 12–13, 2022.
Wangyal, Tsering. Personal interview, Dolanji, India, July 28, 2015.
Yongdzin Lopön Tenzin Namdak Rinpoche. Personal interview, Kathmandu, November 23, 2015.
Yugyal. Personal interviews, Mainpat, India, September 17–19, 2015.

TIBETAN LANGUAGE SOURCES

Choden, Gyaltsen. "A Report by Gyaltsen Chonden, a Tibetan language teacher at Ockenden School." *Bhod-mi Rangwang (Tibetan Freedom)* 2, no. 72/2 (June 2, 1966): 2.

———. *Bhod kyi gyalrab dang drel we mitsei logue dentam drimed sershun tseg pe lhunpo/Bod kyi rgyal rabs dang 'brel ba'i mi tshe'i lo rgyus bden gtam dri med gser gzhun brtsegs pa'i lhun po* (*A History of Tibet and a Stainless Truthful Biography.*) Self-published: Karnataka, India, 2016.

Dhondup, Amdo. *Gyalkhab sum gyi mangmi/Rgyal khab gsum gyi dmag mi* (*A Soldier of Three Nations*). New Delhi: Denrab Tsomrig Tsogchung, 2019.

Namgyal, Juchen Thupten. *Juchen Thupten gyi kutse logyue/Ju chen rnam rgyal gyi sku tshe'i lo rguys* (*The Autobiography of Juchen Thupten Namyal*). 21 vols. Chauntra, District Mandi, H.P., India: Juchentsang, 2014.
Tendar. Testimony. *Tibetan Freedom* 2, no. 74 (June 7, 1966).
Tibetan Institute of Performing Arts and Tibet Writes. *Bhod Shung Dokar Tsogpae logyue kunsang shing gyi choting mikyid nawae gaton* (*History of the Tibetan Institute of Performing Arts 1959–2009*). Dharamsala: Tibetan Institute of Performing Arts, 2016.
Tibetan United Association. *Cholsum Chigdril Tsogpai logyue ngoeden jhungrim debther drangsong gyepae choetin she jawa shugso/Chol gsum chig bsgril tshogs pa'i lo rgyus dngos bden byung rim deb ther drang srong dgyes pa'i mchod sprin zhes bya ba bzhugs so* (*Truthful History of the Tibetan United Association*). Dharamsala: Tibetan United Association, 2005.
———. *Drochoe dhon tsen dun dang dh'e gyab non chey shug so/gros chod don tshan bdun dang de'i rgyab gnon bcas bzhugs so* (*Seven Resolutions and Supporting Documents*). Darjeeling, India: Tibetan United Association, 1965.
———. *Bhod Cholsum Chigdril Tsogpae mig yul dontsen gna/ Bhod Chol gsum chig sdril tsogs pa'i dmigs yul don tshen lgna* (*Five Aims of the Tibetan United Association*), Darjeeling, India: Tibetan United Association, April 23, 1964.
Tibetan Welfare Association. *Ngo yoe denpay sel dag/Dngos yod bden pa'i gsal bsgrags.* (*A Statement of the Real Truth*). N.p.: Tashijong, 1979.
Tsering, Jho. Testimony. *Bhod-mi Rangwang* (*Tibetan Freedom*) 2, no. 75 (June 8, 1966).
Tsering, Yidam. "I, 14-Year-Old Yidam Tsering's Statement." *Bhod-mi Rangwang* (*Tibetan Freedom*) 2, no. 74 (June 7, 1966).
Wangdu, Kalsang. "Statement of 14-year-old Kalsang Wangdu." *Bhod-mi Rangwang* (*Tibetan Freedom*) 2, no. 75 (June 8, 1966).

EUROPEAN LANGUAGE SOURCES

Adrian, Bailey, Richard Wright A., Alison Mountz, and Ines M. Miyares. "(Re)producing Salvadoran Transnational Geographies." *Annals of the Association of American Geographers* 92, no. 1 (published online March 2010): 125–144.
Agnew, John. *Making Political Geography*. London: Arnold, 2002.
Amin, Shahid. *Event, Metaphor, Memory: Chauri Chaura 1922–1992*. Berkeley: University of California Press, 1995.
Anand, Dibyesh. "The Tibet Question and the West: Issues of Sovereignty, Identity and Representation." In *Contemporary Tibet: Politics, Development and Society in a Disputed Region*, ed. Sautman and Dreyer, 285–304. New York: East Gate, 2006.
Anderson, Benedict. *Imagined Communities*. New York: Verso, 2006. First published by Verso 1983.
Anderson, Bridget. *Us and Them? The Dangerous Politics of Immigration Control*. Oxford: Oxford University Press, 2013.

Anderson, Bridget, and Vanessa Hughes, eds. *Citizenship and Its Others: Migration, Diasporas and Citizenship*. London: Palgrave Macmillan, 2015.
Andrugtsang, Gompo Tashi. *Four Rivers, Six Ranges: Reminiscences of the Resistance Movement in Tibet*. Dharamsala, India: Information and Publicity Office of H.H. the Dalai Lama, 1973.
Arendt, Hannah. *The Origins of Totalitarianism*. New York: Harcourt, 1966.
Aris, Michael, and Aung San Suu Kyi, eds. *Tibetan Studies: In Honor of Hugh Richardson*. New Delhi: Vikas Publishing House, 1980.
Arora, Vibha, and N. Jayaram. *Routeing Democracy in the Himalayas: Experiments and Experiences*. New Delhi: Routledge, 2013.
Avedon, John F. *In Exile from the Land of Snows*. New York: Knopf, 1984.
Arya, Tsewang Gyalpo. "Yungdrung-bon, the Religion of Eternal Truth in the Land of Snow: A Note to Dispel the Misunderstanding and Misinterpretation of the Religion." *The Tibet Journal* 41, no. 2 (Autumn/Winter 2016): 63–71.
Balakrishnan, Gopal. *Mapping the Nation*. New York: Verso, 2012. First published 1996.
Baogang, He. "The Dalai Lama's Autonomy Proposal: A One-Sided Wish?" In *Contemporary Tibet: Politics, Development and Society in a Disputed Region*, ed. Barry Sautman and Jane Teufel Dreyer, 67–84. New York: M. E. Sharpe, 2006.
Barnett, Robert. "Introduction." In *The Struggle for Tibet*, ed. Wang Lixiong and Tsering Shakya, 1–34. London: Verso, 2009.
Basu, Sudeep. "Interrogating Tibetan Exilic Culture: Issues and Concerns." *Sociological Bulletin* 61, no. 2 (May–August (2012): 232–254.
Battacharya, Sabyasachi, ed. *The Mahatma and the Poet: Letters and Debates Between Gandhi and Tagore 1915–1941*. New Delhi: National Book Trust, 1977.
Bauer, Otto. "The Nation." In *Mapping the Nation*, ed. Gopal Balakrishnan, 39–77. New York: Verso, 2012.
——. *The Question of Nationalities and Social Democracy*. Minneapolis: University of Minnesota Press, 2000.
Beckwith, Christopher I. *The Tibetan Empire in Central Asia*. Princeton, NJ: Princeton University Press, 1987.
——. "The Tibetan Empire in the West." In *Tibetan Studies*, ed. Michael Aris and Aung San Suu Kyi, 30–38. New Delhi: Vikas Publishing House, 1980.
Bernstorff, Dagmar, and Hubertus von Welck, eds. *Exile as Challenge: The Tibetan Diaspora*. Hyderabad, India: Orient Longman Private Ltd., 2004.
——. "An Interview with Tenzin Gyatso, the Fourteenth Dalai Lama." In *Exile as Challenge: The Tibetan Diaspora*, ed. Dagmar Bernstorff and Hubertus von Welck, 107–124. Hyderabad, India: Orient Longman Private Ltd., 2004.
Bhabha, Homi K., ed. *Nation and Narration*. New York: Routledge, 1990.
Bhoil, Shelly, and Enrique Galvan-Alvarez, eds. *Tibetan Subjectivities on the Global Stage: Negotiating Dispossession*. New York: Lexington Books, 2018.
Billig, Michael. *Banal Nationalism*. London: Sage Publications, 1995.

Blondeau, Ann-Marie. "How Does the Chinese Government Value the Idea of a 'Greater Tibetan Autonomous Region' Suggested by Some People Around the Dalai Lama?" In *Authenticating Tibet: Answers to China's 100 Questions*, ed. Ann-Marie Blondeau and Katia Buffetrille, 123–124. Berkeley: University of California Press, 2008.

——. "When Did Tibetan Buddhism Come Into Being? How Many Sects Does It Have?" In *Authenticating Tibet: Answers to China's 100 Questions*, ed. Ann-Marie Blondeau and Katia Buffetrille, 181–185. Berkeley: University of California Press, 2008.

Blondeau, Ann-Marie, and Katia Buffetrille, eds. *Authenticating Tibet: Answers to China's 100 Questions*. Berkeley: University of California Press, 2008.

Bloom, Tendayi, Katherine Tonkiss, and Phillip Cole, eds. *Understanding Statelessness*. Oxford: Routledge, 2017.

Bongsar, Tsodi. *Nangchen Sremo: The Story of Tsodi Bongsar from Nangchen*. Self-published: India, 2023. Digital.

Boyd, Helen R. *The Future of Tibet: The Government-in-Exile Meets the Challenge of Democratization*. New York: Peter Lang, 2004.

Boyarin, Jonathan, and Daniel Boyarin. *Powers of Diaspora: Two Essays on the Relevance of Jewish Culture*. Minneapolis: University of Minnesota Press, 2002.

Brown, Jeremy, and Paul Pickowicz, eds. *Dilemmas of Victory*. Cambridge, MA: Harvard University Press, 2008.

Brown, Wendy. *Undoing the Demos: Neoliberalism's Stealth Revolution*. New York: Zone Books, 2015.

Brox, Trine. "Democracy in the Words of the Dalai Lama." *The Tibet Journal* 33, no. 2 (Summer 2008): 65–90.

——. *Tibetan Democracy: Governance, Leadership and Conflict in Exile*. London: I. B. Tauris, 2016.

Buffetrille, Katia. "The Increasing Visibility of the Tibetan 'Borderlands.'" In *Frontier Tibet: Patterns of Change in the Sino-Tibetan Borderlands*, ed. Stéphane Gros, 85–114. Amsterdam: Amsterdam University Press, 2019.

Butler, Judith, and Gayatri Spivak. *Who Sings the Nation State?* Calcutta: Seagull Books, 2010.

"The Buxa Lama Ashram." *Tibetan Review* 1, no. 3 (March 1968): 10–12.

Central Tibetan Administration. *The Constitution of Tibet*. Dharamsala, 1963.

——. "Green Book (Chatrel)." Dharamsala. http: //tibet.net/support-tibet/pay-green-book/.

——. *Middle Way Policy and All Related Documents*. Dharamsala: Department of Information and International Relations, 2010.

Central Tibetan Administration, Information and Publicity Office of His Holiness the Dalai Lama. Press Release. "Kashag's Statement on the 80th birth anniversary of the Great 14th Dalai Lama." Dharamsala: Central Tibetan Administration, July 6, 2015. http: //tibet.net/2015/07/Kashags-statement-on-the-eightieth-birth-anniversary-of-his-holiness-the-great-14th-dalai-lama-2/.

Chakrabarty, Dipesh. *Provincializing Europe: Postcolonial Thought and Historical Difference*. Princeton, NJ: Princeton University Press, 2000.
Chatterjee, Partha. *Lineages of Political Society: Studies in Postcolonial Democracy*. New York: Columbia University Press, 2011.
——. *The Nation and Its Fragments: Colonial and Postcolonial Histories*. Princeton, NJ: Princeton University Press, 1993.
——. *Nationalist Thought and the Colonial World: A Derivative Discourse*. Minneapolis: University of Minnesota, 1993.
——. "Whose Imagined Community?" In *Mapping the Nation*, ed. Gopal Balakrishnan, 214–225. New York: Verso, 2012.
Chattopadhya, Ray, and Jayant Kumar, D. P., eds. *Aspects of India's International Relations 1700–2000: South Asia and the World*, vol. X, part 6. New Delhi: Pearson Longman, 2007.
Chayet, Anne. "The Qing Dynasty (1644–1911)." In *Authenticating Tibet: Answers to China's 100 Questions*, ed. Ann-Marie Blondeau and Katia Buffetrille, 21–40. Berkeley: University of California Press, 2008.
Chen, Jian. "The Chinese Communist 'Liberation' of Tibet, 1949–51." In *Dilemmas of Victory: The Early Years of the People's Republic of China*, ed. Jeremy Brown and Paul G. Pickowicz, 130–159. Cambridge, MA: Harvard University Press, 2008.
Choedon, Yeshi. "The Unintended Consequences of India's Policy on Citizenship for Tibetan Refugees." New Delhi: Institute for Defence Studies and Analyses, February 23, 2018.
Choedup, Ugyan. "Competing Visions: Schooling the Nation and the 'Revolt' at the Ockenden Tibetan School." *International Journal of Asian Studies* 20 (2022): 497–512.
Chung, Lawrence. "Taiwan Calls Time on Mongolian and Tibet Affairs Commission." *South China Morning Post*, August 16, 2017.
Clapham, Christopher. "Sovereignty and the Third World State." *Political Studies* XVII (1999): 522–537.
Cuevas, Bryan J. "Some Reflections on the Periodization of Tibetan History." In *The Tibetan History Reader*, ed. Gray Tuttle and Kurtis R. Schaeffer, 67–78 (ebook 49–63). New York: Columbia University Press, 2013.
"Current Magazine's apology." *Tibetan Review* XIII, no. 8 (August 1978): 4.
"Dalai Lama Aide Strikes to Kill." *The Current*, July 22, 1978. Reprinted in *Tibetan Review* XIII, no. 8 (August 1978): 22.
Dalal, Nergis. "The Tragedy of Tibetans." Reprinted in *Tibetan Review* XIII, no. 8 (August 1978): 23. First published in *The Tribune*, Chandigarh, July 14, 1978.
Dalton, Jacob P. *The Taming of the Demons: Violence and Liberation in Tibetan Buddhism*. New Haven, CT: Yale University Press, 2011.
Das, Veena. *Critical Events: An Anthropological Perspective on Contemporary India*. Oxford: Oxford University Press, 1995.
——. *Life and Words: Violence and the Descent into the Ordinary*. Berkeley: University of California Press, 2006.

Das, Veena, and Deborah Poole, eds. *Anthropology in the Margins of the State.* Santa Fe: School of American Research Press, 2004.

Dayal, Samir. *Resisting Modernity: Counternarratives of Nation and Masculinity in Pre-Independence India.* Newcastle: Cambridge Scholars Publishing, 2007.

"Declaration of the Association of Thirteen Groups." *Tibetan Bulletin* X, no. 4 (July–August 1978): 24–26.

Department of Information and International Relations. *Tibet and the Tibetan Struggle: 10 March Statements of His Holiness the Dalai Lama (1961–2005).* Dharamsala: Central Tibetan Administration, 2005.

Dhargye, Dawa. "Letters." *Tibetan Review* XIII, no. 11 (November 1978): 27.

Dhondup, K. "The Unveiling of Old Tibet." "Letters," *Tibetan Review* XII, no. 7 (July 1977): 24.

Dickie, Tenzin, ed. *The Penguin Book of Modern Tibetan Essays.* Gurugram: Penguin Random House, 2023.

Di Cosmo, Nicola. "Kirghiz Nomads on the Qing Frontier: Tribute, Trade, or Gift Exchange?" In *Political Frontiers, Ethnic Boundaries, and Human Geographies in Chinese History,* ed. Nicola Di Cosmo and Don J. Wyatt, 351–372. London: RoutledgeCurzon, 2003.

Dilgo Khyentse Rinpoche. *Brilliant Moon: The Autobiography of Dilgo Khyentse.* Trans. Ani Jimba Palmo. Boston: Shambhala, 2008.

Dodin, Thierry. "The Ladakh Budh Vihar of Delhi: The Fate of a Ladakhi Outpost in the Indian Capital." In Proceedings of the Ninth Seminar of the IATS, 2000, *Tibet, Past and Present. Tibetan Studies 1,* vol. 2/1, ed. Henk Blezer, 387–414. Leiden: Brill, 2002.

Dorjee, M. "Letters." *Tibetan Review* XIII, no. 8 (August 1978): 8.

Dorjee, Tenzin. "Diplomacy or Mobilization: The Tibetan Dilemma in the Struggle with China." In *China's Internal and External Relations and Lessons for Korea and Asia,* ed. Jung-Ho Bae and Jae H. Ku, 63–112. Seoul: Korea Institute for National Unification, 2013.

———. *The Tibetan Nonviolent Struggle: A Strategic and Historical Analysis.* Washington, DC: International Center on Nonviolent Conflict, 2015.

Duara, Prasenjit. "Civilization and Realpolitik." *India International Centre Quarterly* 36, no. 3/4 (Winter 2009/Spring 2010): 20–33.

———. "De-Constructing the Chinese Nation." *The Australian Journal of Chinese Affairs* 30 (July 1993): 1–26.

———. *The Global and Regional in China's Nation-Formation.* Oxon: Routledge, 2009.

———. "History and Globalization in China's Long Twentieth Century." *Modern China, the Nature of the Chinese State: Dialogues Among Western and Chinese Scholars* 34, no. 1 (January 2008): 152–164.

———. *Rescuing History from the Nation.* Chicago: University of Chicago Press, 1995.

Ekvall, Robert B. "Law and the Individual among the Tibetan Nomads." *American Anthropologist,* New Series, 66, no. 5 (October 1964): 1110–1115.

———. "Peace and War among the Tibetan Nomads." *American Anthropologist*, New Series, 66, no. 5 (October 1964): 1119–1148.

Epstein, Lawrence, ed. *Khams Pa Histories: Visions of People, Place and Authority*. Leiden: Brill, 2002.

Fairbank, John K., and Ssu-yu Teng. "On the Ch'ing Tributary System." *Harvard Journal of Asiatic Studies* 2 (1941): 135–246.

Fanon, Frantz. *The Wretched of the Earth*. New York: Grove Press, 2004.

Fletcher, Joseph F. "China and Central Asia, 1368–1884." In *The Chinese World Order: Traditional China's Foreign Relations*, ed. John K. Fairbank, 206–224. Cambridge, MA: Harvard University Press, 1968.

Foucault, Michel. *Discipline and Punish: The Birth of the Prison*. New York: Vintage, 1995.

Frank, Mark E. "Planting and Its Discontents: Or How Nomads Produced Spaces of Resistance in China's Erstwhile Xikang Province." *Resilience: A Journal of the Environmental Humanities* 3 (Winter/Spring/Fall 2015–16): 112–126.

Frechette, Ann. *Tibetans in Nepal: The Dynamics of International Assistance Among a Community in Exile*. New York: Berghahn, 2002.

"Freedom Given Only for Religious Activities: Mr. Nehru on Dalai Lama's Privileges." *Times of India*, April 21, 1959, 1 and 7, col. 3.

French, Rebecca R. "The New Snow Lion: The Tibetan Government-in-Exile in India." In *Governments-in-Exile in Contemporary World Politics*, ed. Yossi Shain, 188–201. New York: Routledge, 1991.

Gardner, Alex. Review article, "Khams pa histories: Visions of People, Place and Authority." *The Tibet Journal* 28, no. 3 (2000): 61–96.

Geertz, Clifford. *The Interpretation of Cultures*. New York: Basic Books, 1973.

Gelek, Tashi, Dorjee Damdul, and Tashi Dhondup. *Resistance and Unity: The Chinese Invasion, Makchi Shangri Lhagyal, and a History of Tibet (1947–1959)*, ed. Carole McGranahan. Chennai: Notion Press, 2019.

Gellner, Ernest. "The Coming of Nationalism and Its Interpretation: The Myths of Nation and Class." In *Mapping the Nation*, ed. Gopal Balakrishnan, 98–145. New York: Verso, 2012.

Gernet, Jacques. *Ancestry of Chinese Civilization*. Cambridge: Cambridge University Press, 1982.

Geshe Lhundup Sopa. *Lectures on Tibetan Religious Culture*, vol. 1. Delhi: Library of Tibetan Works and Archives, 1983.

Gierke, Otto von. *Community in Historical Perspective*. Trans. Mary Fischer. Cambridge: Cambridge University Press, 1990. First published in German in 1968.

Glees, Anthony. *Exile Politics during the Second World War*. Oxford: Clarendon Press, 1982.

Gold, Peter. *Tibetan Reflections: Life in a Tibetan Refugee Community*. Somerville, MA: Wisdom, 1984.

Goldberg, David Theo. "Disposable Citizenship." In *Citizenship and Its Others: Migration, Diasporas and Citizenship*, ed. Bridget Anderson and Vanessa Hughes, 199–125. London: Palgrave Macmillan, 2015.

Goldstein, Melvyn C. *A History of Modern Tibet, Volume 1: 1913–1951: The Demise of the Lamaist State*. Berkeley: University of California Press, 1989.

———. *A History of Modern Tibet, Volume 2: The Calm before the Storm: 1951–1955*. Berkeley: University of California Press, 2007.

———. *A History of Modern Tibet, Volume 3: The Storm Clouds Descend: 1955–1957*. Berkeley: University of California Press, 2014.

———. *The Snow Lion and the Dragon: China, Tibet, and the Dalai Lama*. Berkeley: University of California Press, 1997.

Goldstein, Melvyn C., Dawei Sherap, and William R. Siebenschuh. *A Tibetan Revolutionary: The Political Life and Times of Bapa Phuntso Wangye*. Berkeley: University of California Press, 2004.

Gordon, Andrew, and Trevor Stack. "Citizenship Beyond the State: Thinking with Early Modern Citizenship in the Contemporary World." *Citizenship Studies* 11, no. 2 (2007): 117–133.

Grant, Thomas D. *The Recognition of States: Law and Practice in Debate and Evolution*. Westport, CT: Praeger, 1999.

Gros, Stéphane. "Frontier (of) Experience: Introduction and Prolegomenon." In *Frontier Tibet: Patterns of Change in the Sino-Tibetan Borderlands*, ed. Stéphane Gros, 41–84. Amsterdam: Amsterdam University Press, 2019. *JSTOR*, www.jstor.org/stable/j.ctvt1sgw7.6.

———. *Frontier Tibet: Patterns of Change in the Sino-Tibetan Borderlands*. Amsterdam: Amsterdam University Press, 2019.

———. "Introduction." In *Frontier Tibet: Patterns of Change in the Sino-Tibetan Borderlands*, ed. Stéphane Gros, 38–40. Amsterdam: Amsterdam University Press, 2019.

Guha, Ranajit. *The Small Voice of History*. Ranikhet: Permanent Black, 2009.

"Gungthang Tsultrim—A Political Victim?" *Tibetan Review* XIII, no. 8 (August 1978): 5–9.

Guo, Rongxing. *China's Regional Development and Tibet*. Singapore: Springer, 2016.

Gyari, Lodi Gyaltsen. *The Dalai Lama's Special Envoy: Memoirs of a Lifetime in Pursuit of a Reunited Tibet*. New York: Columbia University Press, 2022.

———. "Status and Position of the Tibetan Youth Congress." *Tibet.net*, October 6, 2014.

Gyatsho, Karma. "Putting the Record Straight." *Rangzen* III, no. 2 (Summer 1978): 7–8.

Gyatso, Janet. "Down With the Demoness: Reflections on a Feminine Ground in Tibet." *The Tibet Journal* XII, no. 4, A Special Issue on Women and Tibet (Winter 1987): 34–46.

Gyatso, Tenzin, the 14th Dalai Lama of Tibet. *Freedom in Exile*. New York: HarperCollins, 1990. First published by Hodder and Stoughton Ltd.

Gyatso, Tenzin, the 14th Dalai Lama of Tibet. *My Land and My People*. New York: Hachette Book Group, 1997.

Gyatso, Tenzin, the 14th Dalai Lama of Tibet. *The Political Philosophy of the Dalai Lama: Selected Speeches and Writings*. Ed. Subash C Kashyap. New Delhi: Rupa Publications, 2014.

Gyatso, Tenzin, the 14th Dalai Lama of Tibet. *Speeches of His Holiness the XIV Dalai Lama (1959–1989) Vol. 1.* Trans. Sonam Gyatso. Dharamsala: Library of Tibetan Works and Archives (LTWA), 2011.

Gyatso, Tenzin, the 14th Dalai Lama of Tibet, and Arthur C. Brooks. "Behind Our Anxiety, The Fear of Being Unneeded." *New York Times*, November 4, 2016, A29.

Habermas, Jurgen. "The European Nation-state—Its Achievements and Its Limits. On the Past and Future of Sovereignty and Citizenship." In *Mapping the Nation*, ed. Gopal Balakrishnan, 268–294. New York: Verso, 2012.

Hall, Norman C. "The United States, Tibet and China: A Study of the American Involvement in Tibet and its Role in Sino-American and Sino-Tibetan Relations." *Tibetan Review* XIII, no. 1 (January 1978): 12–18.

Harrer, Heinrich. "Flight in a Sandstorm: A Miraculous Escape." *Life Magazine*, May 4, 1959.

Hess, Julia Meredith. *Immigrant Ambassadors: Citizenship and Belonging in the Tibetan Diaspora*. Stanford, CA: Stanford University Press, 2009.

Hevia, James. "Lamas, Emperors, and Rituals: Political Implications in Qing Imperial Ceremonies." *Journal of the International Association of Buddhist Studies* 2 (1993): 243–278.

Hobsbawm, Eric. J. *The Age of Extremes: A History of the World, 1914–1991*. New York: Vintage 1996.

———. "Ethnicity and Nationalism in Europe Today." In *Mapping the Nation*, ed. Gopal Balakrishnan, 255–266. New York: Verso, 2012.

———. *Nations and Nationalisms since 1780*. Cambridge: Cambridge University Press, 1990.

Hobsbawm, Eric J., and Terence Ranger. *The Invention of Tradition*. Cambridge: Cambridge University Press, 1983.

Hroch, Miroslav. "From Nationalist Movement to the Fully Formed Nation: The Nation-Building Process in Europe." In *Mapping the Nation*, ed. Gopal Balakrishnan, 78–97. New York: Verso, 2012.

———. *Social Preconditions of National Revival in Europe: A Comparative Analysis of Social Composition of Patriotic Groups Among the Smaller European Nations*. Trans. Ben Fowkes. Cambridge: Cambridge University Press, 1985.

Hyndman, Jennifer, and Wenona Giles. *Refugees in Extended Exile: Living on the Edge*. Oxon: Routledge, 2017.

Information Office of His Holiness the Dalai Lama. *Tibetans in Exile: 1959–1969*. Dharamsala: Information Office of His Holiness the Dalai Lama, 1969.

Isin, Engin F., and Greg M. Nielsen. *Acts of Citizenship*. London: Zed Books, 2008.

Isin, Engin F., and Patricia K. Wood. *Citizenship and Identity*. London: Sage Publications, 1999.

Jabb, Lama. *Oral and Literary Continuities in Modern Tibetan Literature*. London: Lexington Books, 2015.

Jagou, Fabienne. "The Dispute between Sichuan and Xikang over the Tibetan Kingdom of Trokyab (1930s–1940s)." In *Frontier Tibet: Patterns of Change in the*

Sino-Tibetan Borderlands, ed. Stephane Gros, 337–362. Amsterdam: Amsterdam University Press, 2019.
Jayal, Niraja Gopal. *Citizenship and Its Discontents*. Cambridge, MA: Harvard University Press, 2013.
Johnson, Ian. "Beyond the Dalai Lama: An Interview With Woeser and Wang Lixiong." *New York Review of Books*, August 7, 2017. http: //www.nybooks.com /blogs/nyrblog/2014/aug/07/interview-tsering-woeser-wang-lixiong/?insrc =hpbl.
Kapstein, Matthew T. *The Tibetans*. Malden, MA: Blackwell, 2006.
Karmay, Samten G. *The Arrow and the Spindle: Studies in History, Myths, Rituals and Beliefs in Tibet*, Vol. III. Kathmandu: Mandala Book Point, Reprint Edition 2014.
———. "Coalition of Religion and Politics." In *The Arrow and the Spindle, Studies in History, Myths, Rituals and Beliefs in Tibet, Vol. III*, ed. Samten G. Karmay 193–197. Kathmandu: Mandala Book Point, 2014.
———. "The Exiled Government and the Bonpo Community in India." In *The Arrow and the Spindle: Studies in History, Myths, Rituals and Beliefs in Tibet, Vol. I,*. ed. Samten G. Karmay, 532–536. Kathmandu: Mandala Book Point, 2014. Originally published in *Lungta* 7 (1993): 21–23.
———. "Introduction." In *A Survey of Bonpo Monasteries and Temples in Tibet and the Himalaya*, eds. Samten G. Karmay and Yasuhiko Nagano, 1–16. Osaka: National Museum of Ethnology, 2003. https: //texts.shanti.virginia.edu/thl /monasteries/bonpo#.
———. "A Historical Overview of the Bon Religion." In *Bon: The Magic Word*, ed. Samten G. Karmay and Jeff Watt, 55–82. New York: Rubin Museum of Art, 2007.
———. "King Glang Dar-ma and His Rule." In *The Arrow and the Spindle: Studies in History, Myths, Rituals and Beliefs in Tibet, Vol. II*, ed. Samten Gyaltsen Karmay, 15–29. Kathmandu: Mandala Book Point, 2014. First published by Mandala Publications in 2005.
———. "Religion: A Major Cause of Tibetan Disunity." *Tibetan Review* XII, vol. 5 (May 1977): 54–26.
———. "Who are the Amdowas: Letters." *Tibetan Review* XIII, no. 9 (September 1978): 26–27.
Kauffman, Thomas. *The Agendas of the Tibetan Refugees*. New York: Berghahn, 2015.
Kedourie, Elie. *Nationalism*. London: Century Hutchinson Publishing Group, 1966.
Kharat, Rajesh. "Gainers of a Stalemate: The Tibetans in India." In *Refugees and the State: Practices of Asylum and Care in India, 1947–2000*, ed. Ranabir Samaddar, 281–320. New Delhi: Sage Publications, 2003.
Khashitsang, Loten. "Letters." *Tibetan Review* XII, vol. 7 (July 1977): 24.
Khenpo Tsewang Dongyal Rinpoche. *Light of Fearless Indestructible Wisdom: The Life and Legacy of His Holiness Dudjom Rinpoche*. Boulder: Snow Lion, 2008.
Kim, Hanung. "Renaissance Man from Amdo: The Life and Scholarship of the Eighteenth-Century Amdo Scholar Sum Pa Mkhan Po Yeshe Dpal 'Byor." PhD diss., Harvard University, 2018.

Kingston, Lindsey N. "Worthy of Rights: Statelessness as a Cause and Symptom of Marginalization." In *Understanding Statelessness*, ed. Tendayi Bloom, Katherine Tonkiss, and Phillip Cole, 17–34. Oxford: Routledge, 2017.

Klieger, P. Christiaan. "Ideology and the Framing of Tibetan History." *The Tibet Journal*, vol. 14, no. 4 (Winter 1989): 3–16.

——. "Riding High on the Manchurian Dream: Three Paradigms in the Construction of the Tibetan Question." In *Contemporary Tibet: Politics, Development and Society in a Disputed Region*, ed. Barry Sautman and Jane Teufel Dreyer, 214–229. New York: East Gate, 2006.

Knaus, John Kenneth. *Orphans of the Cold War*. New York: PublicAffairs, 1999.

Kvaerne, Per. "The Bon Religion of Tibet." In *Bon, Buddhism and Democracy: The Building of a Tibetan National Identity*, ed. Per Kvaerne and Rinzin Thargyal, 10–26 (ebook 183–195). Copenhagen: Nordic Institute of Asian Studies, 1993.

——. "The Study of Bon in the West: Past, Present, and Future." In *New Horizons in Bon Studies: Bon Studies 2*, ed. Samten G. Karmay and Yasuhiko Nagano, 7–18. Osaka: National Museum of Ethnology, 2000.

——. "Zhangzhung, Bon, and China: The Construction of an Alternative Tibetan Historical Narrative." In *Tibetan Subjectivities on the Global Stage*, ed. Shelly Bhoil and Enrique Galvan-Alvarez, 3–24. Lanham, MD: Lexington Books, 2018.

Kvaerne, Per, and Dan Martin. *Drenpa's Proclamation: The Rise and Decline of the Bon Religion in Tibet*. Kathmandu: Vajra Books, 2023.

Lama, Jigme Yeshe. "Exile Tibetans and the Dance of Democracy." In *Tibetan Subjectivities on the Global Stage: Negotiating Dispossession*, ed. Shelly Bhoil and Enrique Galvan-Alvarez. New York: Lexington Books, 2018.

Lan, Mei-hua. "From Lifanyuan to the Mongolian and Tibetan Affairs Commission." In *Managing Frontiers in Qing China: The Lifanyuan and Libu Revisited*, ed. Dittmar Scholrkowitz and Ning Chia. Leiden: Koninklijke Brill, 2017.

Langenbacher, Eric, and Yossi Shain, eds. *Power and the Past: Collective Memory and International Relations*. Washington, DC: Georgetown University Press, 2010.

Litzinger, Ralph A. *Other Chinas: The Yao and the Politics of National Belonging*. Durham, NC: Duke University Press, 2000.

Lloyd, David. *Anomalous States: Irish Writing and the Post-Colonial Moment*. Durham, NC: Duke University Press, 1993.

Mamdani, Mahmood. *Define and Rule: Native as Political Identity*. Cambridge, MA: Harvard University Press, 2012.

Mancall, Mark. "The Ch'ing Tribute System: An Interpretive Essay." In *The Chinese World Order: Traditional China's Foreign Relations.*, ed. John K. Fairbank, 63–89. Cambridge, MA: Harvard University Press, 1968.

Marshall, T. H. *Class, Citizenship, and Social Development*. New York: Doubleday, 1964.

Marston, Sallie A. "The Private Goes Public: Citizenship and the New Spaces of Civil Society." *Political Geography* 14, no. 2 (1995): 194–198.

McClennen, Sophia A. *The Dialectics of Exile: Nation, Time, Language, and Space in Hispanic Literatures*. West Lafayette, IN: Purdue University Press, 2004.

McConnell, Fiona. "De Facto, Displaced, Tacit: The Sovereign Articulations of the Tibetan Government-in-Exile." *Political Geography* 28, no. 6 (August 2009): 343–352.

———. "Government-in-Exile: Statehood, Statelessness and the Reconfiguration of Territory and Sovereignty." *Geography Compass* 3, no. 5 (September 2009): 1902–1919.

———. *Rehearsing the State: The Political Practices of the Tibetan Government-in-Exile.* London: Wiley, 2016.

McGranahan, Carole. "Afterword: Chinese Settler Colonialism: Empire and Life in the Tibetan Borderlands." In *Frontier Tibet: Patterns of Change in the Sino-Tibetan Borderlands*, ed. Stéphane Gros, 517–540. Amsterdam: Amsterdam University Press, 2019.

———. *Arrested Histories: Tibet, the CIA, and Memories of a Forgotten War.* Durham, NC: Duke University Press, 2010.

———. "In Rapga's Library: The Texts and Times of a Rebel Tibetan Intellectual." *Cahiers d'Extrême-Asie* 15 (2005): 253–274.

———. "On Social Death: The Spang mda' tsang Family and 20th-Century Tibetan History." In *Trails of the Tibetan Tradition: Papers for Elliot Sperling*, ed. Roberto Vitali, 199–206. Dharamsala: Amyen Machen Institute, 2014.

———. "Tibet's Cold War." *Journal of Cold War Studies* 8, no. 3 (2006): 102–130.

Modood, Tariq. "A Basis for and Two Obstacles in the Way of a Multiculturalist Tradition." *British Journal of Sociology* 59, no. 1 (2008): 47–52.

Mote, F. W. *Imperial China: 900–1800.* Cambridge, MA: Harvard University Press, 1999.

Mountcastle, Amy. "The Question of Tibet and the Politics of the 'Real.'" In *Contemporary Tibet: Politics, Development and Society in a Disputed Region*, ed. Barry Sautman and Jane Teufel Dreyer, 85–106. New York: East Gate, 2006.

"MTAC." *Tibetan Review* XXXVIII, no. 2 (February 2003): 9.

Mulla, Arvind. "The Dalai Lama Speaks Out." *Tibetan Review*, April 18, 1971, 4–7. Originally published in *Times Weekly*.

Nandy, Ashis. *Bonfires of Creeds: The Essential Ashis Nandy.* New Delhi: Oxford University Press, 2004.

———. *Traditions, Tryanny and Utopias: Essays in the Politics of Awareness.* Calcutta: Oxford University Press, 1987.

Narayan, Jayaprakash. *A Revolutionary's Quest: Selected Writings.* Ed. Bimal Prasad. Delhi: Oxford University Press, 1980.

Nebesky-Wojkowitz, De Rene. *Oracles and Demons of Tibet: The Cult and Iconography of the Tibetan Protective Deities.* Varanasi: Book Faith India, 1996.

Norbu, Dawa. *China's Tibet Policy.* Surrey: Curzon Press, 2001.

———. *Culture and the Politics of Third World Nationalism.* New York: Routledge, 1992.

———. "Editorial: Toward Sectarian Harmony and National Unity." *Tibetan Review* XI, no. 9 (September 1976): 3–4.

———. "Four Rivers Have the Same Water," Interview with T. G. Dhongthok. *Tibetan Review* XI, no. 9 (September 1976): 24–25, 29.

———. "Han Hegemony and Tibetan Ethnicity." *International Studies* 32, no. 3 (July 1995): 299–314.

———. "The Murder of Gungthang Tsultrim." *Tibetan Review* XIII, no. 7 (July 1978): 9–10.

———. "The 1959 Tibetan Rebellion: An Interpretation." *The China Quarterly* 77 (March 1979): 74–93.

———. *Red Star Over Tibet*. London: William Collins & Sons, 1974.

———. "The Settlements: Participation and Integration." In *Exile as Challenge: The Tibetan Diaspora*, ed. Dagmar Bernstorff and Hubertus von Welck, 186–212. Hyderabad: Orient Longman Private Ltd., 2004.

———. "Sifting Facts out of Scriptures." Interview with Tsepon W.D. Shakabpa. *Tibetan Review* XI, no. 6–7 (June–July 1978): 26–27.

———. *Tibet: The Road Ahead*. London: Rider, 1998.

———. "TIRS: Not a Success Story." *Tibetan Review*, Editorial, VIII, no. 6 (July 1973).

Norbu, Jamyang. *Echoes from Forgotten Mountains*. Gurugram: Penguin Random House, 2023.

———. "Extinguishing the Embers of Freedom" (Part 1). *Shadow Tibet* (blog). January 17, 2019. https://www.jamyangnorbu.com/blog/2019/01/17/extinguishing-the-embers-of-freedom-part-1/.

———. "The Political Vision of Andrugtsang Gompo Tashi." *Shadow Tibet* (blog). September 27, 2014. https://www.jamyangnorbu.com/blog/2014/09/27/the-political-vision-of-andrugtsang-gompo-tashi/.

———. "Untangling a Mess of Petrified Noodles II." *Shadow Tibet* (blog). September 13, 2016. https://www.jamyangnorbu.com/blog/2016/09/13/untangling-a-mess-of-petrified-noodles-ii/.

Norbu, Namkhai, and K. Dhondup. "Tibetan Culture." *The Tibet Journal* 3, no. 3 (Autumn 1978): 38–40.

Norbu, Tseten. "Rebels: The Tibetan Youth Congress." In *Exile as Challenge: The Tibetan Diaspora*, ed. Dagmar Bernstorff and Hubertus von Welck, 391–408. Hyderabad: Orient Longman Private Ltd., 2004.

Nyers, Peter. *Rethinking Refugees: Beyond States of Emergency*. New York: Routledge, 2006.

Painter, Joe. "Prosaic Geographies of Stateness." *Political Geography* 25, no. 7 (September 2006): 752–774.

———. "Spaces of Citizenship: an Introduction." *Political Geography* 14, no. 2 (February 1995): 107–120.

Pardesi, Ghanshyam. "Some Observations on the Draft Constitution of Tibet." *The Tibet Journal* 1. no. 1 (July/September 1975): 63–69.

Patterson, George N. *Requiem for Tibet*. London: Aurum Press, 1990.

———. *Tibet in Revolt*. London: Faber and Faber, 1960.

———. *Tragic Destiny*. London: Faber and Faber, 1959.

Pema, Jetsun. "Caring for the Weakest: The Children's Villages." In *Exile as Challenge: The Tibetan Diaspora*, ed. Dagmar Bernstorff and Hubertus von Welck, 279–294. Hyderabad: Orient Longman Private Ltd., 2004.

Pema Shastri. "Opinion: What Tibetans Expect from Exile Leadership." *Tibetan Review* XXXVIII, no. 3 (March 2003): 21.

Perdue, Peter C. *China Marches West: The Qing Conquest of Central Eurasia*. Cambridge, MA: Harvard University Press, 2005.

Petech, Luciano. "The Administration of Tibet During the First Half-Century of Chinese Protectorate." In *The Tibetan History Reader*, ed. Gray Tuttle and Kurtis R. Schaeffer, 389–410 (ebook).

———. *China and Tibet in the Early Eighteenth Century: History of the Establishment of Chinese Protectorate in Tibet*, T'oung pao, Monographie 1, Leiden: Brill, 1950.

———. "The Mongol Census in Tibet." In *Tibetan Studies: In Honor of Hugh Richardson*, ed. Michael Aris and Aung San Suu Kyi, 233–238. New Delhi: Vikas Publishing House, 1980.

———. "The Rise of the Pakmodru Dynasty." In *The Tibetan History Reader*, ed. Gray Tuttle and Kurtis R. Schaeffer, 249–265 (ebook). New York: Columbia University Press, 2013.

Phuntso, Tsewang. "Government in Exile." In *Exile as Challenge: The Tibetan Diaspora*, ed. Dagmar Bernstorff and Hubertus von Welck, 125–149. Hyderabad: Orient Longman, 2004.

Pirie, Fernanda. "Segmentation Within the State: The Reconfiguration of Tibetan Tribes in China's Reform Period." Special Issue: Pastoralists in Post-socialist Asia New Series. *Nomadic Peoples* 9, no. 1/2 (2005): 83–102.

Pradhan, Atul Chandra. "The Sarvoday Movement in Odisha after Independence." *Odisha Review*, August 2014.

Pye, Lucien W., and Sidney Verba, eds. *Political Culture and Political Development*. Princeton, NJ: Princeton University Press, 1965.

Rawski, Evelyn S. *The Last Emperors: A Social History of Qing Imperial Institutions*. Berkeley: University of California Press, 1998.

Regional Working Committee, Tibetan Youth Congress. "Blasphemy Against Buddhism.""Letters," *Tibetan Review* XIII, no. 8 (August 1978): 4–5.

Reisman, Michael. "Governments-in-Exile: Notes Toward a Theory of Formation and Operation." In *Governments-in-Exile in Contemporary World Politics*, ed. Yossi Shain, 238–248. New York: Routledge, 1991.

Renan, Ernest. "What is a Nation?" In *Nation and Narration*, ed. Homi Bhabha, 8–22. London: Routledge, 1990.

"Reprint of Current Magazine's article." *Tibetan Review*, "From the Press," XIII, no. 8 (August 1978): 3–4.

Richardson, Hugh E. *High Peaks, Pure Earth*. London: Serindia, 1998.

Rigzin Tsepak. "The Tibetan Schools in the Diaspora." In *Exile as Challenge: The Tibetan Diaspora*, ed. Dagmar Bernstorff and Hubertus von Welck, 266–278. Hyderabad: Orient Longman Private Ltd., 2004.

Rinpoche, Jigme, Phagpa Tshering, Mrs. Gha Yonden, et al. "Tibetans in India." "Readers' Views," *The Times of India*, June 12, 1971.

Roebert, Donovan, ed. *Samdhong Rinpoche: Uncompromising Truth for a Compromised World*. Bloomington, IN: World Wisdom, 2006.

Roemer, Stephanie. *The Tibetan Government-in-Exile: Politics at Large.* London: Routledge, 2008.
Rossabi, Morris, ed. *China Among Equals: The Middle Kingdoms and Its Neighbors, 10th–14th Centuries.* Berkeley: University of California Press, 1983.
Ruegg, David Seyfort. "The Preceptor-Donor Relation in Thirteenth-Century Tibetan Society and Polity." In *The Tibetan History Reader*, ed. Gray Tuttle and Kurtis R. Schaeffer, 211–232 (ebook). New York: Columbia University Press, 2013.
Said, Edward W. *Culture and Imperialism.* New York: Vintage, 1994.
——. *The Politics of Dispossession.* New York: Vintage, 1995.
——. *Power, Politics and Culture.* New York: Vintage, 2001.
——. *Orientalism.* New York: Vintage, 1979.
Samaddar, Ranabir, ed. *Refugees and the State: Practices of Asylum and Care in India, 1947–2000.* New Delhi: Sage Publications, 2003.
Samdhong Rinpoche. "Democracy and Future Tibet." His Eminence Professor Samdhong Rinpoche, Speeches. July 18, 2014. http: //samdhongrinpoche.com/en/democracy-and-future-tibet/.
——. "Education for Non-Violence." In *Exile as Challenge: The Tibetan Diaspora*, ed. Dagmar Bernstorff and Hubertus von Welck, 167–185. Hyderabad: Orient Longman Private Ltd., 2004.
——. "Modernity and Tradition." His Eminence Professor Samdhong Rinpoche, Speeches. October 10, 2014. http://samdhongrinpoche.com/en/modernity-and-tradition/.
——. *Selected Writings and Speeches.* Sarnath: Central Institute of Higher Studies, 1999.
——. *The Social Philosophy of Buddhism.* Sarnath: Central Institute of Higher Tibetan Studies, 1972.
Samphel, Thubten. "Statement of the Kashag on the 53rd Anniversary of Tibetan Democracy Day." Dharamsala: Central Tibetan Administration, September 2, 2013.
——. "Statement of the Kashag on the 55th Anniversary of Tibetan Democracy Day," Dharamsala: Central Tibetan Administration, September 2, 2015.
——. "Virtual Tibet: The Media." In *Exile as Challenge: The Tibetan Diaspora*, ed. Dagmar Bernstorff and Hubertus von Welck, 167–185. Hyderabad: Orient Longman, 2004.
Sautman, Barry, and He Baogang. "The Politics of the Dalai Lama's New Initiative for Autonomy." *Pacific Affairs* 4 (2005/2006): 601–629.
Sautman, Barry, and Jane Teufel Dreyer, eds. *Contemporary Tibet: Politics, Development and Society in a Disputed Region.* New York: East Gate, 2006.
Schaeffer, Kurtis R., Matthew T. Kapstein, and Gray Tuttle. *Sources of Tibetan Tradition.* New York: Columbia University Press, 2013.
Schaeffer, Kurtis R. "The Fifth Dalai Lama." In *The Tibetan History Reader*, ed. Gray Tuttle and Kurtis R. Schaeffer, 348–362 (ebook). New York: Columbia University Press, 2013
Schaik, Sam van. *Tibet: A History.* New Haven, CT: Yale University Press, 2011.

Schmitz, Gerarld. "Tibet's Position in International Law." In *Exile as Challenge: The Tibetan Diaspora*, ed. Dagmar Bernstorff and Hubertus von Welck, 45–71. Hyderabad: Orient Longman Private Ltd., 2004.
Schurmann, H. F. "Organization and Response in Communist China." *The Annals of the American Academy of Political and Social Science* 321 (January 1959): 51–61.
Schwieger, Peter. *The Dalai Lama and the Emperor of China*. New York: Columbia University Press, 2015.
———. "History as Myth: On the Appropriation of the Past in Tibetan Culture." In *The Tibetan History Reader*, ed. Gray Tuttle and Kurtis R. Schaeffer, 64–85 (ebook). New York: Columbia University Press, 2013.
Scott, James C. *The Art of Not Being Governed*. New Haven, CT: Yale University Press, 2009.
Shain, Yossi. "Collective Memory and the Logic of Appropriate Behavior." In *Power and the Past: Collective Memory and International Relations*, ed. Eric Langenbacher and Yossi Shain, 213–224. Washington, DC: Georgetown University Press, 2010.
———. *The Frontiers of Loyalty*. Middletown, CT: Wesleyan University Press, 1989.
———, ed. *Governments-in-Exile in Contemporary World Politics*. New York: Routledge, 1991.
———. "Governments-in-Exile and International Legitimation." In *Governments-in-Exile in Contemporary World Politics*, ed. Yossi Shain, 219–237. New York: Routledge, 1991.
———. "Introduction: Governments-in-Exile and the Age of Democratic Transitions." In *Governments-in-Exile in Contemporary World Politics*, ed. Yossi Shain, 1–17. New York: Routledge, 1991.
———. *Kinship and Diasporas in International Affairs*. Minneapolis: University of Minnesota Press, 2007.
Shain, Yossi, and Juan J. Linz. *Between States: Interim Governments and Democratic Transitions*. Cambridge: Cambridge University Press, 1995.
Shakabpa, Tsepon W. D. *Tibet: A Political History*. New Delhi: Potala Publications, 1967.
Shakya, Tsering. *The Dragon in the Land of Snows: A History of Modern Tibet Since 1947*. New York: Penguin, 1999.
———. "The Genesis of the Sino-Tibetan Agreement of 1951." In *The Tibetan History Reader*, ed. Gray Tuttle and Kurtis R. Schaeffer, 609–632 (ebook). New York: Columbia University Press, 2013.
Shiromany, A. A., and Tibetan Parliamentary and Policy Research Center, eds. *The Spirit of Tibet: Universal Heritage. Selected Speeches and Writings of HH The Dalai Lama XIV*. New Delhi: Allied Publishers Ltd., 1995.
Smith, Warren W. *Tibetan Nation: A History of Tibetan Nationalism and Sino-Tibetan Relations*. Boulder, CO: Westview Press, 1996.

Snellgrove, David L. "The Rulers of Western Tibet." In *The Tibetan History Reader*, ed. Gray Tuttle and Kurtis R. Schaeffer, 166–182 (ebook). New York: Columbia University Press, 2013.

Söderbaum, Fredrik. *Rethinking Regionalism*. London: Palgrave, 2016.

Sperling, Elliot. "The Chinese Venture in K'am, 1904–1911, and the Role of Chao Erh-feng." *The Tibet Journal* 1, no. 2 (April–June 1978): 10–25.

——. "The Yuan Dynasty." In *Authenticating Tibet: Answers to China's 100 Questions*, ed. Ann-Marie Blondeau and Katia Buffetrille, 14–17. Berkeley: University of California Press, 2008.

Stein, R. A. "The Evolution of Monastic Power." In *The Tibetan History Reader*, ed. Gray Tuttle and Kurtis R. Schaeffer, 196–207 (ebook). New York: Columbia University Press, 2013.

Stoddard, Heather. "Progressives and Exiles." In *The Tibetan History Reader*, ed. Gray Tuttle and Kurtis R. Schaeffer, 583–608. New York: Columbia University Press, 2013.

——. "Tibetan Publications and National Identity." In *Resistance and Reform in Tibet*, ed. Robert Barnett and Shivin Arkiner, 121–156. London: Hurst, 1994.

"STOP PRESS." *Tibetan Review* XIII, no. 8 (August 1978): 9.

Suzuki, Chusei. "China's Relations with Inner Asia: The Hsiung-Nu, Tibet." In *The Chinese World Order*, ed. John K. Fairbank, 180–197. Cambridge, MA: Harvard University Press, 1968.

Tapper, Richard. *Frontier Nomads of Iran: A Political and Social History of the Shahsevan*. Cambridge: Cambridge University Press, 1997.

Tashi Tsering. *The Struggle for Modern Tibet: The Autobiography of Tashi Tsering*. New York: East Gate, 1997.

Tethong, Wangpo. "Tibet's Future—Options for Self-Governance." In *Exile as Challenge: The Tibetan Diaspora*, ed. Dagmar Bernstorff and Hubertus von Welck, 409–418. Hyderabad: Orient Longman Private Ltd., 2004.

Thapar, Romila. *The Past Before Us: Historical Traditions of Early North India*. Cambridge, MA: Harvard University Press, 2013.

——. *The Past as Present*. London: Seagull Books, 2019.

"13-Groups Deny Taiwanese Connection." *Tibetan Review* XIII, no. 10 (October 1978): 6.

Thondup, Gyalo, and Anne F. Thurston. *The Noodle Maker of Kalimpong*. New York: PublicAffairs, 2015.

Tibet Documentation. *Exile: A Photo Journal (1959–1989)*. Dharamsala: Tibet Documentation, 2017.

"Tibetan Leader Murdered." *Vanguard* XXIV, no. 20 (June 25, 1978).

"Tibetan refugees seek Indian citizenship." *The Times of India*, August 5, 1971, 16.

Tibetan Welfare Association. *The Assasination [sic] of Gungthang Tsultrim: Black Friday*. Self-published, June 1978.

Tololyan, Khachig. "Exile Governments in the Armenian Polity." In *Governments-in-Exile in Contemporary World Politics*, ed. Yossi Shain, 166–187. New York: Routledge, 1991.

"The Tragedy of Tibetans." Reprint of Nergis Dalal's article in the *Tribune*. *Tibetan Review* XIII, no. 8 (August 1978): 23.
Tsarong, Dundul Namgyal. *In the Service of His Country: The Biography of Dasang Damdul Tsarong*. Ithaca, NY: Snow Lion, 2000.
Tsomo, Tsering. "Parliament in Exile." In *Exile as Challenge: The Tibetan Diaspora*, ed. Dagmar Bernstorff and Hubertus von Welck, 150–166. Hyderabad: Orient Longman Private Ltd., 2004.
Tsomu, Yudru. *The Rise of Gonpo Namgyel in Kham: The Blind Warrior of Nyarong*. New York: Lexington Books, 2016.
——. "The Rise of a Political Strongman in Derge in the Early Twentieth Century: The Story of Jago Topden." In *Frontier Tibet: Patterns of Change in the Sino-Tibetan Borderlands*, ed. Stéphane Gros, 363–410. Amsterdam: Amsterdam University Press, 2019.
——. "Taming The Khampas: The Republican Construction of Eastern Tibet." *Modern China* 39, no. 3. (May 2013): 319–344.
Turek, Maria. "Return of the Good King: Kingship and Identity among Yushu Tibetans since 1951." In *Frontier Tibet: Patterns of Change in the Sino-Tibetan Borderlands*, ed. Stéphane Gros, 453–488. Amsterdam: Amsterdam University Press, 2019.
Tuttle, Gray. *Tibetan Buddhists in the Making of Modern China*. New York: Columbia University Press, 2005.
Tuttle, Gray, and Kurtis R. Schaeffer, eds. *The Tibetan History Reader*. New York: Columbia University Press, 2013.
"Unusual and Exotic Fare: Tibetan Dance-Drama." *The Times of India*, January 28, 1962, 3.
Veg, Sebastian. "Tibet, Nationalism, and Modernity: Two Chinese Contributions." *China Perspectives* 3 (2009): 98–107.
Viswanathan, Gauri. *Outside the Fold: Conversion, Modernity, and Belief*. New Haven, CT: Yale University Press, 1998.
Vitali Roberto, ed. *Trails of the Tibetan Tradition: Papers for Elliot Sperling*. Dharamsala: Amyen Machen Institute, 2014.
Walter, Michael L. *Buddhism and Empire: The Political and Religious Culture of Early Tibet*. Leiden: Brill, 2009.
Wang, Gungwu. "The Rhetoric of a Lesser Empire: Early Sung Relations with Its Neighbors." In *China Among Equals*, ed. Morris Rossabi, 47–65. Berkeley: University of California Press, 1983.
Wang, Hui. *China from Empire to Nation-State*. Trans. Michael Gibbs Hill. Cambridge, MA: Harvard University Press, 2014.
——. *The Politics of Imagining Asia*. Cambridge, MA: Harvard University Press, 2011.
Wang, Lixiong, and Tsering Shakya. *The Struggle for Tibet*. London: Verso, 2009.
Wangyal, Tsering. "The Enemy Within." Editorial, *Tibetan Review* XVI, no. 5 (May 1981): 3–4.
——. "Politics of Sorrow." *Tibetan Review* XIII, no. 8 (August 1978): 1, 20.

——. "A Time for Introspection." *Tibetan Review* XII, no. 5 (May 1977): 3–4.
Williams, Gwyn A. *When was Wales? A Hisory of the Welsh*. Middlesex: Penguin, 1985.
Wylie, Turrell V. "Monastic Patronage in Fifteenth-Century Tibet." In *The Tibetan History Reader*, ed. Gray Tuttle and Kurtis R. Schaeffer, 266–277 (ebook). New York: Columbia University Press, 2013.
Yang, Eveline. "Tracing the *Chol kha gsum*: Reexamining a Sa skya-Yuan Period Administrative Geography." *Revue d'Etudes Tibetaines* 37 (December 2016): 551–568.
Yuthok, Jigmie Dorje. "Yuthok's Rejoinder to the Noodle Maker." *Tibetan Political Review*, July 30, 2016.

INDEX

Locators in *italics* refer to figures.

Akhu Tsultrim. *See* Gungthang Tsultrim
Amdo and Amdowa identity: armed struggle against the Chinese in Kham and Amdo (1950s), 8, 39, 42; drama troupe formed by Gungthang Tsultrim in, 112, 197; the Fourteenth Dalai Lama as a native of, 170, 302n37; Gungthang Tsultrim, Tongkhor Rinpoche, and Trochupon Dorje Pasang as representatives of Amdo in the CTA, 60; Gungthang Tsultrim as a native of, 60, 112, 170, 195, 222; Gyalo Thondup as a native of, 170; historical and religious autonomy of eastern Tibetan regions, 12–14, 61, 222–223; Labrang Tashikhyil located in, 2, 112, 290n38
Anderson, Benedict, 20
Anderson, Bridget, 141, 245
Andrugtsang, Gompo Tashi: Chushi Gangdrug founded by, 58; meeting at his house in Lhasa to pledge support to fight the Chinese (Feb. 1958), 52; oath to work in harmony taken at Chushi Gangdrug's regrouping in Mustang, 299n27; Tibetan resistance movement following his death, 92; at Wangdu Dorjee and Jagoetsang Namgyal Dorjee's address in Bodh Gaya, 46
Assasination [sic] of Gungthang Tsultrim, The (*Pasang Nagpo [The Black Friday]*): on the appointment of the sixteenth Karmapa, 241–242; the CTA criticized by, 222–223; the Dalai Lama's concern over, 235–237, 248–249; Declaration of the Association of Thirteen Groups in response to criticism of, 236–237, 303–304n14; discussion in letters addressed to Moraji Desai from Tibetans in Dharamsala, 246–247; English version reproduced in the *Tibetan Review* (August 1978), 221–222; Gungthang Tsultrim's personality described in, 198, 222; publication by the Tibetan Welfare Association, 5, 211–212, *256*; revisions and clarifications made by the Thirteen with the Tibetan government, 247; the three regions

Assasination [sic] *of Gungthang Tsultrim (continued)* in, 222, 239; the Tibetan government's condemnation of, 246

Avedon, John F.: on the challenging of reforms by chieftains, 37; on the thirteen members of the Commission of Tibetan People's Deputies, 36

Bakula Rinpoche (or Kushok Bakula), 113–114, 116, 117

Barchungtsang, Dorjee Lhamo, 193, 287n44

Barchungtsang, Thutop Gompo, 89, 91, 182, 183, 193

Bauer, Otto, 242

Bawa Chakzoe Kalsang Tashi, 94, 284n21

Bhabha, Homi K., 65

Bhave, Vinobha, 115–116

Bhod Dedon Tsogpa. *See* Tibetan Welfare Association (Bhod Dedon Tsogpa, Tsokhag Chusum, the Group of Thirteen)

Bhod-mi Rangwang (Tibetan Freedom): Gyaltsen Choden as a writer for, 295n23; Gyari Rinpoche as a writer for, 107; six-point resolution printed in, 75–76; the United Party affiliated with, 80, 81, 91

Bhod-mi Rangwang (Tibetan Freedom)— testimonies regarding Ockenden: "The Reason Why Kelsang Left Ockenden," 155; "A Report by Gyaltsen Choden" published by, 152, 154–155, 295n23; students on their reasons for leaving Ockenden, 155–156

Bhoodan Movement, 115–116

Bir Nangchen settlement. *See* Tibetan Khampa Industrial Society (or Bir Nangchen settlement)

Black Friday. *See Assasination* [sic] *of Gungthang Tsultrim*

Bongsar, Tsodi: on her family's journey to exile, 67–70; on Khampas not receiving aid from exile officials, 129; meetings with Indian officials attended with her father, 192; with members of Tsokhag Chusum, *184*

Bongsartsang, Drakpa Namgyal (Bongsarpon Drakpa Namgyal), 67–70

Bongsartsang, Namkha Dorje (Bongsarpon Namkha Dorje): author's personal relation to, ix; as Bongsarpon, 67, 259; as a founding member of the Tibetan Welfare Association, 183, *184, 185*, 301n20; his daughter Tsodi as his translator, 192; journey from Yeyonsumdo in Nangchen into exile, 67–70; loan arranged for by Tsering Choden Dhompa, 193; meeting with Prime Minister Nehru, 284n9; petition to Prime Minister Nehru for aid for his people, 129; petition to Prime Minister Nehru for help to establish a settlement, 73–74, 117, 284n9; rejection of his request to form a work unit, 72; relations with the United Party, 74; settlement established in Mainpat (1965), 73, 74, 117; settlements led by their own leaders viewed as important, 71, 127, 188, 258, 260; work building roads, 70

Bongsartsang Namkha Dorje— Mainpat Settlement: aborted attempt to relocate to Bhutan, 189; challenges faced by his clan, 188, 298n17

Bonpos and Bon. *See also* Lungtok Tenpai Nyima Rinpoche; Pon Sangye Namgyal; Yongdzin Lopon Tenzin Namdak: election of a Bon religious representative to the Tibetan parliament (1977), 219–220;

Lang Darma's association with, 163; Zhangzhung, 164–165

Bonpo settlement in Dolanji (Tibetan Bonpo Foundation). *See also* Gyatso, Lobsang; Sangye Namgyal, Bongsarpon; Wangyal, Tsering; Yongdzin Lopon Tenzin Namdak: author's visit to (2015), 71, 108, 159–160, 260; funds received from the Catholic Relief agency to buy land (1966), 158–159; protesting of allegations made by Taiwan, 206; role of the Thirteen in its establishment, 261; Tibetans settled in, 186; Ugyan Choedup's visit to, 161–162

Boyarin, Jonathan, and Daniel Boyarin, 296n53

Brewster, Pat, *187*; on challenges associated with distributing aid, 130; on challenges of working in India in the 1960s, 217; letter to the NCC on rehabilitating Tibetan refugees in India, 173; on the need to train Tibetans in basic administrative skills, 216; the refugee department at CORAGS run by, 171–172; relationship with the Thirteen, 174, *185*; on the Thirteen and international aid, 218; TIRS established by, 173

Brox, Trine, 25, 285n25

Buxa Choegar, 126–127, 291n11

Bylakuppe settlement: as the first Tibetan agricultural settlement, 73, 283n8; Namdroling Monastery in, 263; stories from Bylakuppe, 127–128; United Party representatives in, 18, 138

Central Relief Committee of India: aid distributed by, 129; Pat Brewster as a member of, 173; the Kripalani Committee's establishment of (1959),

131; report by Kalyan Singh Gupta on the Thirteen settlements, 215–216

Central Tibetan Administration (CTA). *See also* Information and Publicity Office of His Holiness the Dalai Lama: Academy of Music, Dance, and Drama formed by (1959), 197, 300n1; electoral process divided according to the *chol kha sum* (three regions), 59; establishment in Dharamsala (1960), 34–35; initiatives to rehabilitate dispossessed Tibetans, 24; proposed meeting with the Thirteen (July 1978), 210, 301n29; Taiwan and the People's Republic of China denounced as enemies, 106, 208–209

Central Tibetan Administration (CTA)—Kashag: Gelug authority, 23; selection of cabinet members by the Dalai Lama, 35–36

Cheme Dorjee (Dege Cheme): journey to Bodh Gaya for the Great Oath, 45–46, 52; as a member of the Tibetan parliament, 45; as Ontul Karma Dechen's assistant, 279n29; on the printing machines at Rangwang Parkhang, 91

Chen, Jian, 282n69

Chinese Communist Party (CCP): denounced as an enemy by the Tibetan exile government, 106, 124–125, 208–209, 210; shift from national self-determination to "uniting all nationalities into a big family," 62, 282n69

Choden, Gyaltsen: analysis of the events at Ockenden School, 152, 154–155, 162, 295n23; Dexter's accusations against, 148–149, 150, 151, 294n10; influence in the Tibetan government, 79–80; Ockenden School appointment, 148; Ockenden School left by, 161

Choedup, Ugyan, 161–162
Chokling Rinpoche: as a native of Derge, Kham, 290n39; as president of the Derge settlement in Bir, 187; as a Tsokhag Chusum/Group of Thirteen leader, *185, 186, 187*
Choklingtsang, Jamyang Gyaltsen, 116, *184*, 215
chol kha sum (three regions; Greater Tibet): in *The Black Friday* pamphlet, 222, 239; as a concept during the Sakya-Yuan period, 59, 281n58; map of, *xix*; "political" Tibet and "ethnographic" Tibet used to distinguish regions of, 38; primacy of their unity in the national narrative, 11, 61, 222–223; in a verse attributed to Sumpa Khenpo Yeshe Peljor, 59
Cholsum Chigdril Tsogpa. *See* United Party (Cholsum Chigdril Tsogpa [Tibetan United Association])
Chushi Gangdrug. *See also* McGranahan, Carole—on the Chushi Gangdrug: as both relied upon and dismissed by the Lhasa government, 8; disbanding of (1974), 94; establishment in the mid-1950s, 8, 39, 42; Gungthang Tsultrim as a member of, 2; protection of the Dalai Lama during his escape to India, 34; regrouping in Mustang, 299n27; relationships formed with members of the Thirteen, 90; views of veterans of, 249–250, 303n10
Chushi Gangdrug—rift in the leadership: authority over funds as an issue, 92, 286–287n44, 287n46; embezzlement charges against its leaders, 90–91, 92; Gyari Rinpoche on the styles of Chushi Gangdrug's main leaders, 95; merging of Sungkyob Parkhang with Rangwang Parkhang, 91–92,

286–287n44; Sonam Damdul's explanation of, 95; support for Gyen Yeshi among the leaders of, 94
Current, The magazine: article on Gungthang Tsultrim's assassination, 2, 223, 224, 302n41

Dalai Lama: Altan Khan's creation of the title "Dalai Lama," 10; arguments for the Dalai Lama to be a nonsectarian lama, 110; as the incarnation of the bodhisattva Avalokitesvara, 25
Dalai Lama—The Fifth Dalai Lama (Losang Gyatso): Nangchen under the authority of, 58–59; political and religious authority over Tibet established by (1642), 9, 10
Dalai Lama—The Thirteenth Dalai Lama: Chinese efforts to counter Tibet's claim to sovereignty over Kham, 282n68; declaration of independence (1913), 11, 43; initiatives to modernize Tibet, 23; and the Pangdatsang family, 133
Dalai Lama—The Fourteenth Dalai Lama (Tenzin Gyatso): on Amdo at the time he lived there with his family, 302n37; on the dissolution of the Chushi Gangdrug, 94; escape from Tibet, 8, 33–34; Gungthang Tsultrim encouraged to help establish a settlement for Tibetans, 197; on Gyen Yeshe, 94; initiatives to modernize Tibet, 23, 24; knowledge of *The Black Friday* pamphlet gained from Wangdu Dorjee, 237; on the Nechung oracle, 76; private meeting with Peter Woodard from Ockenden Venture, 152, 154; realization of the Thirteenth Dalai Lama's proclamation of independence, 43; recognition and enthronement as,

INDEX 335

22; renunciation of his practice of Shugden (1975), 109

Dalai Lama—The Fourteenth Dalai Lama (Tenzin Gyatso)—government in exile. *See also* Central Tibetan Administration (CTA); Information and Publicity Office of His Holiness the Dalai Lama: approval of the goals of the United Party, 80, 84; on democracy and centralization, 285–286n33; democracy viewed by Tibetans as his gift to them, 25–26, 56, 141; Draft Constitution of Tibet (March 1963), 63–64, 80; endeavor to ceaselessly preserve, promote, and act upon traditional Tibetan values, 298n19; on the exile government as a new polity where all *tsampa*-eaters were equal, 281n57; help establishing settlements requested from the Indian prime minister, 73; Kashag leaders nominated by, 27–28; positioning by the United Party as both the symbol and motivation of the Tibetan struggle for freedom, 81–85; Seventeen-Point Agreement with China repudiated, 34; speech to representatives of Domey (28 September 1978), 247–249, 281n57; as the symbol of Tibetan culture, religion, and sovereignty, 48; Tibetan unity associated with him, 22, 25–26, 35, 55–57

Dalton, Jacob P., 280n43

Damdul, Sonam (Sodam): on Dzongnang Rinpoche, 252; Gungthang Tsultrim described by, 253; as a member of the Thirteen, *184*; on raising funds to find Gungthang Tsultrim's murderer(s), 22; on the rift in the Chushi Gangdrug between Gyalo Thondup and Gyen Yeshe, 95; as secretary for the settlement in Kamrao, 21, 301n19, 304n14; on the third formal meeting of the Thirteen, 182–183; on why the Thirteen was formed, 21–22

Davinson, William (Bill), 174, *185*

Declaration of the Association of Thirteen Groups, 236–237, 303–304n14

Derge, Kham: Chokling Rinpoche as a native of, 290n39; the Derge kingdom as an alliance between secular and religious powers, 40, 181; Kathok Monastery in, 102; Khampa uprising in (1956), 68

Derge (or Dege) settlement in Bir. *See also* Cheme Dorjee (Dege Cheme); Jagoetsang Namgyal Dorjee: administration of, 187–188; families from Tibet settled in, 187; Tibetan Khampa Industrial Society in, 174, 177

Dexter, Malcolm: correspondence with Joyce Pearce, 130, 148–149, 153; criticism from Ockenden students for teaching "wrong history," 144, 145, 148–153, 156, 158, 166; the Dalai Lama's encouragement of, 157, 294n7; decision to expel ten students, 295n21; hiring of, 147

Dhondup, Amdo (or Gyemi Dhondup): accused by Gungthang Tsultrim as plotting his murder, 1, 212; claim that Gungthang Tsultrim took money from Taiwan, 207–208; position as a senior army officer, 1; the Thirteen's criticism of, 258

Dhondupling Tibetan Colony, Clement Town settlement: establishment of, 170; Mindrolling Monastery as an education center in, 263; Mindrolling Monastery cofounded by Dzongnang Rinpoche and Khochhen Rinpoche

Dhondupling Tibetan Colony (*continued*) (1965), 170; murder of Gawa Zamkhen Tashi Yarphel in, 199–200; registration of land with the Lucknow court (Nov. 1964), 116
Dhongthok, T. G., 110, 290n32
Dorje, Pema, 128–129, 284n21
Dorzong Rinpoche: dedication to developing the Khampagar Tashi Jong settlement, 216; as a founding member of the Tibetan Welfare Association, 182, 183, *184*, *186*, 301n19, 304n14; questions raised on belonging during a meeting with the CTA, 233, 235, 237; response to the government's receptivity to excoriations against the Thirteen, 229
Drawutsang, Rinchen Tsering (or Drawupon Rinchen Tsering): as the chieftain of Ga Kyekudo in Nangchen, 169; documents signed for camps established by TIRS, 297n15; false accusations and posters by the United Party defaming him, 111, 304n16; founding of the Taopon settlement in Kamrao, 169, 186; Gyen Yeshi defended by, 94; as a leader of Chushi Gangdrug, 79, 89, 94–96, 193; as a leader of the Group of Thirteen, 4, 181, 182, 183, *184*, 185, *185*, 233; meeting with the Dalai Lama to discuss the *Black Friday* pamphlet, 237; as a member of parliament in exile, 60, 233; memories of him by his wife and daughter, 193; on Phenpo Lobsang Yeshi, 79; reconciliation with Jagoetsang Namgyal Dorjee, 299n27
Drayabtsang, Tashi Namgyal, 252–253
Duara, Prasenjit: on citizens of frontier races in China, 282n68; on defining national territories between China and India, 61; on national unity and national integration, 28, 29; on the relationship between the nation-state and nationalism, 296n52; on studying twentieth-century China, 285n24
Dudjom Rinpoche: disrespectful treatment of him at a United Party meeting in Dharamsala, 86, 100; imprisonment in India, 103, 104; as a member of the standing committee of the United Party, 80; Orissa settlement established by, 102, 139
Dzongnang Rinpoche (Patrul Jampal Lodroe Dzongnang Rinpoche): address to the exile government in Dharamsala (July 25, 1978), 228–230, 233–234; criticized by Tibetans in letters to the cabinet, 251–252; friendship with Gungthang Tsultrim, 170; as a member of the Thirteen, 182, 183, *185*, *186*, 301n19, 304n14; Mindrolling Monastery cofounded in the Dhondupling settlement with Khochhen Rinpoche (1965), 170

exile government. *See* Central Tibetan Administration (CTA): Academy of Music, Dance, and Drama formed by (1959), 197, 300n1

Five Aims of the Tibetan United Association. *See* United Party (Cholsum Chigdril Tsogpa [Tibetan United Association])—five aims of its manifesto
Frank, Mark E., 40–41

Gandhi, Indira: Gungthang Tsultrim's letter to (June 23, 1971), 198–201, 300n10; photo with the Thirteen leaders, *184*, *186*, 190
Gardner, Alex, 283n77
Geertz, Clifford, 28–29

INDEX 337

Gelug school. *See also* Dalai Lama; Gungthang Tsultrim (or Akhu Tsultrim): dominance of, 23, 110; Labrang Tashikhyil, 2, 112, 290n38; as the norm in Central Tibet since the seventeenth century, 23; rise of its popularity in the fifteenth century, 10; struggle for power between Kagyu and Gelug lamas, 110

Geshe Lhundup Sopa, 163

Goldstein, Melvyn C., 23, 43

Greater Tibet. *See chol kha sum* (three regions)

Great Oath (*nagen thumo che*): Dege Cheme's account of his journey to Bodh Gaya, 45–46; as a pledge to the Dalai Lama's personhood, 44, 48–49, 55, 57–58; pledging by sixty representatives in Bodh Gaya (Feb. 3, 1960), 46–47, 49–50, 58; Wangdu Dorjee and Jagoetsang Namgyal Dorjee's address prior to it, 46

Gros, Stéphane: Central Tibet identified as Xikang, 278n16; on the multifaceted composition of Kham, 12; on the spatial division of Tibet before the idea of a Great Tibet, 59; on the *tusi* system of indirect rule, 64

Gungthang, Sonam Wangyal, 193–194

Gungthang Ngodup. *See also* Dhondupling Tibetan Colony, Clement Town settlement: described as a "Chinese spy" by the Kham Amdo Youth Organization, 247; letter to the district magistrate in Dehra Dun (June 1979), 213; as a member of the Thirteen, 2, *184, 185,* 186; as possibly the author of the English version of the pamphlet, 221; return to Tibet after Gungthang Tsultrim's death, 302n35

Gungthang Tsultrim (or Akhu Tsultrim): Amdo drama troupe formed by, 112, 197; Bhoodan Movement ideas introduced to, 115–116; the Dalai Lama's encouragement of his establishing settlements for Tibetans, 197, 199; denouncing as a traitor by parliamentarians, 202–203, 209, 210; federation-style settlement ideas, 113, 223; as general secretary of the Tibetan Welfare Association, 183; as the head administrator for Gungthang Rinpoche in Labrang Tashikhyil, 2, 112; as head of the Thirteen, xiii, 3; on the inclusion of Nangchen in Amdo, 60; Khamo (his wife), *185,* 193, 211, 212; letter to PM Indira Gandhi (June 23, 1971), 198–201, 300n10; Nehru Memorial Foundation established by, 115, 116; network of social reformers, 115–116; opinion about Tibet's independence, 114–115; *Roof of the World* directed and produced by, 212–213

Gungthang Tsultrim (or Akhu Tsultrim)—assassination of. *See also Assasination [sic] of Gungthang Tsultrim, The* (*Pasang Nagpo [The Black Friday]*): alleged assassin, Tenzin, 6–7, 212, 220–221, 301n20, 301n34; article in *The Current,* 2, 223, 224, 302n41; circumstances, 211–212; concerns expressed by Gungthang Tsultrim, 1, 198; coverage in Indian newspapers, 223–224; Declaration of the Association of Thirteen Groups in response to criticism of the *Black Friday* pamphlet, 236–237, 303–304n14; designation as "The Black Friday," 221; funds raised by the Thirteen to find his murderer(s), 22; his application for

Gungthang Tsultrim (*continued*)
Indian citizenship in 1971 viewed as a motive for, 2; impact of, 15, 214, 221
Gyalo Thondup: animosity toward Surkhang Wangchen Gelek and Taktra Rinpoche, 134–135; *Bhod-mi Rangwang (Tibetan Freedom)* overseen by, 80, 135, 295n23; criticism of his leadership by members of the Thirteen, 89, 198–203; on the Dalai Lama's escape from Tibet (1959), 34; embezzlement charges against, 90–91, 92; Gyari Rinpoche's description of, 79, 200–201; as head of Tibetan intelligence, 120; as a native of Amdo, 170; power and influence of, 79–80, 104; relations with Taiwan, 286n40; relations with the Pangdatsang family, 133, 135, 137; rift in the Chushi Gangdrug between him and Gyen Yeshe, 95; the United Party allegedly lead by, xii, xiii, 20–21, 78–80; as the United Party's founder, 78; unity encouraged by, 284n14
Gyamtso, Khedup, 160, 161
Gyari, Lodi Gyaltsen (Gyari Rinpoche): on the Great Oath as a vow to the Dalai Lama's personhood, 57; Gyalo Thondup described by, 79, 200–201; on the response of Khampa chieftains to oath taking events in Bodh Gaya, 53–54; on the Sixteenth Karmapa as the head of the Thirteen, 298n25; on the styles of Chushi Gangdrug's main leaders, 95; Surkhang Wangchen Gelek described by, 136; as a translator for Chushi Gangdrug leaders, 287n44; on the United Party's discourse of Tibetan Unity, 111; on the United Party's leadership, 79; on why the Thirteen sought Indian citizenship, 300n3

Gyari Nyima Gyaltsen (Nyarong Pon Nyima Gyaltsen): response to oath taking events in Bodh Gaya, 53–54; the United Party's aims presented in Dharamsala, 80, 284n21

gyashok (collectives of 100 workers): Chokling *gyashok*, 72, 130; Nangchen *gyashok*, 72; organization and management of, 70

Gyatso, Janet, 288n3

Gyatso, Lobsang: on the election of a Bon religious representative to the Tibetan parliament (1977), 219; on the formation of the Thirteen, 22; on his experience as a minority within the Thirteen, 192

Gyen Yeshi: support for him among leaders of the Chushi Gangdrug, 94; at Wangdu Dorjee and Jagoetsang Namgyal Dorjee's address in Bodh Gaya, 46

Harrer, Heinrich, 33
Hobsbawm, Eric. J., 26, 243, 299
Hou, Joseph, 134–135

Indian settlements. *See* Orissa settlement; settlements associated with the Thirteen

Information and Publicity Office of His Holiness the Dalai Lama: autobiographies published by, 166; circulation of the *Young Army Journal* article to the Thirteen settlements, 205; inquiry to the Thirteen re the Tibetan New Year greeting published in MTAC's publication, 207; Juchen Thupten Namgyal as Minister of Information, 218

Information and Publicity Office of His Holiness the Dalai

Lama—August 9, 1978 press release: confirmation of the Karmapa as head of the Thirteen (August 9, 1978), 182; on harmful "untruths" in *The Black Friday*, 239; on the 1971 attempt by the Thirteen to seek Indian citizenship, 205

Jadur, Sonam Zangpo (or Jadurtsang Sonam Sangpo), 18, 188
Jagoetsang Namgyal Dorjee: acquaintance with Ontrul Rinpoche in Derge, 181; address to the Chushi Gangdrug prior to the Great Oath, 46; arrest and imprisonment of, 204; on the boundaries of Kham and Amdo, 60; Gyen Yeshi defended by, 94; as a leader of the Chushi Gangdrug, 89, 94; reconciliation with Drawutsang, Rinchen Tsering, 299n27; as steward of the clan leader Jagoetsang Topden, 183; as treasurer of the Tibetan Welfare Association, 183, *186*; as vice president of the Derge settlement in Bir, 187
Jagou, Fabienne, 282n68
Jayal, Niraja Gopal, 140, 141
Jigme, Alak (Alak, Jigme Rinpoche): article in the *Times of India*, 202; as a member of the Tibetan parliament, ix, 199; role of the Thirteen raised at the annual general meeting, 231, 252, 304n16; the Thirteen's critique of, 258
Jigme Lingtsang: as the king of Lingtsang in Kham, 177, 184; as a leader of the Lingtsang settlement, 177, 185, *185*, 304n14
Jinpa, *185*; on Gungthang Tsultrim's assassination, 211–212; on Gungthang Tsultrim's interest in Vinobha Bhave's ideas, 115–116; performance with the Amdo drama troupe, 197; on the screening of *Roof of the World*, 212–213; search for Gungthang Tsultrim's assassin, 301n20; on why local Tibetans faulted Gungthang Tsultrim, 213

Kagyu school. *See also* Karmapa—The Sixteenth Gyalwang Karmapa; Khamtrul Rinpoche Dongyu Nyima: in Bhutan, 104; Kagyud lamas in Buxa Choegar, 126–127, 291n11; struggle for power between Kagyu and Gelug lamas, 110; Tai Situ Jangchup Gyaltsen, 10
Kapstein, Matthew T., 9, 10, 164
Karmapa—The Sixteenth Gyalwang Karmapa: approached to be the patron of the Thirteen, 180, 182; as head of the Tibetan Welfare Association, 182–183, 241–242, 298n25; settlement established in Rumtek, 139
Karma Tsultrim, 178, 185
Karmay, Samten G.: analysis of Gungthang Tsultrim and the Group of Thirteen, 7–9; on the historiographical portrait of Lang Darma, 163–164; work with Tibetan Bonpo scholars, 151
Kathok Ontrul Rinpoche: as a founding member of the Tibetan Welfare Association, 183; as head lama of Kathok Monastery in Palyul, Derge, 102
Kathok settlement in Sataun: hydrated lime plant in, 177; Kathok Ontrul Rinpoche as the founder of, 218, 297n15; Shingkyong Rinpoche (Kathok Drimed Shingkyong Rinpoche), 213, 215, 304n14; Tibetans settled in, 186
Kelsang Liushar: Dexter's accusations against, 148–149, 150, 151, 294n10; Ockenden School appointment,

Kelsang Liushar (*continued*)
148; Ockenden School left by, 161; "The Reason Why Kelsang Left Ockenden," 155
Kham Amdo Youth Organization: letter to the Kashag (Aug. 20, 1978), 247, 254
Kham and Khampa identity. *See also* Derge, Kham; Derge (or Dege) settlement in Bir; Lingtsang; Markham; Nangchen; Nyarong: armed struggle against the Chinese in Kham and Amdo (1950s), 8, 39, 42, 68; clan identification among nomadic communities in Kham, 37–38, 41–42, 86–87; clan identification and regionalism among Khampas in exile, 259–260; Dokham described in Dilgo Khyentse Rinpoche's autobiography, 64; historical and religious autonomy of eastern Tibetan regions, 12–14, 38–39, 61, 222–223; Sadutshang Lobsang Nyendak, Jangtsetsang Tsering Gonpo, and Drawupon Rinchen Tsering as representatives of Kham in the CTA, 60; upper and lower Golok as part of, 60; Xizang used as a term for, 278n16
Kham Kathok Tibetan Society: hydrated lime plant in, 177
Khampagar Tashi Jong Tibetan Settlement. *See also* Dorzong Rinpoche: Khampagar Monastery established by Khamtrul Rinpoche, 262–263; report on by K. Singh Gupta (general secretary of the Central Relief Committee of India), 216
Khamtrul Rinpoche Dongyu Nyima: dedication to developing the Khampagar Tashi Jong settlement, 216; as a founding member of the Tibetan Welfare Association, 183, *184, 185, 186*; Khampagar Monastery in Lhathog, Kham led by, 112–113; Martham Thoesam supported by his monks, 286n40; as a native of Nangchen, 290n39

Kharat, Rajesh, 283n8

Khenpo Tsewang Dongyal Rinpoche: on Dudjom Rinpoche's popularity, 103; on Dudjom Rinpoche's request to join his followers in Orissa, 103; on the heterogeneous religious practices and players in the exile community in India, 103–104

Kvaerne, Per: on Bon, 146, 164–165; letter to Joyce Pearce, 295n17

Lama, Jigme Yeshe, 25–26

Lama Asi, 74, 189

Lang Darma: in the history curriculum at the Ockenden School, 156–157, 164; persecution of Buddhism associated with, 44, 156, 163–164

Lhalungpa, Lobsang Phuntsok, 114, 171; draft of a report on the Thirteen, 175–177

Library of Tibetan Works and Archives (LTWA), 166

Lingtsang: Lingtsang Choegyal Jigme Wangdu, king of Lingtsang, 177, 184

Lingtsang settlement in Munduwala, Uttarakhand. *See also* Jigme Lingtsang; Yarling Dorje Wangyal: establishment by Yarling Dorje Wangyal (1974), 177, 184–185; handicraft industry, 262; Tibetans settled in, 156, 177

Lloyd, David, 29–30

Lungtok Tenpai Nyima Rinpoche: author's audience with, 161; as the spiritual head of Bon monasteries in Tibet and Nepal, 161; as the thirty-third abbot of Menri (1968), 294n8

Lungtok Tenpai Nyima Rinpoche—as Sangye Tenzin Jongdong: birth of, 295n27; concerns for his safety expressed in the Bon community, 161; criticism by Ockenden students for teaching "wrong history," 148–156, 158, 166, 180; the Dalai Lama's encouragement of his hiring, 157, 294n7; *geshe* degree and studies at SOAS, 147–148; hiring by the Ockenden school, 147; work with Tibetan Bonpo scholars, 151

Luthoktsang, Chime, 22, *184*, 213

Maclehose, Diana, 295n17

Markham: Khampa uprising in (1956), 68; tension between Markham and Bawa groups within the Chushi Gangdrug, 93, 287n51

Marong, Adak Choje, 108, 260–261, 289n29

Martham Thoesam (or Marnang Thoesum), 46, 90, 171, 286n40

McGranahan, Carole: on national identity of Tibetans in exile, xi; on the Pangdatsang brothers, 133–134, 292n21; on the relationship between the Thirteen and the Tibetan government, 259; on Tibetans use of the term *chol kha sum* (three regions), 59; on the United Party, 78; when Tibetans from Kham defined themselves as Tibetan raised as a question, 75

McGranahan, Carole—on the Chushi Gangdrug: on the creation of the Chushi Gangdrug, 42; on the "native-place" affiliations of Chushi Gangdrug's units, 93; tensions within the Chushi Gangdrup related to views of Gyalo Thondup, 94–95; on the views of Chushi Gangdrug veterans, 249–250, 303n10; on views of nationalism within the organization, 90

Modood, Tariq, 293n47

Mongolian and Tibetan Affairs Commission (MTAC): establishment by the KMT, 106, 289n21; relations with the Group of Thirteen, 3, 106, 179, 202, 205–209, 228, 230–231, 232; the Thirteen leaders accused of receiving money from, 193; Tibetan New Year greeting in Chinese bearing felicitations to the MTAC from the Thirteen published by (Feb. 6, 1978), 207

Namgyal, Juchen Thupten: on the arrest and death of Amdo Dolma Kyab, 287n51; on Gungthang Tsultrim's inclusion of Nangchen as part of Amdo, 60; on Gyalo Thondup as the leader of both the Chushi Gangdrug and the United Party, 180; influence on Thirteen leaders reconciling with the CTA, 301n25; as Minister of Information, 218; on rumors by the United Party regarding Penor Rinpoche, 298n18; on the United Party's national ambitions, 86

Nangchen. *See also* Drawutsang, Rinchen Tsering (or Drawupon Rinchen Tsering); Tibetan Khampa Industrial Society (or Bir Nangchen settlement); Yugyal: fear of the impact of democratic reforms imposed by the Chinese, 68; *gotakpa* (seeking refuge in another clan), 41; Khamtrul Rinpoche as a native of, 290n39; lineage of Nangchen kings traced to the Yarlung dynasty, 13; multiple historical changes of authority over, 59–60; Orgyen Nyima and Ratro terton, 69;

Nangchen (*continued*)
  twenty-five clans as part of the Kham-in-exile polity, 60
Narayan, Jayaprakash, 115–116
national consciousness: attack on two teachers in the Ockenden School related to narratives about Tibet, 144, 165–166; attitudes towards unity, 85–86, 242; the Dalai Lama as pivotal to Tibetan national identity, 81–85; existence of a Tibetan ethos and feeling of nation, 12–13, 44; force of national sentiment, 242; forgetting as crucial to the creation of a nation, 189, 299n33; integrated Tibetan identity in exile, xi, 21, 30–31, 44, 113, 165–166; lack of diversity in models of unity expressed in letters criticizing the Thirteen, 243–244, 254–255; nationalist sentiment in quotidian life, 143; nationalist sentiments undermined in the *Tibetan Freedom*, 143; national loyalty associated with, 253–254; primacy of the unity of the three regions in the national narrative, 11, 61, 222–223
Nechung oracle: building unity within the community advised by, 75–76, 119; the Dalai Lama advised to leave Tibet (1958), 33–34; tradition of consulting him, 75–76, 284n12; warning about potential danger to the Dalai Lama, 75, 119, 120
Nehru, Jawaharlal: Bakula Rinpoche selected to lead a delegation to Tibet (1956), 114; death of, 115; Namkha Dorje's petition to, 74, 117, 284n9; support for the Dalai Lama's religious activities—not political activities, 120
Nehru Memorial Foundation, 115, 116
Nepal: Bon monasteries in, 161; Gungthang Tsultrim's assassin caught in, 6, 220–221, 301n20; military base in Mustang headed by Gyen Yeshi, 92; resolutions of the United Party addressed at Tibetans living in, 122, 123–134; Sakya school in, 104; support for the Thirteen from the Derge group in, 252; Tibetans ostracized for following Shugden, 289–290n30; Tsodi Bongsar's clan settled in, 70; United Party representatives in, 18, 119
Neten Chokling (Pema Gyurme) Rinpoche: aid secured for his group, 129–130; Bir Nangchen settlement established by, 78; meeting with Gungthang Tsultrim, 113; as vice president of the Tibetan Welfare Association, 183; work unit (*gyashok*) formed by, 72–73
nomads (*drokpas*) and nomadic communities: *drokpa* agency, 40–41; impact of Chinese democratic reforms on nomads in Nangchen, 68; Khampa clan identification, 73–74, 86–87, 189–190; leaders of the Thirteen as members of, 181; mobility associated with power by, 41–42; tribes distinguished from, 298n23
Norbu, Dawa: China's claim that Tibet was incorporated into China during the Yuan contested by, 276n17; on the CTA as different from the older Lhasa government, 37; on cultural sovereignty at the core of national identity, 47–48; Dhongthok Tulku interviewed about sectarianism, 110, 290n32; editorial "TIRS: Not a Success Story" (July 1973), 214–215; editorial "Toward Sectarian Harmony and National Unity" (Sept. 1976), 109–110; on the regionally specific political formation of Kham, 12; on Tibetan

nationalism as a history of "rising social consciousness," 26; on uprisings in Kham, 53–54

Norbu, Jamyang: on elements of the KMT in the United Party, 110; on the Fourteenth Dalai Lama's escape from Tibet, 33–34; on Gyalo Thodup's power in the Indian government, 104; on intelligence activity in Kalimpong, 58; on Mimang, 286n40; on Surkhang Wangchen Gelek and Yuthok Tashi Dhondup, 136; on Topgyal and Rapga Pangdatsang, 292n21; on U.S. concerns about Gyen Yeshi, 93; on Yamphel forced to leave India, 292n29

Norbu, Rinchen, 92, 286–287n44

Nyarong. *See also* Gyari Nyima Gyaltsen (Nyarong Pon Nyima Gyaltsen): Great Khampa Uprising (Feb. 1956), 68; Yudru Tsomu's study of Gönpo Namgyel, 40, 282n82

Nyingma school. *See also* Dudjom Rinpoche; Dzongnang Rinpoche (Patrul Jampal Lodroe Dzongnang Rinpoche); Gyari, Lodi Gyaltsen (Gyari Rinpoche); Kathok Ontrul Rinpoche; Neten Chokling (Pema Gyurme) Rinpoche; Pema Norbu Rinpoche (Penor Rinpoche); Tenzin Norbu; Ugyen Topgyal Rinpoche: fear of religious homogenization by the United Party, 98, 100, 109, 139; Gelugpa scholars' criticism of during the Thirteenth Dalai Lama's rule, 110; Rewalsar Monastery established in Himachal Pradesh, 128; in Sikkim, 104

oaths and oath making. *See also* Great Oath (*nagen thumo che*): in the courts of early Tibetan kings, 280–281n55; the establishment of Buddhism in Tibet based on, 47; oath to work in harmony taken at Chushi Gangdrug's regrouping in Mustang, 299n27; the Tibetan refugees pressed to take the Unity Party's oath of unity, 97–99

Ockenden School. *See also Bhod-mi Rangwang (Tibetan Freedom)*— testimonies regarding Ockenden; Dexter, Malcolm: attack on two teachers in the Ockenden School related to narratives about Tibet, 144, 165–166; closing of, 166; establishment of, 117, 146–147; letters to Joyce Pearce from students who had left Ockenden, 149–150; Peter Woodard's report on the mutiny at the Ockenden School, 152–153, 154

Ockenden Venture: Ockenden School established by, 117, 146–147; Joyce Pearce as one of three founders of, 127; Peter Woodard's report on the mutiny at the Ockenden School, 152–153, 154

Orissa settlement: Dudjom Rinpoche based in, 102, 139; United Party branch office in, 119

Pangdatsang family—Lobzang Yamphel ("Pom"): identification in the sixth resolution, 133, 143; perceived as a Chinese spy, 143; possible identification in the third resolution, 125; relations with Gyalo Thondup and Pangdatsang, 133, 135, 137

Pangdatsang family—Rapga: accused as being a Chinese agent, 135, 292n21; attempted assassination of, 134; relations with Gyalo Thondup and Pangdatsang, 133, 135; Tibetan Improvement Party founded by, 291–292n21

Pangdatsang family—Topgyal: possible identification in the third resolution, 125; revolt against the Tibetan government's army, 292n21

Pangdatsang family—Wangmo: ostracizing due to views about her father Yamphel, 143; request to have an audience with the Dalai Lama, 143, 293n48

parliament in exile. *See also* Tsering Choden Dhompa—as a member of parliament: Bon representation in, 219–220; changes including seats reserved for women, 278n7; Cheme Dorjee as a member of, 45; Drawutsang Rinchen Tsering as a member of, 60, 233; Gungthang Tsultrim denounced as a traitor by parliamentarians, 202–203, 209, 210

Patterson, George N., 130–131

Pearce, Joyce: correspondence with Malcolm Dexter, 130, 148–149, 153; correspondence with T. N. Taka, 151–152; as a founder of the Ockenden Venture, 127; Per Kvaerne's letter to Pearce, 295n17; letter from the Bureau of the Dalai Lama concerning boys expelled from Ockenden, 150; letters from students who had left Ockenden, 149–150; letter to Peter Woodard, 153; letter to T. C. Tara, 153

Pema, Jetsun: denunciation of the Tsokhag Chusum (Group of Thirteen), 210, 229, 231; the Thirteen's response to her, 251, 258, 304n16

Pema Norbu Rinpoche (Penor Rinpoche): Namdroling Monastery in Bylakuppe founded by, 263

People's Republic of China: denounced as an enemy by the Tibetan exile government, 106; integration strategies toward the Kham Frontier, 282n68

Phakte (or Gara Phatkte): accused by Gungthang Tsultrim as plotting his murder, 1, 212

Phenpo Tsedung Lobsang Yeshi, 78, 79, 80, 284n21

Pon Sangye Namgyal: the Bonpo community in India led by, 72; as a chief in Sogh Geimar, 184, 299n26; funding for the Bonpo settlement in Dolanji secured by, 178; as a member and treasurer of the Tibetan Welfare Association, 182, 183, 184, *184, 185, 187*

Qing dynasty (1644–1911): Kham referred to as a frontier regime during, 12; Lifanyuan of, 289n21; *tusi* system, 64, 181, 283n77; Xikang used as a term for Kham during, 278n16

Rashi Karma Kandor (Rashi Kandor), 89–90

Regional Working Committee of the Tibetan Youth Congress, 224

Renan, Ernest, 299n33

Rumtek settlement, Sikkim: establishment by the Sixteenth Gyalwang Karmapa, 139; Tsurphu Monastery completed in, 182

Sakya school: adherents in Mustang in Nepal, 104; Derge Gonchen, 181; domain of power during the Ming (1368–1644), 10; Sakya monks in Buxa Choegar, 126–127, 291n11; Sakyapa-Mongol rule of U and Tsang, 9–10; Sakya Pandita, 9, 276n17

Samdhong Rinpoche: Bhod Rangwang Denpai Legul (Righteous Tibetan Freedom Movement) formed by, 218

Sandutshang Lobsang Nyendrak, 46, 94, 204, 299n25
Sangye Tenzin. *See* Lungtok Tenpai Nyima Rinpoche—as Sangye Tenzin Jongdong
Schurmann, H. F., 290n36
Scott, James C., 41
settlements associated with the Thirteen. *See also* Bongsartsang Namkha Dorje—Mainpat Settlement; Bylakuppe settlement; Derge (or Dege) settlement in Bir; Dhondupling Tibetan Colony, Clement Town settlement; Kathok settlement in Sataun; Khampagar Tashi Jong Tibetan Settlement; Lingtsang settlement in Munduwala, Uttarakhand; Rumtek settlement, Sikkim; Taopon Gapa Welfare Society, Kamrao; Tibetan Khampa Industrial Society (or Bir Nangchen settlement): the fourth resolution of the United Party on, 126–128; self-administered settlements, 113; TIRS funding of (1966), 177–178
Seven Resolutions and Supporting Documents. *See* United Party (Cholsum Chigdril Tsogpa [Tibetan United Association])—Seven Resolutions
Seventeen-Point Agreement, 11, 34, 38–39
Sey Dhonyo Jagoetsang, 89, 210, 301n19
Sey Jigme: as a member of the Thirteen, *184*, 301n19; move from Lingtsang to Rajpur after Yarling Wangyal's death, 297n2
Shain, Yossi, 253–254
Shakabpa, Tsepon W. D, 163, 287n46
Shakya, Tsering: on the Communist Chinese needing Khampas to enter Central Tibet, 278n17; on information in autobiographies published by the exile government, 166; on the monk officials in the Tibetan government in Lhasa, 23; on the transformation of the relationship between China and Tibet, 11
Shangri Lhagyal, 96
Shelkar Drungyik Tsering Wangdu, 284n21, 285n22
Shingkyong Rinpoche (Kathok Drimed Shingkyong Rinpoche), 213, 215, 304n14
Simla Convention, 38, 278n16
Snellgrove, David L.: analysis of events at Ockenden, 162; and Malcolm Dexter, 150, 294n7; work with Tibetan Bonpo scholars, 151
Sperling, Elliot, 281n67
Surkhang Wangchen Gelek: Gyalo Thondup's criticism of, 135–136; as a Lhasa official, 125, 135; Taiwan Kalon Office run by with Yuthok Tashi Dhondup, 135, 136, 208

Taiwan. *See also* Mongolian and Tibetan Affairs Commission (MTAC): the Kuomintang denounced as an enemy by the Tibetan exile government, 106, 124–125, 208–209, 210; Phala Thupten Woeden's and Gyalo Thondup's relations with, 286n40; Surkhang Wangchen Gelek's move to, 135, 136–137, 143; Tibet viewed as part of China by the Taiwanese government, 2
Takla, T. N., 151–153
Taopon Gapa Welfare Society, Kamrao: Drawutsang Rinchen Tsering's founding of, 169, 186; lime quarry established by TIRS, 174, 177
Tapper, Richard, 298n23nomads
Tara, T. C., 153
Tenkyab, Lama, 262, 263

Tenpa, Chanzoe Ngawang: on Pat Brewster's influence on leaders of the Thirteen, 174; on Gyalo Thondup as the United Party's founder, 78; on the Thirteen, 88, 297n8

Tenzin Norbu: as a monk and practitioner of the Nyingma School, 98; as a skeptic of unity, 110; the Thirteen described by, 97; on the United Party and its definition of unity (*chigdril*), 97–101

Thapar, Romila, 56–57

Thirteen, the. *See* Tibetan Welfare Association (Bhod Dedon Tsogpa, Tsokhag Chusum, the Group of Thirteen)

Thonmi Sambhota, 156–157, 164, 165

three regions. *See chol kha sum* (three regions)

Tibetan Buddhist schools. *See also* Gelug school; Kagyu school; Nyingma school; Sakya school: first conference in exile led by heads of the four schools (1963), 122–123

Tibetan Empire (seventh to ninth centuries). *See also* Lang Darma: lineages of indigenous leaders across the Tibetan plateau traced to, 13; national narratives traced to, 44; U-Tsang as corresponding to the boundaries of, 9

Tibetan Freedom. See Bhod-mi Rangwang (Tibetan Freedom)

Tibetan Industrial Rehabilitation Society (TIRS): Davinson and Bob as members of its team, 178; establishment of, viii; industrial programs and settlements set up by, 132; registration as a Charitable Society by Brewster, 173

Tibetan Khampa Industrial Society (or Bir Nangchen settlement). *See also* Neten Chokling (Pema Gyurme) Rinpoche: administration of, 116, 188; establishment in Bir (1966), 174, 187; as the first Thirteen settlement run by the CTA (1976), 218; people from Nangchen drawn to the camp in Bir, 186–187; tea estate and factory in, 215; woolen mill in, 177, 217

Tibetan terms for modern concepts: definitions derived from Chinese, 81, 285n24; *A Statement of the Real Truth* (*Ngo yoe denpay sel dag*, 1978), 255–256, 257, 258; terms for democracy in Tibetan, 81, 285n24

Tibetan United Association. *See* United Party (Cholsum Chigdril Tsogpa [Tibetan United Association, TUA])

Tibetan United Association—*Truthful History of the Tibetan United Association:* the Fourteenth Dalai Lama's address (Sept. 28, 1978), 281n57; on the importance of uniting the people of the three provinces, 284n21; on Pomda (Pangdatsang) Wangmo, 292n28; on Yamphel Pangdatsang, 135{292n28}

Tibetan Welfare Association (Bhod Dedon Tsogpa, Tsokhag Chusum, the Group of Thirteen). *See also* Gungthang Tsultrim: *The Assasination* [sic] *of Gungthang Tsultrim* published by, 5, 211–212, 256; brought together because of the United Party's accusations, 117; Declaration of the Association of Thirteen Groups in response to the Black Friday pamphlet, 236–237, 303–304n14; diminishment of, 260–261; establishment of (1966), viii–ix, 3; first formal meeting of the Thirteen leaders (April 1966), 179–180; Gungthang Tsultrim's murder as the concluding chapter of, 15, 214; inclusion of Khampas, Amdowas, and Tibetans from U-Tsang, 240; location of its head office in Jangpura, Delhi, 183; objection by leaders of the Thirteen to the United Party's method, 85, 87–88; as part of Tibetan history, xiii, 195; prominent religious and secular members of, 183–186, *184, 185, 186, 187*; registration of the Thirteen leaders as (1966), viii, 15–16, 181–183; relationships formed with members of the Chushi Gangdrug, 90, 194; similarities with the United Party, 194; standing committee of, 183; struggle against the United Party, 189–192

Tibetan Welfare Association (Bhod Dedon Tsogpa, Tsokhag Chusum, the Group of Thirteen)—antigovernment narrative: as centers of power in their roles as leaders in eastern regions of the Tibetan plateau, 12; criticism by the Cholsum Mimang (Dharamsala People's United), 250–251; Indian citizenship sought by, 3, 198–202, 300n3, 300n11; the Kham Amdo Youth Organization's denunciation in their letter to the Kashag, 247, 254; lack of tolerance in letters expressing criticism, 243–244, 254–255; relations with Taiwan and MTAC, 3, 106, 179, 202, 205–209, 228, 230–231, 232; strategies discussed to protect themselves from accusations of, 180; Tibetans working for the Chinese referred to as "running dogs," 82, 295n30; the United Party identified as responsible for, 194

Tobden, Sonam: acquaintance with Tenzin (Gungthang Tsultrim's assassin) in the Bylakuppe settlement, 220; performance with the Amdo drama troupe, 197; search for Gungthang Tsultrim's assassin in Nepal, 220–221, 301n20; on the United Party's criticism of Gungthang Tsultrim, 197–198; on why local Tibetans were upset with Gungthang Tsultrim, 213

Trochupon Dorje Pasang (or Trochu Dorje Pasang): assertion of Gyalrong as its own region, 60; as a founding member of the Tibetan Welfare Association, 183, 185, *185, 187*; Ladakh Budh Vihar as an outpost for him and his people, 113; as a representative of Amdo in the Tibetan Parliament, 60; sons sent to Taiwan in the mid-1960s, 170; time in Gyarong Rokor, 297n2; the United Party's campaign against him in the *Seven Resolutions*, 133, 138–139, 143, 170, 178; visit to Clement Town, 169

Tsarong, Dundul Namgyal, 287n46

Tsering Choden Dhompa: death of, vii–viii; decades-long history of governmental work and community service, vii–viii, ix; journey from Kathmandu to Dharamsala (1961–1962), 45; *phayul* (fatherland) used to speak of her village in Nangchen, 67

Tsering Choden Dhompa—as a member of parliament: exile officials pushed to refrain from accusing the Thirteen, 207; meeting in Dharamsala with the Thirteen (July 1978), 228; meeting to discuss *The Assasination* [sic] *of Gungthang Tsultrim* (August 1978), 235; terms of service, vii, ix; vote in favor of the Bon community having representation in parliament, 219

Tsokhag Chusum. *See* Tibetan Welfare Association (Bhod Dedon Tsogpa, Tsokhag Chusum, the Group of Thirteen)
Tsomu, Yudru, 39–40, 62, 181, 282n68
Turek, Maria, 13, 40, 59–60, 67

Ugyen Topgyal Rinpoche, 174, 230, 237; on Chokling Rinpoche and his *gyashok*, 129–130; on Gungthang Tsultrim, 112, 114–115; as the son of Chokling Rinpoche, 78; on the United Party, 78–79, 85
United Party (Cholsum Chigdril Tsogpa [Tibetan United Association, TUA]). *See also* Gyalo Thondup; *Tibetan United Association—Truthful History of the Tibetan United Association*: campaign against Trochupon Dorje Pasang, 133, 138–139, 143, 178; criticism of the Thirteen leaders, viii; Dedhon Tsokpa (Welfare Association) as its framework, 284n14; feared for having plans to homogenize Tibetan identity, 98, 100–101, 107, 139; fears of retribution for opposing them, 120; founders of, 80; lamas and chiefs suspected by, 74; membership at the end of their first year, 80–81; the Nyingma school deemed unnecessary by, 98, 100; promotion of education and democracy, 31, 80–81, 83; standing committee, 80, 284–285n22; warning to Tibetans against building their own settlements and schools, viii, 170
United Party (Cholsum Chigdril Tsogpa [Tibetan United Association, TUA])—five aims of its manifesto: the Dalai Lama's approval of its goals, 80, 84; evidence of its effect even today, 56; objection by leaders of the Thirteen to its manifestos, 85, 169–171; positioning of the Dalai Lama as both the symbol and motivation of the Tibetan struggle for freedom, 81–85; publication as *Bhod Cholsum Chigdril Tsogpae mig yul dontsen gna* (1964), 76, 80; signing at a meeting in Dharamsala (1965), 76–77; standing committee of, 80, 284–285n22; Tenzin Norbu's criticism of, 100–101
United Party (Cholsum Chigdril Tsogpa [Tibetan United Association, TUA])—*Seven Resolutions and Supporting Documents:* on following the path of the democratic politico-religious system established by the Dalai Lama, 123–124; the Kuomintang and the CCP denounced as enemies in the third resolution, 124–125; non-Gelug religious communities addressed in the first resolution, 121–122{First resolution}; Tibetans discouraged from seeking aid from international organizations, 128–129, 132; Trochupon Dorje Pasang targeted in, 133, 138–139, 143, 170, 178; as a unifying force, 55–56, 117
U-Tsang: the boundaries of the Tibetan Empire as, 9; Gelug rule in Central Tibet since the seventeenth century, 23; as part of the Tibetan Autonomous Region (TAR), 38; Phala Thupten Woeden as a native of, 286n40; Sakyapa-Mongol rule of U and Tsang, 9–10; U-Tsang social and political forms recast as pan-Tibetan identity, xi, 102

Walter, Michael L., 280–281n55
Wang, Hui, 62–63, 282n70
Wangdu Dorjee: accused by Gungthang Tsultrim as plotting his

murder, 1, 212, 304n16; address to Tibetans prior to the Great Oath, 46, 189; meeting with the Dalai Lama concerning his fear the Thirteen would harm him, 237; the Thirteen's criticism of, 258; as the Tibetan home minister, 1, 71, 74, 237, 304n16

Wangyal, Tsering: on moving from Kham to India, 159–160; as a religious skeptic of unity, 110

Wangyal, Tsering, editorial "Politics of Sorrow," 6

Wiederkehr, Ernest, 174

Woeden, Phala Thupten, 33, 38, 166, 286n40

Woodard, Peter, 152–153, 154

Yang, Eveline, 59, 281n58

Yarling Dorje Wangyal: death of, 297n2; as a founding member of the Tibetan Welfare Association, 183, *185*; as the leader of the Lingtsang settlement, 177, 184–185; Lingtsang settlement in Munduwala established by, 177, 184–185

Yongdzin Lopon Tenzin Namdak, 4; Bonpo group under, 176, 178; as general secretary of the Tibetan Welfare Association, 183; as member of the Thirteen, 4, 176, 181, 301n19

Yugyal: dream of returning to Nangchen, 188, 238; on the early years in exile, 67; on identification with clans, 259, 261; as a member of the Thirteen, *185, 187,* 301n19; on problems with the second resolution, 134; on the registration of the Thirteen's land in Mainpat with the Lucknow court, 116; on why the Thirteen organized as a group, 111–112

Yuthok, Jigmie Dorje, 137

Yuthok, Tashi Dhondup: as a Lhasa official, 125; Taiwan Kalon Office run by, with Surkhang Wangchen Gelek, 135, 136, 208

STUDIES OF THE WEATHERHEAD EAST ASIAN INSTITUTE COLUMBIA UNIVERSITY

Selected Titles

(Complete list at: https://weai.columbia.edu/content/publications)

In Search of Admiration and Respect: Chinese Cultural Diplomacy in the United States, 1875-1974, by Yanqiu Zheng. University of Michigan Press, 2024.

Perilous Wagers: Gambling, Dignity, and Day Laborers in Post-Fukushima Tokyo, by Klaus K. Y. Hammering. Cornell University Press, 2024.

The Chinese Computer: A Global History of the Information Age, by Thomas S. Mullaney. The MIT Press, 2024.

Beauty Matters: Modern Japanese Literature and the Question of Aesthetics, 1890-1930, by Anri Yasuda. Columbia University Press, 2024.

Revolutionary Becomings: Documentary Media in Twentieth-Century China, by Ying Qian. Columbia University Press, 2024.

Waiting for the Cool Moon: Anti-imperialist Struggles in the Heart of Japan's Empire, by Wendy Matsumura. Duke University Press, 2024.

Beauty Regimes: A History of Power and Modern Empire in the Philippines, 1898–1941, by Genevieve Clutario. Duke University Press, 2023.

Afterlives of Letters: The Transnational Origins of Modern Literature in China, Japan, and Korea, by Satoru Hashimoto. Columbia University Press, 2023.

Republican Vietnam, 1963–1975: War, Society, Diaspora, edited by Trinh M. Luu and Tuong Vu. University of Hawai'i Press, 2023.

Territorializing Manchuria: The Transnational Frontier and Literatures of East Asia, by Miya Xie. Harvard East Asian Monographs, 2023.

Takamure Itsue, Japanese Antiquity, and Matricultural Paradigms that Address the Crisis of Modernity: A Woman from the Land of Fire, by Yasuko Sato. Palgrave Macmillan, 2023.

Rejuvenating Communism: Youth Organizations and Elite Renewal in Post-Mao China, by Jérôme Doyon. University of Michigan Press, 2023.

From Japanese Empire to American Hegemony: Koreans and Okinawans in the Resettlement of Northeast Asia, by Matthew R. Augustine. University of Hawai'i Press, 2023.

Building a Republican Nation in Vietnam, 1920-1963, edited by Nu-Anh Tran and Tuong Vu. University of Hawai'i Press, 2022.

China Urbanizing: Impacts and Transitions, edited by Weiping Wu and Qin Gao. University of Pennsylvania Press, 2022.

Common Ground: Tibetan Buddhist Expansion and Qing China's Inner Asia, by Lan Wu. Columbia University Press, 2022.

GPSR Authorized Representative: Easy Access System Europe, Mustamäe tee
50, 10621 Tallinn, Estonia, gpsr.requests@easproject.com

www.ingramcontent.com/pod-product-compliance
Lightning Source LLC
Chambersburg PA
CBHW022026290426
44109CB00014B/771